April 3–6, 2016
Santa Rosa, CA, USA

I0041883

Association for Computing Machinery

Advancing Computing as a Science & Profession

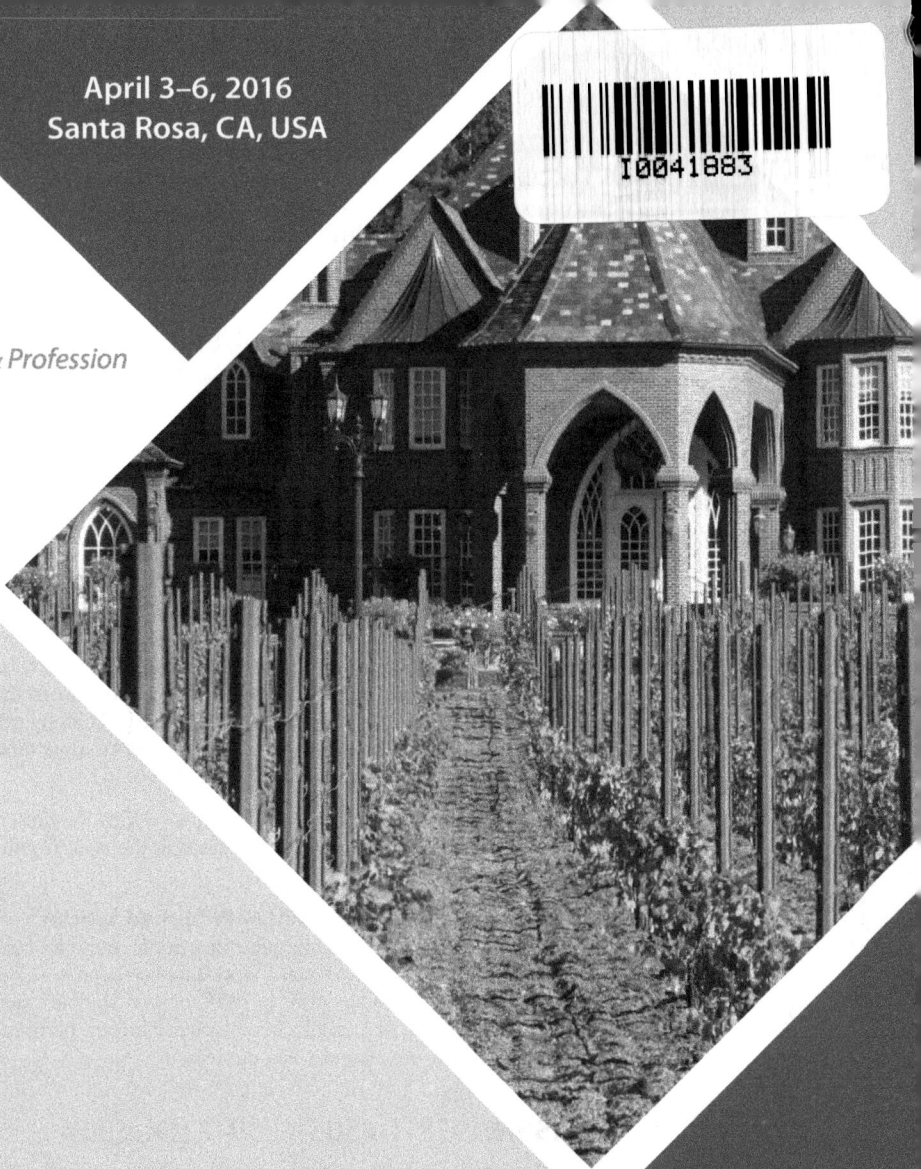

ISPD'16

Proceedings of the 2016
International Symposium on Physical Design

Sponsored by:
ACM SIGDA

Technical Co-Sponsor:
IEEE Circuits and Systems Society

Supported by:
ALTERA, ATopTech, Cadence, IBM Research, Intel, Mentor Graphics, Oracle, Xilinx, Synopsys, & TSMC

Association for Computing Machinery

Advancing Computing as a Science & Profession

The Association for Computing Machinery
2 Penn Plaza, Suite 701
New York, New York 10121-0701

Notice to Past Authors of ACM-Published Articles
ACM intends to create a complete electronic archive of all articles and/or other material previously published by ACM. If you have written a work that has been previously published by ACM in any journal or conference proceedings prior to 1978, or any SIG Newsletter at any time, and you do NOT want this work to appear in the ACM Digital Library, please inform permissions@acm.org, stating the title of the work, the author(s), and where and when published.

ISBN: 978-1-4503-4039-7 (Digital)

ISBN: 978-1-4503-4475-3 (Print)

Additional copies may be ordered prepaid from:

ACM Order Department
PO Box 30777
New York, NY 10087-0777, USA

Phone: 1-800-342-6626 (USA and Canada)
+1-212-626-0500 (Global)
Fax: +1-212-944-1318
E-mail: acmhelp@acm.org
Hours of Operation: 8:30 am – 4:30 pm ET

Printed in the USA

Foreword

On behalf of the organizing committee, we are delighted to welcome you to the 2016 ACM International Symposium on Physical Design (ISPD), held at Santa Rosa, California. Continuing the great tradition established by its twenty-four predecessors, which includes a series of five ACM/SIGDA Physical Design Workshops held intermittently in 1987-1996 and nineteen editions of ISPD in the current form since 1997, the 2016 ISPD provides a premier forum to present leading-edge research results, exchange ideas, and promote research on critical areas related to the physical design of VLSI and other related systems.

The regular papers in the ISPD 2016 program were selected after a rigorous, month-long, double-blind review process and a face-to-face meeting by the Technical Program Committee (TPC). The papers selected exhibit latest advancements in a variety of topics in physical design, including 3D integration, directed self-assembly, timing and clock optimization, reliability, adaptability, and the latest machine-learning based techniques for computer-aided design.

The ISPD 2016 program is complemented by two keynote addresses, twelve invited talks and a tribute session, all of which are delivered by distinguished researchers from both industry and academia. Dr. Kevin Zhang, vice president at Intel Corporation, will talk about circuit design in nano-scale CMOS technologies in the Monday keynote speech. In the Tuesday keynote speech, Dr. Antun Domic, executive vice president at Synopsys, will present his observations on the physical design problems of the next decade. A commemorative session on Tuesday afternoon will pay tribute to Prof. Ralph Otten. His collaborators will share with us Dr. Otten's exceptional contributions to EDA research, including his pioneering effort in automated floorplanning and layout generation. There will be two special sessions and other invited talks interspersed with the presentations of the regular papers. The topics of the invited papers range from emerging technologies such as 3D ICs, directed self-assembly, neurosynaptic chips, sub-7nm designs, as well as the latest challenges in physical design of ICs and FPGAs.

Since 2005, ISPD has organized highly competitive contests to promote and advance research in placement, global routing, clock network synthesis, discrete gate sizing, and detailed routing-driven placement. Unlike previous years' contests which are mostly on ASIC designs, this year's contest, organized by Xilinx, is on routability-driven FPGA placement. This is the first large-scale worldwide contest on FPGA placement optimizing towards important real-world objectives based on a realistic heterogeneous FPGA architecture. The contest evaluates the quality of an FPGA placement with an advanced commercial FPGA routing tool making the problem even more challenging and practical. It is expected to lead and motivate more research and contributions on FPGA physical design. Continuing the tradition of all the past contests, a new large-scale real-world benchmark suite for FPGA circuits based on an advanced heterogeneous FPGA architecture will be released in the ISPD website: http://www.ispd.cc

We would like to take this chance to express our gratitude to the authors, the presenters, the keynote/invited speakers for contributing to the high-quality program, and the session chairs for moderating the sessions. We would like to thank our program committee and external reviewers, who provided insightful constructive comments and detailed reviews to the authors. We greatly appreciate the exceptional set of invited talks put together by the Steering Committee, which is chaired by Azadeh Davoodi. We also thank the Steering Committee for selecting the best paper. Special thanks go to the Publications Chair Chris Chu and the Publicity Chair Ismail Bustany for their tremendous services. We would like to acknowledge the team organizing the contest led by

Stephen Yang. We are also grateful to our sponsors. The symposium is sponsored by the ACM SIGDA (Special Interest Group on Design Automation) with technical co-sponsorship from the IEEE Circuits and Systems Society. Generous financial contributions have also been provided by (in alphabetical order): Altera, ATopTech, Cadence, IBM Research, Intel Corporation, Mentor Graphics, Oracle, Synopsys, TSMC, and Xilinx. Last but not least, we thank Lisa Tolles and others from Sheridan Communications for their expertise and enormous patience during the production of the proceedings.

The organizing committee hopes that you will enjoy ISPD. We look forward to seeing you again in future editions of ISPD.

Evangeline Young   **Mustafa Ozdal**

ISPD 2016 General Chair   *Technical Program Chair*

Table of Contents

ISPD 2016 Symposium Organization..viii

ISPD 2016 Sponsors & Supporters...x

Welcome and Keynote Address
Session Chair: Evangeline Young *(Chinese University of Hong Kong)*

- **Circuit Design in Nano-Scale CMOS Technologies** 1
  Kevin Zhang *(Intel Corporation)*

Session: 3D Circuits
Session Chair: David Chinnery *(Mentor Graphics)*

- **Physical Design Automation for 3D Chip Stacks - Challenges and Solutions**......................3
  Johann Knechtel *(Masdar Institute of Science and Technology)*, Jens Lienig *(Dresden University of Technology)*

- **ePlace-3D: Electrostatics based Placement for 3D-ICs** 11
  Jingwei Lu *(Cadence Design Systems, Inc.)*, Hao Zhuang, Ilgweon Kang *(University of California, San Diego)*,
  Pengwen Chen *(National Chung Hsing University)*, Chung-Kuan Cheng *(University of California, San Diego)*

- **A Compressive-sensing based Testing Vehicle for 3D TSV Pre-bond and Post-bond
  Testing Data**.. 19
  Hantao Huang, Hao Yu *(Nanyang Technological University)*, Cheng Zhuo *(Intel Corporation)*,
  Fengbo Ren *(Arizona State University)*

- **PLATON: A Force-Directed Placement Algorithm for 3d Optical Networks-on-Chip** 27
  Anja von Beuningen, Ulf Schlichtmann *(Technische Universität München)*

Session: Monday Lunch
Session Chair: Qi Zhu *(University of California, Riverside)*

- **Optimizing for Power, Speed, Cost and Emissions in Automotive Drivetrains** 35
  Patrick R. Groeneveld *(Synopsys Inc.)*

Session: Directed Self Assembly
Session Chair: Dwight Hill *(Synopsys)*

- **Cell-Based Design Methods for Directed Self-Assembly**... 37
  Karl K. Berggren, Caroline A. Ross, Hyung Wan Do, Jae-Byum Chang,
  Hong Kyoon Choi *(Massachusetts Institute of Technology)*

- **Concurrent Guiding Template Assignment and Redundant via Insertion for DSA-MP
  Hybrid Lithography** 39
  Jiaojiao Ou *(University of Texas at Austin)*, Bei Yu *(Chinese University of Hong Kong)*,
  David Z. Pan *(University of Texas at Austin)*

- **Double-Patterning Aware DSA Template Guided Cut Redistribution for Advanced 1-D
  Gridded Designs** 47
  Zhi-Wen Lin, Yao-Wen Chang *(National Taiwan University)*

Special Session
Session Chair: Mahesh A. Iyer *(Intel Corporation)*

- **Technology Inflection Points** 55
  Victor Moroz *(Synopsys, Inc.)*

- **Challenges and Opportunities with Place and Route of Modern FPGA Designs** 57
  Raymond Nijssen *(Achronix Semiconductor Corporation)*

- **Design and Tool Flow of IBM's TruenNorth: An Ultra-Low Power Programmable
  Neurosynaptic Chip with 1 Million Neurons** 59
  Filipp A. Akopyan *(IBM)*

Tuesday Keynote Address

Session Chair: Yao-Wen Chang *(National Taiwan University)*

- **Some Observations on the Physical Design of the Next Decade**..61
  Antun Domic *(Synopsys, Inc.)*

Session: Timing and Clock Optimization

Session Chair: Gustavo Wilke *(Synopsys)*

- **A Designer's Perspective on Timing Closure**...63
  Greg Ford *(GlobalFoundries)*
- **Cell Selection for High-Performance Designs in an Industrial Design Flow**..........................65
  Tiago J. Reimann *(Universidade Federal do Rio Grande do Sul)*, Cliff C. N. Sze *(IBM Research)*,
  Ricardo Reis *(Universidade Federal do Rio Grande do Sul)*
- **Drive Strength Aware Cell Movement Techniques for Timing Driven Placement**.................73
  Guilherme Flach, Mateus Fogaça, Jucemar Monteiro, Marcelo Johann, Ricardo Reis *(UFRGS)*
- **Construction of Latency-Bounded Clock Trees**...81
  Rickard Ewetz, Chuan Yean Tan, Cheng-Kok Koh *(Purdue University)*

Session: PD for Reliability and Adaptability

Session Chair: Shuai LI *(Cadence)*

- **Scaling Beyond 7nm: Design-Technology Co-optimization at the Rescue**............................89
  Julien Ryckaert *(IMEC)*
- **Proximity Optimization for Adaptive Circuit Design**..91
  Ang Lu, Hao He, Jiang Hu *(Texas A&M University)*
- **Load-Aware Redundant via Insertion for Electromigration Avoidance**..................................99
  Steve Bigalke *(Institute of Electromechanical and Electronic Design (IFTE))*,
  Jens Lienig *(Institute of Electromechanical and Electronic Design (IFTE))*

Session: Commemoration for Prof. Ralph Otten

Session Chair: Michael Burstein *(MediaBoost)*

- **Early Days of Automatic Floorplan Design**..107
  Martin D. F. Wong *(University of Illinois at Urbana-Champaign)*
- **The Annealing Algorithm revisted**...109
  Lukas P.P.P. van Ginneken *(DigiPen Institute of Technology)*
- **Trailblazing Physical Design Flows: Ralph Otten's Impact on Design Automation**...........113
  Patrick R. Groeneveld *(Synopsys Inc.)*
- **Complexity and Diversity in IC Layout Design**...115
  Ralph Otten *(Technische Universiteit Eindhoven)*

Session: FPGA Physical Design

Session Chair: Sabya Das *(Xilinx)*

- **An Interactive Physical Synthesis Methodology for High-Frequency FPGA Designs**.......117
  Sabya Das, Rajat Aggarwal, Zhiyong Wang *(Xilinx Inc)*
- **Power Optimization of FPGA Interconnect via Circuit and CAD Techniques**......................123
  Safeen Huda, Jason H. Anderson *(University of Toronto)*
- **Scaling Up Physical Design: Challenges and Opportunities**..131
  Guojie Luo *(Peking University & PKU-UCLA Joint Research Institute)*,
  Wentai Zhang, Jiaxi Zhang *(Peking University)*,
  Jason Cong *(University of California, Los Angeles, PKU-UCLA Joint Research Institute & Peking University)*
- **Routability-Driven FPGA Placement Contest**...139
  Stephen Yang, Aman Gayasen, Chandra Mulpuri, Sainath Reddy, Rajat Aggarwal *(Xilinx Inc.)*

Session: Statistical and Machine Learning-Based CAD

Session Chair: Jackey Yan *(Cadence)*

- **Generating Routing-Driven Power Distribution Networks with Machine-Learning Technique** 145

  Wen-Hsiang Chang, Li-De Chen, Chien-Hsueh Lin, Szu-Pang Mu,
  Mango C.-T. Chao *(National Chiao-Tung University)*,
  Cheng-Hong Tsai, Yen-Chih Chiu *(Global Unichip Corporation (GUC))*

- **Hyperspherical Clustering and Sampling for Rare Event Analysis with Multiple Failure Region Coverage** 153

  Wei Wu *(University of California, Los Angeles)*, Srinivas Bodapati *(Intel Corporation)*,
  Lei He *(University of California, Los Angeles)*

- **A Machine Learning Based Framework for Sub-Resolution Assist Feature Generation** 161

  Xiaoqing Xu *(University of Texas at Austin)*,
  Tetsuaki Matsunawa, Shigeki Nojima, Chikaaki Kodama, Toshiya Kotani *(Toshiba Corporation)*,
  David Z. Pan *(University of Texas at Austin)*

Author Index 169

ISPD 2016 Symposium Organization

General Chair: Evangeline Young *(The Chinese University of Hong Kong)*

Technical Program Chair: Mustafa Ozdal *(Bilkent University)*

Past Chair: Azadeh Davoodi *(University of Wisconsin - Madison)*

Steering Committee Chair: Azadeh Davoodi *(University of Wisconsin - Madison)*

Steering Committee: Chuck Alpert *(Cadence)*
Yao-Wen Chang *(National Taiwan University)*
Azadeh Davoodi (Chair) *(University of Wisconsin-Madison)*
Patrick Groeneveld *(Synopsys)*
David Pan *(University of Texas at Austin)*
Cliff Sze *(IBM)*
Martin Wong *(University of Illinois at Urbana-Champaign)*

Program Committee: Yongchan Ban *(LG)*
Aiqun Cao *(Synopsys)*
David Chinnery *(Mentor Graphics)*
Salim Chowdhury *(Oracle)*
Chris Chu *(Iowa State University)*
Sabya Das *(Xilinx)*
Stephan Held *(University of Bonn)*
Iris Hui-Ru Jiang *(National Chiao Tung University)*
Andrew Kennings *(Univ. of Waterloo)*
Taemin Kim *(Intel)*
Jens Lienig *(Dresden Univ. of Technology)*
Guojie Luo *(Peking University)*
David Newmark *(AMD)*
Mark Po-Hung Lin *(National Chung Cheng University)*
Sherief Reda *(Brown Univ.)*
Kambiz Samadi *(Qualcomm)*
Natarajan Viswanathan *(IBM)*
Jackey Yan *(Cadence)*
Hailong Yao *(Tsinghua University)*

Publication Chair: Chris Chu *(Iowa State University)*

Publicity Chair: Ismail Bustany *(Mentor Graphics)*

Contest Chair: Stephen Xiaojian Yang *(Xilinx)*

Additional Reviewers:

Sarvesh Bhardwaj
Steve Bigalke
Ismail Bustany
Tuck Boon Chan
Chin-Chih Chang
Ching-Yu Chin
Duo Ding
Jerrica Gao
John Gilchrist
Dwight Hill
Andrew Kahng
Johann Knechtel
Andreas Krinke

Shuai Li
Jingwei Lu
Laurent Masse-Navette
Pavlos Matthaiakis
Parijat Mukherjee
Sergii Osmolovskyi
Shreepad Panth
Xiang Qiu
Ankur Sharma
Matthias Thiele
Linfu Xiao
Stephen Sangho Youn
Bei Yu

ISPD 2016 Sponsors & Supporters

Sponsor:

Technical Co-sponsor:

Supporters:

Circuit Design in Nano-Scale CMOS Technologies

Kevin Zhang
Circuit Technology
Technology & Manufacturing Group
Intel Corporation
Hillsboro, Oregon 97124, USA

Abstract

CMOS technology scaling has followed Moore's law well into the nano-scale regime now. The technology scaling is no longer just about geometric reduction but more about innovation in the use of new materials and transistor architectures. Relentless feature size reduction along with the innovations in transistor architecture and new material have created both challenges and opportunities for circuit designers to fully realize the technology scaling benefits. In this talk, an overview on the technology scaling will first be presented. The talk will then explore many advanced circuit design techniques that are key to achieve product-level scaling benefits. It will start with SRAMs, the work-horse for embedded memories. The state-of-the-art read-write-assist (RWA) techniques in SRAMs will be discussed for achieving adequate margins for low-voltage operation. Analog and mixed signal (AMS) circuits are long considered "not scalable" due to many unique design requirements and process sensitivities. In this talk, several novel digital-assist techniques are explored to illustrate how they can help achieve excellent power, performance, and area scaling in some common AMS circuits such as phase-lock-loop (PLL) and high-speed serial IO. Adaptive design concept has become a focal point in advanced circuits today to augment the process variations. A couple of design examples will be given to demonstrate the benefits of these advanced circuit techniques. To further improve system-level performance, more intelligent integration schemes are becoming more important. Again, real product examples, including integrated-voltage-regulator and in-package-memory, will be given on how they can help address the power/performance challenges at system-level. In conclusion, as CMOS technology scaling continues, novel circuit topologies and integration schemes will play an increasingly more important role in driving the power and performance scaling for future products.

Keywords

Circuit design; Nano-scale CMOS technologies; CMOS technology scaling; Moore's law.

Short Bio

Kevin Zhang is a Vice President of Technology and Manufacturing Group and an Intel Fellow at Intel Corporation. He is responsible for advanced circuit technology development for the company's future products. Zhang oversees the development of process design rules, circuit & device modeling, digital circuit libraries, key analog and mixed-signal circuits, high-speed I/O and embedded memories. Zhang has published more than 60 papers at international conferences and in technical journals and is the editor of Embedded Memory for Nano-Scale VLSIs, published by Springer in 2009. He holds more than 50 U.S. patents in the field of integrated circuit technology. Zhang is 2016 ISSCC Program chair and also serves on IEEE VLSI Executive Committee. Zhang is a Fellow of the Institute of Electrical and Electronics Engineers. He received his bachelor's degree from Tsinghua University in Beijing in 1987 and his Ph.D. from Duke University in 1994, both in electrical engineering.

ISPD'16, April 3–6, 2016, Santa Rosa, California, USA.
ACM 978-1-4503-4039-7/16/04.
DOI: http://dx.doi.org/10.1145/2872334.2878629

Physical Design Automation for 3D Chip Stacks – Challenges and Solutions

Johann Knechtel
Masdar Institute of Science and Technology
Abu Dhabi, UAE
knechtel@ieee.org

Jens Lienig
Dresden University of Technology
Dresden, Germany
jens@ieee.org

ABSTRACT

The concept of 3D chip stacks has been advocated by both industry and academia for many years, and hailed as one of the most promising approaches to meet ever-increasing demands for performance, functionality and power consumption going forward. However, a multitude of challenges has thus far obstructed large-scale transition from "classical" 2D chips to stacked 3D chips. We survey major design challenges for 3D chip stacks with particular focus on their implications for physical design. We also derive requirements for advances in design automation, such as the need for a unified workflow. Finally, we outline current promising solutions as well as areas needing further research and development.

Keywords

Electronic design automation; physical design; through-silicon via-based 3D ICs; interposer stacks; monolithic 3D ICs; high-level design challenges; power delivery; thermal management; clock delivery; partitioning; floorplanning; placement; routing; testing; pathfinding; chip-package co-design; multi-physics simulation; assembly design kit; design standards

1. INTRODUCTION

3D chip stacks offer the potential to meet current and future requirements of electronic circuits, such as for performance, functionality, and power consumption. Two design paradigms, namely "More Moore" (shrinking device nodes) and "More-than-Moore" (heterogeneous integration), are advocating 3D chip stacks in particular [1] (Fig. 1). Despite significant projected benefits over 2D chips, the overall adoption of 3D stacks still lags behind expectations. What are reasons for the current lack of industrial adoption, and what are specific implications for physical design?

Successful adoption of 3D chip stacks requires addressing different classical and novel challenges which simultaneously affect the manufacturing processes, design practices and physical design tools. If not properly addressed, the fairly complex challenges may render 3D chip stacks commercially unviable, despite recent advances in manufacturing yield and cost reduction. Physical design automation partially meets these challenges at present, but further efforts are needed to fully exploit the potential of 3D chip stacks and to facilitate their commercial breakthrough.

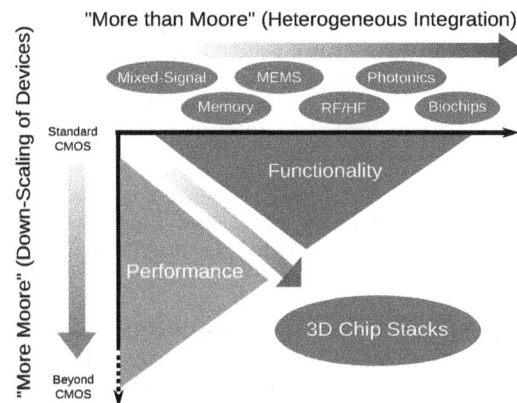

Figure 1: The well-known "More Moore" trend is slowly but surely reaching its limits for CMOS technology. "More than Moore", i.e., exploiting heterogeneous integration, has been identified as novel, important direction. 3D chip stacks offer the potential to meet both trends at the same time.

In this paper, we will first review the diversity of stacking options for 3D chips and formulate related high-level design challenges. Then, along with further needs for design automation, we discuss the following classical challenges and related promising solutions:

- Power delivery and thermal management;
- Clock delivery;
- Partitioning and floorplanning;
- Placement;
- Routability estimation and routing; and
- Testing.

It is important to understand that these challenges are much more complex for 3D chip stacking, and that existing design tools for 2D chips cannot be directly applied.

We also elaborate on novel challenges that are currently (at least partially) addressed, but which require further efforts, such as:

- Pathfinding and design-space exploration;
- Chip-package co-design; and
- Multi-physics simulation and verification.

Our paper concludes with promising trends for physical design of 3D stacks, which meet the identified open challenges, and whose application can ease the adoption of 3D stacks.

2. 3D-CHIP STACKING OPTIONS AND HIGH-LEVEL DESIGN CHALLENGES

3D-chip stacking falls into four categories (Fig. 2): (*i*) package stacking, (*ii*) interposer stacks, (*iii*) through-silicon via (TSV)-based 3D ICs, and (*iv*) monolithic 3D ICs. Each option has its

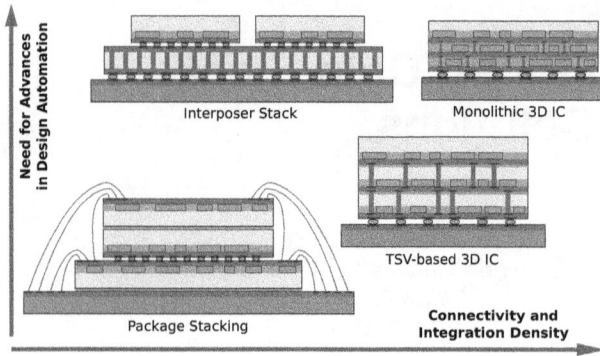

Figure 2: Implementation options for 3D chip stacks. Originating with package stacking, 3D integration has evolved through interposer stacks (also known as "2.5D integration") towards TSV-based and monolithic 3D ICs. Advances in design automation are typically called for the latter two options but are also required for modern, large-scale interposer stacks.

scope of application, with distinctive benefits and drawbacks as well as requirements for design and manufacturing processes [1,2]. In the following, related key aspects are reviewed and design challenges are outlined.

2.1 Options for 3D Chip Stacking

Package stacking, based on wire bonding and/or flip-chip bonding, has been widely adopted and thus is not reviewed here.

TSV-based 3D ICs have initially attracted the most attention and efforts; many academic/industrial prototypes/products nowadays are based on TSV technology [3–7]. TSVs are metal plugs (copper or tungsten) that penetrate whole dies—which are stacked and bonded—to interconnect those dies. Different stacking scenarios are applicable, such as face-to-back die-to-wafer stacking [2].

Depending on the TSV type, different challenges arise: via-first and via-middle TSVs obstruct the device layer and result in placement obstacles; via-last TSVs obstruct the device layer and the metal layers, resulting in placement and routing obstacles. Due to their relatively large size and intrusive character, TSVs cannot be deployed excessively and/or arbitrarily but have to be optimized in count and arrangement [8,9]. Note that TSVs do not scale at the same rate as transistors, thus the TSV-to-cell mismatch will remain for future nodes and may even increase [10].

Interposer stacks are a cost-efficient but only seemingly straightforward option for 2.5D or 3D integration [11–13]. Mainly pre-designed dies are stacked in lateral and/or vertical fashion on interposer where redistribution layers and TSVs realize the connectivity. Interposer are typically fabricated as passive carriers, but may also embed components like decaps or even "glue logic" [11]. The concept of interposer stacks supports various applications and is thus widely acknowledged in the industry. Notable products include the Xilinx *Virtex-7 FPGA* family [14] and a GLOBALFOUNDRIES prototype with two *ARM Cortex-A9* chips [15].

The design of interposer stacks is obstructed by the lack of dedicated design tools [12]. For example, routing highly-interconnected interposer and the related design of large-scale NoCs requires further research [16]. Other challenges such as simulation and verification of signal integrity across an interposer stack have been recently addressed [17], but require further integration efforts [18].

Monolithic 3D ICs have recently gained more attention [19], thanks to advances of the processing technology. The key feature of monolithic integration is that active layers are sequentially manufactured into one stack rather than bonded using separate dies. Due to their relatively small vias, monolithic 3D ICs enable fine-grain transistor-level integration, which is especially sought-after for high-density logic integration [19].

As for design challenges, routing becomes notably more complex due to high congestion along with increased delays [19]. Novel approaches covering partitioning, placement and routing for monolithic integration are required; such a holistic approach has recently been proposed in [20]. Furthermore, thermal properties differ from "classical" TSV-based 3D ICs: on the one hand, the small vias are not as effective as TSVs for conducting heat towards the heatsink; on the other hand, monolithic stacks do not exhibit "thermal barriers" in form of bonding layers. Thus, the thermal coupling within monolithic stacks is larger and more uniform than for TSV-based 3D ICs. This, in turn, calls for dedicated thermal management [21].

2.2 High-Level Design Challenges

Exploring and selecting the most suitable chip-stacking options for a particular design is much more complex than handling the decisions required for classical 2D-IC design. Given an abstract design description in early planning phases, one has to consider the following challenges, among others:

- How can intellectual property (IP) blocks, pre-designed modules or even whole dies be effectively reused in the stack?
- Into how many dies/layers should the design be split up, and how is the design performing after being spread across multiple dies? What is an appropriate partitioning strategy?
- What are the bandwidth, power and integrity requirements for global interconnects? What is an appropriate system-level interconnect structure for separated components/dies?
- Which bonding and packaging technologies are applicable, and what technology/device node should be considered for each die? Are constraints (such as thermal design, power and signal integrity) satisfiable with the chosen technologies?
- How are heterogeneous components such as MEMS or HF modules designed and properly integrated along with digital modules? (This challenge is especially relevant for 3D chip stacks targeting widely-anticipated and multifunctional applications such as Internet of Things, IoT.)
- How to test separate components/dies and the overall stack?

Most of these challenges are interacting, and any respective decision does impact the overall performance, reliability and cost of the 3D chip stack. It is apparent that solving such a convoluted set of challenges requires sophisticated design know-how, EDA capabilities and well-defined project structures. Specifically, methodologies and tools are required that enable (*i*) an accurate (yet fast) exploration of the design space and (*ii*) rapid prototyping/evaluation of different stacking configurations (see Sec. 4).

3. CLASSICAL DESIGN CHALLENGES: AGGRAVATED BUT SOLVABLE

Classical challenges such as power delivery, floorplanning and placement become much more complex when designing 3D chip stacks instead of 2D chips. Existing methodologies and tools for 2D-chip design cannot be directly applied and are only to some degree extendible. During the recent years, however, many efforts in academia and industry have been undertaken which render those classical challenges still aggravated but solvable. In the following, key challenges and promising solutions are discussed.

3.1 Power Delivery and Thermal Management

High integration density—a key benefit of 3D stacking—notably complicates both power delivery and thermal management. A stack of d dies/layers potentially exhibits a d-fold power density compared to 2D chips. This implies that approximately $d\times$ power has to be delivered through the stack, without excessive static and dynamic voltage drop, despite the notable parasitics of 3D power-distribution networks (PDNs) [22]. At the same time, approximately $d\times$ of heat has to be removed from the stack. Solutions for power delivery and thermal management are discussed next.

Arrangement of TSVs: For power/ground (PG) TSVs, a distributed, irregular topology is superior to both regularly placed (single) TSVs and clustered TSVs in order to limit power noise [22,23]. Proper planning of TSVs may also serve power delivery and thermal management at the same time. For example, aligned PG-TSV stacks may simultaneously increase heat dissipation and reduce power noise [23, 24]. Regular signal TSVs can be similarly arranged into (possibly aligned) TSV cluster for improved heat conduction without excessive routing overheads [25–27].

Design of PDN and PG grids: A promising (yet expansive) PDN architecture is the "multi-story power delivery" [28], where several power supplies (e.g., one per die) distribute the load more effectively compared to a single power supply. As for decaps, their allocation has to be carefully investigated to manage their complex impact on the power-noise distribution in 3D chip stacks [29].

The design of PG grids should generally account for the overall 3D PDN, not only for the dies each grid is attached to [24, 30].

Low-power design: Consumed power and, in turn, generated heat can be reduced by deployment of low-power circuitry. In this context, sub-/near-threshold circuitry for 3D chip stacks has gained attention; detailed studies and prototypes are available [31,32]. Arrangement of multiple voltages domains in order to reduce power and temperature has been recently proposed as well [33].

Thermal-aware design: Spreading high-power modules in an orchestrated manner, e.g., during thermal-aware floorplanning [27, 34–36] or placement [37], is a simple but effective measure. Along with high temperature comes a strong impact on transistor behaviour; thermal-aware design is thus also important for reliability.

Technological approaches: In order to limit package impedance and external current supply, one can bring voltage converters closer to the logic by "sandwiching" dedicated converter dies into the 3D stack [38]. To reduce power noise, classical CMOS decaps and/or metal-insulator-metal (MIM) decaps can be deployed within each die [39] or even in dedicated "decap dies" as well [30]. As for thermal paths, internal paths (i.e., paths across and within dies) as well as external paths (i.e., paths to the heatsink and the package) can be improved by introducing micro-fluidic channels [40].

3.2 Clock Delivery

The key challenge when designing 3D clock networks is to ensure reliable, uniform and high-speed delivery of clock signals to all sinks which are spread across different dies. Besides thermal management, this is one of the main challenges for "real logic-on-logic stacking" and has many implications for physical design. These concerns, along with promising solutions, are discussed next.

Redundancy and arrangement of TSVs: Since the advent of TSV technology, their reliability has been a major concern—failure of any clock or signal TSV would render the whole stack defective. Thus, different redundancy architectures have been proposed in general [41,42] and for clock networks in particular [43,44].

The optimized assignment of clock signals to TSV arrays—which are generally more practical than separate TSVs [8]—has also been proposed for design of reliable and low-power clock networks [45]. Another flow [46] accounts for PG- and signal-TSV obstacles during placement of clock TSVs, but neglects their co-optimization while arranging those different types of TSVs.

Holistic and variation-aware design: The design of clock networks is highly coupled to most physical-design stages like placement, routing and timing optimization. All stages should account for the 3D clock network's properties, e.g., arrangement of clock TSVs and clock-trees on individual dies. Capabilities for tuning the network and to provide feedback to other stages are also needed.

Another requirement for clock delivery is the analysis of timing variations and parameter variations, which are a general concern for 3D chip stacks with their inter-die variations. These variations can be mitigated by implementation of multiple clock domains [47]. Note that variations are exacerbated in interposer stacks and TSV-based 3D ICs, mainly due to thermo-mechanical stress [48].

Clock-network synthesis: Minimizing the clock skew is a key objective for clock-network synthesis. It is considered by most previous studies such as [43–45, 49–51]. Variation-aware timing simulation [49, 52], statistical clock-skew models [53] or post-silicon techniques such as body biasing [50] have been applied as well.

As for network topologies, it has been shown that H-trees are superior to classical grid networks in terms of power and mean skew but may suffer from larger maximum skew due to variations [52]. Other proven approaches such as the method of means and medians (MMM) and deferred-merge embedding (DME) have been successfully extended as well [51]. The related approach in [51] allows to effectively trade-off TSV count and power consumption, to manage slew variations and to insert buffers, all within low runtime.

Testability and yield management: Stacking only known-good dies is essential in order to manage the overall yield of 3D chips. This stacking paradigm requires the clock networks to be tailored for pre-bond testability which can be achieved by encapsulating separate, fully functional clock networks into individual dies.[1] These separate networks should be subsequently linked by multiple TSVs to improve wirelength and clocking performance [43].

3.3 Partitioning and Floorplanning

Traditionally, the main objectives for partitioning are to (*i*) minimize the cuts/connections between partitions and to (*ii*) reduce the overall design complexity by means of divide-and-conquer. For 3D stacks, however, the objective (*i*) has to be carefully adapted. For example, min-cut partitioning is not practical since it cannot account for the stacking order of partitioned layers/dies which, in turn, impacts the overall number of vertical interconnects [56]. Furthermore, depending on other, more pressing criteria such as thermal management, the minimization of cuts/connections may not be the primary concern.

In general, partitioning tools need to become more technology-aware in order to properly account for different stacking scenarios and their implications. For example, monolithic stacks are vertically interconnected by very small vias which can (and should) be employed in large numbers, to enable high-performance and low-power transistor-level integration [19]. Nevertheless, related partitioning must account for routing congestion [20]. For TSV-based 3D ICs, it depends on the particular dies' stacking interface whether interconnects should be limited: a face-to-back (or back-to-back) interface requires TSVs which may need to be restricted, while a face-to-face interface allows for a large number of interconnects, comparable to monolithic stacks. Practical approaches for 3D partitioning must also address other design concerns such as power-density constraints [57] or performance-aware logic splitting [6].

Floorplanning determines the module arrangement within (nowadays mainly pre-fixed) die outlines. For 3D chip stacks, the module arrangement is interdependent across the whole stack, rendering 3D floorplanning much more complex than 2D floorplanning.[2]

Existing floorplanning methodologies already address key challenges such as thermal management [27, 34–36], co-arrangement of modules and TSVs [59] or planning of system-level buses [27, 36, 60]. Still, 3D floorplanning is a highly technology-dependent and iterative process—fast, accurate and configurable design evaluation is currently targeted but still to be enhanced [61,62]. So far, only few tools offer high-level, multi-objective exploration, which is needed for microarchitecture-focused 3D design [55, 63]. Furthermore, splitting and folding modules across multiple dies—to potentially reduce power and wirelength even more—has to be also

---

[1]Modules are preferably (re)used as is—splitting them across dies is only warranted for particular scenarios [8, 54, 55]. Thus, timing paths remain mostly within dies which implies that embedding of functional clock networks into separate dies is practical.

[2]Wang *et al.* [58] have shown the NP-complete nature of both 2.5D floorplans (zero-height modules; emulated 3D arrangements) with more than two dies and for 3D floorplans (non-zero height modules; native 3D arrangements) in general.

explored during floorplanning (and during placement, see below). Related tools/flows are available [54, 55, 64, 65], but they tend to neglect properties of stacking interfaces and/or apply stochastic optimization where results are largely irreproducible and unsteady.

3.4 Placement

As with floorplanning, placement for 3D chips becomes much more challenging. The main objectives are (i) wirelength minimization, (ii) thermal management, and (iii) vertical-interconnect-aware placement or co-placement of cells and vertical interconnects (applies for TSV-based 3D ICs). Placement may further account for specific properties of 3D stacks, e.g., thermo-mechanical stress induced by TSVs (which can even be exploited for timing [66]). There are three categories for placement approaches, discussed next.

Folding-based placement reuses 2D placement solutions/tools and derives a 3D placement by folding modules and applying local refinements [67]. The main benefit is that proven 2D placers can be applied; the disadvantage is the limited consideration of implications arising from die stacking, e.g., increased routing congestion. Recall that folding has been recently advocated for 3D floorplanning as well; the potential of orchestrated folding for floorplanning and placement, however, has not been addressed yet.

Analytic placement is based on numerical analysis of non-linear equations which encode objectives such as minimization of wirelength and cell overlap. In the context of 3D chips, analytic placement is either tailored as 2.5D or 3D placement: the 2.5D approach encodes cell-die assignments as fixed variables, but still accounts for any interdependencies of cells across different dies [37, 66, 68–70]; the 3D approach sets cell-die assignments as flexible variables to be optimized as part of the overall placement solution [37, 71, 72].

Analytic placement suggests itself for placement of 3D chips—cells are distributed optimally ("only" with respect to the tailored equations) throughout the 2.5D/3D domain. However, it has some drawbacks: its complexity calls for techniques such as clustering and coarsening [72] which may lower the final design quality; some formulations (e.g., Huber functions) offer only local smoothness which requires further efforts for global smoothing across the third dimension [37]; any issue/objective not readily accounted within the placement equations (such as thermo-mechanical stress induced by TSVs) may be notably exacerbated and difficult to post-process. Thus, analytic placement is usually not applied as stand-alone but rather as integrated stage (for global placement), as described next.

Hierarchical placement typically applies three stages: global placement, legalization and detailed placement. For 3D chip stacks, most hierarchical placers invoke partitioning and/or floorplanning before actual placement [37, 66, 68–70, 73]. This way, related efforts for module arrangement are acknowledged and cells are pre-assigned to particular dies (but not necessarily fixed to them). This, in turn, helps to improve the convergence of 3D placement. Note that hierarchical placement is not restrictive in terms of applicable placement techniques. For example, Kim et al. [69] apply force-directed (2.5D/3D) global placement, Goplen et al. [73] promote 3D recursive-bisection placement, and Lu et al. [71] propose (globally smooth) electrostatics-based 3D placement.

For placement of TSV-based 3D ICs, different thermal- and TSV-aware 3D placers have been proposed [68, 70, 73]. In this context, the co-placement of cells and TSVs has proven beneficial for thermal management [68, 70] as well as for reducing wirelength [69] and critical delays [66]. In order to avoid potentially opposing and/or unsteady TSV arrangement across partitioning, floorplanning and placement, a closer integration of those stages with dedicated feedback loops to orchestrate TSV (co-)placement is required.

3.5 Routability Estimation and Routing

Routability estimation provides fast but limited local and global predictions of routing supply and demand, without invoking actual routing. This is particularly relevant when designing 3D stacks in order to fully exploit their potential for massive interconnectivity and to enable high-performance and low-power 3D chips. The key challenge for both routability estimation and routing of 3D stacks arises from the 3D arrangement of nets, i.e., nets are spanning more than one die, which requires to account for vertical interconnects. Related EDA techniques are reviewed next.

Analytic estimation is mainly based on simple geometric and/or global estimates and, thus, not effective for controlling physical-design stages, e.g., to avoid local routing congestion. Nevertheless, analytic estimates are helpful for fast design evaluation; the well-known half-perimeter wirelength (HPWL) is such an estimate. However, note that the HPWL should be determined step-wise in 3D chips to achieve reasonable accuracy; all partial nets (i.e., net segments encapsulated in separate dies/layers) are to be independently estimated and subsequently summed up [8]. Kim et al. [74] proposed an interconnect model which is TSV-aware and emulates optimal buffer insertion. Thus, this model helps to efficiently evaluate wirelength, delay and power consumption of 3D chips.

Heuristic estimation applies computationally-inexpensive probabilistic models to capture local routing demand or congestion. Models for 3D chips have to account for vertical interconnects, along with their capacities, distribution and potential blockages. Fischbach et al. [75] extended the well-known concept of routing graphs which may serve as generic data structure or "backbone" for any model of choice. Depending on the desired accuracy-runtime trade-off, their extended graph encodes each die's multiple metal layers as one merged graph layer or as separate layers. In any case, the stacking and interconnects technology defines the graph's vertical capacities. Panth et al. [20] use such a 3D routing graph along with simplified construction of 3D rectilinear Steiner trees for efficient routability estimation in monolithic 3D chips.

Global routing for 3D chips has already been implicitly addressed by conventional methodologies due to the routing layers' "3D arrangement" in 2D chips. Nevertheless, dedicated global routers have been proposed for TSV-based 3D ICs to account for routing obstacles (induced by TSVs) and to facilitate thermal management [26, 76–79]. Most of these routers construct Steiner or minimum spanning trees, use thermal-RC-network analysis, and (re)arrange signal TSVs, possibly along with dummy thermal TSVs and/or thermal wires. In general, accounting for signal, PG, clock and thermal TSVs along with their networks—all competing for placement and routing area—poses a major design challenge [80]. Thus, global routing (along with partitioning, floorplanning and placement) has to implement an orchestrated (re)arrangement of TSVs to enable design closure.

As for global routing of interposer stacks, early work by Minz et al. [81] focused on delay-, congestion- and crosstalk-aware redistribution of pins and nets to properly access and utilize the interposer's routing channels. In order to reduce TSV usage, Wang et al. [82] developed a 3D NoC with shared vertical links, and Foroutan et al. [83] optimized the assignment of such shared links in "vertically-partially-connected 3D NoCs". Loh et al. [16] outlined open challenges for large-scale and heterogeneous 3D NoCs, such as the synchronization of routers across sub-networks with potentially different topologies.

Detailed routing is not fundamentally different for 3D stacks; its task remains routing the net segments within metal layers (of individual dies). Assuming that multiple types of interconnects and obstacles may be modeled, available detailed routers can be reused.

3.6 Testing

As indicated when discussing testability of clock networks (see Sec. 3.2), stacking known-good dies is essential for 3D chips. Further testing approaches of 3D chip stacks are described next.

Fault models and at-speed testing has been proposed for both interposer stacks [84–86] and TSV-based 3D ICs [43, 87, 88]. These studies are typically focused on specific scenarios. For example, Taouil et al. [87] developed a methodology tailored for testing of memory-on-logic stacks and Deutsch et al. [88] applied thermo-mechanical-stress-aware generation of test patterns for TSV-based 3D ICs. Offering a more holistic approach, Wang *et al.* [84] enabled unified testing of wires, microbumps and TSVs for interposer stacks, with low overhead and compliance to the *IEEE 1149.1* standard. Agrawal *et al.* [89] proposed an efficient heuristic for test-flow selection which can be applied for different configurations of 3D chip stacks; it is notably more efficient and qualitatively competitive to an optimal approach when stacking up to three dies.

Since Design-for-Test (DfT) architectures require access to all modules within 3D chip stacks, such architectures should be based on well-defined components and testing interfaces (see Sec. 5).

3.7 Needs for Advances in Design Automation

We discussed how classical challenges become much more complex when designing 3D chip stacks, and we reviewed promising and available solutions. There is nevertheless a need to further improve "classical" design automation, with particular focus on:

- Synchronized arrangement of all types of TSVs during floorplanning, placement, design of clock networks and routing;
- Perpetual consideration of variations—mainly induced by chip stacking in general and/or by thermo-mechanical stress around TSVs in particular;
- Technology- and stacking-aware design planning and evaluation, in particular for partitioning and floorplanning;
- Measures for 3D design-space exploration, e.g., by exploring options for module folding during partitioning and/or floorplanning, or by system-level arrangement of components and dies within the 3D stack; and
- System-level design of global interconnects. This requires to optimize buses and vertical interconnects (mainly relevant for TSVs) along with design objectives/constraints for, e.g., bandwidth, power consumption, delay and signal integrity.

Note that some of these needs (e.g., 3D design-space exploration) have recently been addressed to some degree by high-level design automation (see Sec. 4).

As outlined in Fig. 3, EDA tools should be unified into a workflow in order to meet (3D-specific) classical as well as novel design challenges. This calls for, among others, extensive code modularization, the design/use of internal/external APIs and for file formats tailored for exchanging 3D-chip designs (see Sec. 5 for the latter).

4. NOVEL DESIGN CHALLENGES AND EMERGING SOLUTIONS

With the aforementioned classical design challenges of 3D chip stacks being addressed at least to some degree by today's tools, the focus for EDA R&D is shifting towards more high- and system-level challenges such as simulation of multi-physics effects. These challenges are especially pressing for heterogeneous stacks, comprising components such as MEMS or photonics along with "regular" digital modules. We outline promising approaches and trends suitable to address such novel challenges next.

4.1 Pathfinding and Design Exploration

Due to the complex and diversified nature of 3D chip stacks, the automation of their high-level design is extremely challenging. Novel tools are required to explore (at an early stage) the complex impact arising from any decision/step taken in the design flow on criteria such as functionality and power consumption. *Pathfinding* is addressing this need by stepwise passing down high-level descriptions within customized EDA suites. Feedback loops are essential for this purpose, to pass down specifications (e.g., physical constraints) as well as to annotate findings back (e.g., simulation results). Pathfinding flows should cover the following three stages:

1. **System-Level Design:** A high-level description (e.g., in SystemC) is generated and/or iteratively adapted. Technology

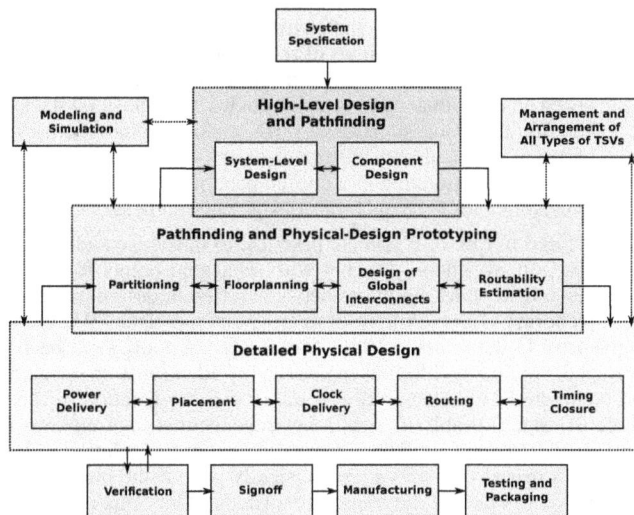

Figure 3: Workflow for designing 3D chip stacks. Pathfinding and prototyping link system-level and IC-level design; this link eases the design closure for the highly iterative process. Modeling and simulation as well as management of TSVs must interact with multiple design stages. Most stages require thermal- and variation-aware optimization; feedback loops are essential.

and stacking configurations have to be already considered, e.g., stacking impacts the options for high-level partitioning.

2. **Component Design**: Components are abstract design modules such as RTL modules—they serve as "bridging" parts between system design and physical design. Components must be modularized in order to encapsulate the high-level design and to enable design reuse for different 3D stacks.

3. **Physical-Design Prototyping:** The components are then fed to (customized) physical-design stages. In contrast to classical physical design, the focus lies initially on fast design exploration, i.e., to obtain "coarse layouts". The components are also to be annotated (e.g., with their power consumption) to facilitate guidance of subsequent pathfinding iterations.

Pathfinding for 3D chip stacks has been initially proposed in 2009 by Milojevic *et al.* [90]. They applied automated synthesis of RTL modules and physical-design prototyping using feedback loops. More recently, Martin *et al.* [18] proposed to encapsulate TSV arrays using parameterized multi-port modules. They do so in order to feed 3D chip stacks containing such and other components to electromagnetic solvers for analysis of crosstalk across the whole stack. Yazdani and Park [91] automated and optimized the arrangement of buffers, Cu pillars and package bumps for *Wide I/O* memory integration [92] in interposer stacks. Priyadarshi *et al.* [93] proposed transaction-level-based and thermal-aware pathfinding, complementing previous RTL-based approaches.

Besides these mainly academic efforts, commercial tool chains have been becoming available as well, for example *Sphinx 3D Path Finder* (used in [18]) or *Mentor Graphics Xpedition Path Finder Suite* [94].

4.2 Chip-Package Co-Design

The diverse nature of 3D chip stacking, along with its manifold technology configurations, calls for co-design of chip and package. Ideally, the whole 3D stack should be designed within one EDA suite. However, this is not necessarily practical due to several reasons such as:

1. The design of complex 3D chip stacks is typically the effort of a large team, with several engineers (potentially working

in separate companies and/or different locations) being responsible for different parts of the whole stack.

2. Existing design know-how and EDA tools are mainly focused on individual parts or technologies, not whole 3D stacks.

3. The multitude of interfaces in 3D stacks require—both in terms of physical and functional design—measures for design orchestration and/or a unified data base; this is difficult to establish for heterogeneous design environments.

As illustrated in Fig. 3, it is more practical to introduce and agree on a common workflow, possibly with dedicated points for data handover and feedback iterations between different design parties.

An elaborate example for co-designing a mixed-signal 3D stack is given by Cederström in [95]. Multiple EDA tools have been leveraged, applied by different engineers, linked via custom scripts, and configured to exchange design data. A representation of the whole 3D stack, usable in such a heterogeneous design environment, is called for (see Sec. 5 for a related, novel solution). It has been stressed that TSVs are physically part of the interposer but functionally part of the transceivers (in the ICs). This required multiple iterations for design closure, along with notable manual effort. Cederström hence proposes that the top metal layers, pins and bumps of the ICs are managed by packaging engineers. This way, the iterations for designing the package and the transceiver-TSV links are eased and IC designers are involved more effectively.

Analysing TSVs more efficiently for their impact on whole 3D chip stacks has been successfully pursued for some time; the related modeling and simulation techniques (see "medium" design phases, Sec. 4.3) can also be extended for chip-package co-design [96].

Pathfinding tools may be helpful for co-design as well; for example, *Mentor Graphics Xpedition Path Finder* [94] is tailored for chip-package design with features such as a "virtual die model" (to encapsulate details of IC design) or the generation of pin arrays.

4.3 Multi-Physics Simulation and Verification

Simulation is an integral part of design automation while verification is traditionally separated from the actual physical design. Because of strong coupling of the different physical domains—especially but not exclusively occurring in complex, heterogeneous stacks—simulation and verification for 3D chip stacks should account for multi-physics effects (Fig. 4). Such a framework has been proposed by Schneider *et al.* [97]. They advocate tailoring simulation techniques for each design level; they further promote the (re)use of parameterizable models.

Next, we review measures for simulation and verification of 3D chip stacks across different design levels.

At transistor level, i.e., the lowest level of abstraction, very detailed simulation models are required—they must capture all active and passive devices along with their physical properties. For the thermal and mechanical domains, models are implemented as fine-grain meshes which are fed to finite element/difference analysis, e.g., using tools from ANSYS or COMSOL. These models are also used to verify the reliability and performance of 3D interconnects in detail, e.g., for TSV arrays [98–100]. For the electrical domain, well-known techniques such as SPICE simulations, LVS or ERC verification are applied as well, but with additional consideration of 3D interconnects and multi-physics effects [101]. Some tools (e.g., *Mentor Calibre*) have also been tailored for this need.

For "medium" design phases, such as placement and routing, models are more abstract and capture the system behaviour. Here, the main challenge for simulation is to survey the complex, multi-physics coupling between individual components and to evaluate the overall system behaviour, all in relatively short runtime. Models are often derived from detailed simulations of small components, e.g., single IP blocks or few TSVs. These "characterizing simulations for base components" are independent from the actual design process and can be conducted in advance by experienced engineers, who then encapsulate their findings, typically into parameterizable modules or analytical models. A prominent example for this is

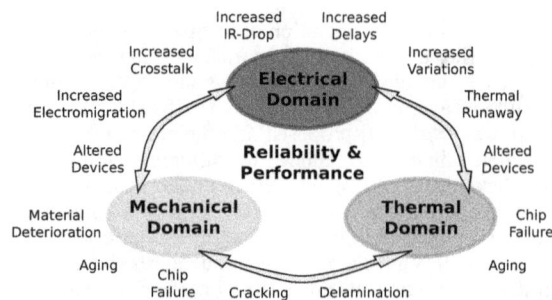

Figure 4: Coupling of various domains in 3D chips, along with potential implications for reliability and performance, require simulation and verification to account for multi-physics effects.

the simulation of TSV arrays—they have been successfully modeled using manifold approaches: as multi-port components along with S-parameters for simulation of signal coupling [17, 18, 102]; as MIMO channels to regulate equalization of such coupling [103]; via superposition of TSV's stress components to capture their impact on power and/or timing [48, 96]; and via superposition of stress components to determine thermo-mechanical stress itself [9, 96, 100]. The automated generation of such models, also for other components than TSV arrays, remains an open challenge [104].

High-level design renders simulation challenging due to its abstract nature; 3D chips are typically described as a chip-package stack in SystemC, VHDL or Verilog, or even in custom languages. As with pathfinding (Sec. 4.1), simulations are initially approximative (and rely on design experience); more accurate simulations will become feasible after subsequent design/simulation stages fed their findings back. In general, models have to be scalable to support 3D stacks with diverse, multi-scale geometries [102]. Regarding needs for EDA tools, a unified data handling of high-level descriptions is sought after, to ease streaming the 3D-chip configuration to and from different simulation and design tools [105]. A flexible configuration or even the generation of PDKs is required to streamline verification at this chip-package system level [105]; Cibrario *et al.* [106] released such a PDK generator for the (currently widely adopted) 3D stacking technologies from CEA-LETI.

5. PROMOTING 3D CHIPS VIA DESIGN STANDARDS AND FILE FORMATS

Design standards and file formats for seamless data exchange are important measures to achieve the advances required in design automation for 3D chip stacks more efficiently. As for standardization, recent progress covers memory integration and testing:

- The JESD229 standard [92], commonly known as *Wide I/O*, considers one up to four memory dies stacked on top of a controller die, with four up to eight 128-bit-wide memory channels. The standard further covers details on AC and DC characteristics, packages, and bump assignments. First *Wide I/O* stacks and design flows are available [12, 91, 96, 107].
- JESD235A [108], better known as *High Bandwidth Memory (HBM)*, is an alternative standard for memory integration and adopted by industry, e.g., by Hynix [109] and Nvidia [110].
- Yet another standard, the *Hybrid Memory Cube (HMC)* [3], has recently gained more attention as well. It is backed by Altera, Micron, Open-Silicon, Samsung and Xilinx.
- As for testing, standards are currently under development; *IEEE P1838* evolves as the most promising option [111]. The therein proposed wrapper circuitry enables controllability and observability at the die boundaries. Besides the novel wrapper, existing test facilities are considered for reuse whenever possible: *IEEE 1149.x* for test access, *IEEE 1500* for die test, and *IEEE P1687* for internal debugging.

These standardization efforts are crucial for adoption of 3D chip stacks since they facilitate first commercial products (i.e., memory stacks) and are streamlining DfT, which is a pressing concern from industrial perspective. However, further aspects such as thermal management and power delivery (along with related analysis/verification) also call for standardization efforts [102].

As indicated before, another essential need is the seamless data exchange between different parties. Heinig and Fischbach [112] proposed an *assembly design kit (ADK)* for this purpose, which is analogous to the well-known PDK but tailored for 3D chip stacks. An ADK serves the exchange of both design data as well as manufacturing requirements. Using input from all parties, it encodes details of manufacturing steps and procedures, material properties, geometrical descriptions of the stack along with its components and interconnects, as well as assembly rules such as minimal pitches. Besides, an ADK contains customized data converters to "translate" any 3D-stack design into appropriate settings/commands for the manufacturing equipment. Ferguson and Ramadan (*Mentor Graphics*) also advocate the concept of ADKs [113]. They highlight its potential for simplified verification and sign-off procedures, especially for interfaces between dies and/or the package.

6. SUMMARY

In this paper, we discuss the most relevant aspects of automating the physical-design process for 3D chip stacks. We highlight how this process becomes increasingly difficult and demanding as compared to well-engineered design automation for 2D chips, and we review the state-of-art for such 3D-chip design automation.

Classical challenges such as thermal management, clock delivery and placement also became notably more complex, and have seen much academic and industrial R&D in the past. Novel, 3D-specific challenges, such as pathfinding or multi-physics simulation, have undergone similar progress recently. However, further problems remain such as the system-level design of global interconnects and stacking-aware partitioning. Other challenges to be addressed are more technology-dependent, e.g., the synchronized arrangement of all different types of TSVs. Finally, the automation and data management for high-level design is of particular importance—such measures are essential for initial design exploration, collaborative and distributed design teamwork, and final design closure.

We conclude that design automation for 3D chip stacks is challenging and not yet fully solved, though more and more sophisticated EDA solutions are being proposed. Recent efforts such as ADKs and pathfinding tools, among others, help to streamline the design process and, thus, render 3D chip stacks more applicable.

7. ACKNOWLEDGMENTS

This work was supported by *Mubadala*, Abu Dhabi, UAE, under the *TwinLab 3D Stacked Chips* collaboration between the Masdar Institute of Science and Technology, UAE, and the Dresden University of Technology, Germany, Ref. 372/002/6754/102d/146/64947. The authors are thankful to Prof. Ibrahim (Abe) M. Elfadel (Masdar Institute) for fostering the *TwinLab* collaboration and for his feedback on this paper.

8. REFERENCES

[1] W. Arden *et al.*, ""More-than-Moore" White Paper," ITRS, Tech. Rep., 2010.
[2] R. R. Tummala, *System on Package: Miniaturization of the Entire System.* McGraw-Hill Professional, 2008.
[3] (2014, Feb) Hybrid Memory Cube specification 2.0. [Online]: http://hybridmemorycube.org/files/SiteDownloads/20141119_HMCC_Spec2.0Release.pdf
[4] S. Borkar, "3D integration for energy efficient system design," in *Proc. DAC*, 2011, pp. 214–219.
[5] D. H. Kim *et al.*, "3D-MAPS: 3D massively parallel processor with stacked memory," in *Proc. ISSCC*, 2012, pp. 188–190.
[6] G. Neela and J. Draper, "Logic-on-logic partitioning techniques for 3-dimensional integrated circuits," in *Proc. ISCAS*, 2013, pp. 789–792.

[7] T. Thorolfsson, S. Lipa, and P. D. Franzon, "A 10.35 mW/GFlop stacked SAR DSP unit using fine-grain partitioned 3D integration," in *Proc. CICC*, 2012, pp. 1–4.
[8] J. Knechtel, I. L. Markov, and J. Lienig, "Assembling 2-D blocks into 3-D chips," *Trans. CAD*, vol. 31, no. 2, pp. 228–241, 2012.
[9] C. Zhang and L. Li, "Characterization and design of through-silicon via arrays in three-dimensional ICs based on thermomechanical modeling," *Trans. ED*, vol. 58, no. 2, pp. 279–287, 2011.
[10] V. S. Nandakumar and M. Marek-Sadowska, "Layout effects in fine-grain 3-D integrated regular microprocessor blocks," in *Proc. DAC*, 2011, pp. 639–644.
[11] J. H. Lau, "TSV interposer: The most cost-effective integrator for 3D IC integration," SEMATECH Symposium Taiwan, 2011.
[12] D. Milojevic *et al.*, "Design issues in heterogeneous 3D/2.5D integration," in *Proc. ASPDAC*, 2013, pp. 403–410.
[13] C. Zhang and G. Sun, "Fabrication cost analysis for 2D, 2.5D, and 3D IC designs," in *Proc. 3DIC*, 2012, pp. 1–4.
[14] P. Dorsey, "Xilinx stacked silicon interconnect technology delivers breakthrough FPGA capacity, bandwidth, and power efficiency," Xilinc, Inc., Tech. Rep., 2010.
[15] (2013, Nov) Open-Silicon and GLOBALFOUNDRIES demonstrate custom 28nm SoC using 2.5D technology. [Online]: http://www.open-silicon.com/2013/11/open-silicon-globalfoundries-demonstrate-custom-28nm-soc-2-5d-technology/
[16] G. H. Loh *et al.*, "Interconnect-memory challenges for multi-chip, silicon interposer systems," in *Proc. MEMSYS*, 2015, pp. 3–10.
[17] W. Yao *et al.*, "Modeling and application of multi-port TSV networks in 3-D IC," *Trans. CAD*, vol. 32, no. 4, pp. 487–496, 2013.
[18] B. Martin, K. Han, and M. Swaminathan, "A path finding based SI design methodology for 3D integration," in *Proc. ECTC*, 2014, pp. 2124–2130.
[19] Y.-J. Lee and S. K. Lim, "Ultrahigh density logic designs using monolithic 3-D integration," *Trans. CAD*, vol. 32, no. 12, pp. 1892–1905, 2013.
[20] S. Panth *et al.*, "Placement-driven partitioning for congestion mitigation in monolithic 3D IC designs," *Trans. CAD*, vol. 34, no. 4, pp. 540–553, 2015.
[21] S. K. Samal *et al.*, "Fast and accurate thermal modeling and optimization for monolithic 3D ICs," in *Proc. DAC*, 2014, pp. 1–6.
[22] M. B. Healy and S. K. Lim, "Distributed TSV topology for 3-D power-supply networks," *Trans. VLSI*, vol. 20, no. 11, pp. 2066–2079, 2012.
[23] H.-T. Chen *et al.*, "A new architecture for power network in 3D IC," in *Proc. DATE*, 2011, pp. 1–6.
[24] J. Knechtel *et al.*, "Multiobjective optimization of deadspace, a critical resource for 3D-IC integration," in *Proc. ICCAD*, 2012, pp. 705–712.
[25] Y. Chen *et al.*, "Through silicon via aware design planning for thermally efficient 3-D integrated circuits," *Trans. CAD*, vol. 32, no. 9, pp. 1335–1346, 2013.
[26] P. Hsu, H. Chen, and T. Hwang, "Stacking signal TSV for thermal dissipation in global routing for 3-D IC," *Trans. CAD*, vol. 33, no. 7, pp. 1031–1042, 2014.
[27] J. Knechtel, E. Young, and J. Lienig, "Planning massive interconnects in 3D chips," *Trans. CAD*, vol. 34, no. 11, pp. 1808–1821, 2015.
[28] P. Jain *et al.*, "A multi-story power delivery technique for 3D integrated circuits," in *Proc. ISLPED*, 2008, pp. 57–62.
[29] K. Kim *et al.*, "Effects of on-chip decoupling capacitors and silicon substrate on power distribution networks in TSV-based 3D-ICs," in *Proc. ECTC*, 2012, pp. 690–697.
[30] G. Huang *et al.*, "Power delivery for 3D chip stacks: Physical modeling and design implication," in *Proc. EPEPS*, 2007, pp. 205–208.
[31] S. Samal *et al.*, "Ultralow power circuit design with subthreshold/near-threshold 3-D IC technologies," *Trans. CPMT*, vol. 5, no. 7, pp. 980–990, 2015.
[32] D. Fick *et al.*, "Centip3De: A cluster-based NTC architecture with 64 ARM Cortex-M3 cores in 3D stacked 130 nm CMOS," *J. Solid-State Circ.*, vol. 48, no. 1, pp. 104–117, 2013.
[33] S. Jin *et al.*, "On optimizing system energy of voltage-frequency island based 3-D multi-core SoCs under thermal constraints," *Integration*, vol. 48, pp. 36–45, 2015.
[34] J. Cong and Y. Ma, "Thermal-aware 3D floorplan," in *Three Dimensional Integrated Circuit Design*, Y. Xie, J. Cong, and S. Sapatnekar, Eds. Springer US, 2010, ch. 4, pp. 63–102.
[35] P. Budhathoki *et al.*, "Integrating 3D floorplanning and optimization of thermal through-silicon vias," in *3D Stacked Chips – From Emerging Processes to Heterogeneous Systems*, I. A. M. Elfadel and G. Fettweis, Eds. Springer, 2016, ch. 10.
[36] J. Knechtel, E. F. Y. Young, and J. Lienig, "Structural planning of 3D-IC interconnects by block alignment," in *Proc. ASPDAC*, 2014, pp. 53–60.
[37] G. Luo, Y. Shi, and J. Cong, "An analytical placement framework for 3-D ICs and its extension on thermal awareness," *Trans. CAD*, vol. 32, no. 4, pp. 510–523, 2013.
[38] J. Sun *et al.*, "3D power delivery for microprocessors and high-performance ASICs," in *Proc. Appl. Power Electr. Conf.*, 2007, pp. 127–133.
[39] P. Zhou, K. Sridharan, and S. S. Sapatnekar, "Congestion-aware power grid optimization for 3D circuits using MIM and CMOS decoupling capacitors," in *Proc. ASPDAC*, 2009, pp. 179–184.
[40] D. Sekar *et al.*, "A 3D-IC technology with integrated microchannel cooling," in *Proc. IITC*, 2008, pp. 13–15.
[41] A.-C. Hsieh and T. Hwang, "TSV redundancy: Architecture and design issues in 3-D IC," *Trans. VLSI*, vol. 20, no. 4, pp. 711–722, 2012.

[42] I. Loi *et al.*, "A low-overhead fault tolerance scheme for TSV-based 3D network on chip links," in *Proc. ICCAD*, 2008, pp. 598–602.

[43] C.-L. Lung *et al.*, "Through-silicon via fault-tolerant clock networks for 3-D ICs," *Trans. CAD*, vol. 32, no. 7, pp. 1100–1109, 2013.

[44] H. Park and T. Kim, "Synthesis of TSV fault-tolerant 3-D clock trees," *Trans. CAD*, vol. 34, no. 2, pp. 266–279, Feb 2015.

[45] X. Zhao and S. K. Lim, "TSV array utilization in low-power 3D clock network design," in *Proc. ISLPED*, 2012, pp. 21–26.

[46] X. Zhao and S. K. Lim, "Through-silicon-via-induced obstacle-aware clock tree synthesis for 3D ICs," in *Proc. ASPDAC*, 2012, pp. 347–352.

[47] S. Garg and D. Marculescu, "Mitigating the impact of process variation on the performance of 3-D integrated circuits," *Trans. VLSI*, vol. 21, no. 10, pp. 1903–1914, 2013.

[48] S. Marella and S. Sapatnekar, "A holistic analysis of circuit performance variations in 3-D ICs with thermal and TSV-induced stress considerations," *Trans. VLSI*, vol. 23, no. 7, pp. 1308–1321, 2015.

[49] J.-S. Yang *et al.*, "Robust clock tree synthesis with timing yield optimization for 3D-ICs," in *Proc. ASPDAC*, 2011, pp. 621–626.

[50] T.-Y. Kim and T. Kim, "Post silicon management of on-package variation induced 3D clock skew," *J. Semicond. Technol. Scie*, vol. 12, no. 2, pp. 139–149, 2012.

[51] X. Zhao, J. Minz, and S. K. Lim, "Low-power and reliable clock network design for through-silicon via (TSV) based 3D ICs," *Trans. CPMT*, vol. 1, no. 2, pp. 247–259, 2011.

[52] H. Xu, V. F. Pavlidis, and G. De Micheli, "Effect of process variations in 3D global clock distribution networks," *J. Emerg. Technol. Comput. Syst.*, vol. 8, no. 3, pp. 20:1–20:25, 2012.

[53] X. Zhao, S. Mukhopadhyay, and S. K. Lim, "Variation-tolerant and low-power clock network design for 3D ICs," in *Proc. ECTC*, 2011, pp. 2007–2014.

[54] M. Jung *et al.*, "On enhancing power benefits in 3D ICs: Block folding and bonding styles perspective," in *Proc. DAC*, 2014, pp. 1–6.

[55] Y. Ma *et al.*, "Investigating the effects of fine-grain three-dimensional integration on microarchitecture design," *J. Emerg. Technol. Comput. Syst.*, vol. 4, no. 4, pp. 17:1–17:30, 2008.

[56] Y.-S. Huang, Y.-H. Liu, and J.-D. Huang, "Layer-aware design partitioning for vertical interconnect minimization," in *ISVLSI*, 2011, pp. 144–149.

[57] H.-L. Chang *et al.*, "A 3D IC designs partitioning algorithm with power consideration," in *Proc. ISQED*, 2012, pp. 137–142.

[58] R. Wang, E. F. Y. Young, and C.-K. Cheng, "Complexity of 3-D floorplans by analysis of graph cuboidal dual hardness," *Trans. DAES*, vol. 15, no. 4, pp. 33:1–33:22, 2010.

[59] C.-R. Li, W.-K. Mak, and T.-C. Wang, "Fast fixed-outline 3-D IC floorplanning with TSV co-placement," *Trans. VLSI*, vol. 21, no. 3, pp. 523–532, 2013.

[60] A. Quiring, M. Olbrich, and E. Barke, "Fast global interconnnect driven 3D floorplanning," in *Proc. VLSISOC*, 2015, pp. 313–318.

[61] R. Fischbach, J. Lienig, and J. Knechtel, "Investigating modern layout representations for improved 3D design automation," in *Proc. GLSVLSI*, 2011, pp. 337–342.

[62] S. K. Lim, "Research needs for TSV-based 3D IC architectural floorplanning," *J. Inf. Commun. Converg. Eng.*, vol. 12, no. 1, pp. 46–52, 2014.

[63] M. Healy *et al.*, "Multiobjective microarchitectural floorplanning for 2-D and 3-D ICs," *Trans. CAD*, vol. 26, no. 1, pp. 38–52, 2007.

[64] R. K. Nain and M. Chrzanowska-Jeske, "Fast placement-aware 3-D floorplanning using vertical constraints on sequence pairs," *Trans. VLSI*, vol. 19, no. 9, pp. 1667–1680, 2011.

[65] Y. Liu *et al.*, "Fine grain 3D integration for microarchitecture design through cube packing exploration," in *Proc. ICCD*, 2007, pp. 259–266.

[66] K. Athikulwongse *et al.*, "Stress-driven 3D-IC placement with TSV keep-out zone and regularity study," in *Proc. ICCAD*, 2010, pp. 669–674.

[67] J. Cong *et al.*, "Thermal-aware 3D IC placement via transformation," in *Proc. ASPDAC*, 2007, pp. 780–785.

[68] J. Cong, G. Luo, and Y. Shi, "Thermal-aware cell and through-silicon-via co-placement for 3D ICs," in *Proc. DAC*, 2011, pp. 670–675.

[69] D. H. Kim, K. Athikulwongse, and S. K. Lim, "Study of through-silicon-via impact on the 3-D stacked IC layout," *Trans. VLSI*, vol. 21, no. 5, pp. 862–874, 2013.

[70] K. Athikulwongse, M. Pathak, and S. K. Lim, "Exploiting die-to-die thermal coupling in 3D IC placement," in *Proc. DAC*, 2012, pp. 741–746.

[71] J. Lu *et al.*, "ePlace-3D: electrostatics based placement for 3D-ICs," *ArXiv e-prints*, Dec. 2015.

[72] M.-K. Hsu, V. Balabanov, and Y.-W. Chang, "TSV-aware analytical placement for 3-D IC designs based on a novel weighted-average wirelength model," *Trans. CAD*, vol. 32, no. 4, pp. 497–509, 2013.

[73] B. Goplen and S. Sapatnekar, "Placement of 3D ICs with thermal and interlayer via considerations," in *Proc. DAC*, 2007, pp. 626–631.

[74] D. Kim, S. Mukhopadhyay, and S. Lim, "TSV-aware interconnect distribution models for prediction of delay and power consumption of 3-D stacked ICs," *Trans. CAD*, vol. 33, no. 9, pp. 1384–1395, 2014.

[75] R. Fischbach, J. Lienig, and T. Meister, "From 3D circuit technologies and data structures to interconnect prediction," in *Proc. SLIP*, 2009, pp. 77–84.

[76] J. Cong and Y. Zhang, "Thermal-driven multilevel routing for 3-D ICs," in *Proc. ASPDAC*, 2005, pp. 121–126.

[77] T. Zhang, Y. Zhan, and S. S. Sapatnekar, "Temperature-aware routing in 3D ICs," in *Proc. ASPDAC*, 2006, pp. 1–6.

[78] M. Pathak and S. K. Lim, "Performance and thermal-aware Steiner routing for 3-D stacked ICs," *Trans. CAD*, vol. 28, no. 9, pp. 1373–1386, 2009.

[79] P.-Y. Hsu, H.-T. Chen, and T. Hwang, "Stacking signal TSV for thermal dissipation in global routing for 3D IC," in *Proc. ASPDAC*, 2013, pp. 699–704.

[80] Y.-J. Lee and S. K. Lim, "Co-optimization and analysis of signal, power, and thermal interconnects in 3-D ICs," *Trans. CAD*, vol. 30, no. 11, pp. 1635–1648, 2011.

[81] J. R. Minz and S. K. Lim, "Block-level 3-D global routing with an application to 3-D packaging," *Trans. CAD*, vol. 25, no. 10, pp. 2248–2257, 2006.

[82] Y. Wang *et al.*, "Economizing TSV resources in 3-D network-on-chip design," *Trans. VLSI*, vol. 23, no. 3, pp. 493–506, 2015.

[83] S. Foroutan, A. Sheibanyrad, and F. Petrot, "Assignment of vertical-links to routers in vertically-partially-connected 3-D-NoCs," *Trans. CAD*, vol. 33, no. 8, pp. 1208–1218, 2014.

[84] R. Wang, K. Chakrabarty, and S. Bhawmik, "Interconnect testing and test-path scheduling for interposer-based 2.5-D ICs," *Trans. CAD*, vol. 34, no. 1, pp. 136–149, 2015.

[85] L.-R. Huang *et al.*, "Parametric fault testing and performance characterization of post-bond interposer wires in 2.5-D ICs," *Trans. CAD*, vol. 33, no. 3, pp. 476–488, 2014.

[86] S. Huang *et al.*, "Pulse-vanishing test for interposers wires in 2.5-D IC," *Trans. CAD*, vol. 33, no. 8, pp. 1258–1268, 2014.

[87] M. Taouil *et al.*, "Post-bond interconnect test and diagnosis for 3-D memory stacked on logic," *Trans. CAD*, vol. 34, no. 11, pp. 1860–1872, 2015.

[88] S. Deutsch *et al.*, "TSV stress-aware ATPG for 3D stacked ICs," in *Proc. ATS*, 2012, pp. 31–36.

[89] M. Agrawal, K. Chakrabarty, and B. Eklow, "Test-cost optimization and test-flow selection for 3D-stacked ICs," Duke University, Tech. Rep., 2012.

[90] D. Milojevic *et al.*, "Automated pathfinding tool chain for 3D-stacked integrated circuits: Practical case study," in *Proc. 3DIC*, 2009, pp. 1–6.

[91] F. Yazdani and J. Park, "Pathfinding methodology for optimal design and integration of 2.5D/3D interconnects," in *Proc. ECTC*, 2014, pp. 1667–1672.

[92] (2011, Dec) JEDEC standard: JESD229 Wide I/O. [Online]: http://www.jedec.org/standards-documents/results/jesd229

[93] S. Priyadarshi *et al.*, "Thermal pathfinding for 3-D ICs," *Trans. CPMT*, vol. 4, no. 7, pp. 1159–1168, 2014.

[94] (2014, June) Mentor Graphics launches Xpedition Path Finder suite for efficient IC/Package/PCB design optimization, assembly, and visualization. Mentor Graphics. [Online]: https://www.mentor.com/company/news/mentor-xpedition-path-finder

[95] L. Cederström, "EDA environments for 3D chip stacks," in *3D Stacked Chips – From Emerging Processes to Heterogeneous Systems*, I. A. M. Elfadel and G. Fettweis, Eds. Springer, 2016, ch. 9.

[96] M. Jung, D. Z. Pan, and S. K. Lim, "Chip/package mechanical stress impact on 3-D IC reliability and mobility variations," *Trans. CAD*, vol. 32, no. 11, pp. 1694–1707, 2013.

[97] P. Schneider *et al.*, "Towards a methodology for analysis of interconnect structures for 3D-integration of micro systems," in *DTIP*, 2007, pp. 162–168.

[98] K. H. Lu *et al.*, "Thermo-mechanical reliability of 3-D ICs containing through silicon vias," in *Proc. ECTC*, 2009, pp. 630–634.

[99] H. M. Lee *et al.*, "Impact of TSV induced thermo-mechanical stress on semiconductor device performance," in *Proc. EDAPS*, 2012, pp. 189–192.

[100] Y. S. Chan, H. Y. Li, and X. Zhang, "Thermo-mechanical design rules for the fabrication of TSV interposers," *Trans. CPMT*, vol. 3, no. 4, pp. 633–640, 2013.

[101] R. Fischbach, A. Heinig, and P. Schneider, "Design rule check and layout versus schematic for 3D integration and advanced packaging," in *Proc. 3DIC*, 2014, pp. 1–7.

[102] M. Swaminathan, "Electrical design and modeling challenges for 3D system integration," in *DesignCon Tutorial*, 2012, pp. 1–31.

[103] T. Seifert, F. Pauls, and G. Fettweis, "Multi-TSV crosstalk channel equalization with non-uniform quantization," in *3D Stacked Chips – From Emerging Processes to Heterogeneous Systems*, I. A. M. Elfadel and G. Fettweis, Eds. Springer, 2016, ch. 4.

[104] P. Schneider *et al.*, "Integration of multi physics modeling of 3D stacks into modern 3D data structures," in *Proc. 3DIC*, 2010, pp. 1–6.

[105] A. Heinig and R. Fischbach, "Overview of 3D CAD design tools," in *Physical Design for 3D Integrated Circuits*, A. Todri-Sanial and C. S. Tan, Eds. CRC Press, Taylor & Francis, 2016, ch. 14, pp. 311–320.

[106] G. Cibrario *et al.*, "A 3D process design kit generator based on customizable 3D layout design environment," in *Proc. 3DIC*, 2013, pp. 1–5.

[107] A. Heinig, R. Fischbach, and M. Dittrich, "Thermal analysis and optimization of 2.5D and 3D integrated systems with Wide I/O memory," in *Proc. ITHERM*, 2014, pp. 86–91.

[108] (2015, Nov) JEDEC standard: JESD235A high bandwidth memory (HBM). [Online]: http://www.jedec.org/standards-documents/docs/jesd235a

[109] SK HYNIX INC. (2014, Dec) SK Hynix HBM graphics memory. [Online]: http://www.skhynix.com/inc/pdfDownload.jsp?path=/datasheet/Databook/Databook_Q4'2014_Graphics.pdf

[110] H. Reiter. (2014, Dec) 3D ASIP 2014: All aboard the 3D IC train! [Online]: http://www.3dincites.com/2014/12/3d-asip-2014-addresses-3d-benefits-challenges-solutions/

[111] E. J. Marinissen, "Status update of IEEE Std P1838," in *Proc. Int. Workshop Testing 3D Stack. Integr. Circ.*, 2014.

[112] A. Heinig and R. Fischbach, "Enabling automatic system design optimization through assembly design kits," in *Proc. 3DIC*, 2015, pp. TS8.31.1–TS8.31.5.

[113] J. Ferguson and T. Ramadan. (2015, Nov) Why do we need assembly design kits for packages? [Online]: http://www.3dincites.com/2015/11/why-do-we-need-assembly-design-kits-for-packages/

ePlace-3D: Electrostatics based Placement for 3D-ICs

Jingwei Lu
Cadence Design Systems, Inc.
francesco.ljw@gmail.com

Hao Zhuang
Dept. CSE of UCSD
hao.zhuang@cs.ucsd.edu

Ilgweon Kang
Dept. CSE of UCSD
igkang@ucsd.edu

Pengwen Chen
Dept. Applied Maths of NCHU
pengwen@nchu.edu.tw

Chung-Kuan Cheng
Dept. CSE of UCSD
ckcheng@ucsd.edu

ABSTRACT

We propose a flat, analytic, mixed-size placement algorithm *ePlace-3D* for three-dimension integrated circuits (3D-ICs) using nonlinear optimization. Our contributions are (1) electrostatics based 3D density function with globally uniform smoothness (2) 3D numerical solution with improved spectral formulation (3) 3D nonlinear pre-conditioner for convergence acceleration (4) interleaved 2D-3D placement for efficiency enhancement. Our placer outperforms the leading work mPL6-3D and NTUplace3-3D with 6.44% and 37.15% shorter wirelength, 9.11% and 10.27% fewer 3D vertical interconnects (VI) on average of IBM-PLACE circuits. Validation on the large-scale modern mixed-size (MMS) 3D circuits shows high performance and scalability.

1. INTRODUCTION

Placement remains dominant on the overall quality of physical design automation [29, 30]. Based on logic synthesis [31], back-end design on timing [45], power [9, 44], routability [8,38], variability [3,42] etc. are highly impacted by placement performance. The emerging 3D-IC [28] challenges the traditional 2D placers [1,2,5,17,19,25,41] to produce 3D circuit layout with minimum wirelength yet limited vertical interconnects (through-silicon vias (TSVs), monolithic inter-tier vias (MIVs), etc.). Innovations of mixed-size 3D-IC placement become quite desirable.

Previous **combinatorial** 3D-IC placers form two categories. Folding based methods [4] folds the 2D-IC placement layout to produce 3D solution with local refinement. Partitioning based approaches [7,18] minimize the usage of vertical resources. Kim et al. [18] partitions the netlist followed by tier assignment, then applies 2D quadratic placement [40] simultaneously over all the tiers. **Analytic** placers achieve better 3D-IC placement performace versus combinatorial algorithms. Goplen et al. [6] models the 3D-IC placement by a quadratic framework [5]. Hsu et al. [10] extends the 2D-IC placement prototype [11] and uses Bell-shape function [34] to smooth the vertical dimension. Luo et al. [27] utilizes the

2D algorithm in [1] and relaxes the discrete tiers via Huber function [12]. However, these modeling functions are only locally smooth. Moreover, their hierarchical cell clustering and grid coarsening would degrade the quality [25]. Separately, prior 3D placement benchmarks [13,15] are of up to only 210K cells, which are too small to represent modern design complexity. Large-scale bookshelf 3D-IC placement benchmarks become desirable.

In this work, we extend the 2D placers ePlace [22,23,25] and ePlace-MS [22,26] to the 3D domain. Our algorithm is named **ePlace-3D** and focused on **wirelength minimization** and **density equalization**, while other 3D-IC objectives like thermal are not covered. To the best of our knowledge, this is the first work in literature achieving analytically **global smoothness** along all the three dimensions. In contrast, previous analytic works [10,27] only ensure (partially) local smoothness in their density functions [12,34], while their less continuous cell movement would slow down placement convergence and cause more penalty on wirelength. We conduct analytic global placement and stochastic legalization in the entire 3D cuboid domain, which maximizes the search space thus further boost the solution quality. ePlace-3D well demonstrates the applicability of the electrostatic density model **eDensity** [23,24] in various physical dimensions. Our specific contributions are listed as follows.

- **eDensity-3D**: an electrostatics based 3D density function ensuring global smoothness.

- A 3D numerical solution based on fast Fourier transform (FFT) and improved spectral formulation.

- A nonlinear 3D preconditioner to equalize all the moving objects in the optimization perspective.

- Interleaving coarse-grained 3D placement with fine-grained 2D placement to enhance efficiency.

- Our mixed-size 3D-IC placement prototype **ePlace-3D** outperforms the leading placers mPL6-3D [27] and NTUplace3-3D [10] with 6.44% and 37.15% shorter wirelength, 9.11% and 10.27% fewer 3D vertical interconnects, while runs 2.55× and 0.30× faster on average of all the ten IBM-PLACE benchmarks [13],

The remainder is organized as follows. Section 2 introduces the background knowledge. Section 3 discusses our 3D placement density function eDensity-3D, numerical solution, and nonlinear precondition. Section 4 provides an overview of ePlace-3D algorithm. Experiments and results are shown in Section 5. We conclude in Section 6.

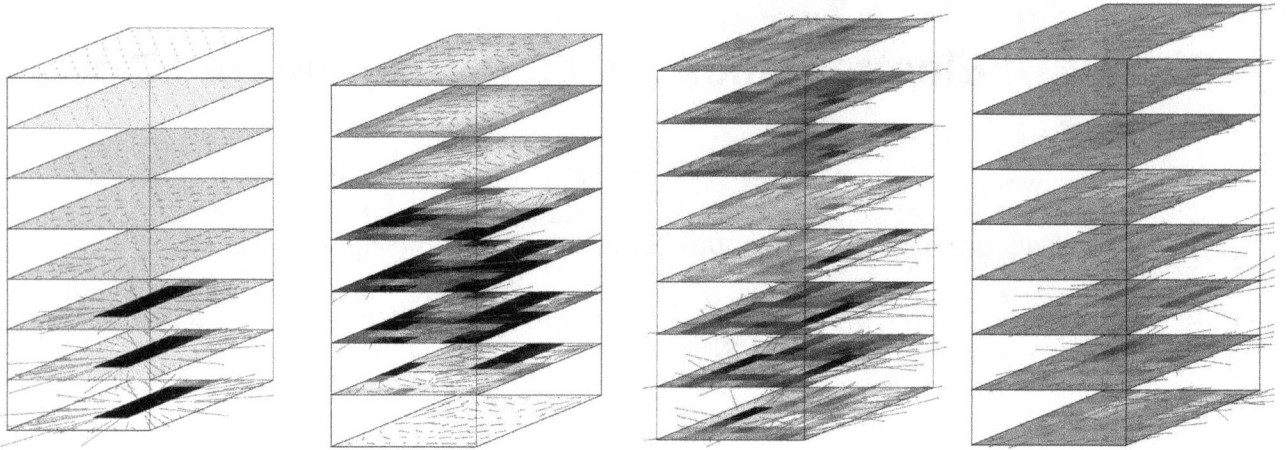

(a) Iter=0, U=6.18e17, τ = 90.13%.   (b) Iter=3, U=5.84e16, τ = 47.56%.   (c) Iter=6, U=3.56e15, τ = 11.75%.   (d) Iter=20, U=2.07e14, τ = 2.53%.

Figure 1: Iterative density-driven global placement (wirelength force disabled) with potential U and density overflow τ on the MMS ADAPTEC1 benchmark with three tiers and resolution of $8 \times 8 \times 8$. Electric density and field are shown by gray scale and red arrows. All the movable objects are initialized at the bottom tier where all IO blocks locate. eDensity-3D iteratively spreads all the movable objects evenly within the entire 3D domain to equalize the placement density.

2. BACKGROUND

Given a set V of n objects, net set N and 3D cuboid core region $R = [0, d_x] \times [0, d_y] \times [0, d_z]$, global placement is formulated as constrained optimization. The **constraint** desires all the objects to be accommodated with zero overlap. Let $\mathbf{v}$ denote the placement solution, which consists of the physical coordinates of all the objects. The region R is uniformly decomposed into $m_x \times m_y \times m_z$ 3D bins denoted as set B. For every bin $b \in B$, the density $\rho_b(\mathbf{v})$ should not exceed the target density ρ_t. The **objective** is to minimize the total half-perimeter wirelength (HPWL) of all the nets. Let $HPWL_{e_x} = \max_{i,j \in e} |x_i - x_j|$ denote the horizontal wirelength of net e (similar for $HPWL_{e_y}$), the total 2D HPWL is $HPWL(\mathbf{v}) = \sum_{e \in N} \left(\beta_x HPWL_{e_x}(\mathbf{v}) + \beta_y HPWL_{e_y}(\mathbf{v}) \right)$. We use β_x, β_y and β_z as dimensional weighting factors. 3D-IC placement needs **vertical interconnects**, such as through-silicon via (TSV) and monolithic inter-tier via (MIV), to penetrate silicon tiers. Diverse types of connects have different physical and electrical properties. However, ePlace-3D is compatible with any types of connects, which can be reflected on the weight of β_z. *In the remainder of this manuscript, we name all types of 3D vertical interconnects uniformly as* **VI** *for simplicity. The number of vertical interconnect units ($\#VI$) is computed as how many times silicon tiers have been penetrated, e.g., one vertical connect between tier one and tier three is counted as two VI.* The nonlinear placement optimization is formulated as

$$\min_{\mathbf{v}} \ (HPWL(\mathbf{v}) + \beta_z \#VI) \ \text{s.t.} \ \rho_b(\mathbf{v}) \leq \rho_t, \ \forall b \in B. \quad (1)$$

Analytic methods conduct placement using gradient-directed optimization. As $HPWL(\mathbf{v})$ is not differentiable, we use **wirelength smoothing** by weighted-average (WA) model [10].

$$W_{e_x}(\mathbf{v}) = \frac{\sum_{i \in e} x_i \exp(x_i/\gamma_x)}{\sum_{i \in e} \exp(x_i/\gamma_x)} - \frac{\sum_{i \in e} x_i \exp(-x_i/\gamma_x)}{\sum_{i \in e} \exp(-x_i/\gamma_x)} \quad (2)$$

Here $W_e(\mathbf{v}) = \beta_x W_{e_x}(\mathbf{v}) + \beta_y W_{e_y}(\mathbf{v}) + \beta_z W_{e_z}(\mathbf{v})$ and $W(\mathbf{v}) = \sum_e W_e(\mathbf{v})$. γ_x, γ_y and γ_z control the modeling accuracy.

Density function relaxes all the $|B|$ constraints in Eq. (1). Most 2D and 3D **quadratic** placers [6,18,19] follow the linear density force formulation by [5]. **Nonlinear** placers [1, 10,11,27] have their dedicated density functions. NTUplace3-3D [10] leverages bell-shape curve [34] for local smoothness in 3D domain. mPL6-3D [1] uses Helmholtz function to globally smoothen the 2D plane and Huber's function to locally smoothen the vertical dimension. The **electrostatics** based density function [25] converts objects to charges. By the Lorentz law, the electric repulsive force spreads charges away towards the electrostatic equilibrium state, which produces a globally even density distribution. Let $U(\mathbf{v})$ denote the density cost function, the constraints in Eq. (1) can be relaxed by the penalty factor λ, while the unconstrained optimization is shown as below.

$$\min_{\mathbf{v}} f(\mathbf{v}) = W(\mathbf{v}) + \lambda U(\mathbf{v}), \quad (3)$$

In this work, we set vertical connects as zero-volumed thus do not consider them in eDensity-3D[1]. Therefore, the optimization of electrostatics will not be affected and can be still achieved based on the movement of netlist objects. **Density overflow** is used to terminate global placement and denoted as τ, which is

$$\tau = \frac{\sum_{b \in B} \max \left(V_b^m - \rho_t V_b^{WS}, 0 \right)}{V_m}. \quad (4)$$

Here V_m is the total volume of all the movable objects, V_b^m is the total volume of objects in the bin b, and V_b^{WS} is the total whitespace in bin b. The volume of each cell is computed as its planar area multiplied by the depth of each tier.

---

[1]Practically, vertical connects can never be zero volumed. However, for academic research we are able to simplify the engineering problems to boost scientific innovations. Similarly, state-of-the-art 2D placement academic works [1,2,17, 19,25,40,41] target wirelength only and ignore other objectives like timing, power and routability. As vertical connects may be of large volume thus significantly contribute to the placement density, we will put it in our future work.

3. EDENSITY-3D: 3D DENSITY FUNCTION

In this section, we introduce our novel 3D density function **eDensity-3D**, a fast numerical solution by spectral methods, and approximated 3D nonlinear preconditioner. The key insight is, *we treat the third dimension equally as the other two dimensions, such that vertical cell movement will be as smooth as the planar movement in 2D placement.* The behavior of eDensity-3D is visualized in Figure 1.

3.1 3D Density Function

Extending the planar function eDensity in [25], eDensity-3D models the entire placement instance as a 3D electrostatic field. Every placement object (standard cells, macros and fillers) is converted to a positively charged cuboid. The electric repulsive force spreads all the objects away from the high-density region. The 3D density cost U is modeled as the total potential energy of the system and defined as below

$$U(\mathbf{v}) = \sum_{i \in V} U_i(\mathbf{v}) = \sum_{i \in V} q_i \Phi_i(\mathbf{v}). \qquad (5)$$

q_i denotes the electric quantity of the charge i and is set as the physical volume of placement object i. Φ_i is the electric potential at charge i. Charges with high potential will reduce the placement overlap by moving towards the direction of largest energy descent. Unlike the spatial density distribution $\rho(x, y, z)$ (Figure 1) which is coarse and non-differentiable, the electric potential distribution $\Phi(x, y, z)$ is globally smooth. We use the potential gradient (thus electric field), $\nabla\Phi(x, y, z) = \mathbf{E}(x, y, z)$, to direct cell movement for density equalization. Given a placement layout $\mathbf{v}$, we generate the density map $\rho(x, y, z)$, then compute the potential map $\Phi(x, y, z)$ by solving the **3D Poisson's equation**

$$\begin{cases} \nabla \cdot \nabla\Phi(x, y, z) = -\rho(x, y, z), \\ \hat{\mathbf{n}} \cdot \nabla\Phi(x, y, z) = 0, \ (x, y, z) \in \partial R, \\ \iiint_R \Phi(x, y, z) = \iiint_R \rho(x, y, z) = 0. \end{cases} \qquad (6)$$

Here $\hat{n}$ is the outer unit normal of the placement cube R. ∂R is the boundary and consists of orthogonal rectangular planes to enclose the placement cuboid. In Eq. (6), the first equation has $\nabla \cdot \nabla \equiv \frac{\partial^2}{\partial x^2} + \frac{\partial^2}{\partial y^2} + \frac{\partial^2}{\partial z^2}$. Neumann condition by the second equation requires that when any object i reaches any boundary plane, its density force vector will have the component perpendicular to the plane reduced to zero, in order to prevent i from penetrating the plane. The third equation shows that the integral of density $\rho(x, y, z)$ and potential $\Phi(x, y, z)$ within R are set to zero to ensure that (1) electric force drives all the charges towards even density distribution rather than pushing them to infinity, which matches the placement objective (2) the 3D Poisson's equation would have a unique solution by satisfying the Neumann condition. We differentiate the potential Φ_i on each charge i to generate the electric field $\nabla\Phi_i = \mathbf{E_i} = (E_{i_x}, E_{i_y}, E_{i_z})$. The electric (density) force is $\nabla U_i = q_i \nabla\Phi_i = q_i \mathbf{E_i}$.

3.2 3D Numerical Solution

Based on the 2D solution in [25], we solve the 3D Poisson's equation by spectral methods using frequency decomposition [39]. To satisfy the Neumann condition of zero gradients at the boundaries, we use sinusoidal wave to express the electric field $\mathbf{E}(x, y, z)$. We construct an odd and periodic field distribution by negatively mirroring itself w.r.t. the origin, then periodically extending it towards positive and negative infinities. Electric potential and density distributions are then expressed by cosine waveforms, which are the integration and differentiation of the field. Let $a_{j,k,l}$ denote the 3D coefficients of the density frequency.

$$a_{j,k,l} = \frac{1}{n^3} \sum_{x,y,z} \rho(x, y, z) \cos(w_j x) \cos(w_k y) \cos(w_l z) \qquad (7)$$

eDensity [25] sets $w_j = \pi\frac{j}{m_x}$, which equals the discrete index for the jth frequency component. However, as we are conducting placement in a continuous domain, the multiplication of x and w_j induces inconsistency. In this work, we propose **improved spectral methods** for the 3D placement density function. Specifically, we set $w_j = \pi\frac{j}{d_x}$ since x ranges within $(0, d_x)$. As a result, $w_j x = \pi j \frac{x}{d_x}$ well matches the original unit of discrete frequency index, and we have all the frequency indexes defined as $\{w_j, w_k, w_l\} = \{\frac{\pi j}{d_x}, \frac{\pi k}{d_y}, \frac{\pi l}{d_z}\}$. As mentioned in Section 2, here d_x, d_y and d_z represent the dimensions of the cuboid placement core region. $d_{\{x,y,z\}}$ can be set as any value since $w_{\{j,k,l\}}$ will be normalized by $\frac{\{x,y,z\}}{d_{\{x,y,z\}}}$. j, k and l range in $[0, n-1]$, which is only half of a cosine function period. In contrast, one complete function period centered at the origin is $[-n, n-1]$. Therefore, we have π rather than 2π in the above frequency index. We set $a_{0,0,0} = 0$ to remove the zero-frequency component. The spatial density distribution $\rho(x, y, z)$ is

$$\rho(x, y, z) = \sum_{j,k,l} a_{j,k,l} \cos(w_j x) \cos(w_k y) \cos(w_l z). \qquad (8)$$

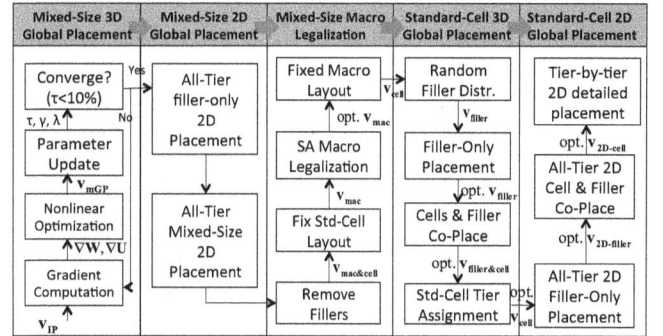

Figure 2: the flowchart of ePlace-3d.

To achieve $\nabla \cdot \nabla\Phi(x, y, z) = -\rho(x, y, z)$, the solution to the potential can be expressed as

$$\Phi(x, y, z) = \sum_{j,k,l} \frac{a_{j,k,l}}{w_j^2 + w_k^2 + w_l^2} \cos(w_j x) \cos(w_k y) \cos(w_l z). \qquad (9)$$

By differentiating Eq. (9), we have the electric field distribution $\mathbf{E}(x, y, z) = (E_x, E_y, E_z)$ shown as below

$$\begin{cases} E_x(x, y, z) = \sum_{j,k,l} \frac{a_{j,k,l} w_j}{w_j^2 + w_k^2 + w_l^2} \sin(w_j x) \cos(w_k y) \cos(w_l z), \\ E_y(x, y, z) = \sum_{j,k,l} \frac{a_{j,k,l} w_k}{w_j^2 + w_k^2 + w_l^2} \cos(w_j x) \sin(w_k y) \cos(w_l z), \\ E_z(x, y, z) = \sum_{j,k,l} \frac{a_{j,k,l} w_l}{w_j^2 + w_k^2 + w_l^2} \cos(w_j x) \cos(w_k y) \sin(w_l z). \end{cases} \qquad (10)$$

Let $|B| = m_x \times m_y \times m_z$ denote the total number of bins in global placement. Instead of quadratic complexity, above spectral equations can be efficiently solved using FFT algorithms [36] with $O(|B|log|B|)$ complexity.

13

3.3 3D Nonlinear Precondition

Theoretically, preconditioning improves convergence rate rather than solution quality. However, as placement is a highly nonlinear, non-convex and ill-conditioned problem, the Hessian matrix with improved condition number would reshape the search direction for the nonlinear solver to follow. As a result, preconditioning would open the gate for unexplored high-dimension search space, while surprising quality enhancement would be expectable.

Preconditioned mixed-size placement should tolerate the huge physical and topological differences between all the standard cells, macros, and dummy fillers. In [25], the nonlinear preconditioner H for 2D placement is modeled as

$$H_{i_x} = \frac{\partial^2 f}{\partial x_i^2} = \frac{\partial^2 W}{\partial x_i^2} + \lambda \frac{\partial^2 U}{\partial x_i^2} \approx |N_i| + \lambda A_i. \quad (11)$$

Here N_i are all the nets incident to the object i, A_i is the 2D area of the object i. In 3D placement, we use V_i to denote the volume of i instead. The preconditioned gradient $\nabla f_{pre} = H^{-1} \nabla f$ then improves and accelerates the placement. Our studies show that Eq. (11) relies on the assumption of $\frac{\partial^2 W / \partial x_i^2}{\partial^2 U / \partial x_i^2} \approx \frac{|N_i|}{A_i}$. However, the third dimension weakens $\frac{\partial^2 W}{\partial x_i^2}$ and breaks the above assumption. As a result, $|N_i|$ dominates λV_i and makes fillers and macros with small $|N_i|$ spread faster than standard cells, as Eq. (12) shows

$$\left\| H_{i_x}^{-1} \nabla U \right\| = \left\| \frac{\partial U / \partial x_i}{\lambda V_i} \right\| \gg \left\| \frac{\partial f / \partial x_i}{|N_i| + \lambda V_i} \right\| = \left\| H_{i_x}^{-1} \nabla f \right\|. \quad (12)$$

Instead, we propose a new preconditioner as below

$$H_{i_x} = \frac{\partial^2 f}{\partial x_i^2} \approx \lambda \frac{\partial^2 U}{\partial x_i^2} \approx \lambda V_i, \quad (13)$$

The noise factors introduced by $|N_i|$ is resolved, where all the objects are being equalized in the optimizer's perspective and simultaneously spread over the entire domain. Experiments show that our 3D preconditioner reduces the global placement iterations by 15% and improves the wirelength by 30% over all the 16 MMS benchmarks.

3.4 Complexity

Complexity significantly impacts the placement runtime. In each iteration, we traverse all the bins to reset their density in $O(|B|)$ time, then traverse all the placement objects in $O(n)$ time to update the superimposed density map. By Eq. (7), (9) and (10), five times of 3D FFT computation are invoked, which costs $O(5n \log n)$ time. By our grid sizing strategy in Eq. (14), $|B|/n$ is limited to constant. The overall complexity is thus $O(|B| + n + 5n \log n) \approx O(n \log n)$,

In ePlace-3D, the placement domain is geometrically transformed from $R = [0, d_x] \times [0, d_y] \times [0, d_z]$ to $R' = [0, 1] \times [0, 1] \times [0, 1]$. We set the density resolutions $m_x = m_y = m_z = m_{3D}$ to make the placement domain R' uniformly decomposed into $|B| = m_{3D}^3$ cubic bins. Let V_R denote the total volume of R and $V_{C_{avg}}$ denote the average area of all standard cells. The grid sizing is set as

$$|B| = \frac{V_R}{k \times V_{C_{avg}} \times \rho_t^{-1}}. \quad (14)$$

Here every k standard cells are accommodated by one bin. Placement quality (efficiency) is determined by the value of k. In this work, we constantly set $k = 1.0$.

4. EPLACE-3D: OVERVIEW

ePlace-3D is built upon the infrastructure of ePlace-MS [26]. Figure 2 shows the flowchart of our algorithm. Given a placement instance, our algorithm minimizes the quadratic wirelength over the 3D domain to produce the initial solution $\mathbf{v_{IP}}$. To approach the optimum solution in the end, we make $\mathbf{v_{IP}}$ as minimum-wirelength violation-tolerant.

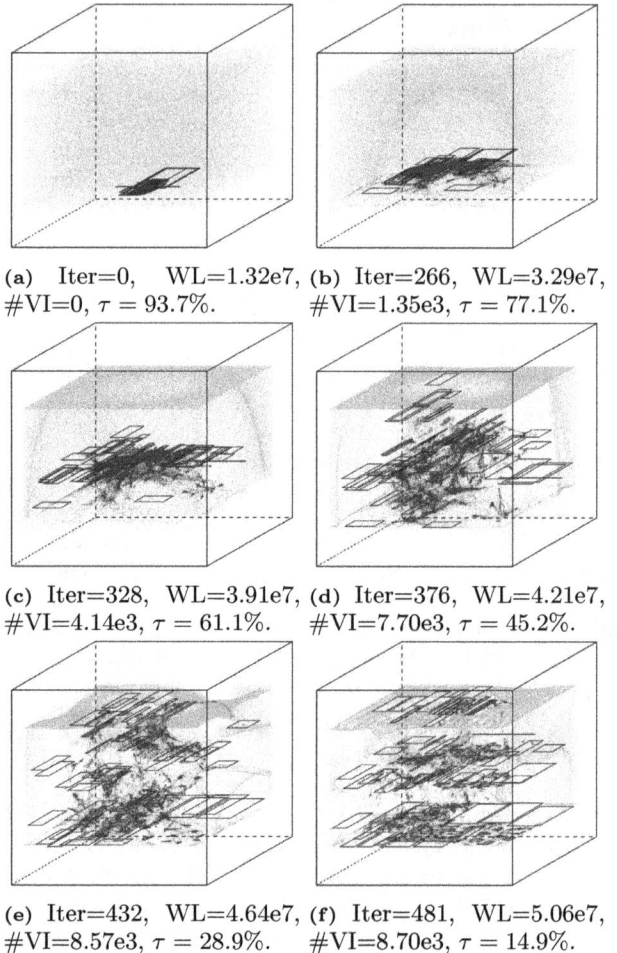

(a) Iter=0, WL=1.32e7, #VI=0, $\tau = 93.7\%$.

(b) Iter=266, WL=3.29e7, #VI=1.35e3, $\tau = 77.1\%$.

(c) Iter=328, WL=3.91e7, #VI=4.14e3, $\tau = 61.1\%$.

(d) Iter=376, WL=4.21e7, #VI=7.70e3, $\tau = 45.2\%$.

(e) Iter=432, WL=4.64e7, #VI=8.57e3, $\tau = 28.9\%$.

(f) Iter=481, WL=5.06e7, #VI=8.70e3, $\tau = 14.9\%$.

Figure 3: 3D-IC mixed-size global placement on MMS ADAPTEC1 with three tiers. Standard cells, macros and fillers are denoted by red dots, blue rectangles and cyan dots.

Our 3D-IC global placement is visualized in Figure 3. Unconnected fillers [1, 25] are inserted to populate up extra whitespace. All the fillers are equally sized by the average dimensions of all the standard cells. *The optimum solution of 3D global placement will have all the cells, macros and fillers orient towards discrete tiers.* Otherwise, some cuboid placement sites will be partially wasted, degrading the solution quality. Figure 3(f) illustrates the beauty of our approach, i.e., the analytic 3D placer is visually approaching density evenness from the vertical dimension, which ensures *negligible quality overhead during tier assignment.* We use Nesterov's method [35] as the nonlinear solver and determine the steplength by [25].

A multi-tier 2D-IC mixed-size global placement follows by assigning all the macros and standard cells to the closest tiers and separately filling the remaining whitespace on each tier with fillers. Planar placement is conducted simultaneously over all the tiers. As wirelength smoothing is homogeneous over all the tiers (with the same γ), heterogeneous grid sizing is not feasible as density force is dependent on resolution by Eq. (10). We set all the tiers with the same density resolution m_{2D}, which is the maximum of that of all the tiers by Eq. (14) with $k = 1$. In practice, we have $O(m_{2D}^2) \approx O(m_{3D}^3)$. Figure 4 illustrates the progression.

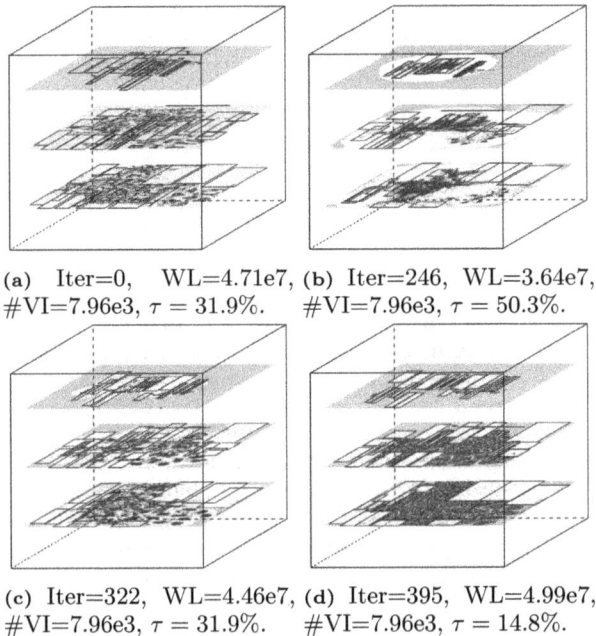

(a) Iter=0, WL=4.71e7, #VI=7.96e3, $\tau = 31.9\%$.

(b) Iter=246, WL=3.64e7, #VI=7.96e3, $\tau = 50.3\%$.

(c) Iter=322, WL=4.46e7, #VI=7.96e3, $\tau = 31.9\%$.

(d) Iter=395, WL=4.99e7, #VI=7.96e3, $\tau = 14.8\%$.

Figure 4: 2D-IC mixed-size global placement on MMS ADAPTEC1 with three tiers. Initial and final overflow are both larger than the final overflow of 3D placement due to finer granularity ($m_{2D} \gg m_{3D}$).

Our 3D-IC macro legalizer generates a legal macro layout with zero macro overlap and small wirelength overhead. The algorithm is stochastic based on simulated annealing [20]. A 3D-IC standard-cell global placement follows to mitigate the quality loss due to sub-optimal macro legalization. We assign standard cells to their closest tiers and conduct simultaneous 2D-IC standard-cell placement on all the tiers. The standard-cell layouts of all the tiers are locally refined. Figure 5 shows the respective placement progressions, more details can be found in [26]. The detailed placer from [37] is then invoked for a tier-by-tier standard-cell legalization and detailed placement from the bottom to the top tier.

In general, we have fine-grained 2D placement interleaved with coarse-grained 3D placement, which achieves a good trade-off between quality and efficiency. On average of all the ten IBM-PLACE circuits, the application of 2D refinement reduces the wirelength by more than 4%.

5. EXPERIMENTS AND RESULTS

We implement ePlace-3D using C programming language in the single-thread mode and execute the program in a Linux machine with Intel i7 920 2.67GHz CPU and 12GB memory. There is no benchmark specific parameter tuning in our work. #VI are controlled by the weighting factor β_z based on capacitance ratio. By [16], one TSV (VI) has

the capacitance of $C_{VI} = 30fF$ at 45nm tech-node. ITRS annual reports [14] show that unit capacitance of interconnects at intermediate routing layers is constantly $2pF/cm$ across various tech-nodes. Placement row height is $1.4um$ at 45nm tech-node ($70nm$ M1 half-pitch, ten M1 tracks per row), capacitance becomes $C_{ROW} = 0.3fF$ for 2D interconnect spanning one-row height. Based on the length units for each benchmark, as well as our geometric transformation of the placement core region to be $[0, 1] \times [0, 1] \times [0, 1]$ as discussed in Section 3.4, we compute the respective capacitance ratio of one VI versus one unit wirelength and use it as the VI weight. Specifically, we have

$$\beta_z = \frac{\#tiers \times C_{VI}}{\#rows \times C_{ROW}} \tag{15}$$

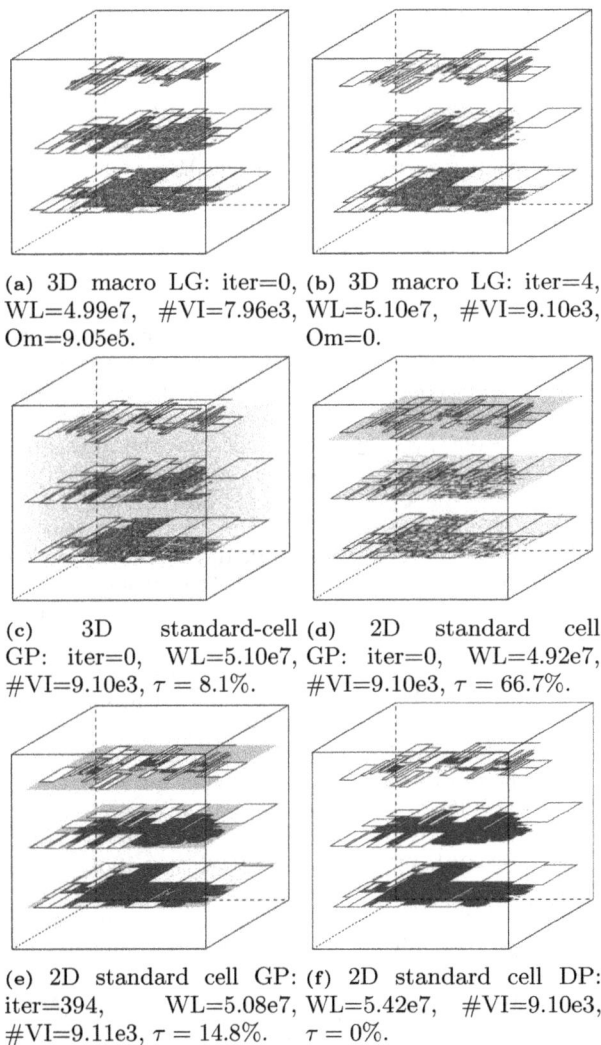

(a) 3D macro LG: iter=0, WL=4.99e7, #VI=7.96e3, Om=9.05e5.

(b) 3D macro LG: iter=4, WL=5.10e7, #VI=9.10e3, Om=0.

(c) 3D standard-cell GP: iter=0, WL=5.10e7, #VI=9.10e3, $\tau = 8.1\%$.

(d) 2D standard cell GP: iter=0, WL=4.92e7, #VI=9.10e3, $\tau = 66.7\%$.

(e) 2D standard cell GP: iter=394, WL=5.08e7, #VI=9.11e3, $\tau = 14.8\%$.

(f) 2D standard cell DP: WL=5.42e7, #VI=9.10e3, $\tau = 0\%$.

Figure 5: Post-placement on MMS ADAPTEC1 with three tiers. Standard cells, macros and fillers are denoted by red dots, blue rectangles and cyan dots. Om denotes the total macro overlap.

Notice that the focus of this work is the algorithm framework of 3D placement, not the accurate weight modeling of vertical connects. The weighting factor can be adjusted by VLSI designers for their particular needs, e.g., vertical

Table 1: HPWL (e7), #VI (vertical interconnect) (e3) and runtime (minutes) on the IBM-PLACE benchmark suite [13]. Cited results are marked with *. All the experiments are conducted under single-thread mode. The results are evaluated by the same scripts and normalized to ePlace-3D. The best result for each case is in bold-face.

Categories			NTUplace3-3D [10]			mPL6-3D* [27]			ePlace-3D		
Benchmarks	# Cells	# Nets	HPWL	#VI	CPU	HPWL	#VI	CPU	HPWL	#VI	CPU
IBM01	12K	12K	0.34	**0.69**	0.20	0.26	1.04	2.95	**0.25**	1.31	0.58
IBM03	22K	22K	0.76	3.32	0.50	0.59	**3.11**	4.72	**0.56**	3.27	1.33
IBM04	27K	26K	1.00	**2.60**	0.60	0.81	2.95	6.41	**0.74**	3.53	1.88
IBM06	32K	33K	1.30	3.99	0.80	1.05	**3.97**	6.20	**0.92**	4.50	2.98
IBM07	45K	44K	1.92	5.73	1.30	1.59	4.68	8.64	**1.50**	**4.39**	3.87
IBM08	51K	48K	2.08	4.90	1.70	1.71	**3.94**	11.23	**1.54**	4.90	4.75
IBM09	52K	50K	1.92	3.88	1.50	1.45	3.24	14.61	**1.40**	**3.18**	5.63
IBM13	82K	84K	3.69	**3.98**	2.60	2.88	5.59	19.62	**2.67**	4.73	8.65
IBM15	158K	161K	9.16	15.67	7.20	6.79	10.52	46.82	**6.39**	9.16	40.25
IBM18	210K	201K	13.41	12.19	13.60	**9.16**	15.22	52.09	9.47	**6.83**	63.07
Avg.	69K	68K	37.15%	10.27%	0.30×	6.44%	9.11%	2.55×	0.00%	0.00%	1.00×

connects of different electric and physical attributes (TSVs, MIVs, super contacts, etc.).

We conduct experiments on IBM-PLACE [13] standard-cell benchmarks without macros or blockages, all of which are derived from real IC design. We include two state-of-the-art 3D-IC placers, mPL6-3D [27][2], and NTUplace3-3D [10], in our experiments on IBM-PLACE. As other categories of algorithms (e.g., folding and partition based approaches) have been outperformed by analytic placement in literature, we do not include them in our experiments. We have obtained the binary of NTUplace3-3D from the original authors and executed it on our machine for experiments[3]. mPL6-3D is not available (as notified by the author), so we cite the performance from their latest publication [27]. We use exactly the same benchmark transformation as that by mPL6-3D and NTUplace3-3D. I.e., we insert four silicon tiers into each benchmark, scale down each tier to $\frac{1}{4}$ of the original 2D placement area, add 10% whitespace to each tier, and keep the aspect ratio of each tier to be the same as the original 2D design. As a result, all the experiments on the three placers, including those from [27], are conducted on exactly the same **IBM-PLACE-3D** benchmarks. As HPWL and #VI are being computed in exactly the same way, the performance comparison among the three placers are fair. The results on IBM-PLACE cases are shown in Table 1. On average of all the ten circuits, ePlace-3D outperforms mPL6-3D and NTUplace3-3D with 6.44% and 37.15% shorter wirelength together with 9.11% and 10.27% fewer VIs. ePlace-3D runs 2.55× faster than mPL6-3D but 0.30× slower than NTUplace3-3D, nevertheless, the improvement on wirelength (37.15%) and VI (10.27%) is significant.

To validate the scalability of ePlace-3D, we also conduct experiments on the large-scale **modern mixed-size (MMS)** benchmarks [43] with on average 829K and up to 2.5M netlist objects. MMS benchmarks was first published in DAC 2009. The circuits inherit the same netlists and den-

sity constraints ρ_t from ISPD 2005 [33] and ISPD 2006 [32] benchmarks but have all the macros freed to place. The original planar placement domain is geometrically transformed to be of 2, 3 and 4 silicon tiers, each tier is equally down-sized to keep both the aspect ratio and total silicon area unchanged. All the standard cells and macros keep their original dimensions and span only one tier. MMS circuits have all their fixed objects with zero area (volume) and outside the placement boundaries, and we geometrically transform them to the boundary of the bottom (first) tier. Also, as macros are all free to move, we skip the geometrical transformation of the fixed macro layout from 2D to 3D, which is suboptimal and usually causes quality loss. Similar to mPL6-3D [27] and NTUplace3-3D [10], we add 10% extra whitespace to each tier, in order to relieve the placement dilemma due to the increased area ratio between large macros and silicon tiers[4]. There are benchmark-dependent target density ρ_t for eight out of the sixteen MMS circuits. Detailed circuit statistics can be found in Table 1 of [43]. We create evaluation scripts to compute the total wirelength, number of vertical interconnects, and legality of the produced 3D-IC placement solution. The results on the MMS benchmarks are shown in Table 2. Notice that here HPWL is the original half-perimeter wirelength. It is not penalized by the amount of density overflow, since the density overflow in 3D domain is of one more dimension thus hard to compare with that of 2D domain. The binary of NTUplace3-3D does not work with these benchmarks, while the binary of mPL6-3D is not available for use. As a result, we compare the 3D MMS placement solutions with the best published (golden) 2D results in literature [26]. By using two, three and four tiers, ePlace-3D outperforms the golden 2D placement with on average 13.67%, 20.50% and 27.54% shorter wirelength. On the other side, the average ratio between the number of vertical interconnect units versus the number of placement objects (standard cells and macros) are only 2.17%, 4.30% and 6.10%, respectively. These vertical connect ratios are much smaller than the average VI ratio on IBM-PLACE, which are more than 9% for all the three placers in Table 1.

---

[2]Although mPL6-3D has extension to thermal-aware placement, its experiments on the IBM-PLACE cases are based on their original prototype driven by only wirelength and density but not thermal.

[3]There is a small quality gap on NTUplace3-3D between our local experiment results and that published in [10], which may be due to the differences in computing platforms.

---

[4]BIGBLUE3, NEWBLUE2 and NEWBLUE3 have very large macros. For the tier insertion of two, three and four, we add 20%, 30% and 40% whitespace to each tier to make sure that the largest macro can be accommodated.

Table 2: HPWL (e6), #VI (vertical interconnect) and runtime (mins) on MMS circuits. Cited results are marked with *. All the experiments are in single-thread mode. The HPWL and CPU results are normalized to the best published 2D placement results [26], #VI are normalized to # objects.

# tiers			ePlace-MS* [26]		ePlace-3D w/ 2 tiers			ePlace-3D w/ 3 tiers			ePlace-3D w/ 4 tiers		
Benchmarks	# Objs	# Nets	HPWL	CPU	HPWL	#VI	CPU	HPWL	#VI	CPU	HPWL	#VI	CPU
ADAPTEC1	211K	221K	67.15	5.47	59.51	5733	24.63	54.19	9104	14.65	51.3	13568	16.03
ADAPTEC2	255K	266K	77.37	7.43	73.97	9269	39.67	75.38	9929	25.18	59.97	18085	24.57
ADAPTEC3	451K	466K	164.50	27.23	141.97	5557	95.48	136.85	18203	88.55	120.29	28694	94.42
ADAPTEC4	496K	515K	148.38	29.35	126.94	8149	107.15	113.22	13811	121.40	106.34	14527	118.13
BIGBLUE1	278K	284K	86.82	7.82	76.06	8272	40.63	71.34	10508	36.17	63.64	19403	38.05
BIGBLUE2	557K	577K	130.18	13.70	109.27	2565	70.25	97.1	5347	63.58	90.14	9241	64.95
BIGBLUE3	1096K	1123K	302.29	72.98	251.77	24466	268.47	271.27	42053	291.38	295.38	62669	388.08
BIGBLUE4	2177K	2229K	657.92	204.15	577.98	21263	491.97	537.2	50552	563.98	500.25	113590	420.17
ADAPTEC5	843K	867K	310.54	48.35	258.18	22705	170.90	244.57	27764	146.22	223.44	50732	149.22
NEWBLUE1	330K	338K	61.85	10.87	56.36	5901	28.15	53.05	7295	24.08	48.85	12346	25.07
NEWBLUE2	441K	465K	162.93	62.40	179.82	25571	67.27	143.5	43642	77.20	169.78	53487	72.98
NEWBLUE3	494K	552K	304.15	17.53	240.47	7686	308.62	365.10	48979	410.73	397.46	51597	265.67
NEWBLUE4	646K	637K	228.54	29.73	197.21	11372	110.02	177.82	29767	112.80	171.21	35067	101.78
NEWBLUE5	1233K	1284K	392.27	63.40	344.95	45995	202.12	303.05	64336	195.52	280.42	95768	216.22
NEWBLUE6	1255K	1288K	408.36	69.65	379.59	10901	222.72	325.35	50487	194.57	298.82	66983	180.88
NEWBLUE7	2507K	2636K	894.31	191.47	814.79	18615	363.30	696.27	92943	375.65	670.51	111562	353.92
Avg.	829K	859K	0.00%	1.00×	13.67%	2.17%	3.13×	20.50%	4.30%	3.03×	27.54%	6.10%	2.94×

Due to the introduction of the third dimension, the search space of placement optimization is substantially enlarged. However, the runtime increase is just 3×, which indicates high efficiency of ePlace-3D.

We also study the trends of HPWL and #VI by linearly sweeping the number of tiers and exponentially sweeping the VI weight. We select eight out of the sixteen MMS benchmarks (ADAPTEC1, ADAPTEC4, BIGBLUE1, BIGBLUE2, BIGBLUE3, BIGBLUE4, NEWBLUE6, NEWBLUE7), all of which could accommodate the maximum macro block after inserting ten tiers. Keeping the same aspect ratio, the area of each tier is scaled down by ten times with the insertion of 10% extra whitespace. Figure 6 shows that ePlace-3D is able to reduce the total 2D wirelength by up to 40% (with the insertion of up to ten tiers), while #VI is roughly scaled up by the number of tiers. VI weight sweeping is conducted

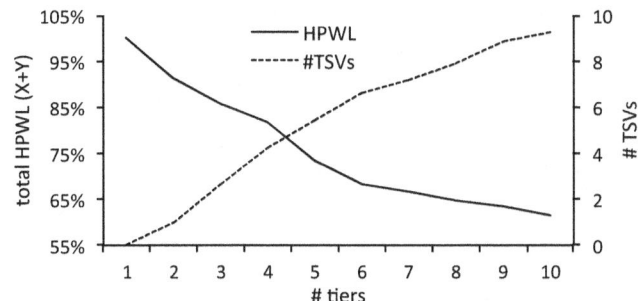

Figure 6: Avg. HPWL and #VI of eight selected MMS cases w.r.t. number of silicon tiers.

on all the sixteen MMS benchmarks. Figure 7 shows the trends of average HPWL and #VI by dividing the normal VI weight by up to 32 times (i.e. × 0.03125). The total 2D HPWL saturates at the reduction of 7%, while #VI is scaled up by roughtly 2.5×.

Our 3D-IC placement algorithm shows significant quality improvement while limited runtime overhead. BIGBLUE4 and NEWBLUE7 are the largest circuits with 2.2M and 2.5M cells, and they consume the longest runtime on the 3D-

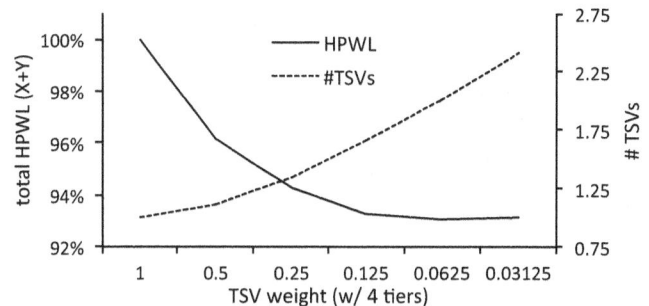

Figure 7: Avg. HPWL and #VI of all the sixteen MMS cases w.r.t. VI weights.

IC placement. However, compared to the respective golden 2D placement solutions, the runtime ratio is upper-bounded by 2.5×, which is still less than the average runtime ratios of 3.13× for two tiers, 3.03× for three tiers and 2.94× for four tiers, respectively. To this end, ePlace-3D shows good scalability and acceptable efficiency on the large cases.

In this work, we do not test ePlace-3D on circuits with fixed macros, as geometrically transforming the 2D floorplan into 3D is difficult and usually error-prone. However, ePlace-3D shows high performance and scalability on MMS benchmarks with lots of movable large macros, which is more difficult to place than fixed-macro layouts. As a result, we are confident on the performance of ePlace-3D on any circuits with fixed macros. The advantage of 3D tier insertion vanishes if there are large macros to accommodate (BIG-BLUE3, NEWBLUE3, etc.). Transformation of 2D planar macros into 3D cuboid macros would resolve this issue and ensure the consistent benefits by inserting more tiers. However, it is beyond this work and will be covered in future.

6. CONCLUSION

We propose the first electrostatics based placement algorithm **ePlace-3D**, which is effective and efficient for 3D-ICs with uniform exploration over the entire 3D space. Our 3D-IC density function leverages the analogy between placement spreading and electrostatic equilibrium, while global and uniform smoothness is realized at all the three dimensions. Our balancing and preconditioning techniques prevent solution oscillation or divergence. The interleaved 3D coarse-grained optimization followed by 2D fine-grained post processing obtains a good trade-off between quality and efficiency. The experimental results validate the high performance and scalability of our approach, indicating the benefits of placement smoothness. In future, we will develop 3D density function to address the volume of vertical interconnects (VI). We would also like to explore advanced technology for 3D-IC placement/routing with patterning and graph coloring technology [21].

7. ACKNOWLEDGMENT

The authors acknowledge (1) Prof. Dae Hyun Kim and Prof. Sung Kyu Lim for providing the 3D-IC flow scripts and IWLS testcases (2) Dr. Meng-Kai Hsu and Prof. Yao-Wen Chang for providing the binary of NTUplace3-3D (3) Dr. Guojie Luo and Prof. Jason Cong for providing the binary of mPL6-3D (4) the support of NSF CCF-1017864.

8. REFERENCES

[1] T. F. Chan, J. Cong, J. R. Shinnerl, K. Sze, and M. Xie. mPL6: Enhanced Multilevel Mixed-Size Placement. In *ISPD*, pages 212–214, 2006.

[2] T.-C. Chen, Z.-W. Jiang, T.-C. Hsu, H.-C. Chen, and Y.-W. Chang. NTUPlace3: An Analytical Placer for Large-Scale Mixed-Size Designs with Preplaced Blocks and Density Constraint. *IEEE TCAD*, 27(7):1228–1240, 2008.

[3] Y.-G. Chen, T. Wang, K.-Y. Lai, W.-Y. Wen, Y. Shi, and S.-C. Chang. Critical Path Monitor Enabled Dynamic Voltage Scaling for Graceful Degradation in Sub-Threshold Designs. In *DAC*, pages 1–6, 2014.

[4] J. Cong, G. Luo, J. Wei, and Y. Zhang. Thermal-Aware 3-D IC Placement Via Transformation. In *ASPDAC*, pages 780–785, 2007.

[5] H. Eisenmann and F. M. Johannes. Generic Global Placement and Floorplanning. In *DAC*, pages 269–274, 1998.

[6] B. Goplen and S. Sapatnekar. Efficient Thermal Placement of Standard Cells in 3D ICs using a Force Directed Approach. In *ICCAD*, 2003.

[7] B. Goplen and S. Sapatnekar. Placement of 3-D ICs with Thermal and Interlayer Via Considerations. In *DAC*, pages 626–631, 2007.

[8] S. K. Han, K. Jeong, A. B. Kahng, and J. Lu. Stability and Scalability in Global Routing. In *SLIP*, pages 1–6, 2011.

[9] Q. He, D. Chen, and D. Jiao. From Layout Directly to Simulation: A First-Principle Guided Circuit Simulator of Linear Complexity and Its Efficient Parallelization. *IEEE CPMT*, 2(4):687–699, 2012.

[10] M.-K. Hsu, V. Balabanov, and Y.-W. Chang. TSV-Aware Analytical Placement for 3D IC Designs Based on a Novel Weighted-Average Wirelength Model. *IEEE TCAD*, 32(4):497–509, 2013.

[11] M.-K. Hsu and Y.-W. Chang. Unified Analytical Global Placement for Large-Scale Mixed-Size Circuit Designs. *IEEE TCAD*, 2012.

[12] P. J. Huber. *Robust Statistics*. John Wiley and Sons, 1981.

[13] IBM-PLACE. http://er.cs.ucla.edu/benchmarks/ibm-place. 2001.

[14] ITRS. http://www.itrs.net/Links/2012ITRS/Home2012.htm. 2012.

[15] IWLS. http://iwls.org/iwls2005/benchmarks.html. 2005.

[16] M. Jung et al. How to Reduce Power in 3D IC Designs: A Case Study with OpenSPARC T2 Core. In *CICC*, 2013.

[17] A. B. Kahng and Q. Wang. A Faster Implementation of APlace. In *ISPD*, pages 218–220, 2006.

[18] D. H. Kim, K. Athikulwongse, and S. K. Lim. A Study of Through-Silicon-Via Impact on the 3-D Stacked IC Layout. In *ICCAD*, 2009.

[19] M.-C. Kim and I. Markov. ComPLx: A Competitive Primal-dual Lagrange Optimization for Global Placement. In *DAC*, 2012.

[20] S. Kirkpatrick, C. D. G. Jr., and M. P. Vecchi. Optimization by Simulated Annealing. *Science*, 220(4598):671–680, 1983.

[21] W. Lin, M. McGrath, I. Ramzy, T. H. Lai, and D. Lee. Detecting Job Interference in Large Distributed Multi-Agent Systems - A Formal Approach. In *IEEE IM*, 2013.

[22] J. Lu. *Analytic VLSI Placement using Electrostatic Analogy*. Ph.D. Dissertation, University of California, San Diego, 2014.

[23] J. Lu, P. Chen, C.-C. Chang, L. Sha, D. Huang, C.-C. Teng, and C.-K. Cheng. ePlace: Electrostatics based Placement using Fast Fourier Transform and Nesterov's Method. *ACM TODAES*, 20(2):article 17, 2015.

[24] J. Lu, P. Chen, C.-C. Chang, L. Sha, D. J.-H. Huang, C.-C. Teng, and C.-K. Cheng. FFTPL: An Analytic Placement Algorithm Using Fast Fourier Transform for Density Equalization. In *ASICON*, pages 1–4, 2013.

[25] J. Lu, P. Chen, C.-C. Chang, L. Sha, D. J.-H. Huang, C.-C. Teng, and C.-K. Cheng. ePlace: Electrostatics based Placement using Nesterov's Method. In *DAC*, pages 1–6, 2014.

[26] J. Lu, H. Zhuang, P. Chen, H. Chang, C.-C. Chang, Y.-C. Wong, L. Sha, D. Huang, Y. Luo, C.-C. Teng, and C.-K. Cheng. ePlace-MS: Electrostatics based Placement for Mixed-Size Circuits. *IEEE TCAD*, 34(5):685–698, 2015.

[27] G. Luo, Y. Shi, and J. Cong. An Analytical Placement Framework for 3-D ICs and Its Extension on Thermal Awareness. *IEEE TCAD*, 2013.

[28] P.-W. Luo, T. Wang, C.-L. Wey, L.-C. Cheng, B.-L. Sheu, and Y. Shi. Reliable Power Delivery System Design for Three-Dimensional Integrated Circuits (3D ICs). In *ISVLSI*, pages 356–361, 2012.

[29] I. L. Markov, J. Hu, and M.-C. Kim. Progress and Challenges in VLSI Placement Research. In *DAC*, 2012.

[30] J. Miao, A. Gerstlauer, and M. Orshansky. Approximate Logic Synthesis under General Error Magnitude and Frequency Constraints. In *ICCAD*, pages 779–786, 2013.

[31] J. Miao, A. Gerstlauer, and M. Orshansky. Multi-Level Approximate Logic Synthesis under General Error Constraints. In *ICCAD*, pages 504–510, 2014.

[32] G.-J. Nam. ISPD 2006 Placement Contest: Benchmark Suite and Results. In *ISPD*, pages 167–167, 2006.

[33] G.-J. Nam et al. The ISPD2005 Placement Contest and Benchmark Suite. In *ISPD*, pages 216–220, 2005.

[34] W. C. Naylor, R. Donelly, and L. Sha. Non-Linear Optimization System and Method for Wire Length and Delay Optimization for an Automatic Electric Circuit Placer. In *US Patent 6301693*, 2001.

[35] Y. E. Nesterov. A Method of Solving A Convex Programming Problem with Convergence Rate $O(1/k^2)$. *Soviet Math*, 27(2):372–376, 1983.

[36] T. Ooura. General Purpose FFT Package, http://www.kurims.kyoto-u.ac.jp/~ooura/fft.html. 2001.

[37] M. Pan, N. Viswanathan, and C. Chu. An Efficient and Effective Detailed Placement Algorithm. In *ICCAD*, pages 48–55, 2005.

[38] C.-W. Sham, E. F.-Y. Young, and J. Lu. Congestion Prediction in Early Stages of Physical Design. *ACM TODAES*, 14(1):12:1–18, 2009.

[39] G. Skollermo. A Fourier Method for the Numerical Solution of Poisson's Equation. *Mathematics of Computation*, 29(131):697–711, 1975.

[40] P. Spindler, U. Schlichtmann, and F. M. Johannes. Kraftwerk2 - A Fast Force-Directed Quadratic Placement Approach Using an Accurate Net Model. *IEEE TCAD*, 27(8):1398–1411, 2008.

[41] N. Viswanathan, M. Pan, and C. Chu. FastPlace3.0: A Fast Multilevel Quadratic Placement Algorithm with Placement Congestion Control. In *ASPDAC*, pages 135–140, 2007.

[42] T. Wang, C. Zhang, J. Xiong, and Y. Shi. Eagle-Eye: A Near-Optimal Statistical Framework for Noise Sensor Placement. In *ICCAD*, pages 437–443, 2013.

[43] J. Z. Yan, N. Viswanathan, and C. Chu. Handling Complexities in Modern Large-Scale Mixed-Size Placement. In *DAC*, 2009.

[44] X. Zhang, J. Lu, Y. Liu, and C.-K. Cheng. Worst-Case Noise Area Prediction of On-Chip Power Distribution Network. In *SLIP*, pages 1–8, 2014.

[45] H. Zhuang, J. Lu, K. Samadi, Y. Du, and C.-K. Cheng. Performance-Driven Placement for Design of Rotation and Right Arithmetic Shifters in Monolithic 3D ICs. In *ICCCAS*, pages 509–513, 2013.

A Compressive-sensing based Testing Vehicle for 3D TSV Pre-bond and Post-bond Testing Data

Hantao Huang, Hao Yu
School of Electrical and
Electronic Engineering
Nanyang Technological
University
50 Nanyang Avenue,
Singapore
haoyu@ntu.edu.sg

Cheng Zhuo
Intel Corporation
Hillsboro, OR 97124 U.S.A
cheng.zhuo@intel.com

Fengbo Ren
School of Computing,
Informatics, Decision Systems
Engineering
Arizona State University
699 S Mill Ave, Tempe,
Arizona, U.S.A
renfengbo@asu.edu

ABSTRACT

Online testing vehicle is required for 3D TSV pre-bond and post-bond testing due to high probability of TSV failures. It has become a challenge to deal with large sets of generated testing data with limited probing when transmitting the data out. In this paper, a lossless compressive-sensing based testing vehicle is developed for online testing of TSVs. By exploring sparsity of the testing data under constraint of failure bound of TSV, sparse-representation based encoding can be deployed by XOR and AND network on chip to deal with large volume of testing data. Experimental results (with benchmarks) have shown that 89.70% pre-bond data compression rate can be achieved under 0.5% probability of failures; and 88.18% post-bond data compression rate can be achieved with 5% probability of failures.

1. INTRODUCTION

With the introduction of vertical through silicon via (TSV), 3D-IC provides energy efficient interconnect for memory and logic integration [1]. However, 3D-IC has low yield with high probability of TSV manufacturing defects [2]. TSV may be shorted to substrate due to pin-hole or open because of micro-void or partial filling [3]. To increase the yield, online TSV testing vehicle is thereby required to provide just-in-time diagnosis to detect faulty TSVs and replace them with redundant TSVs [4, 5] to achieve self-healing (TSV repair).

Due to the stacking nature of 3D-IC, TSV testing is needed for every layer before stacking. However, the testing data can be only collected from specially designed probe pad as shown in Fig. 1a, which are limited in number due to area limitation. After bonding, the bottom die can communicate with the external tester. Therefore, as shown in Fig. 1b, the testing data has to be transferred from bottom die to upper die through the so-called TSV elevator [6]. As the 3D-stacking is mainly applied for high-volume I/O circuits

(with TSV density of $10,000/mm^2$ or more) [7, 8], it poses a grand challenge for TSV pre-bond and post-bond testing because the bandwidth of TSV testing data becomes the primary bottleneck [5, 9] for online TSV testing vehicle. As such, one needs to develop an efficient yet low-loss method to compress TSV testing-data with preserved fault detection information.

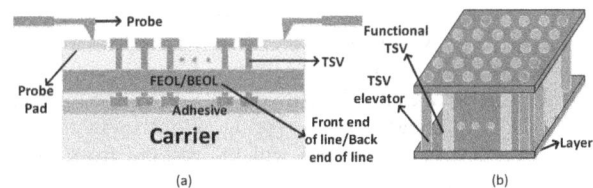

Figure 1: (a) Probing on extra DFT pads in pre-bond testing (b) TSV elevator in post-bond testing

Conventional testing data compression is widely used with according simple compaction circuits. It can be categorized as space compression and time compression. For space compression, XOR network is used to reduce many testing bits into single bit, which is however, limited by high aliasing rate because any even number of faulty responses could cancel error with a 'correct' response. For time compression such as multiple input signature register (MISR) method, it can achieve lower aliasing effect for conventional testing but cannot be directly deployed in the TSV testing because of the clustering effect [10, 11]. Furthermore, such a many-to-one compression method provides less online diagnosis information for TSV self-healing, which is a critical to improve the TSV yield.

In this paper, to perform online testing with improved bandwidth, we propose a lossless data compression method based on compressive-sensing for both pre-bond and post-bond TSV testing. It has no aliasing rate with on-chip data compression and off-chip lossless data recovery with according online hardware implementation for testing data compression. The problem of compressive-sensing based TSV testing data compression is formulated to find the maximum compression rate with lossless recovery under the constraint of TSV failure probability. For the pre-bond TSV testing, the failure probability refers to TSV failure probability due to variation of manufacturing [7]; whereas for the post-bond TSV testing, the failure probability is the faulty IC probability resulting in error output during functional testing

[12]. Experiment results show that with the testing data compression, 89.70% data compression rate can be achieved under 0.5% failure probability and 88.18% post-bond data compression rate with 5% failure probability.

The rest of the paper is organized as follows. Section II provides the TSV online testing vehicle architecture with the according problem formulation. Section III discusses the compressive-sensing based testing data compression and recovery. Section IV shows the application in pre-bond and post-bond TSV testing. Section V presents the numerical results with conclusion drawn in Section VI.

2. COMPRESSIVE 3D-IC TESTING PROBLEM

In this section, we will present the 3D-IC testing architecture for pre-bond and post-bond online TSV testing with the probe pad and TSV elevator. Moreover, the problem of the testing data compression is formulated based on this testing architecture.

2.1 TSV Testing Vehicles

The online TSV testing vehicle architecture can support pre-bond die testing, post-bond stack testing and board level interconnect testing based on [6]. Pre-bond testing is mainly designed to detect TSV manufacturing faults; while post-bond testing is not only for TSV interconnect testing but also for scan-chain and functional testing. As shown in Fig. 2, the testing wrapper will provide testing access mechanism (TAM) and send/receive testing signal to/from I/Os of external stack. Testing data will be injected from probe pad for pre-bond testing or from bottom die to upper die through TSV elevator for post-bond testing. Decoder will decode the input testing data and function as Automatic Testing Pattern Generator (ATPG) to cover the sequential and combinational circuits. The testing data is collected from the scan chain and compressed by the testing data compression (TDC) block. Then, such compressed testing data will be transported from the upper die to the bottom and eventually collected by the tester or probe pad. For pre-bond TSV testing, the expected output is the same as the input testing data, whereas for post-bond TSV testing the expected output is collected from output bandwidth based on time-division multiplexing technique, in which the first slot is used for expected output and the remaining slots are for compressed testing data output [13]. Therefore, no additional bandwidth is required for expected output.

For the pre-bond TSV testing, testing each TSV is time consuming and impractical [5, 7], groups of TSVs are tested. The TSV groups are formed based on the pitch of probe head such that the probe can contact the whole TSV group at once. The faulty TSV interconnect can be detected by the difference between the received signal and expected signal. The target of pre-bond TSV testing data compression is to minimize the output bits to save testing time while be able to lossless recover original signal to provide diagnostic information for TSV repair. Probe pad is used to collect the pre-bond TSV testing data.

For the post-bond TSV testing, as there are only TSV elevators and probe pads to provide input and output data for non-bottom die, the testing time is constrained by the bandwidth, given a large volume of testing data. Moreover, increasing the number of TSV elevator will incur more

die area and reduce the functional TSV densities. Therefore, data compression is needed to reduce the bandwidth requirement of TSV elevator and save testing time.

2.2 Problem Formulation

As previously discussed, lossless testing data compression is required to provide diagnostic information for TSV repair. The main proposed solution here is to fully utilize the compressive-sensing to compress the TSV testing data with high data compression rate under the given failure probability while being able to losslessly recover the original signal. Here, we assume that the TSV failure probability is known prior. As such, the TSV testing data compression problem can be formulated.

Problem: Find minimum number of output bits OB to locate faulty TSV/IC $E_{fault} \in \mathbb{R}^N$

$$\begin{aligned} Min. &< OB = MLog_2(Max(Y)) > \\ S.T.(i)\ & X_r = (I + E_{fault})X_e \\ (ii)\ & Y = \Phi(X_r - X_e) \\ (iii)\ & \|E_{fault}\|_0 \le K \end{aligned} \qquad (1)$$

where $X_r \in \mathbb{R}^N$ and $X_e \in \mathbb{R}^N$ denote the received and expected testing data through TSV for pre-bond testing or scan chain for post-bond testing and $Y \in \mathbb{R}^M$ is the compressed output testing data. $\Phi \in \mathbb{R}^{M \times N}$ is the compressive-sensing matrix generated from TDC block using XOR-AND networks. M and N is the compressed testing data length and original testing data length respectively. $E_{fault} \in \mathbb{R}^N$ are the defective TSV location in the pre-bond testing, while for the post-bond testing, E_{fault} represents the error bits introduced by faulty ICs. Sparsity K represents the maximum number of non-zero values in E_{fault}, which can be estimated by the TSV failure probability or IC failure probability. The lossless compression thereby means that when given the compressed result Y and sensing matrix Φ, we can losslessly recover E_{fault} such that no TSV testing data information is lost. By making use of sparsity of E_{fault}, an unique sparse solution can be found for the undetermined linear system [14, 15]. Please note that only compression process performed as $Y = \Phi(X_r - X_e)$ is on-chip. The rest

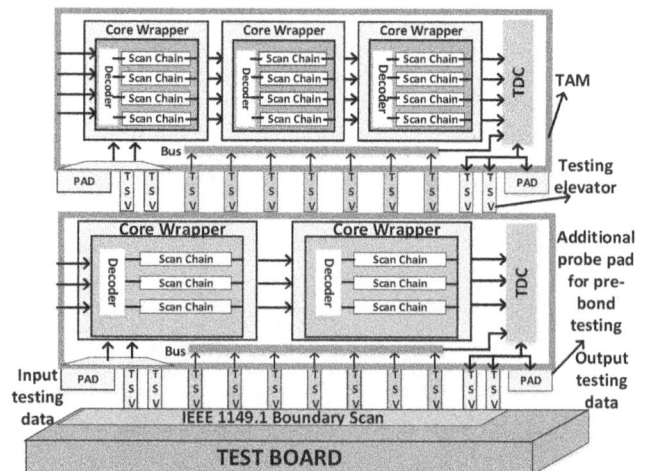

Figure 2: TSV testing vehicle with compressive-sensing based testing circuits

computation including testing data recovery is performed off-chip.

3. COMPRESSIVE-SENSING BASED COMPRESSION ALGORITHM

In this section, we discuss the sparsity of the testing data which is the foundation to perform compressive-sensing. Moreover, orthogonal matching pursuit is introduced here to solve undetermined equations. Please note that this section focuses on testing data analysis and recovery.

3.1 Sparsity of Testing data

Traditional lossless testing data compression methods such as length run (LR) coding and Golomb coding (GLC) are limited by the hardware implementation complexity for high volume of testing data. Compressive-sensing is one recently developed compression technique with sparse-representation of data by finding the most sparse solution of undetermined linear systems [14, 16]. Such a compression method results in simple encoding with comparable hardware implementation complexity as MISR since only XOR and AND network is required on-chip with data reconstruction off-chip.

To perform compressive-sensing, sparsity of testing data is estimated based on its yield. For TSV testing, signal is sparse in nature as only $1 - yield$ portion of data is nonzero if we compare the received result to expected outcome using XOR operation. For a common TSV yield such as 99% under pre-bond testing, there are 99% interconnects functioning properly. The defects are sparse in this sense indicating that the difference between the received and expected outputs are sparse with only 1% non-zero value at locations of faulty TSV interconnects. Similar to the pre-bond testing, the post-bond functional testing data can also be sparse by taking the difference between the received and expected data [12]. In order to know the sparsity, we need to estimate the TSV yield Y_{pre} and IC fault-free probability Y_{post}. Fig. 3 shows the testing data by XOR the expected and received expected output for 1024 TSV under different yields. Signal difference $'1'$ indicates an defective TSV. Thus, we can conclude that the higher yield, the more sparse the testing data will be.

Similar to [11, 17], we assume a uniform failure probability p for TSV under testing following binomial distribution. The overall probability of having x defective TSVs is

$$Y_{pre} = C_{N_{TSV}}^x p^x (1-p)^{N_{TSV}-x} \qquad (2)$$

where N_{TSV} is the number of TSVs. The yield of pre-bond TSV can be calculated as $x = 0$. Similarly for post-bond TSV testing, the fault-free IC probability can be estimated using Poisson distribution [18].

$$Y_{post} = \frac{(N_{com} * P_{com})^{N_{fault}}}{N_{fault}!} e^{-N_{com}*P_{com}} \qquad (3)$$

where N_{faulty} is the number of faulty components. N_{com} and P_{com} are the number of components and the probability of being faulty components respectively. The IC failure probability is $P_{post} = 1 - Y_{post}(N_{fault} = 0)$.

For post-bond, due to the application of ATPG and different functional testing algorithms, the testing data may not directly reflect the faulty component location. Therefore, the clustering effect is not considered. As the affected output bits due to faulty IC components depends on the testing

algorithm, we assume the affected output signal (error bit probability) is proportional to faulty component probability. For pre-bond TSV testing, TSV testing data is directly related to faulty TSV location. The clustering effect is considered and there exists a spatial correlation between defective TSVs. This indicates that presence of a defective TSV increases the probability of defective TSV nearby. Based on [11, 17], the probability of defect for i-th TSV P_i can be modeled as below.

$$P_i = P(1 + \sum_{j=1}^{N_c} (1/d_{ic})^\alpha) \qquad (4)$$

where P is the single TSV failure rate, d_{ic} is the distance between the TSV_i and cluster center, and α is the clustering coefficients indicating cluster extent. A large α indicates higher clustering effect. In our simulations, we assume the cluster center is injected randomly and only forms a proportion of total defective TSV number. The rest of failure TSV is generated with the combination of failure probability and clustering effect as mentioned in (4). The testing data compression rate N_C and output bandwidth improvement for both pre-bond and post-bond circuit can be defined as follows.

$$Bw_{Imp} = \frac{N}{M * log_2(Max(Y))}, \quad N_C = 1 - \frac{1}{Bw_{Imp}} \qquad (5)$$

where $Max(Y)$ is maximum digital value of the compressed testing data, and N is the original data size. Please note that for a given bandwidth, data compression is equivalent to improve bandwidth, which has the same effect on throughput. We select the maximum code bit size $log_2(Max(Y))$ to ease the decoding after receiving them from probe pad or tester.

3.2 Lossless Compression and Recovery in L_1 Norm

The lossless compression is performed on-chip; whereas recovery is done off-chip. The recovery of compressed testing data can be formulated as L_0 norm minimization problem given below:

$$\begin{array}{ll} \text{argmin} & \|E_{fault}\|_0 \\ \text{subject to} & Y = \Phi E_{fault} \end{array} \qquad (6)$$

where E_{fault} is N dimensional sparse testing data ($E_{fault} \in \mathbb{R}^N$), Φ is the sensing matrix ($\Phi \in \mathbb{R}^{M \times N}$) generated by TDC from XOR-AND network, and Y is the compressed testing data in low dimension ($Y \in \mathbb{R}^M$ and $M \ll N$). Note the solution of L_0 norm is equivalent to L_1 norm with overwhelming probability [14].

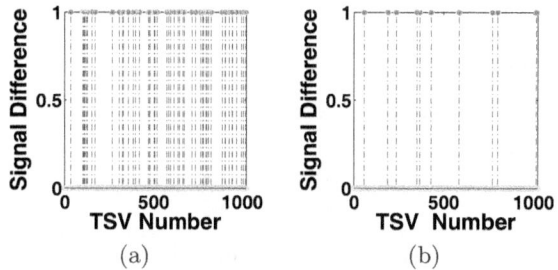

Figure 3: (a) Sparse data for yield (Y_{pre}) of 95% (b) sparse data for yield (Y_{pre}) of 99%

To ensure a successful recovery without loss, the sensing (or sampling) matrix must satisfy the restricted isometry property (RIP) [14]. In this paper, we use random Bernoulli matrix that can be implemented from pseudo number generator in hardware with well recognized RIP property. For the online TSV testing vehicles in Section 2, we can implement a counter to record non-zero values for lossless data compression and reconstruction. The minimum dimension M of compressed testing data [14] is

$$M = O(Klog(N/K)) \qquad (7)$$

where K is the sparsity of data that can be estimated as (8) and N is the total length of original testing data. N has relationship with number of TSV N_{TSV} by $N = N_{TSV} * N_{data}$, where N_{data} is the number signal sent from each TSV. From (7), we can sample the signal based on its sparsity. The sparsity K can be estimated as below.

$$K = Ceil(N - NY_{pre}) \qquad (8)$$

where Y_{pre} is the yield of pre-bond TSV testing. If we replace Y_{pre} by Y_{post}, the sparsity K for the post-bond TSV testing can also be calculated.

3.3 OMP based Compressed Data Recovery

As discussed in Section 3.1, L_0 norm solution can be applied to solve (6). In this paper, we deploy the Orthogonal Matching Pursuit (OMP) solver for the L_0 norm solution, which is a heuristic solver based on greedy algorithm to find the most sparse solution [19]. More details on compressed testing data recovery from OMP are provided in Algorithm 1. The residual is initialized as compressed testing data Y. Index set Λ_0 and chosen matrix Φ_0 are empty. The largest correlated column is found from Step 4, while index and chosen matrix will be updated as Step 5. The new estimated testing data is reconstructed in Step 6 via $L2$ minimization. The residual is updated from the estimated testing data and compressed testing data. The iteration will stop after K iterations. In summary, OMP performs two functions as follows. Firstly, it finds the most correlated column from the sensing matrix Φ by comparing simple dot multiplication. Secondly, the largest correlated column is added to the selected column and by solving a $L2$ norm minimization, the most fitted new estimate testing data is generated. This procedure will repeat K times to find the recovered testing data. Note that K is the sparsity of the testing data E_{faulty}, which can be estimated from the Y_{pre} and Y_{post}.

4. COMPRESSIVE-SENSING BASED HARD-WARE IMPLEMENTATION

In this section, we will discuss the hardware implementation of compressive-sensing with XOR and AND network followed by the application of compressive-sensing to pre-bond and post-bond TSV testing.

4.1 Compressive-sensing based Testing Circuit

To perform the data compression using the proposed algorithm, outputs from the scan chain and expected output are provided as inputs for the testing data compression (TDC), as shown in Fig.2. Note that X-states (unknown states) will be masked to '0' based on the information from testing data controlled by mask controller. The TDC testing can be implemented using adders and XOR gates as shown in Fig. 4.

Algorithm 1 Orthogonal Matching Pursuit Algorithm

Require: An MxN TDC generated sensing matrix $\Phi = [\varphi_1, \varphi_2, ...,\varphi_N]$, an M-dimensional compressed testing data Y and yield Y_{yield}
Ensure: An accurate testing data E_{faulty}
1: Initialize the residual $r_0 = Y$, the index set $\Lambda_0 = \emptyset$, $\Phi_{\Lambda_0} = \emptyset$ and iteration counter $t = 1$.
2: Calculate sparsity $K = Ceil(N - NY_{yield})$
3: While $(t \leq K)$
4: Find column index λ_t of Φ correlates Y most as below
  $\lambda_t = argmax_{j=1,...N} | < r_{t-1}, \varphi_j > |$,
5: Update column index set and matrix of chosen columns
  $\Lambda_t = \Lambda_{t-1} \cup \lambda_t$
  $\Phi_{\Lambda_t} = [\Phi_{\Lambda_{t-1}} \varphi_{\lambda_t}]$
6: Solve a least squares problem to obtain new signal
  $x_t = argmin|| Y - \Phi_{\Lambda_t} x ||_2$
7: Calculate the new approximation and residual
  $a_t = \Phi_{\Lambda_t} x_t$, $r_t = Y - a_t$, $t = t + 1$
8: End While
9: $E_{faulty} = x_t$

The scan chain output and the expected output from the probe pad are XORed to obtain the testing data, E_{faulty} , which is normally sparse with '1' to denote the failure. The Bernoulli function is realized using a linear feedback shift register (LFSR) with M measurements collected after performing M shifts. Here, M is the dimension of compressed testing data Y. Furthermore, the Bernoulli matrix is multiplied with the testing data using AND gates, where bits are added using the adder and fed to the probe pad. This implementation reduces the number of outputs from N dimensions to M dimensions. Note that the above-mentioned TDC implementation is suitable for both pre-bond and post-bond TSV testing on-chip.

4.2 Pre-bond TSV Testing

For pre-bond TSV testing, short or open defects will lead to receive incorrect testing data, which can be used to detect faulty TSVs after comparing to the expected data. Fig. 5a shows an example of TSV failure. In general, the size of probe heads is large compared to the pitch of TSVs. Hence, the probe head will contact a group of TSVs instead of each individual TSV. As shown in Fig. 5b, among the group of TSVs, only a few can have the I/O driving ability, which can be used to output the testing data and the rest can only

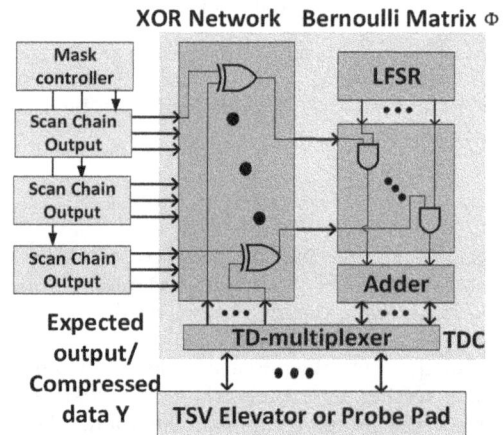

Figure 4: Compressive-sensing based testing circuit diagram for testing data compression

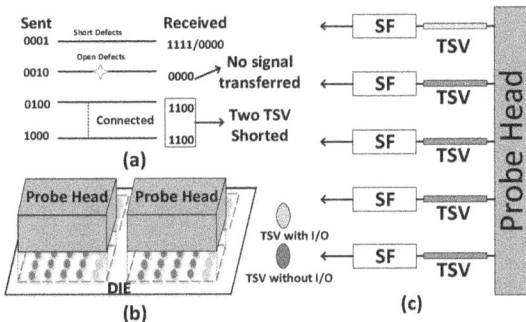

Figure 5: Conceptual diagram for pre-bond TSV testing

receive data from probe. As multiple TSVs are connected to one probe head, it is important to differentiate each TSV in the receiving end. Similar to [20], a scan flip-flop (SF) controlled by digital enable circuit is utilized to differentiate the input from the TSVs as described in Fig. 5c. This received data from top SF is provided as the input to the XOR network of TDC (in Fig. 4) and then the compressed testing data Y is sent through top TSV with I/O. The original testing data E_{fault} can be recovered from compressed testing data Y based on the proposed Algorithm 1.

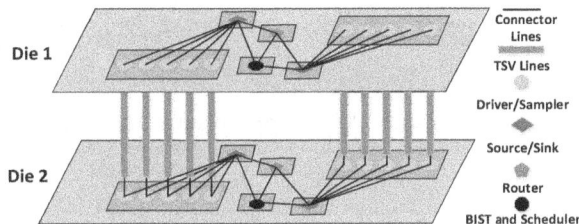

Figure 6: Conceptual diagram for post-bond TSV testing

4.3 Post-bond TSV Testing

For post-bond functional testing, our proposed compression technique can work independently or co-work with conventional MISR techniques to further compress the testing data depending on the lossless/lossy testing requirement. Our proposed compression algorithm provides general solutions to digital signal lossless compression. Fig. 6 shows a conceptual post-bond TSV testing diagram where built-in-self-test (BIST) circuit is shared between different TSV groups. The signal generated from BIST is scheduled and sent to router. Router will send the signal to TSV group driver for testing purposes by a sequence of digital bits similar as in the pre-bond test. Testing data compression (TDC) will receive the expected testing data from the router and compress them. Similarly ATPG can also be performed where the expected output is known. As shown in Fig. 4, the compressed testing data Y is collected and original testing data E_{fault} can be recovered from Y as shown in the proposed Algorithm 1.

4.4 TSV Testing Flow

Fig. 7 depicts the overall testing flow for the proposed TSV online testing vehicle. The input patterns and the expected output will be sent to device under test (DUT) and XOR-AND network respectively through input and output testing pads or elevators as shown in Fig. 2. Note that the expected output will be sent through output testing pads based on time-division multiplexer (TD-multiplexer).

Therefore, no additional bandwidth is required. The testing data compression (TDC) will compress the testing data through XOR-AND network described in Fig. 4. The compressed testing data will be sent to off-chip computational resource for recovery. Note that as for the existing MISR-based compression method, faults are detected from one-in-many testing based on single signature. Insufficient diagnostic information is available to designers. Moreover, detection failure rate of MISR increases due to the error-cancelling effect under the clustering effect and the non-uniform TSV failure probability. In contrast, the proposed method performs the lossless compression without the error-cancelling effect. Moreover, it results in pin-level output of testing data for TSV self-repair or the other debugging capability.

5. SIMULATION RESULTS

In this section, we discuss the experiments set-up, the testing data recovery and compression for pre-bond and post-bond TSV testing. The compressive-sensing based TSV testing simulation platform is implemented in Matlab 2014a on a computer with 3.2 GHz core and 8.0G memory.

5.1 Experiment Set-up

Firstly, we present the compressed testing data of TSVs under different yields and the corresponding reconstructed data. The experiment is performed for 1024 number of TSVs with input as '1' for each TSV to verify whether '1' is received. Faulty TSV is inserted based on (2).

Secondly, for pre-bond TSV testing, 4096, 16384 and 65536 TSVs are tested with a scan signal and a 3-bit testing output [20]. To model defective TSV distribution, 10% defective TSVs are inserted as center in a TSV map; and the rest is generated based on clustering effect presented in (4).

Finally, for post-bond TSV testing, the proposed testing data compression method is applied for ISCAS-85 benchmarks [21] in Verilog based on stuck-at fault model. The testing pattern is generated using Mintest [22], which provides 100% fault coverage. An 8-bit output signal after scan testing is assumed and error bit probability is modeled based on (3) for stuck-at fault model. We select length-run (LR) coding and Golomb coding (GLC) coding for performance comparison as they both perform lossless compression and close to the entropy of information [23]. The area overhead of proposed TDC is synthesized using DC Synopsys

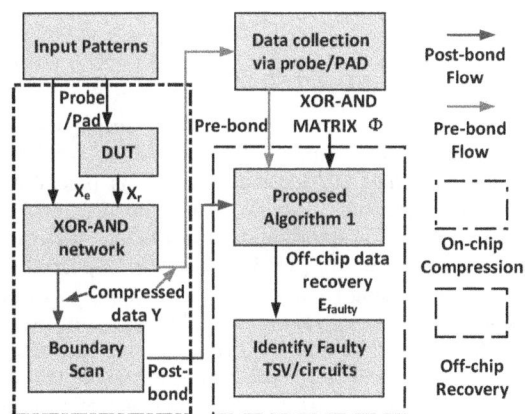

Figure 7: Testing flow for proposed testing vehicle

Table 1: Testing data Compression Rate and Bandwidth Improvement in Pre-bond Testing with 0.5 % (upper row) and 1% (lower row) Failure Rate

TSV Number	Cluster	Proposed		Length Run Coding		Golomb Coding GS= 8		Golomb Coding GS= 16		Golomb Coding GS =32	
		Comp. Rate	Bw Imp.	Comp. Rate	Bw Imp.	Comp. Rate	Bw Imp.	Comp. Rate	Bw Imp.	Comp. Rate	Bw Imp.
4096	$\alpha = 0$	89.45%	9.48 x	81.80%	5.49 x	76.83%	4.32 x	79.98%	5.00 x	81.23%	5.33 x
	$\alpha = 1$	89.70%	9.71 x	81.14%	5.30 x	77.29%	4.40 x	80.18%	5.05 x	81.30%	5.35 x
	$\alpha = 2$	89.32%	9.36 x	81.52%	5.41 x	76.68%	4.29 x	79.76%	4.94 x	80.98%	5.26 x
	$\alpha = 0$	65.29%	2.88 x	50.99%	2.04 x	35.57%	1.55 x	44.38%	1.80 x	48.02%	1.92 x
	$\alpha = 1$	65.03%	2.86 x	50.73%	2.03 x	35.57%	1.55 x	43.80%	1.78 x	47.29%	1.90 x
	$\alpha = 2$	66.48%	2.98 x	51.52%	2.06 x	37.16%	1.59 x	45.85%	1.85 x	49.51%	1.98 x
16384	$\alpha = 0$	89.16%	9.22 x	80.37%	5.09 x	75.95%	4.16 x	79.11%	4.79 x	80.38%	5.10 x
	$\alpha = 1$	89.23%	9.28 x	80.15%	5.04 x	73.99%	3.84 x	77.28%	4.40 x	78.63%	4.68 x
	$\alpha = 2$	89.35%	9.39 x	80.47%	5.12 x	75.59%	4.10 x	78.89%	4.74 x	80.27%	5.07 x
	$\alpha = 0$	64.80%	2.84 x	49.42%	1.98 x	34.08%	1.52 x	43.39%	1.77 x	47.35%	1.90 x
	$\alpha = 1$	64.29%	2.80 x	46.93%	1.88 x	29.49%	1.42 x	38.37%	1.62 x	42.03%	1.73 x
	$\alpha = 2$	64.86%	2.85 x	50.62%	2.03 x	34.51%	1.53 x	43.84%	1.78 x	47.73%	1.91 x
65536	$\alpha = 0$	89.17%	9.24 x	79.77%	4.94 x	73.48%	3.77 x	76.86%	4.32 x	78.26%	4.60 x
	$\alpha = 1$	89.21%	9.27 x	79.73%	4.93 x	73.09%	3.72 x	76.63%	4.28 x	78.12%	4.57 x
	$\alpha = 2$	89.24%	9.30 x	79.38%	4.85 x	73.49%	3.77 x	76.86%	4.32 x	78.26%	4.60 x
	$\alpha = 0$	65.32%	2.88 x	50.03%	2.00 x	34.27%	1.52 x	43.35%	1.77 x	47.17%	1.89 x
	$\alpha = 1$	64.59%	2.82 x	48.57%	1.94 x	34.19%	1.52 x	43.41%	1.77 x	47.28%	1.90 x
	$\alpha = 2$	64.88%	2.85 x	47.08%	1.89 x	26.68%	1.36 x	40.21%	1.67 x	45.34%	1.83 x

(D-2010.03-SP2) and estimated $4522um^2$ using $65nm$ process technology from Globalfoundries.

5.2 Compressive-sensing in TSV Testing

As shown in Fig. 4, the XOR of received and expected data is multiplied by a Bernoulli based sensing matrix Φ, which is generated from a binary pseudo number generator. The TSV with defects will not receive '1' and therefore the XOR result will be '1', indicating the failure of this TSV. Furthermore, one encoded output is generated from the adder based on the row of sensing matrix Φ multiplied by the XOR result. As an example, we collected 200 output measurements and plotted the adder output under different yields in Fig. 8. From Fig. 8(a), one can observe that the adder results are smaller for TSV with 99% yield, compared to adder results shown in Fig. 8(b) for TSV with yield 95%. It indicates that high yield testing data will required less bits for encoding, which results in higher compression rate as per Equation (5).

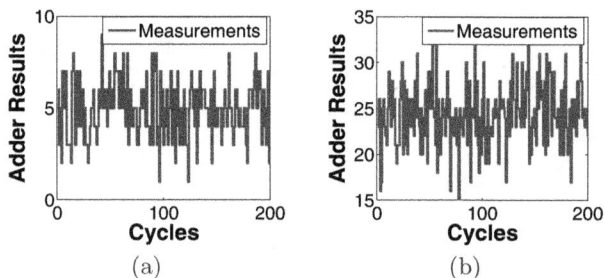

Figure 8: (a) Compressed output for yield of 99% (b) compressed output for yield of 95%

Furthermore, the minimum number of required measurements (dimension of compressed testing data) under different yields to achieve a lossless recovery is presented in Fig. 9. As illustrated in Fig. 9(a), the difference between the recovered and original data decreases dramatically as the measurements (M) increases, as expected from the compressive-sensing theory [14] , indicating a least number of measurements are required for lossless compression. As such, the higher the yield is, the less number of measurements (M) is required. For example, when the yield is as high as 99%, there are nearly 60 measurements good enough to fully recover the testing data; whereas, there are

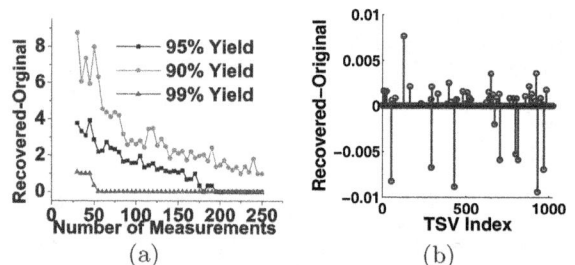

Figure 9: (a) Maximum difference vs. number of output (b) signal reconstruction with 60 measurements for yield of 99%

nearly 190 measurements needed to fully recover the testing data for yield 95%. Since the sparse solution is unique [14], we can confirm the correctness of reconstruction by performing OMP solver twice. For lossless reconstruction, the maximum difference between the recovered and original data should be sufficiently small. As Fig. 9(b) shows, for 99% yield, the maximum difference between the recovered and original data is as small as E^{-2} for 60 measurements to represent 1024 TSVs, corresponding to a 82.42% data compression rate ($1 - 60 \times 3/1024$).

5.3 Compressive-sensing in Pre-bond Testing

In Fig. 10, the red square is the defective TSV cluster center and black circle is the defective TSV generated from failure probability and clustering effect based on (4). X-axis and Y-axis represent the location of TSV. The average failure probability is 20 % and due to the clustering effect, the failure probability can be as high as 81.52% for the TSVs close to the center as Fig. 10c. Table 1 shows the output testing data compression rate for different clustering factor α and the number of TSVs. A compression of nearly 89% is achieved for 4096 TSVs with failure rate of 0.5%, but is reduced to nearly 66% with failure rate of 1%. This indicates that more number of measurements is required for the lossless compression when the failure probability increases. It also shows that despite the existence of clustering effect,the compression rate will be maintained almost the same.

In addition, as shown in Table 1, we compare our compression algorithm with length-run (LR) coding and Golomb coding (GLC) based compression algorithms [23]. Note that Golomb coding is greatly affected by the tunable group size GS. For example, if we consider the case of 16384 TSVs with

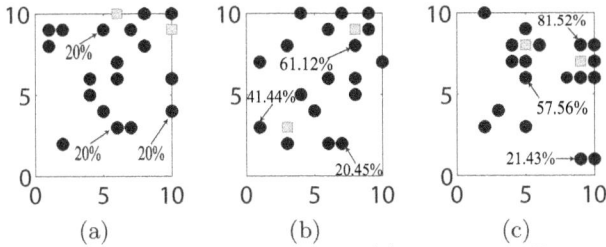

Figure 10: (a) No clustering effect (b) clustering effect with $\alpha = 1$ (c) clustering effect with $\alpha = 2$

failure probability 1% and clustering factor α as 1, our proposed algorithm can successfully compress 64.29%; whereas LR can only compress 46.93%; GLC with $GS = 8, 16, 32$ can only compress 29.49%, 38.37% and 42.03%, respectively. The bandwidth improvement can also be derived from (5) as shown in Table 1. Note that with increasing GS, GLC compression rate of testing-data will converge to the information entropy. However, hardware complexity and decoding time also increase dramatically, which limits us to compare until $GS = 32$.

Table 2: Testing Data Compression in Post-bond Testing

Failure Prob.	Benchmark	Output (bits)	Proposed	LR Coding	GLC $GS =8$	GLC $GS =16$
5%	c499	1696	88.15%	78.22%	73.01%	76.42%
	c432	196	88.18%	77.96%	76.38%	78.57%
	c1908	2475	86.89%	73.69%	72.83%	76.34%
	c2670	6300	82.56%	73.81%	69.77%	73.74%
	c3540	1870	87.76%	80.55%	75.75%	78.72%
	c5315	4674	81.80%	75.31%	71.13%	74.97%
	c6288	416	85.65%	81.15%	82.21%	84.13%
	c7552	7992	80.30%	74.27%	68.26%	72.49%
10%	c499	1696	73.82%	59.53%	50.17%	57.17%
	c432	196	82.19%	68.67%	63.06%	66.94%
	c1908	2475	70.57%	56.00%	45.86%	53.27%
	c2670	6300	61.42%	55.17%	44.25%	51.80%
	c3540	1870	70.82%	56.56%	46.24%	53.76%
	c5315	4674	63.71%	52.38%	40.88%	49.14%
	c6288	416	76.06%	58.51%	49.83%	56.49%
	c7552	7992	60.99%	54.45%	43.95%	51.55%

5.4 Compressive-sensing in Post-bond Testing

We finally discuss the post-bond testing data compression. We assume 5% and 10% probabilities of failure IC for an 8-bit output signal (signature), which mean 0.639% and 1.308% failure probabilities for each bit. Similar to pre-bond testing, we compare our proposed compression algorithm with LR and GLC coding based compression algorithms, and is presented in Table 2. It also shows that the data compression rate outperforms length-run coding and Golomb coding. The testing data compression for 5% failure probability varies from 80.03% to 88.18%, whereas 74.27% to 68.26% for LR coding; and 76.42% to 72.49% for GLC with $GS = 16$. For circuit c7552, our proposed algorithm has a 6.03% and 7.81% improvement compared to LR and GLC, respectively. However, as failure probability increases, our proposed testing data compression rate outperforms further by 6.55% and 9.45% compared to LR and GLC with $GS = 16$ respectively. Moreover, since the proposed algorithm is lossless compression, it can also co-work with MISR or other conventional compression techniques to further compressed the testing data with shared circuit implementations.

6. CONCLUSION

In this paper, the testing data compression is discussed for pre-bond and post-bond TSV testing via compressive-

sensing based method. By exploring the sparsity of the testing data, one can achieve on-chip data compression and lossless off-chip data recovery. The encoding for compression can be easily implemented on-chip using XOR and AND networks with significantly improved bandwidth for the output of the testing data. As such, it can result in an efficient implementation of online TSV testing vehicle to improve TSV yield with TSV self-repair capability. Experiment results with benchmarks have shown that 89.70% pre-bond data compression rate can be achieved under 0.5% failure probability; and 88.18% post-bond data compression rate can be achieved with 5% failure probability.

7. REFERENCES

[1] J. R. Cubillo et al., "Interconnect design and analysis for through silicon interposers (TSIs)," in *IEEE 3DIC*, 2012.

[2] L. Jiang, Q. Xu, and B. Eklow, "On effective TSV repair for 3D-stacked ICs," in *DATE*. ACM/IEEE, 2012, pp. 793–798.

[3] C. Zhang and et.al., "Novel crack sensor for TSV-based 3D integrated circuits: design and deployment perspectives," in *IEEE ICCAD*, 2013.

[4] F.-W. Chen, H.-L. Ting, and T. Hwang, "Fault-tolerant tsv by using scan-chain test tsv," in *IEEE ASP-DAC*, 2014.

[5] B. Zhang and V. D. Agrawal, "An optimal probing method of pre-bond TSV fault identification in 3D stacked ICs," in *IEEE S3S*, 2014.

[6] E. J. Marinissen, "Challenges and emerging solutions in testing TSV-based 1/2D-and 3D-stacked ICs," in *IEEE DATE*, 2012.

[7] B. Noia and K. Chakrabarty, "Pre-bond probing of TSVs in 3D stacked ICs," in *IEEE ITC*, 2011.

[8] E. J. Marinissen and Y. Zorian, "Testing 3D chips containing through-silicon vias," in *IEEE ITC*, 2009.

[9] J. Xie, Y. Wang, and Y. Xie, "Yield-aware time-efficient testing and self-fixing design for TSV-based 3D ICs," in *IEEE ASPDAC*, 2012.

[10] P. H. Bardell, W. H. McAnney, and J. Savir, *Built-in test for VLSI: pseudorandom techniques*. Wiley-Interscience, 1987.

[11] M. Tahoori, "Defects, yield, and design in sublithographic nano-electronics," in *IEEE Defect and Fault Tolerance in VLSI Systems*, 2005.

[12] W. Maly, "Realistic fault modeling for VLSI testing," in *IEEE DAC*, 1987.

[13] B. Sklar, *Digital communications*. Prentice Hall NJ, 2001, vol. 2.

[14] D. L. Donoho and M. Elad, "Optimally sparse representation in general (nonorthogonal) dictionaries via L1 minimization," *Proceedings of the National Academy of Sciences*, 2003.

[15] E. J. Candes and T. Tao, "Near-optimal signal recovery from random projections: Universal encoding strategies?" *IEEE Transactions on Information Theory,*, vol. 52, no. 12, pp. 5406–5425, 2006.

[16] D. L. Donoho, "For most large underdetermined systems of linear equations the minimal L1-norm solution is also the sparsest solution," *Communications on pure and applied mathematics*, vol. 59, no. 6, pp. 797–829, 2006.

[17] Y. Zhao and et.al., "Cost-effective TSV grouping for yield improvement of 3D-ICs," in *IEEE ATS*, 2011.

[18] G. S. May and C. J. Spanos, *Fundamentals of semiconductor manufacturing and process control*. John Wiley & Sons, 2006.

[19] J. A. Tropp and A. C. Gilbert, "Signal recovery from random measurements via orthogonal matching pursuit," *IEEE Transactions on Information Theory,*, vol. 53, no. 12, pp. 4655–4666, 2007.

[20] B. Noia, S. Panth, K. Chakrabarty, and S. K. Lim, "Scan test of die logic in 3D ICs using TSV probing," in *IEEE ITC*, 2012.

[21] M. C. Hansen, H. Yalcin, and J. P. Hayes, "Unveiling the ISCAS-85 benchmarks: A case study in reverse engineering," *IEEE Design and Test of Computers*, vol. 16, no. 3, pp. 72–80, 1999.

[22] I. Hamzaoglu and J. H. Patel, "Testset compaction algorithms for combinational circuits," in *IEEE ICCAD*, 1998.

[23] A. Chandra and K. Chakrabarty, "Test data compression for system-on-a-chip using golomb codes," in *IEEE VTS*, 2000.

PLATON: A Force-Directed Placement Algorithm for 3D Optical Networks-on-Chip

Anja von Beuningen
Institute for Electronic Design Automation
Technische Universität München
anja.boos@tum.de

Ulf Schlichtmann
Institute for Electronic Design Automation
Technische Universität München
ulf.schlichtmann@tum.de

ABSTRACT

Optical Networks-on-Chip (ONoCs) are a promising technology to further increase the bandwidth and decrease the power consumption of today's multicore systems. To determine the laser power consumption of an ONoC, the physical design of the system is indispensible. The only place and route tool for 3D ONoCs already proposed in the literature badly scales with the increasing number of optical devices. Thus, within this contribution we present the first force-directed placement algorithm for 3D optical NoCs. Our algorithm decreases the runtime up to 99.7% compared to the state-of-the-art placer. Using our algorithm large topologies can be placed within a short runtime.

Keywords

Optical Networks-on-Chip; Silicon Photonics; Placement

1. INTRODUCTION

Networks-on-Chip (NoCs) are a promising technology to increase the bandwidth of multicore systems. The usage of optical interconnections instead of metal wires can further increase the bandwidth while minimizing the dynamic power dissipation of NoCs. Recent literature about ONoCs mainly focuses on system level design [22][17][4][9] but rarely discusses placement and routing. Because the laser power consumption strongly depends on the physical design, the layout stage should not be overlooked.

Let the critical path be the optical path with maximum insertion loss, which mainly depends on the waveguide length and the number of waveguide crossings inside the critical path. Then, the laser power consumption is determined by the insertion loss of the critical path. Due to unrealistic assumptions of the positions of the initiators and targets of the optical paths the logic scheme cannot provide a good estimation of the waveguide crossings and waveguide length [14]. In general, the number of waveguide crossings and the waveguide length increase, when the final layout is compared to the original logic scheme.

PROTON [2] is the only automatic placement and routing algorithm for 3D ONoCs. Before PROTON was proposed, designers had to place and route manually, which is time

ISPD'16, April 03 - 06, 2016, Santa Rosa, CA, USA

© 2016 Copyright held by the owner/author(s). Publication rights licensed to ACM.
ISBN 978-1-4503-4039-7/16/04. . . $15.00

DOI: http://dx.doi.org/10.1145/2872334.2872356

consuming and results in suboptimal layouts. PROTON places the optical devices overlap-free inside the footprint area and routes all waveguides on the same layer. Because PROTON does not scale very well with the size of the optical topology, new algorithms, which place and route faster, are needed.

In this contribution we present a force-directed placement algorithm, based on Kraftwerk [20], for 3D ONoCs.

Because the physical design of Wavelength-Routed Optical NoCs (WRONoCs) strongly differs from their logic scheme, these are the most challenging benchmarks for a placement algorithm. We apply our tool to the most significant WRONoCs proposed in the literature. The layouts are compared to the manual design as well as the layouts obtained by PROTON [2]. We will show that the laser power consumption of larger topologies is reduced with the help of PLATON, while the computational effort for all topologies is reduced significantly.

The rest of the paper is structured as follows: In Section 2 we present the background and state-of-the-art of ONoCs. The force-directed placement algorithm is proposed in Section 3. In Section 4, the resulting layouts of different benchmarks are compared to manually designed layouts proposed in the literature as well as to the layouts obtained by PROTON. Finally, in Section 5 a conclusion is drawn.

2. STATE-OF-THE-ART

Similar to [2] we consider a 3D system to integrate the optical devices into the electronic NoC.

2.1 Architecture

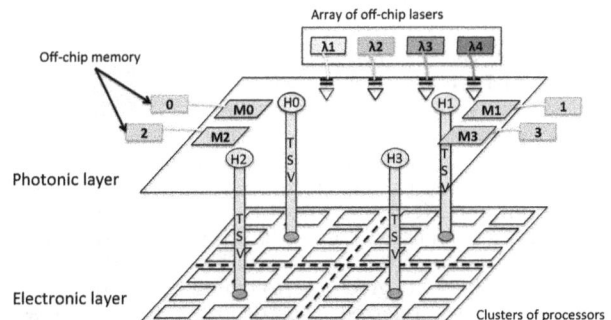

Figure 1: Target architecture

The 3D system consists of a lower, electronic layer and an upper, photonic layer, which are connected by arrays of Through-Silicon-Vias (TSVs) as can be seen in Figure 1. The purely electronic layer is designed using a monolithic

CMOS process and contains all architecture blocks including serializer and deserializer. The electronic circuits for the electronic/optical and optical/electronic communication are split between the electronic and the optical layer. In particular, on the electronic layer a grid of processors partitioned into clusters is located. Each cluster is connected to a network interface on the electronic layer, which guides the signals via a TSV array to the optical interface on the optical layer. We assume a core size of $1.33mm \times 1.33mm$. The die size depends on the total number of cores. In case of 32 cores partitioned into 4 clusters, the die size is assumed to be $8mm \times 8mm$. The rest of the electronic layer is occupied e.g. by I/O peripherals and the electronic interconnect network.

We enable three different kinds of communication: a) between two clusters, b) from a cluster to an off-chip memory connected to the optical layer and c) from a memory to a cluster. The off-chip memory is connected to memory controllers on the optical layer. In Figure 1 the memory controllers are referred to as $M0, \ldots, M3$. The positions of these memory controllers are determined by the location of the off-chip memory [1]. To ensure short interconnections between memory controllers and off-chip memory, the memory controllers are positioned close to the chip boundary. On top of the center point of each cluster a hub, consisting of the optical components of the interface between the electronic and the optical network, is positioned. In Figure 1 the hubs are named $H0, \ldots, H3$. Thus, the communication between all hubs, from all hubs to all memory controllers and from all memory controllers to all hubs has to be enabled. The output pins of hubs and memory controllers are referred to as *initiators*, while the input pins of hubs and memory controllers are named *targets*.

To connect N initiators with N targets a NxN Wavelength-Routed Optical NoC (WRONoC) can be used.

2.2 Wavelength-Routed Optical NoCs

In WRONoCs the principles of wavelength-selective routing and wavelength division multiplexing are used. Let a path be the connection between one initiator and one target. Each path starting at the same initiator uses a different wavelength to reach a specific target. In addition to an initiator and a target, a path consists of several Photonic Switching Elements (PSEs) as shown in Figure 2.

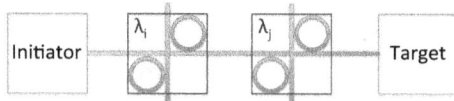

Figure 2: A path connects an initiator and a target via several PSEs.

These are optical switches with either two microring resonators (MRRs) as well as 2 input and 2 output ports (referred to as 2x2 optical switch) or one MRR and one input and 2 output ports (referred to as 1x2 optical switch). In our contribution we focus on passive 2x2 PSEs, e.g. depending on the wavelength of the signal entering the PSE, it is either deflected by 90 degrees due to coupling and resonation processes, which is referred to as drop function, or crosses the PSE as shown in Figure 3. Using passive PSEs allows us to define a contention-free, fully connected network without the overhead of control devices. Furthermore, no time is spent on the activation and deactivation of the PSEs. We assume a PSE size of $70\mu m \times 70\mu m$ [18].

Common use cases are WRONoCs connecting eight initiators and eight targets. The most important 8x8 WRONoC topologies are the following: The 8x8 λ-Router [14] connects

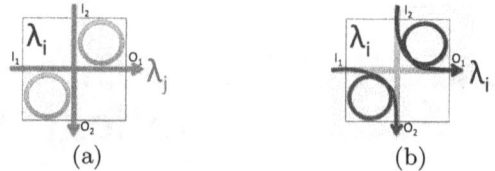

Figure 3: The PSE is sensitive to wavelength λ_i. (a) A signal with wavelength not equal to λ_i crosses the PSE. (b) A signal with wavelength λ_i is coupled into the ring and decoupled into the waveguide perpendicular to the incoming waveguide.

the initiators and targets via 28 2x2 optical switches and uses 8 different wavelengths. The 8x8 Generic Wavelength-Routed Optical Router (GWOR) [21] includes 24 2x2 optical switches and needs 7 different wavelengths. The 8x8 Standard Crossbar [7] uses 64 1x2 optical switches and works with 8 different wavelengths.

2.3 Maximum Insertion Loss

After physical design has been completed, the laser power consumption of the optical NoC can be calculated. Let P be the set of all optical paths. A metric of the laser power required by the system is the maximum insertion loss over all paths $p \in P$.

The insertion loss mainly is determined by four different losses: The propagation loss occurs due to light scattering at the sidewalls of the waveguides when the optical signal propagates through the waveguide. The crossing loss occurs when the optical signal crosses the light signal in any other waveguide either inside or outside a PSE. The bending loss occurs when the optical signal propagates along a waveguide bend, which typically has a 90 degrees curvature. The drop loss describes the loss that occurs if the signal is deflected by 90 degrees inside a PSE due to coupling and resonation processes.

Let $\mathbf{x}$ and $\mathbf{r}$ be the positions of the PSEs and the positions of the waveguides, respectively. Using the loss parameters proposed in [3] the propagation loss $pl_p(\mathbf{x}, \mathbf{r})$, the crossing loss $cl_p(\mathbf{x}, \mathbf{r})$, the drop loss $dl_p(\mathbf{x}, \mathbf{r})$ and the bending loss $bl_p(\mathbf{x}, \mathbf{r})$ of each path p for a resulting layout are calculated as

$$pl_p(\mathbf{x}, \mathbf{r}) = 1.5\frac{dB}{cm} \cdot L_p \tag{1}$$

$$cl_p(\mathbf{x}, \mathbf{r}) = 0.15dB \cdot C_p \tag{2}$$

$$dl_p(\mathbf{x}, \mathbf{r}) = 0.5dB \cdot D_p \tag{3}$$

$$bl_p(\mathbf{x}, \mathbf{r}) = 0.005dB \cdot B_p, \tag{4}$$

where L_p, C_p, D_p and B_p are the waveguide length in cm, the number of crossings, the number of drops and the number of bends in path p, respectively.

In our studies the insertion loss of path p is calculated as the sum of propagation loss, crossing loss, drop loss and bending loss.

$$il_p(\mathbf{x}, \mathbf{r}) = (pl_p(\mathbf{x}, \mathbf{r}) + cl_p(\mathbf{x}, \mathbf{r}) + dl_p(\mathbf{x}, \mathbf{r})$$
$$+ bl_p(\mathbf{x}, \mathbf{r})) \tag{5}$$

We assume equal laser power for each laser source. Thus, the laser source with maximum power consumption determines the power consumption of the entire ONoC. To minimize the laser power consumption, the maximum insertion loss of the critical path, e.g. the path with highest insertion loss, has to be minimized:

$$il_{max}(\mathbf{x}, \mathbf{r}) = max_{p \in P} \quad il_p \tag{6}$$

2.4 Placement and Routing Problem

The physical design of an ONoC strongly influences its laser power consumption, area and reliability. In contrast to digital ICs, the number of optical devices, e.g. PSEs, to be placed and the number of interconnects, e.g. waveguides, to be routed is much smaller, and in contrast to analog circuits no symmetry constraints have to be considered. But the usage of optical interconnects results in new objectives and constraints for placement and routing. The crossing of optical signals does not influence the system's behavior significantly. But each optical signal crossing results in an increase of the insertion loss in the corresponding paths and thereby in an increase of the system's laser power consumption. Hence, in contrast to electronic circuits, waveguide crossings have to be enabled but should be used carefully. The placement and routing problem for ONoCs can be formulated as follows:

Given is a set of optical devices, e.g. PSEs, hubs and/or memory controllers, their dimensions, positions of previously placed optical devices, the list of all paths, and the placement and routing area of the system to be designed. During placement and routing a geometrical description of the system, including the position for each optical device and the waveguides, is determined. At the same time, different objectives are optimized, and specific constraints are considered.

The constraints include the placement of all modules without any overlap inside the predefined placement area, and the routing of all waveguides inside predefined routing regions. During placement and routing, different objectives can be applied: The layout has to be determined such that the total laser power of the ONoC is minimal, which includes the minimization of the waveguide lengths, the number of waveguide crossings, and the number of waveguide bends.

The minimization of the laser power consumption not only improves the system's reliability, but is also important to ensure the correctness of the system, e.g. if the insertion loss of a path is too high, the photodetectors might not be able to detect the signals properly.

In summary, the placement and routing problem for ONoCs can be defined as follows:

Determine a geometrical description of all optical devices and waveguides such that

- all relevant objectives (e.g. maximum insertion loss over all paths including the waveguide length, the number of crossings, and the number of waveguide bends in the critical path, congestion, timing) are minimized and

- all constraints (e.g. no overlap, place all optical devices inside the placement area, place all waveguides inside the routing area) are fulfilled.

2.5 Related Work

Conventional placement and routing algorithms for the design of electronic ICs or NoCs can not be used for the design of ONoCs, because they do not allow any waveguide crossings. Waveguide crossings should be enabled but avoided as far as possible since each crossing results in higher insertion loss.

Only the idea of net overlapping removal for routability-driven placement [8] can be adapted to the waveguide crossing minimization. In this approach the routability-driven placement is integrated into a multilevel placement framework. Because on coarser grids the interconnections between modules within the same cluster are ignored, unrealistic assumption about congestions are made and therefore the routability-driven approach is only performed on the finest grid. However, ignoring the routability on the coarser grids results in suboptimal solutions.

Thus, new algorithms for the physical design of the optical layer of ONoCs are needed, which enable waveguide crossings. At the same time the number of waveguide crossings in the critical path should be minimized to reduce the system's laser power consumption. Manually created layouts have been presented in [13]. Obviously, the creation of manual layouts is time-consuming and error-prone, especially when the number of PSEs to be placed increases. The authors of [11] presented a systematic approach to place $N \times N$ topologies. This approach is restricted to square numbers N of hubs and memory controllers and to hubs and memory controllers placed on a regular grid. To obtain more flexibility and optimality, automatic placement algorithms for the design of ONoCs are needed.

The authors of [15] and [16] presented a stochastic placement algorithm and a maze router for 2D-optoelectronic System-on-Packages (SoPs). The runtime of their algorithm is not presented, but stochastic algorithms suffer from a large number of iterations and thereby a high computation time. In addition, the approach does not utilize wavelength division multiplexing, which would be able to drastically increase the bandwidth, and which is one of the main advantages of optical systems. Several routing algorithms for 3D optical SoPs [12][5] and 2D ONoCs [6] have already been proposed. All of these approaches assume the placement to be given. Because the placement strongly influences the routing result, the placement stage should not be overlooked.

The authors of [2] present the first automatic placement and routing algorithm for 3D ONoCs minimizing the total laser power of the system. The placement problem is solved with the help of nonlinear optimization. But the runtime of the algorithm strongly increases, when the number of optical devices and paths increases slightly. In addition, due to the high memory consumption of this approach, the algorithm is not able to place large topologies. Thus, we present a fast placement algorithm for 3D ONoCs that is able to determine a high-quality layout even for large ONoCs.

3. PLACEMENT ALGORITHM

Given the chip area, the dimensions and positions of hubs and memory controllers, the dimensions of PSEs, and the netlist, PLATON places all PSEs overlap-free inside the chip area. The final layout shall minimize the maximum insertion loss over all paths, which mainly consists of the crossing loss, propagation loss, drop loss and bending loss of the critical path. The drop loss is independent of the layout. In contrast to the crossing loss and propagation loss, the bending loss is very small. Thus, during placement only the propagation loss and crossing loss are considered.

Our quadratic force-directed placer consists of three steps: Initial placement, global placement and legalization.

3.1 Initial Placement

Let $\mathcal{P}$ and $\mathcal{M}$ be the set of all pins and modules, respectively. The set of modules contains all PSEs, hubs, and memory controllers. The PSEs are movable, while hubs and memory controllers are fixed modules. Let net $n_{ij} = (i, j)$ connect pin i and pin j. In the topologies under consideration all nets are two-pin connections, e.g. they connect two pins only. In the first step a placement with minimal total waveguide length

$$\Gamma = \sum_{p \in P} \sum_{n_{ij}=(i,j) \in \mathcal{N}_p} \sqrt{(x_i^{pin} - x_j^{pin})^2 + (y_i^{pin} - y_j^{pin})^2} \quad (7)$$

is determined, where (x_i^{pin}, y_i^{pin}) and $\mathcal{N}_p$ describe the pin position of pin i and the set of all nets in path p, respectively.

The cost function Γ (7) can be reformulated as the quadratic function

$$\Gamma = \frac{1}{2}\sum_{p \in P}\sum_{n_{ij}=(i,j) \in \mathcal{N}_p} \omega_{x,ij}(x_i^{pin} - x_j^{pin})^2 + \omega_{y,ij}(y_i^{pin} - y_j^{pin})^2$$

$$= \sum_{p \in P}\sum_{n_{ij}=(i,j) \in \mathcal{N}_p} \Gamma_{n,x} + \Gamma_{n,y} = \Gamma_x + \Gamma_y \quad (8)$$

with weights

$$\omega_{x,ij} = \frac{2}{\sqrt{(x_i^{pin} - x_j^{pin})^2}}, \quad \omega_{y,ij} = \frac{2}{\sqrt{(y_i^{pin} - y_j^{pin})^2}}. \quad (9)$$

The cost function Γ is separated into x- and y-direction, where $\Gamma_{n,x}$ and $\Gamma_{n,y}$ represent the cost of net n_{ij} in x- and y-direction, respectively. In the following, we focus on the x-direction only. The y-direction is processed analogously.

As proposed in [20], let $\pi : \mathcal{P} \to \mathcal{M}$ be the function that maps a pin to its corresponding module:

$$\pi(i) = m, \text{ if pin } i \in \mathcal{P} \text{ belongs to module } m \in \mathcal{M} \quad (10)$$

Let

$$\mathbf{x} = (x_1, x_2, \ldots, x_M)^T \quad (11)$$

be the vector that represents the x-coordinates of the center positions of all M movable modules, e.g. of all PSEs. With x_i^{off} describing the offset between pin i and the center position of its module $\pi(i)$, it holds: $x_i^{pin} = x_{\pi(i)} - x_i^{off}$. Similar to the apprach proposed in [20], and using (10) and (11), the quadratic cost function in x-direction can be transformed into matrix-vector notation

$$\Gamma_x = \frac{1}{2}\mathbf{x}^T \mathbf{C_x} \mathbf{x} + \mathbf{x}^T \mathbf{d_x} + c. \quad (12)$$

The $M \times M$-matrix $\mathbf{C_x}$ represents the connectivity between all movable modules, the vector $\mathbf{d_x}$ of size M represents the connectivity between fixed and movable modules, and the constant c represents the connectivity between the fixed modules. If there is at least one fixed module, the matrix $\mathbf{C_x}$ is symmetric and positive definite. The minimum of Γ_x is calculated by setting its derivative to zero [20]:

$$\frac{\partial \Gamma}{\partial \mathbf{x}} = \mathbf{C_x} \mathbf{x} + \mathbf{d_x} = 0 \quad (13)$$

The linear equation system is solved by the conjugated gradient method with respect to the center positions $\mathbf{x}$ of all PSEs. The resulting placement has minimal total waveguide length but a lot of module overlap that is removed during the global placement.

In quadratic placement each two-pin connection $n_{ij} = (i,j)$ corresponds to an elastic spring that is spanned between the two pins i and j. The cost function $\Gamma_{n,x}$ of a two-pin connection can be viewed as the energy of the elastic spring. All two-pin connections of a topology correspond to a spring system with the total energy Γ_x proposed in equation (12). The derivative of Γ_x in x-direction represents the force in x-direction. Thus, the derivative is referred to as *net force* [20]:

$$\mathbf{F_x^{net}} = \nabla_x \Gamma_x = \mathbf{C_x} \mathbf{x} + \mathbf{d_x} \quad (14)$$

3.2 Global Placement

The resulting initial placement minimizes the waveguide length, but does not consider module overlap and waveguide crossings. During the global placement the crossings are

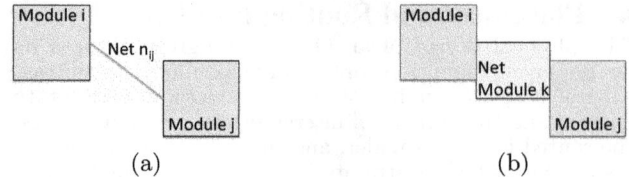

(a)   (b)

Figure 4: Each (a) net connecting two modules defines a (b) net module.

minimized first followed by the reduction of the module overlap.

The paths are split into nets. Let M_n be the total number of nets, where the nets belonging to multiple paths are counted multiple times. Let (x_i^{pin}, y_i^{pin}) and (x_j^{pin}, y_j^{pin}) be the positions of the pins connected by the net $n_{ij} = (i,j)$. For each net $n_{ij} = (i,j)$ we define a *net module* as the rectangle with corners (x_i^{pin}, y_i^{pin}), (x_i^{pin}, y_j^{pin}), (x_j^{pin}, y_j^{pin}) and (x_j^{pin}, y_i^{pin}). An example is shown in Figure 4. To ensure convergence the area of all modules has to be greater than zero. Hence, if the width (height) is smaller than a predefined width (height), the net module is enlarged to the predefined width (height).

If the net modules do not overlap, it is possible to route the waveguides without any crossing. On the other hand, if there is a lot of net module overlap, waveguide crossings are more probable after routing. Thus, in the first step of global placement the module overlap between all net modules is reduced. Let $R(x, y; x_{ll}, y_{ll}, w, h)$ be a rectangle function, which depends on the given width w, height h and lower left corner (x_{ll}, y_{ll}) of a rectangle. The rectangle function R is one for all points (x, y) inside the given rectangle and zero for all points outside. Similar to the definition proposed in [19], let $V_{netmod}(x, y)$ be the *net module distribution*, whose function value at point (x, y) is the total number of net modules at this point:

$$V_{netmod}(x, y) = \sum_{i=1}^{M_n} R\left(x, y; x'_{netmod,i} - \frac{w_{netmod,i}}{2},\right.$$

$$\left. y'_{netmod,i} - \frac{h_{netmod,i}}{2}, w_{netmod,i}, h_{netmod,i}\right), \quad (15)$$

where $(x'_{netmod,i}, y'_{netmod,i})$, $w_{netmod,i}$ and $h_{netmod,i}$ describe the center point of the net module at the beginning of a placement iteration, the width and the height of the net module, respectively.

According to the definition of the module overlap presented in [19], the *net module overlap* Ω_{netmod} represents the area of the union of all net modules $A_{netmod,union}$ normalized by the total net module area $A_{netmod,tot}$:

$$\Omega_{netmod} = 1 - \frac{A_{netmod,union}}{A_{netmod,tot}}, \quad (16)$$

where the area of the union of all net modules is calculated by:

$$A_{netmod,union} = \int_{-\infty}^{\infty}\int_{-\infty}^{\infty} \omega_{netmod}(x, y)dxdy \quad \text{with} \quad (17)$$

$$\omega_{netmod}(x, y) = \begin{cases} 0 & \text{if } V_{netmod}(x, y) \geq 1 \\ 1 & \text{else,} \end{cases} \quad (18)$$

and the total net module area is defined as

$$A_{netmod,tot} = \sum_{i=1}^{M_n} A_{netmod,i}. \quad (19)$$

with $A_{netmod,i} = w_{netmod.i} \cdot h_{netmod,i}$ describing the area of net module i. Obviously, it holds $\Omega_{netmod} = 0$ if there is no overlap between the net modules. If there are a lot of small net modules (e.g. short two-pin connections), and if they are concentrated in a single area on the chip, the net module overlap Ω_{netmod} is close to 1.

Similar to the force-directed placer Kraftwerk [20] for the placement of digital ICs, we define three different forces that act iteratively on the modules: The net force introduced in equation (14) minimizes the waveguide length, the move force attracts the net modules to empty spaces on the chip, and the hold force compensates the net force in each placement iteration.

To define the move force, the placement of the net modules is represented as a demand and supply system [19]:

$$D_{netmod}(x,y) = D_{netmod}^{dem}(x,y) - D_{netmod}^{sup}(x,y), \quad (20)$$

where the demand $D_{netmod}^{dem}(x,y)$ represents the net modules and the supply $D_{netmod}^{sup}(x,y)$ represents the placement area. The demand and supply have to be balanced [19], e.g.:

$$\int_{-\infty}^{\infty} \int_{-\infty}^{\infty} D_{netmod}^{dem}(x,y)dxdy$$
$$= \int_{-\infty}^{\infty} \int_{-\infty}^{\infty} D_{netmod}^{sup}(x,y)dxdy \quad (21)$$

The demand of net module i is defined as

$$D_{netmod,i}^{dem}(x,y) = d_{netmod,i}R\left(x,y;x'_{netmod,i} - \frac{w_{netmod,i}}{2},\right.$$
$$\left. y'_{netmod,i} - \frac{h_{netmod,i}}{2}, w_{netmod,i}, h_{netmod,i}\right), \quad (22)$$

which corresponds to the definition of the module demand of module i given in [19]. Let A_{Large} be a predefined value. In our experiments we assume A_{Large} to be ten times the average PSE area. For small net modules, e.g. for net modules with area smaller than or equal to the value A_{Large}, the factor $d_{netmod,i}$ is chosen to be 1. The choice of the parameter $d_{netmod,i}$ for net modules with area greater than A_{Large} is chosen according to the advanced method for module demand presented in [20]. The total net module demand is the sum of the net module demands of all net modules:

$$D_{netmod}^{dem}(x,y) = \sum_{i=1}^{M_n} D_{netmod,i}^{dem}(x,y). \quad (23)$$

Similar to the definition of the module supply given in [19], the net module supply is defined as

$$D^{netmod,sup}(x,y) = d_{netmod,sup}R(x,y;,x_c,y_c,w_c,h_c), \quad (24)$$

where (x_c, y_c), w_c and h_c are the lower left corner of the chip, its width and height, respectively. The parameter $d_{netmod,sup}$ is determined according to equation (21) [19]:

$$d_{netmod,sup} = \frac{\sum_{i=1}^{M_n} A_{netmod,i}}{A_{chip}}, \quad (25)$$

with $A_{chip} = w_c \cdot h_c$ describing the placement area.

The demand and supply system $D_{netmod}(x,y)$ can be interpreted as a charge distribution that creates an electrostatic potential $\Phi_{netmod}(x,y)$ by Poisson's equation

$$\left(\frac{\partial^2}{\partial x^2} + \frac{\partial^2}{\partial y^2}\right)\Phi_{netmod}(x,y) = -D_{netmod}(x,y) \quad (26)$$

with Neumann boundary conditions [20]. The equation (26) is solved with the help of the multigrid method implemented in the software library DiMEPACK [10]. The move force is modeled with the help of target points and spring connections. For each net module i the x-position $\mathring{x}_{netmod,i}$ of its target point is defined as

$$\mathring{x}_{netmod,i} = x'_{netmod,i}-$$
$$\left. \frac{\partial}{\partial x}\Phi_{netmod}(x,y)\right|_{(x'_{netmod,i},y'_{netmod,i})} \quad [19]. \quad (27)$$

Then, the move force $F_{x,i}^{move,netmod}$ attracts net module i to its target point [19]:

$$F_{x,i}^{move,netmod} = \mathring{\omega}_{netmod,i}(x_{netmod,i} - \mathring{x}_{netmod,i}), \quad (28)$$

where $\mathring{\omega}_{netmod,i} \in \mathbb{R}^+$ are positive weights. The move force attracts the net modules to less congested regions on the placement area. Let n_{kl} be the net represented by net module i, and let k and l be movable modules. Then, the weight $\mathring{\omega}_{netmod,i}$ of the move force determines, how far the net module and thereby the two movable modules k and l are moved. A high weight moves the net module far away from its current position, while a small weight moves the net module just a short distance. The target point is a limit for the movement of the net module, e.g. the net module is at most moved to its target point.

Let $\mathcal{N}$ and $\mathcal{K}$ be the set of all two-pin connections and the set of all net modules, respectively. The function $\psi : \mathcal{N} \rightarrow \mathcal{K}$ maps each two-pin connection to its corresponding net module. As illustrated in Figure 5, the move force of a net module is applied to the (at most) two movable modules that are connected by the two-pin connection represented by the net module. The total move force $F_{x,i}^{move,nm}$ that is applied to the movable module i is given as

$$F_{x,i}^{move,nm} = \sum_{p \in P} \sum_{\substack{n_{kl}=(k,l)\in\mathcal{N}_p \\ n_{kl}\in\mathcal{T}_i}} \mathring{\omega}_{netmod,\psi(n_{kl})} \cdot$$
$$\left(x_{netmod,\psi(n_{kl})} - \mathring{x}_{netmod,\psi(n_{kl})}\right), \quad (29)$$

where $\mathcal{T}_i$ is the set of all two-pin connections that are connected to module i.

Similar to [19], the weights $\mathring{\omega}_{netmod,i}$ are collected in the diagonal matrix $\mathring{\mathbf{C}}_{\mathbf{netmod,x}}$ with

$$\mathring{\mathbf{C}}_{\mathbf{netmod,x}} = diag(\mathring{\omega}_{netmod,i}), \quad (30)$$

the gradients of the potential $\Phi_{netmod}(x,y)$ are collected in the vector $\mathbf{\Phi}_{\mathbf{netmod,x}}$ with

$$\mathbf{\Phi}_{\mathbf{netmod,x}} = \left(\left.\frac{\partial}{\partial x}\Phi_{netmod}(x,y)\right|_{(x'_{netmod,1},y'_{netmod,1})},\right.$$
$$\left.\ldots, \left.\frac{\partial}{\partial x}\Phi_{netmod}(x,y)\right|_{(x'_{netmod,M_n},y'_{netmod,M_n})}\right)^T, \quad (31)$$

and the target points are collected in the vector $\mathring{\mathbf{x}}_{\mathbf{netmod}}$

$$\mathring{\mathbf{x}}_{\mathbf{netmod}} = \mathbf{x}'_{\mathbf{netmod}} - \mathbf{\Phi}_{\mathbf{netmod,x}}. \quad (32)$$

with $\mathbf{x}'_{\mathbf{netmod}} = \left(x'_{netmod,1}, \ldots, x'_{netmod,M_n}\right)$.

A transformation matrix $\mathbf{Q}$ maps the net modules to the modules that are connected by the two-pin connections represented by the net modules. The number of rows of the matrix $\mathbf{Q}$ is equal to the number of movable modules M, and the number of columns of $\mathbf{Q}$ is equal to the number of two-pin connections M_n. The transformation matrix $\mathbf{Q} = (q_{ij})$

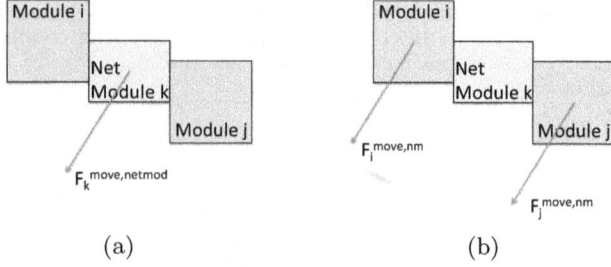

(a)　　　　　　　(b)

Figure 5: Assuming that the two modules i and j defining the net module k are movable, (a) the move force acting on the net module (b) attracts the two movable modules to empty spaces on the chip.

is defined as follows:

$$q_{ij} = \begin{cases} 1 & \text{if module } i \text{ is movable and connected} \\ & \text{by the two-pin connection } j \\ 0 & \text{else} \end{cases}$$

$$(33)$$

Using equation (32) the move force

$$\mathbf{F_x^{move,nm}} = \left(F_{x,1}^{move,nm}, \dots, F_{x,M}^{move,nm} \right) \qquad (34)$$

can be written as

$$\mathbf{F_x^{move,nm}} = \mathbf{Q}\mathring{\mathbf{C}}_{netmod,x} \left(\mathbf{x_{netmod}} - \mathring{\mathbf{x}}_{netmod} \right) \qquad (35)$$

$$= \mathbf{Q}\mathring{\mathbf{C}}_{netmod,x} \left(\mathbf{x_{netmod}} - \mathbf{x'}_{netmod} + \mathbf{\Phi}_{netmod,x} \right) \qquad (36)$$

$$= \mathbf{Q}\mathring{\mathbf{C}}_{netmod,x} \left(\frac{1}{2}\mathbf{Q^T x} - \frac{1}{2}\mathbf{Q^T x'} + \mathbf{\Phi}_{netmod,x} \right) \qquad (37)$$

$$= \frac{1}{2}\mathbf{Q}\mathring{\mathbf{C}}_{netmod,x}\mathbf{Q^T} \left(\mathbf{x} - \mathbf{x'} \right) + \mathbf{Q}\mathring{\mathbf{C}}_{netmod,x}\mathbf{\Phi}_{netmod,x} \qquad (38)$$

The vector $\mathbf{F_x^{move,nm}}$ has size M, which is equal to the total number of movable modules.

If just the move force and the net force would be applied to the modules, the modules would collapse back in each iteration. Thus, the hold force

$$\mathbf{F_x^{hold}} = -(\mathbf{C_x x'} + \mathbf{d_x}) \qquad (39)$$

is used to compensate the net force, where $\mathbf{x'} = (x'_1, \dots, x'_M)$ describe the center positions of the movable modules at the beginning of a placement iteration [20].

In summary, the sum of all three forces is set to zero [19], which gives a linear equation system and is the core of PLATON:

$$\mathbf{F_x^{net}} + \mathbf{F_x^{move,nm}} + \mathbf{F_x^{hold}} = \mathbf{0}, \qquad (40)$$

which is equal to the solution of the linear equation system

$$\left(\mathbf{C_x} + \frac{1}{2}\mathbf{Q}\mathring{\mathbf{C}}_{netmod,x}\mathbf{Q^T} \right) (\mathbf{\Delta x}) = -\mathbf{Q}\mathring{\mathbf{C}}_{netmod,x}\mathbf{\Phi}_{netmod,x}. \qquad (41)$$

The linear equation system is solved with the help of the conjugated gradients method with respect to $\mathbf{\Delta x} = \mathbf{x} - \mathbf{x'}$. Finally, the module positions $\mathbf{x'}$ of the movable modules are updated by $\mathbf{\Delta x}$. To ensure fast convergence the weights $\mathring{\omega}_{netmod,i}$ are adjusted at the end of each iteration by applying a quality control proposed in [20].

The procedure is repeated iteratively until the net module overlap Ω_{netmod} is equal to zero, or until a predefined number of iterations is reached. In our experimental studies we defined the maximum number of iterations to be 25.

After the removal of the overlap of the net modules, the global placement of Kraftwerk [20] is applied to the modules (e.g. PSEs, hubs and memory controllers) to remove module overlap.

In the following we describe te quality control for adjusting the weights. Let M and A_i be the total number of movable modules and the area of module i respectively. One of the degrees of freedom is the choice of the weights $\mathring{\omega}_{netmod,i}$, $i = 1, \dots, M_n$ of the move forces $F_{x,i}^{move,netmod}$. At the beginning they are chosen to be

$$\mathring{\omega}_{netmod,i} = 10^{-2}(M + M_n)^{-0.8}. \qquad (42)$$

Usually, when the number of movable modules increases, the number of two-pin connections between movable modules increases, too. Thus, during the initial placement step the modules are placed more concentrated in the center of the chip, and therefore the module overlap is higher. Hence, the gradient of the potentials are higher, and the target points are located farther away from the modules. To compensate these longer distances and to preserve the move force, the weights are scaled by the factor $(M + M_n)^{-0.8}$.

In general, the net modules are much larger than the movable modules. In contrast to large movable modules, the net modules (and thereby the movable modules connected by the two-pin connection represented by the net module) should not be moved too far to prevent the waveguide length to increase too strongly. Hence, the weights for the net modules are multiplied by a small factor (10^{-2}).

After each placement iteration the weights are adjusted based on the average movement of the modules μ [19] with

$$\mu = \frac{1}{M} \sum_{i=1}^{M} \sqrt{(x_i - x'_i)^2 + (y_i - y'_i)^2}, \qquad (43)$$

where (x'_i, y'_i) and (x_i, y_i) are the positions of module i at the beginning and at the end of each placement iteration, respectively.

Large weights $\mathring{\omega}_{netmod,i}$ result in a high module movement, while the opposite is true for small weights. If the modules are moved far within a placement iteration, the waveguide length and thereby the propagation loss increases drastically. On the other hand, fewer placement iterations are needed to remove the overlap when using large weights. Hence, a good trade-off between quality and runtime has to be determined. We assume a target movement of

$$\mu_T = \frac{w_{mov,avg} + h_{mov_{a}vg}}{2}, \qquad (44)$$

where $w_{mov,avg}$ and $h_{mov_{a}vg}$ describe the average width and height of all movable modules, respectively. Based on the average movement μ and the target movement μ_T a scale factor κ is calculated for the weights $\mathring{\omega}_{netmod,i}$ [19]:

$$\kappa = 1.1 + 0.9 \cdot tanh(atanh(-\frac{1}{9}) + log(\frac{\mu_T}{\mu}) \cdot 1.5) \qquad (45)$$

If the average module movement μ is equal to the target movement μ_T, it holds $\kappa = 1$. If $\mu > \mu_T$, the scale factor κ is smaller than 1. Else the scale factor κ is greater than 1.

Then, the weights of the move force are multiplied by κ [19]:

$$\mathring{\omega}_{netmod,i} = \mathring{\omega}_{netmod,i} \cdot \kappa \qquad (46)$$

Algorithm 1 summarizes the global placement procedure. First, the number of waveguide crossings, e.g. the net module overlap, is minimized (line 2-9). Then, the module overlap is removed (line 13). In both steps a demand-and-supply system is defined that is needed for the calculation of an electrostatic potential. With the help of the potential, the target points are determined. The sum of the three forces is set to zero, which results in two linear equation systems - one in x- and one in y-direction. Finally, the module positions are updated, and the weights of the move forces are adjusted with the help of a quality control.

Algorithm 1: Global Placement

Data: module dimensions, positions of fixed modules, start placement, placement area

1   iter = 0;
2   **while** ($\Omega_{netmod} == 0$) or (iter < 25) **do**
3   Determine demand-and-supply system $D_{netmod}(x, y)$;
4   Calculate potential $\Phi_{netmod}(x, y)$ by solving Poisson's equation (26);
5   **for** x- and y-direction **do**
6   Calculate $\mathbf{C_x}$, $\mathbf{\check{C}_{netmod,x}}$, $\mathbf{Q}$ and $\mathbf{\Phi_{netmod,x}}$;
7   Solve $\left(\mathbf{C_x} + \frac{1}{2}\mathbf{Q\check{C}_{netmod,x}Q^T}\right)(\mathbf{\Delta x}) = -\mathbf{Q\check{C}_{netmod,x}\Phi_{netmod,x}}$ w.r.t. $\mathbf{\Delta x}$;
8   Update $\mathbf{x'}$ by $\mathbf{\Delta x}$;
9   **end**
10   Perform quality control;
11   iter = iter+1;
12   **end**
13   Remove module overlap using global placement of Kraftwerk [20];

3.3 Legalization

After the global placement, there still might be a slight module overlap, which is removed by the quadratic optimization problem solver "Puzzle" [19]. The legalization step hardly influences the insertion loss, but ensures routability and manufacturability of the system.

4. EXPERIMENTAL RESULTS

PLATON is implemented in C++ and all experiments are performed on an Intel Core 2 Quad CPU with 8GB RAM running at 2.33GHz.

We apply PLATON to the 8x8 λ-Router, the 8x8 GWOR, the 8x8 Standard Crossbar as well as the 16x16 λ-Router. For routing we use the PROTON maze router proposed in [2].

We are interested in the required laser power of the system, which is the minimum laser power needed to guarantee a predefined bit error rate at the receivers. We assume an equal laser power for all lasers and thus are interested in the path with maximum required laser power. A measurement for the laser power is the maximum insertion loss il_{max}. We compare the results to a manual layout published in [13] and to the layout obtained by PROTON [2]. Due to complexity reasons the manual layout minimizes the number of crossings only, while PROTON minimizes a weighted sum of propagation loss and crossing loss. The weights are chosen according to the loss parameters given in [3].

The results of our experiments are shown in Table 1. The topology is given in the first column. For each placer we show the maximum insertion loss il_{max} in dB, the number of crossings C and the waveguide length L in μm of the path with highest insertion loss. In addition, the runtime in seconds is given in the columns named *CPU*.

For the 8x8 topologies PLATON significantly reduces the maximum insertion loss compared to the manually designed layout, but it slightly increases compared to PROTON. On the other hand, the insertion loss of the 16x16 topology is reduced by 48.9 % compared to PROTON. To limit the runtime, the nonlinear optimization solver used by PROTON stops after at most 100 iterations. For small topologies, the solver is able to determine an optimal solution of the nonlinear placement problem within fewer than 100 iterations, or the solver obtains a good solution after exactly 100 iterations. Because the cost function in PROTON explicitly considers the maximum insertion loss, e.g. the waveguide length and the number of waveguide crossings in the path with highest insertion loss, instead of the total waveguide length and the total number of waveguide crossings, PROTON obtains slightly better results for small topologies. For large topologies the nonlinear optimization solver used by PROTON needs many more iterations to obtain a high-quality solution. But even the execution of 100 iterations needs more than 6 hours. Thus, the solver is stopped after a predefined number of iterations, which results in suboptimal positions of the PSEs. Hence, PLATON is able to obtain better results. We expect that in the future larger topologies become more important for practical use. Thus, the slight increase for the small topologies can be accepted. A huge improvement can be seen in terms of runtime. For the 16x16 λ-Router we were able to reduce the runtime by 99.7%. Even for the 8x8 topologies the runtime is reduced by at least 86.1%.

The reduction of the maximum insertion loss of the 16x16 topology results in a huge improvement of the system's laser power requirement. In our experiments we assume that the maximum insertion loss over all paths, e.g. the path p with $il_p = il_{max}$ determines the required laser power. For the laser sources we assume a laser-efficiency PLE of 20% and a coupling laser-link PCW of 90%. For the detectors a sensitivity of $S = -17dBm$ and a BER of 10^{-12} is assumed.

For the 16x16 λ-Router the laser power consumption of the layout obtained by PROTON is 44.5 W, while the laser power consumption of the layout obtained by PLATON is 0.3 W. This is an improvement of 99.3%. The resulting layout of the 16x16 λ-Router determined with the help of PLATON is shown in Figure 6.

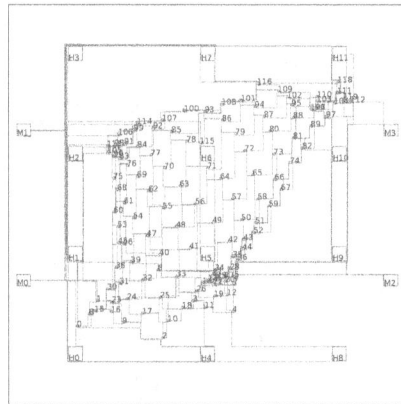

Figure 6: Resulting placement of the 16x16 λ-Router

5. CONCLUSION

We proposed the first force-directed placer for 3D ONoCs. It produces very good results very rapidly especially for larger topologies, which will become more important in the future. With the help of PLATON we are able to decrease the maximum insertion loss of the 16x16 λ-Router by up

Topology	PLATON				Manual layout				PROTON			
	il_{max}	C	L	CPU	il_{max}	C	L	CPU	il_{max}	C	L	CPU
8x8 λ-Router	9.3	29	26865	9.8	17.5	64	49600	-	8.6	41	10413	95.8
8x8 GWOR	9.7	44	15651	10.7	21.4	72	67500	-	8.4	38	13014	77.1
8x8 Standard Crossbar	12.4	50	26478	35.2	-	-	-	-	8.5	36	15255	606.9
16x16 λ-Router	22.5	86	56912	64.3	-	-	-	-	44.0	255	28636	24425.8

Table 1: Results for our algorithm (PLATON), the manually designed layout and PROTON

to 99.3% compared to the state-of-the-art placer and router PROTON. In addition, the runtime decreases by up to 99.7%. With the help of our algorithm even larger topologies can be placed within a suitable runtime.

6. REFERENCES

[1] S. Beamer, C. Sun, Y.-J. Kwon, A. Joshi, C. Batten, V. Stojanović, and K. Asanović. Re-architecting DRAM memory systems with monolithically integrated silicon photonics. *SIGARCH Comput. Archit. News*, 38(3):129–140, June 2010.

[2] A. Boos, L. Ramini, U. Schlichtmann, and D. Bertozzi. Proton: An automatic place-and-route tool for optical networks-on-chip. In *Computer-Aided Design (ICCAD), 2013 IEEE/ACM International Conference on*, pages 138–145, Nov 2013.

[3] J. Chan, G. Hendry, A. Biberman, and K. Bergman. Architectural exploration of chip-scale photonic interconnection network designs using physical-layer analysis. *Journal of Lightwave Technology*, 28(9):1305–1315, May 2010.

[4] M. J. Cianchetti, J. C. Kerekes, and D. H. Albonesi. Phastlane: A rapid transit optical routing network. *SIGARCH Comput. Archit. News*, 37(3):441–450, June 2009.

[5] C. Condrat, P. Kalla, and S. Blair. Crossing-aware channel routing for integrated optics. *Computer-Aided Design of Integrated Circuits and Systems, IEEE Transactions on*, 33(6):814–825, June 2014.

[6] D. Ding, Y. Zhang, H. Huang, R. T. Chen, and D. Z. Pan. O-router: An optical routing framework for low power on-chip silicon nano-photonic integration. In *Design Automation Conference*, 2009.

[7] H. Gu, J. Xu, and W. Zhang. A low-power fat tree-based optical network-on-chip for multiprocessor system-on-chip. In *Design, Automation Test in Europe Conference Exhibition, 2009. DATE '09.*, pages 3–8, April 2009.

[8] Z.-W. Jiang, B.-Y. Su, and Y.-W. Chang. Routability-driven analytical placement by net overlapping removal for large-scale mixed-size designs. In *Design Automation Conference, 2008. DAC 2008. 45th ACM/IEEE*, pages 167–172, June 2008.

[9] S. Koohi, M. Abdollahi, and S. Hessabi. All-optical wavelength-routed noc based on a novel hierarchical topology. In *Networks on Chip (NoCS), 2011 Fifth IEEE/ACM International Symposium on*, pages 97–104, May 2011.

[10] M. Kowarschik and C. Weiß. Dimepack – a cache-optimized multigrid library. In *International Conference on parallel and distributed processing techniques and applications, Volume I*, pages 425–430. CSREA, CSREA Press, 2001.

[11] S. Le Beux, H. Li, G. Nicolescu, J. Trajkovic, and I. O'Connor. Optical crossbars on chip, a comparative study based on worst-case losses. *Concurrency and Computation: Practice and Experience*, 26(15):2492–2503, 2014.

[12] J. R. Minz, S. Thyagara, and S. K. Lim. Optical routing for 3d system-on-package. *IEEE Transactions on Components and Packaging Technologies*, 30(4), 2007.

[13] L. Ramini, D. Bertozzi, and L. Carloni. Engineering a bandwidth-scalable optical layer for a 3d multi-core processor with awareness of layout constraints. In *Networks on Chip (NoCS), 2012 Sixth IEEE/ACM International Symposium on*, pages 185–192, May 2012.

[14] A. Scandurra. Scalable cmos-compatible photonic routing topologies for versatile networks on chip. In *Network on Chip Architecture*, 2008.

[15] C.-S. Seo and A. Chatterjee. A cad tool for system-on-chip placement and routing with free-space optical interconnect. In *Computer Design: VLSI in Computers and Processors, 2002. Proceedings. 2002 IEEE International Conference on*, pages 24–29, 2002.

[16] C.-S. Seo, A. Chatterjee, and N. M. Jokerst. Physical design of optoelectronic system-on-a-package: a cad tool and algorithms. In *International Symposium on Quality of Electronic Design (ISQED)*, pages 567–572, March 2005.

[17] A. Shacham, K. Bergman, and L. Carloni. Photonic networks-on-chip for future generations of chip multiprocessors. *Computers, IEEE Transactions on*, 57(9):1246–1260, Sept 2008.

[18] N. Sherwood-Droz, H. Wang, L. Chen, B. G. Lee, A. Biberman, K. Bergman, and M. Lipson. Optical 4x4 hitless slicon router for optical networks-on-chip (noc). *Opt. Express*, 16(20):15915–15922, Sep 2008.

[19] P. Spindler. *Efficient Quadratic Placement of VLSI Circuits*. PhD thesis, TU München, 2008.

[20] P. Spindler, U. Schlichtmann, and F. M. Johannes. Kraftwerk2: A fast force-directed quadratic placement approach using an accurate net model. *IEEE Transactions on Computer-Aided Design of Integrated Circuits and Systems*, 27(8):1398–1411, Aug 2008.

[21] X. Tan, M. Yang, L. Zhang, Y. Jiang, and J. Yang. On a scalable, non-blocking optical router for photonic networks-on-chip designs. In *Photonics and Optoelectronics (SOPO), 2011 Symposium on*, pages 1–4, May 2011.

[22] D. Vantrease, R. Schreiber, M. Monchiero, M. McLaren, N. Jouppi, M. Fiorentino, A. Davis, N. Binkert, R. Beausoleil, and J. Ahn. Corona: System implications of emerging nanophotonic technology. In *Computer Architecture, 2008. ISCA '08. 35th International Symposium on*, pages 153–164, June 2008.

Optimizing for Power, Speed, Cost and Emissions in Automotive Drivetrains

Patrick R. Groeneveld
Synopsys Inc.
445 North Mary Avenue
Sunnyvale, CA 94085, United States
patrick.r.groeneveld@synopsys.com

ABSTRACT

EDA engineers automate IC design while optimizing speed, power and cost. Though automotive design also has objectives for speed, power and cost, the process is not as well automated. Automotive powertrain engineering has progressed dramatically due to the push for cleaner environment and the pull of more affordable electronics and batteries. This is resulting in ever more electric and efficient gasoline-electric hybrid cars on the road.

This presentation will look at what 'drives' the design optimization of the drive train from the energy source all the way down to where the rubber meets the road. This includes relevant aspects such as energy efficiency, emissions and practicality of gasoline and electrical drivetrains in modern cars. They use 'regenerative' braking that recovers approximately 70% of the kinetic energy. The new generation of hybrid-electric transmissions can hit the fuel consumption 'sweet spot' while delivering a fun high-torque driving experience. This is done by dynamically blending the power of an internal combustion engine with two electric motors using planetary gears. A modern plug-in hybrid may have 5 different drive modes, each optimizing the energy flow for maximum efficiency.

The energy conversion efficiency of an internal combustion engine is only 20%, while electric motors are well over 90% efficient. That seems an unbeatable advantage, but whether electric drive is more environmentally friendly than conventional gasoline depends primarily on the way the electric power is generated in the grid. At the current average of 1.2 lbs CO_2 emissions per kWh in the USA and northern Europe the greenhouse emissions of Electric Vehicles are only very marginally better than comparable gasoline hybrid cars. The electric 'greens' at a glacial rate of 1% per year, and with that EVs slowly become cleaner as well. Current low oil prices, and coal-based electric generation will remain intrinsic challenges for Electric Vehicles for some time. But others can be improved by engineering. The driving range, for instance, is an interesting trade-off between reducing battery wear, energy density and the cost of lithium-ion batteries. Though not as fast as Moore's law, steady battery technology and engineering improvements improve the practicality of EVs. Recharging the battery goes at a leisurely rate of 15 miles per hour vs 3600 miles per hour as a gas station. New 'supercharging' standards may raise charging speeds to over 300 miles per hour.

After 100 years of rather incremental changes in automobile propulsion we have arrived in a new era of a significant innovation. Some methodologies from our field of Electronic Design Automation could be applied to help propel cars into the 21st century.

ISPD'16, April 3–6, 2016, Santa Rosa, California, USA.
ACM 978-1-4503-4039-7/16/04.
DOI: http://dx.doi.org/10.1145/2872334.2872338

Cell-Based Design Methods for Directed Self-Assembly

Karl K. Berggren   Caroline A. Ross   Hyung Wan Do
Jae-Byum Chang   Hong Kyoon Choi
Massachusetts Institute of Technology
50 Vassar Street, Suite 36-219, Cambridge, MA 02139, USA
+1-617-324-0272
berggren@mit.edu

ABSTRACT

Topographic templates can direct the self-assembly of block copolymers to achieve nanoscale patterns with high order. Previously, we have demonstrated well-aligned periodic lines, bends, and meshes using a sparse array of lithographically defined posts [1,2]. However, it is generally challenging to fabricate complex and non-periodic patterns using a sparse post array because the key information contained in the final pattern must be encoded in the sparse template. In this work, we present two cell-based design methods for fabricating complex patterns using directed self-assembly of polystyrene-*b*-polydimethylsiloxane (PS-*b*-PDMS) block copolymer thin films.

For the first approach, we developed a set of template tiles consisting of square post lattices with a restricted range of geometric features. For all possible tile arrangements, we examined the resulting block copolymer patterns. We were able to predict a relatively simple template that will result in a desired complex pattern by combining tiles in different ways. For the second approach, we designed a binary-state system with ladder-shaped block copolymer structures using a square confinement. We developed design-rules for controlling alignment direction of the ladder-shaped structures by introducing openings around the square cells. These methods could provide a new template design method for a complex non-trivial block copolymer patterns.

Keywords

Directed self-assembly; Block copolymer; Rule-based design

REFERENCES

[1] Yang, J. K. W.; Jung, Y. S.; Chang, J.; Mickiewicz, R. A.; Alexander-Katz, A.; Ross, C. A.; Berggren, K. K., Complex self-assembled patterns using sparse commensurate templates with locally varying motifs. *Nat. Nanotechnol.* **2010,** *5,* 256-260.

[2] Tavakkoli, A. K. G.; Gotrik, K. W.; Hannon, A. F.; Alexander-Katz, A; Ross, C. A.; Berggren, K. K., Templating three-dimensional self-assembled structures in bilayer block copolymer films, *Science* **2012,** *336* (6086), 1294-1298.

ISPD'16, April 03-06, 2016, Santa Rosa, CA, USA
ACM 978-1-4503-4039-7/16/04.
http://dx.doi.org/10.1145/2872334.2893445

Concurrent Guiding Template Assignment and Redundant Via Insertion for DSA-MP Hybrid Lithography

Jiaojiao Ou
ECE Department
Univ. of Texas at Austin
jiaojiao@cerc.utexas.edu

Bei Yu
CSE Department
Chinese Univ. of Hong Kong
byu@cse.cuhk.edu.hk

David Z. Pan
ECE Department
Univ. of Texas at Austin
dpan@ece.utexas.edu

ABSTRACT

Directed Self-Assembly (DSA) is a very promising emerging lithography for 7nm and beyond, where a coarse guiding template produced by conventional optical lithography can "magically" generate fine-pitch vias/contacts through self-assembly process. A key challenge for DSA-friendly layout is the guiding template assignment to cover all vias under consideration. Meanwhile, redundant via insertion has been widely adopted to improve yield and reliability of the circuit. In this paper, we propose a comprehensive framework for concurrent DSA guiding template assignment and redundant via insertion with consideration of multiple patterning (MP) in guiding template generation. We first formulate the problem as an integer linear programming (ILP), and then propose a novel approximation algorithm to achieve good performance and runtime trade-off. The experimental results demonstrate the effectiveness of the proposed algorithms. To our best knowledge, this is the first work in concurrent guiding template assignment and redundant via insertion for DSA-MP hybrid lithography.

CCS Concepts

•Hardware → VLSI design manufacturing considerations;

Keywords

Directed Self-Assembly, Multiple Patterning Lithography, Reduant Via Insertion, Guiding Template Assignment

1. INTRODUCTION

As a promising next generation lithography, Directed Self-Assembly (DSA) is gaining interests from both industry and academia, due to its ability to improve the contact/via pitch, as well as its low cost and high throughput [1–3]. A typical DSA process is depicted in Fig. 1, where at first some guiding templates are generated through conventional 193i lithography system. Then block copolymer (BCP) is filled in the guiding templates, followed by block copolymer annealing

ISPD'16, April 03-06, 2016, Santa Rosa, CA, USA

© 2016 ACM. ISBN 978-1-4503-4039-7/16/04. . . $15.00

DOI: http://dx.doi.org/10.1145/2872334.2872352

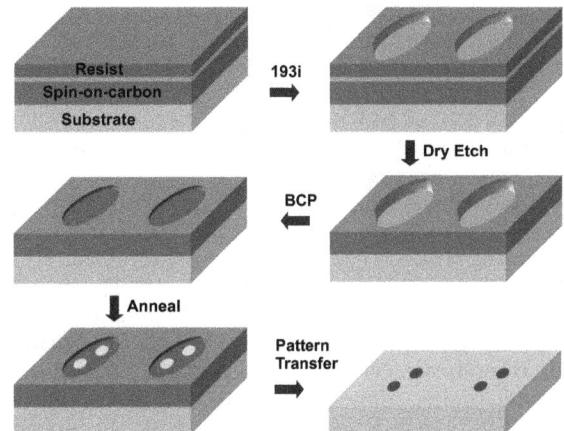

Figure 1: DSA process flow: 193i lithography and etch define the guiding template, the final DSA patterns are generated inside the template.

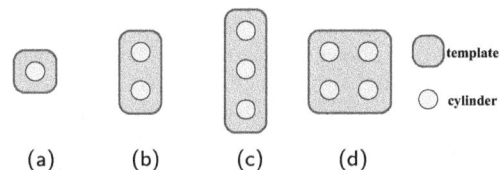

Figure 2: Robust DSA patterns: (a) Singlet. (b) Doublet. (c) Triplet. (d) Quadruplet.

to form cylinders. Since the guiding templates are printed by traditional 193i lithography, the cylinder pitch variation and placement error will deteriorate with the increase of template complexity. Therefore, in order to get better variation control, some regular shaped DSA guiding templates are preferred. Fig. 2 lists some typical regular guiding template examples, which are reported to have less pitch variations and better manufacturability [4]. These guiding templates are singlets, doublets, triplets and quadruplets, which are all in regular shapes.

In recent years, DSA lithography is an emerging candidate for the printing of contact/via layers in $7nm$ technology node and below [5]. There has been significant improvement made on the manufacturing, modeling and simulation of DSA, especially for grapho-epitaxy DSA [6, 7]. On the other hand, multiple patterning is often required for the manufacturing of the dense distributed contacts. It is reported that the application of DSA can also help to reduce the number of mask when contacts/vias are grouped in the same DSA guiding

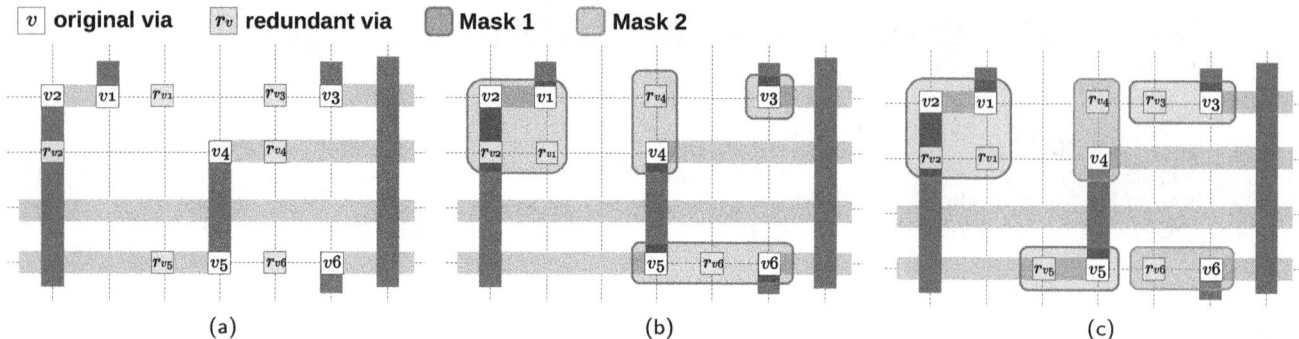

Figure 3: (a) Redundant via insertion result without consideration of DSA pattern compatibility. (b) Concurrent redundant via insertion (RVI) and GTA, insertion rate is reduced due to DSA design rule restrictions. (c) Concurrent GTA and RVI for DSA with double patterning so that the via insertion rate is improved.

template if their distances are within the optical resolution limit [8].

Much previous research has been proposed on contact layer DSA aware design (e.g. [9–11]). There are a lot of work focusing on DSA guiding template assignment (GTA) to minimize manufacturing variations as well. Du et al. [12] proposed a SAT algorithm and bounded approximation algorithm to explore the DSA aware contact layer optimization for 1D standard cell library. Xiao et al. [13] studied the DSA template determination and cut redistribution for cut mask in 1D gridded design, while Ou et al. [14] extended this problem by formulating it to an ILP problem and proposed another heuristic method to solve this problem. Badr et al. [15,16] proposed a set of solutions to resolve the GTA and MP decomposition problem for contacts and vias.

For a long time, Redundant Via Insertion (RVI) has been heavily utilized in industry to improve circuit yield and reliability. Fig. 3(a) shows an example of RVI, where an extra via near the original single via is inserted as the redundant via. RVI has been well studied in routing and post-routing stages, where the major target is to maximize the via insertion rate [17–22]. The redundant via insertion problem has been formulated as a maximum independent set problem in post-routing stage by Lee et al. [17]. In [20], this problem has been formulated as a bipartite matching problem.

For 14nm technology nodes and beyond, it becomes quite difficult to print the lower via layer with 193i lithography single patterning as the density of vias dramatically increases. Thus multiple patterning (MP), such as Double Patterning (DP) and Triple Patterning (TP), is required for via layer fabrication. However, if we use DSA to print the via layer, and continue to use the conventional RVI method without DSA pattern constraints, it is very likely that the dense randomly distributed vias can make the grouping of vias to the regular shaped DSA guiding template very difficult without violating any design rules. Therefore, it is necessary to consider the DSA guiding template patterns and distributions of redundant vias at the insertion stage, to make it compatible when grouping vias to different guiding patterns, as shown in Fig. 3(b). We also notice that as more constraints have been introduced to the DSA redundant via insertion, the insertion rate may be impaired under very strict design rules, v_3 and v_5 are dead vias in Fig. 3(b). In order to maintain

a relatively high insertion rate, multiple patterning for DSA guiding templates and redundant via insertion are considered simultaneously in this work. Fig. 3(c) gives an example of redundant via insertion and DSA GTA under DSA-double patterning hybrid lithography, which could reach 100% insertion rate. In addition, it is also necessary to cover as many vias as possible by using the DSA patterns. Otherwise, we need to use other technique to print the vias that can not be patterned by DSA, which is not cost-effective. But it is still unknown how to solve the problem in DSA-MP hybrid lithography.

In this paper, we investigate the RVI and GTA for DSA lithography with multiple patterning. Our contributions of this paper can be summarized as follows:

- We consider DSA guiding template assignment together with multiple patterning for redundant via insertion.
- We model this problem as a constrained maximum weighted matching for bipartite graph problem, and propose an integer linear programming (ILP) formulation to search for the optimal solutions.
- To improve scalability, we further propose a linear programming (LP) based approximation algorithm to improve the runtime without much loss of solution quality.
- Our experimental results are promising in terms of redundant via insertion rate, total number of patterned vias, and runtime.

The rest of the paper is organized as follows: Section 2 introduces the background of redundant via insertion and the problem formulation. Section 3 proposes the constrained bipartite matching algorithm and general ILP formulation. Section 4 develops an approximation algorithm for further speed-up. Section 5 presents the experimental results, then followed by conclusion in Section 6.

2. PRELIMINARIES

In this section, we first provide some preliminaries on redundant via insertion and DSA guiding template candidates construction. Then we will give the problem formulation.

2.1 Redundant Via Insertion

A redundant via can be inserted in one of the adjacent

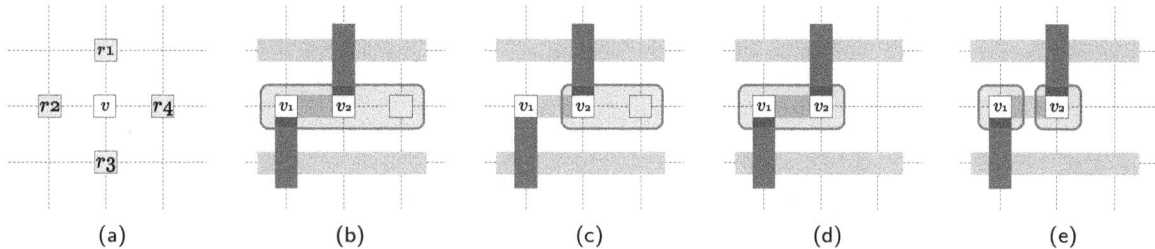

Figure 4: (a) Redundant via positions. (b)-(c) Feasible DSA guiding template candidates that have redundant vias. (d)-(e) DSA guiding template candidates without redundant via.

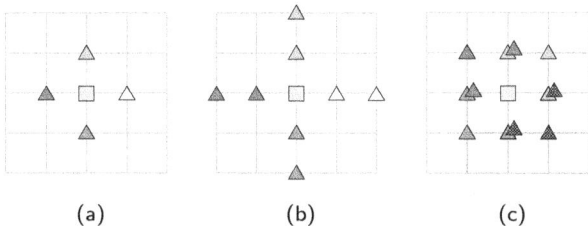

Figure 5: (a) Searched space for doublets, (b) triplets, (c) quadruplets.

four positions of the original single via, as shown in Fig. 4(a). The redundant via is feasible if it does not violate any design rules or overlap with other vias, otherwise it is regarded as infeasible. Generally speaking, if we consider two metal layers in the design, the adjacent position of a single via is feasible to insert redundant via when it satisfies the following conditions: it does not overlap with critical area, it is not occupied by any metal layer, or it is occupied by only one metal layer, and the metal layer is on the same net with the single via. For via that has spaces to insert a redundant via is referred as an alive via. While a via is called as a *dead via* if there is no place to insert a redundant via. The conventional evaluation metric for redundant via insertion is the insertion rate (*IR*), which is the ratio of inserted redundant via number over the original single via number. The ideal insertion is 100%, i.e. each single via has a redundant via. The insertion of redundant via can be performed in the routing stage or post-routing stage. While in this work, we consider the redundant via insertion in the post-routing stage for two routing layers to improve circuit reliability and yield.

2.2 Guiding Template Assignment

Given a post-routing layout and a set of DSA guiding templates, we need to find all the DSA guiding template assignment for all the single vias and feasible redundant vias. For simplicity, it is assumed that the original single via and its redundant via should be included in the same template. We also notice that the insertion rate can not be improved if the template does not include any redundant via, as shown in Fig. 4(d) and Fig. 4(e), but this kind of DSA guiding template assignment could help improve the number of covered vias for some special case, thus we need to include these templates. Figs. 4(b)–(c) illustrate the DSA guiding template candidates which have redundant vias, Figs. 4(d)–(e) illustrate the template candidates with only original single vias. In order to generalize this problem, it is assumed that the metal lines and vias are on grids, and redundant via can be placed at adjacent four grids.

To find DSA guiding template candidates for the entire

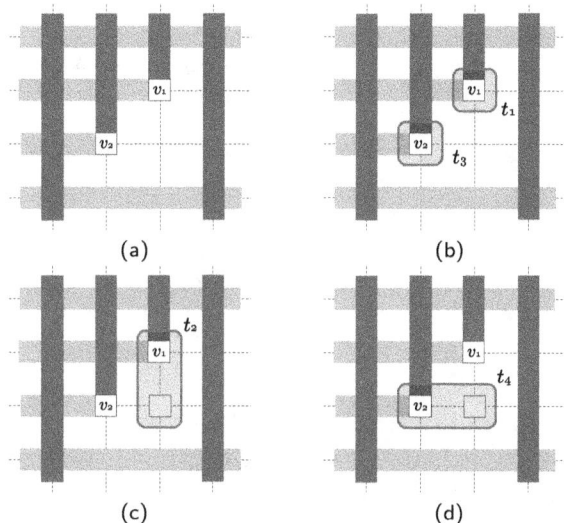

Figure 6: (a) Original layout. (b)-(d) All possible GTA result for the layout.

layout, we iterate all the single vias and verify the adjacent grids of each single via to determine whether the grids can be combined with current single via to form a valid DSA template pattern. The search method for different DSA pattern is as follows. We first explore the adjacent four grids of one single via, as illustrated in Fig. 5(a), we verify the grids one by one to check whether it is feasible to insert a redundant via, or it is another single via, so that it can be combined with the original via to form a doublet DSA pattern. We then explore the adjacent two grids of the single via, and there are four directions that should be checked, as shown in Fig. 5(b), each color indicates the search space in the four directions. The adjacent two grids can be combined with the original via to form a triplet DSA guiding pattern if one of the following conditions can be satisfied:

- The nearest grid contains another single via and the next grid is feasible to insert a redundant via for the second single via;
- The nearest grid is feasible to insert a redundant via for the current single via and the next grid contains another single via;
- Both grids contain single vias.

For the quadruplet DSA guiding pattern, it is a little different from the previous two cases. The search space is the adjacent three grids, and there are four cases to be checked as shown in different colors in Fig. 5(c). The single via and its three adjacent positions can be grouped as a quadruplet DSA guiding template if the adjacent grids have at least one single via and other grids are the feasible positions to

41

insert redundant vias for the single vias. Since two vias can be grouped together in one guiding templates, the via pitch can be reduced compared to traditional lithography.

Fig. 6 shows all the DSA guiding template assignment for the example layout. v_1 and v_2 are the original single vias, and there are four possible groups of the single vias and redundant vias of DSA guiding template: t_1, t_2, t_3, t_4. The DSA guiding templates and vias are stored as rectangles in a R-tree structure for later use.

2.3 Problem Formulation

The primary target of redundant via insertion is to maximize the number of inserted redundant vias in order to improve the yield and reliability of chips. we also consider the number of vias that can been patterned by DSA guiding template for manufacturing compatibility. The application of multiple patterning can help to improve the insertion rate. Thus the guiding template assignment for redundant via insertion of DSA-MP hybrid lithography (GTAR) problem is defined as follows:

Problem 1 (GTAR). *Given a post-routing layout with metal layers and via layer, a predefined DSA guiding template set, and the number of masks for the via layer, our objective is to maximize the redundant via insertion rate and the number of vias patterned by DSA guiding templates.*

3. ALGORITHM

In this section, we model this problem as a constrained weighted matching of bipartite graph problem. Then an ILP formulation for the constrained bipartite matching algorithm is proposed to search for the solutions.

3.1 Constrained Bipartite Graph Matching

The partition in the constrained bipartite graph is the vertex set for single vias and DSA guiding template candidates in this work, which is different from traditional maximum bipartite matching methods mentioned in [17,20], where the partition is the set of single vias and redundant vias in the graph. An edge is added between the original via and the DSA guiding template if the via is covered by the template, as shown in Fig. 7(a), which is the bipartite graph for the example layout in Fig. 6. This bipartite graph is constrained for the reason that the edges are divided into different edge set, and the maximum number of edges for each set is limited. We assume that each edge set has been assigned with a certain color, the edge set constraint is referred as the color constraint in this paper. For each template candidate, if there exists another template that has overlap conflict with it, the corresponding edges are assigned to the same color (edge set), as shown in Fig. 7(b), in which template t_1 overlaps with t_2, so edges connected with t_1 and t_2 are assigned to an edge set with the same color, and at most one edge can be selected from this color. The color constraint assignment is similar for other overlapped templates, as shown in Figs. 7(c)–7(d). If the template has other design rule violation, the corresponding edges are assigned to another color, as shown in Figs. 7(e)–7(f), where t_1 and t_3, t_1 and t_4, t_2 and t_3, have minimum distance violation between the DSA templates. For the ordinary matching, as there is no priority for the edges, it is possible that most of the DSA templates of the matching result does not contain any redundant via, or most of the vias are not patterned by the DSA pattern. In

Table 1: Notation

G	Constrained bipartite graph
V	Vertex in the bipartite graph
V_S	Vertex set of single via
V_T	Vertex set of DSA guiding template assignment
E_i	Edge set with color i
C_i	Color constraint for edge set E_i
V_{TW}	Vertex set of DSA guiding template assignment for MP
e_i	Edge i
e_{ij}	Multiplied edge of e_i on mask j
E_{ij}	Multiplied edge set of E_i on mask j
EO_{ij}	Edge set that has overlap conflict with edge e_{ij}
EV_{ij}	Edge set that has other violations with edge e_{ij}
EV_{k}	Edge set for edges connected with vertex k
W	Multiple patterning number
w_i	Maximum number of edges for C_i
$x_{e_{ij}}$	0/1 variable to indicate the value of edge e_{ij}
$\alpha\backslash\beta$	Weight of DSA template candidate with and without redundant via
$E_w\backslash E_{wo}$	Edge set with and without redundant via

order to obtain a balance between the insertion rate and the number of covered single vias, we can assign different weight to these edges: we assign a large weight α to the edges connecting with template which includes redundant via, and a relatively small weight β to other edges. Thus, we are able to maintain a high insertion rate and a high coverage of vias at the same time.

For simplicity, we first consider the constrained bipartite matching without multiple patterning. Some notations are illustrated in Table 1. The constrained bipartite graph is constructed for single patterning, as shown in Fig. 7.

Problem 2 (Constrained Weighted Matching). *Given a weighted bipartite graph $G = (V, E)$ with partition $V = V_S \cup V_T$, the edge set is partitioned to m set $E_1 \cup E_2 \cup ...E_m$, each set has color C_i. Find the maximum weighted matching M such that there are at most one edge of color C_i, i.e. $|M \cap E_i| \leq 1, \forall i \in [m]$.*

If multiple patterning is considered simultaneously, for DSA guiding templates that have other design rule violations, they can be assigned to different masks to increase the insertion rate. The vertex set for templates V_T and edge set E are multiplied to indicate the masks they are assigned to. Fig. 8 shows the bipartite graph and different color constraints of edge set for double patterning. It is noted that the number of edges and vertexes for templates has been doubled, the color constraints assignment is similar to single patterning. It is easy to extend the bipartite graph and color constraints construction to other multiple patterning in the similar way.

Problem 3 (Constrained Weighted Matching for MP). *Assume it is a W multiple patterning. Given a bipartite graph $G = (V_W, E_W)$ with partition $V_W = V_S \cup V_{TW}$, the number of vertexes and edges in V_{TW} and E_W are multiplied: $|V_{TW}| = W \times |V_T|$, $|E_W| = W \times |E|$. Edge set is partitioned to m set: $E_W = E_1 \cup E_2 \cup ... \cup E_m$, each subset has color C_i. Find the maximum weighted matching M such that there are at most one edge for overlapping color constraint C_i, i.e. $|M \cap E_i| \leq 1, i \in (1, 2, ..., m)$, and at most two edges for other color constraint C_i, i.e. $|M \cap E_i| \leq 2, i \in (1, 2, ..., m)$.*

3.2 ILP Formulation

Since maximum weighted constrained matching in bipartite graph is NP-hard [23,24], we provide an ILP formulation to search for optimal solution.

Let N_v indicate the number of original single via, N_t indicate the number of templates. Let e_{ij} denote edge ij, the

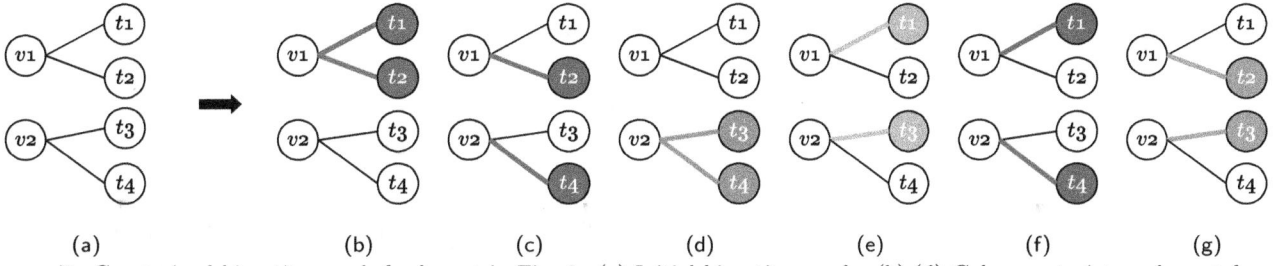

Figure 7: Constrained bipartite graph for layout in Fig. 6. (a) Initial bipartite graph. (b)-(d) Color constraints: edge set for edges connected with overlapped DSA guiding template candidates. (e)-(g) edge set for edges that connected with DSA guiding template candidates which have other design rule violations.

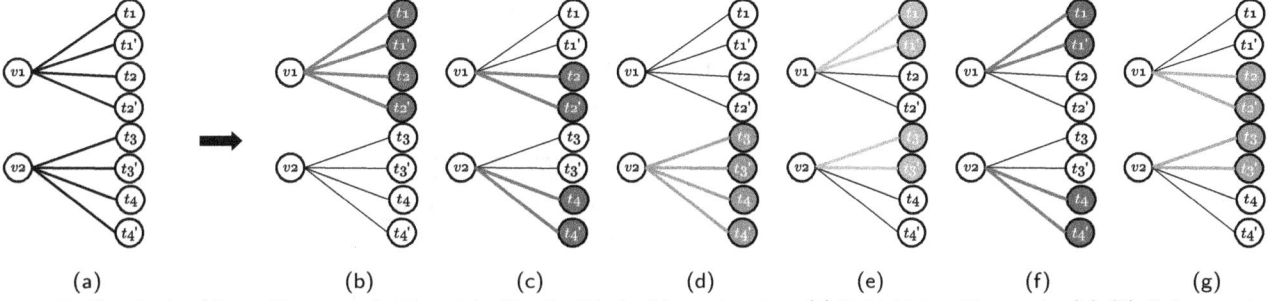

Figure 8: Constrained bipartite graph for layout in Fig. 6 with double patterning. (a) Initial bipartite graph. (b)-(d) Color constraints: edge set for edges connected with overlapped DSA guiding template candidates. (e)-(g) edge set for edges that connected with DSA guiding template candidates which have other design rule violations.

index ij means the primary edge e_i is on mask j. Let $x_{e_{ij}}$ ($e_{ij} \in E$) indicate the binary value for this edge. Other notations are defined in Table 1. The constrained maximum weighted matching for multiple patterning can be formulated as follows:

$$\text{maximize} \quad \alpha \sum_{e_{ij} \in E_w} x_{e_{ij}} + \beta \sum_{e_{ij} \in E_{wo}} x_{e_{ij}} \qquad (1)$$

$$\text{s.t.}$$

$$\sum_{e_{ij} \in E_{V_k}} x_{e_{ij}} \leq 1, \qquad \forall k \in (0, \ldots, N_v)$$

$$\sum_{e_{ij} \in E_{V_h}} x_{e_{ij}} \leq 1, \qquad \forall h \in (0, \ldots, N_t)$$

$$x_{e_{ij}} + x_{e_{\tilde{i}\tilde{j}}} \leq 1, \qquad \forall e_{ij} \in E, \forall e_{\tilde{i}\tilde{j}} \in EO_{ij}$$

$$x_{e_{ij}} + x_{e_{\tilde{i}\tilde{j}}} \leq 2, \qquad \forall e_{ij} \in E, \forall e_{\tilde{i}\tilde{j}} \in EV_{ij}, \tilde{j} \neq j$$

$$x_{e_{ij}} + x_{e_{\tilde{i}\tilde{j}}} \leq 1, \qquad \forall e_{ij} \in E, \forall e_{\tilde{i}\tilde{j}} \in EV_{ij}, \tilde{j} = j$$

The target is to maximize the number of edges in the matching. The first constraint indicates that there is at most one edge that can be selected for each vertex, which corresponds to the matching. The second constraint indicates that if two edges, e_{ij} and $e_{\tilde{i}\tilde{j}}$, have overlap conflict, then at most one edge can be selected. $e_{\tilde{i}\tilde{j}}$ belongs to the edge set EO_{ij} which contains edges that have overlap conflict with edge e_{ij}. The third constraint indicates that for any two templates that have other design rule violations, they can be selected at the same time if they are assigned to different masks ($j \neq \tilde{j}$), here EV_{ij} indicates edge set which contains edges that have design rule violation with edge e_{ij}. However, they are not allowed on the same mask, as illustrated in the last constraint.

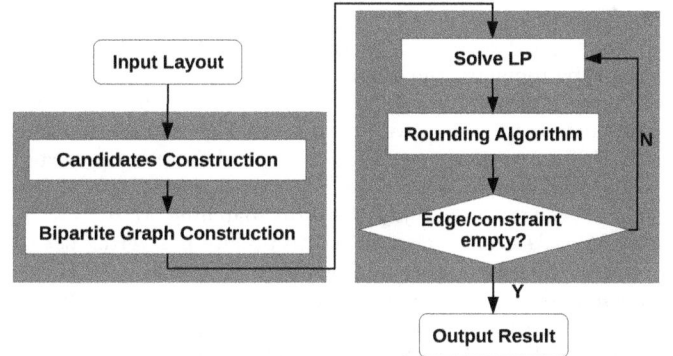

Figure 9: Basic flow for LP approximation algorithm.

We notice that edges which connecting with the same template or vias are also overlapping with each other, which is the same as the third constraint. Thus the simplified ILP formulation is as follows:

$$\text{maximize} \quad \alpha \sum_{e_{ij} \in E_w} x_{e_{ij}} + \beta \sum_{e_{ij} \in E_{wo}} x_{e_{ij}} \qquad (2)$$

$$\text{s.t.}$$

$$x_{e_{ij}} + x_{e_{\tilde{i}\tilde{j}}} \leq 1, \qquad \forall e_{ij} \in E, \forall e_{\tilde{i}\tilde{j}} \in EO_{ij}$$

$$x_{e_{ij}} + x_{e_{\tilde{i}\tilde{j}}} \leq 2, \qquad \forall e_{ij} \in E, \forall e_{\tilde{i}\tilde{j}} \in EV_{ij}, \tilde{j} \neq j$$

$$x_{e_{ij}} + x_{e_{\tilde{i}\tilde{j}}} \leq 1, \qquad \forall e_{ij} \in E, \forall e_{\tilde{i}\tilde{j}} \in EV_{ij}, \tilde{j} = j$$

4. APPROXIMATION ALGORITHM

Since ILP is an NP-hard problem, the runtime penalty is quite large with the increase of problem size, especially

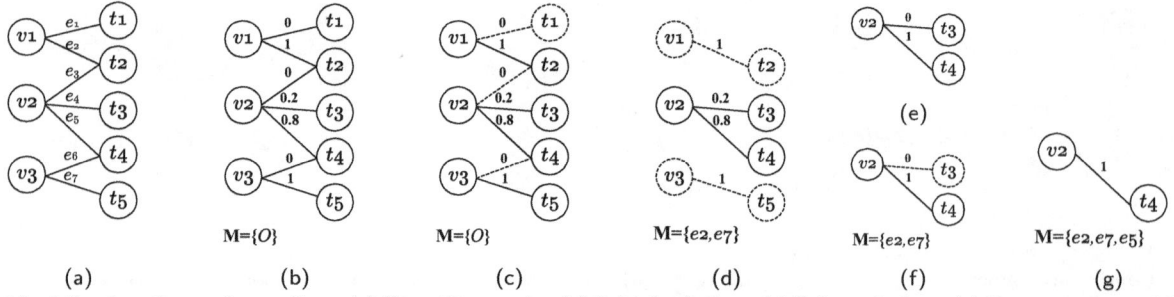

Figure 10: LP relaxation and rounding. (a) Bipartite graph. (b) Initial solution of LP formulation. (c) Remove edges with 0 value, then remove corresponding vertexes with zero degree. Edges and vertexes to be removed are marked as dashed lines. (d) Add edges with value 1 to the final matching M, then remove these vertexes and edges. (e) For tight vertex, round its edge to 1 if the edge value is greater than $\frac{1}{2}$, otherwise round the edge value to 0. (f)-(g) Remove edges with 0 value and vertexes with zero degree, add edges with value 1 to the final matching M.

for multiple patterning where the number of edges has been multiplied. We apply an LP approximation algorithm to solve the constrained maximum weighted matching in bipartite graph problem more efficiently without much loss of solution quality. Our approximation algorithm is inspired by paper [23], which talks about the constrained maximum weighted matching in bipartite graphs. The basic flow of our approximation method is shown in Fig. 9. Our approximation flow consists of two steps: LP relaxation and rounding. Some of the notations used in the algorithm are also defined in Table 1. For generality, we use e to denote an edge, $v \backslash t$ to denote a vertex for via\template in the bipartite graph, and $e = (v, t)$.

For the LP relaxation, we relax the ILP formulation into an LP by replacing the binary variable of edge e with continuous variable $x_e \in [0, 1]$, to obtain a feasible solution x for the current LP. Then we first remove edge e from the edge set E if its value is zero, i.e. $x_e = 0$, and remove the vertex if its degree value is zero, i.e. $deg(v) = 0$ or $deg(t) = 0$. We add the edge to our final bipartite matching M if $x_e = 1$, i.e. $M = M \cup e$. Then we need to update the vertex set to remove the edge $e = (v, t)$ when $x_e = 1$, i.e. $V = V \backslash \{v, t\}$; Then update the maximum number of edges for different color constraints: if the value of the edge $x_e = 1$, all its corresponding color constraints should reduce the maximum number by one, if $e \in E_i$, then $w_i = w_i - 1$. Generally speaking, as the initial value of w is 1 or 2 in the ILP formulation, w usually decreases to zero very quickly. If the maximum number of edges for color constraint is zero, i.e. $w = 0$, we then remove this color constraint and all the edges connected with this constraint. The removal of these edges can introduce more zero degree vertexes, we then delete the newly generated zero degree vertexes.

For the rounding step, we round some edges to 1 and others to 0: If there exists a tight vertex $v \in V$ such that $deg(v) = 2$, assume the two edges connected with vertex v are e_1 and e_2, and $e_1 = (v, t_1), e_2 = (v, t_2)$. If $x_{e_1} \geq \frac{1}{2}$, we round x_{e_1} to 1, and add e_1 to our final matching set M. Then round x_{e_2} and all the other edges connected with t_1 to zero. Then update the maximum number of edges for the color constraint: if $e_1 \in E_i$, thus $w_i = w_i - x_{e_1} - \lambda(1 - x_{e_1})$, $\lambda \in [0, 1]$. And vice versa. We should note that λ can be different in different iterations. We then update the vertex set to remove the rounded edges and vertexes from bipartite graph. Then iterate the algorithm from the LP relaxation. The details of relaxation and rounding algorithm is shown

in Algorithm 1,

Algorithm 1 Approximation for Constrained Weighted Matching in Bipartite Graph

---

Input: Final matching $M = \emptyset$
1: **while** $C \neq \emptyset$ or $E \neq \emptyset$ **do**
2:     Obtain basic feasible solution x for current LP;
3:     Remove edge e from the graph when $x_e = 0$;
4:     Remove node when $deg(v) = 0$;
5:     **if** $x_e = 1$ **then**
6:         add edge $e = (v, t)$ to M, $M = M \cup e$;
7:     **end if**
8:     Iterate from 1;
9:     Remove corresponding nodes $V = V \backslash \{v, t\}$;
10:    Update constraint, $w = w - 1$ if $x_e = 1$;
11:    **if** $w = 0$ and $w \in C_i$ **then**
12:        update constraints set $C = C \backslash C_i$;
13:    **end if**
14:    Update edge set $E = E \backslash \{e : e \in E_i\}$;
15:    Remove nodes with zero degree;
16:    **(Rounding)**
17:    **if** $\exists v$ such that $deg(v) = 2$, assume $e_1 = (v, t_1), e_2 = (v, t_2)$ **then**
18:        **if** x_{e_1} or $x_{e_2} \geq 1/2$ **then**
19:           Rounding x_{e_1} or x_{e_2} to 1, add it to M;
20:           Rounding x_{e_2} or x_{e_1} and all other edges connected with t_1 or t_2 to zero;
21:           If e_1 or $e_2 \in E_i$, then $w_i = w_i - x_{e_1} - \lambda(1 - x_{e_1})$ or $w_i = w_i - x_{e_2} - \lambda(1 - x_{e_2})$;
22:           Remove (v, t_1) or (v, t_2) and all rounded edges from the graph;
23:        **end if**
24:    **end if**
25: **end while**
26: Return M;

Fig. 10 gives a simple example for the relaxation and rounding algorithm, in which Fig. 10(a) shows the original bipartite graph. We first obtain the solution of LP, the value for each edge is shown in Fig. 10(b). Then remove edges e_1, e_3, and e_6 as their values are zero, as shown in Fig. 10(c). Then remove vertex t_1 as its degree is zero. Because the values of edges e_2, e_7 equal to one, we then add them to the matching M, $M = \{e_2, e_7\}$, and remove corresponding edges and vertexes, as shown in Fig. 10(d). For edges e_4 and e_5 that connect with tight vertex v_2, round the value of edge e_5 to one as its value is greater than $\frac{1}{2}$, and round e_4 to zero as its value is smaller than $\frac{1}{2}$. Remove edge e_4, then remove vertex t_3 as its degree is zero. At last add edge e_5 to matching M, $M = \{e_2, e_7, e_5\}$. The process is done when the edge set is empty.

It should be noted that there might be some violations of the color constraints during the updating of maximum number of edges. There may be more color violation for smaller λ value, but better objective performance. Thus in order to prevent the color constraints violations, we can set $\lambda = 1$. Once an edge is rounded, the maximum number of edges decreases by one.

5. EXPERIMENTAL RESULT

All algorithms in this work are implemented in C++, and they are performed on a Linux workstation with Intel Core i7 3.4GHz CPU and 32GB memory. CBC [25] is used as the solver for ILP and LP. Benchmarks used in the experiments are based on the OpenSPARC T1 design [26]. Different modules in OpenSPARC T1 are synthesized with Design Compiler [27]. We then place and route the benchmarks with NanGate 45nm open cell library [28] by using Cadence SOC encounter [29], where the utilization rate is set to 0.7. The weight ratio ($\frac{\alpha}{\beta}$) of DSA template candidates with and without redundant via is set to 250. In order to ensure that no violation is generated during the approximation, the coefficient λ used in the updating of maximum number of edges for color constraints is set to 1. Metal two and metal three layers are used for the redundant via insertion, as they are the most dense metal layers among all the routing layers. We first convert the GDSII layout into grid, and then search for DSA guiding template candidates based on the grids. We assume that there are two units for one metal pitch, and the minimum distance requirement between different DSA guiding template is two metal pitch. Our algorithm is adaptable to more advanced technology node as it is graph based and can be applied to different layout.

In order to compare the performance of our algorithm for DSA and multiple patterning aware redundant via insertion, we implement the DSA aware redundant via insertion with single patterning (SP), double patterning (DP), and triple patterning (TP) to evaluate the improvement of inserted redundant via (insertion rate). We implement the ILP for single patterning (SP-ILP), double patterning (DP-ILP) and triple patterning (TP-ILP), and corresponding approximation algorithms for DP and TP (DP-Ap and TP-Ap). We also implement the ILP formulation for un-constrained redundant via mentioned in [21] (Un-constrained) as comparison, since this algorithm inserts the redundant via without any DSA pattern constraints, it can reach the ideal maximum insertion rate for the layout, but with a lot of vias that can not be patterned by DSA. We use the insertion rate of un-constrained RVI as the ideal target for DSA aware RVI. We assume the design rule is the same for all implementations. In order to evaluate the performance of these methods, we define the coverage rate (CR) to indicate the ratio of patterned single vias and original single vias, we would like to achieve a high insertion rate IR and high coverage rate CR.

The insertion rate (IR) is compared in Table 2. The second column is the total number of original vias for each benchmark. The third column shows the insertion rate for

Table 3: Coverage Rate (CR) Comparison

Bench	#Vias	SP-ILP	DP-ILP	DP-Ap	TP-ILP	TP-Ap
efc	4983	76.33	100	98.63	100	99.53
ecc	5523	80.10	100	98.55	100	99.67
ffu	7026	78.49	100	98.83	100	99.45
alu	7046	74.65	100	98.14	100	99.16
byp	28847	75.14	N/A	97.29	N/A	98.89
mul	62989	70.23	N/A	96.39	N/A	98.31
Avg.	19402	75.82	N/A	97.97	N/A	99.17

Table 4: Runtime Comparison (s)

Bench	#Vias	SP-ILP	DP-ILP	DP-Ap	TP-ILP	TP-Ap
efc	4983	0.85	68.85	3.36	85.07	7.38
ecc	5523	0.84	56.26	3.80	119.43	7.93
ffu	7026	1.17	88.64	4.99	98.22	12.02
alu	7046	1.33	107.34	5.40	399.38	11.55
byp	28847	6.31	N/A	41.41	N/A	136.69
mul	62989	30.98	N/A	417.76	N/A	1613.23
Avg.	19402	6.91	N/A	79.45	N/A	298.13

un-constrained RVI, it represents the ideal maximum insertion rate for each benchmark without DSA pattern constraints, but it contains many vias that can not be patterned by DSA. When DSA pattern is considered in the redundant via insertion process with single pattering (SP), the insertion rate decreases about 24.00% on average due to the design rule violations between DSA guiding template when compared to the un-constrained method with ideal insertion rate. If double patterning process is considered simultaneously in the insertion process, since the violated templates can be assigned to different masks, its IR improves more than 20.00% based on available data when compared to the one with single patterning. When compared with the un-constrained method, the reduction of IR are less than 0.30% and 2.10% for solutions of DP-ILP and DP-Ap. For triple patterning process, when compared with the un-constrained method with ideal insertion rate, the reduction on the insertion rate are less than 0.05% and 0.86% for solutions of TP-ILP and TP-Ap. Therefore, the insertion rate of DSA-MP is quite comparable to un-constrained redundant via insertion, and the final insertion result is DSA compatible.

The coverage rate (CR) is shown in Table 3. As we can see from the table, the single patterning can cover most of the vias, but there are still 24% of vias that can not be patterned. For DP-ILP and TP-ILP, we can reach a hundred percent coverage. For DP-Ap and TP-Ap, the coverage rate can reach 97.97% and 99.17% on average.

The runtime is compared in Table 4. Here the runtime is the time consumption of CPU time to solve the problem, which excludes I/O processing time. The runtime of DP-ILP and TP-ILP increases dramatically because of more variables and constraints for large benchmarks, and the runtime of byp and mul is too long to be collected. Our approximation algorithm, DP-Ap and TP-Ap, are much faster. As the runtime of ILP for byp and mul is not available, we compare the result with largest available benchmark alu, DP-Ap is more than 20× faster than DP-ILP, and TP-Ap is more than 34× faster than TP-ILP.

6. CONCLUSION

Directed Self-Assembly is the potential candidate for the next generation lithography technique, which arouses a lot of interests in the DSA aware design and guiding template optimization. In this paper, we propose a general integer linear programming (ILP) formulation to solve the DSA aware

Table 2: Insertion Rate (IR) Comparison

Bench	#Vias	Un-constrained	SP-ILP	DP-ILP	DP-Ap	TP-ILP	TP-Ap
efc	4983	98.45	75.15	98.29	96.84	98.41	97.89
ecc	5523	99.02	78.68	98.80	97.44	98.98	98.62
ffu	7026	98.57	76.77	98.47	97.35	98.54	97.93
alu	7046	98.32	72.79	98.15	96.39	98.29	97.44
byp	28847	93.88	70.21	N/A	91.35	N/A	92.88
mul	62989	98.55	68.59	N/A	94.91	N/A	96.86
Avg.	19402	97.80	73.70	N/A	95.71	N/A	96.94

redundant via insertion with multiple patterning simultaneously. To improve scalability, we propose an approximation algorithm with LP relaxation and rounding to solve the problem efficiently. The experimental results demonstrate that our methods can insert redundant via with the consideration of DSA guiding template shapes without much loss of insertion rate. Our methods can be adaptive to different technology nodes as well.

Acknowledgment

This work is supported in part by National Science Foundation (NSF), Semiconductor Research Corporation (SRC), and CUHK Direct Grant for Research.

7. REFERENCES

[1] Yuriko Seino, Hiroki Yonemitsu, Hironobu Sato, Masahiro Kanno, Hirokazu Kato, Katsutoshi Kobayashi, Ayako Kawanishi, Tsukasa Azuma, Makoto Muramatsu, Seiji Nagahara, Takahiro Kitano, and Takayuki Toshima. Contact hole shrink process using graphoepitaxial directed self-assembly lithography. *JM3*, 12(3), 2013.

[2] Seong-Jun Jeong, Ju Young Kim, Bong Hoon Kim, Hyoung-Seok Moon, and Sang Ouk Kim. Directed self-assembly of block copolymer for next generation nanolithography. *Materials Today*, 16(12):468–476, 2013.

[3] David Z Pan, Bei Yu, and J-R Gao. Design for manufacturing with emerging nanolithography. *IEEE TCAD*, 32(10):1453–1472, 2013.

[4] H.-S. Philip Wong, Chris Bencher, He Yi, Xin-Yu Bao, and Li-Wen Chang. Block copolymer directed self-assembly enables sublithographic patterning for device fabrication. In *Proc. SPIE*, volume 8323, 2012.

[5] Yuansheng Ma, Junjiang Lei, Juan Andres Torres, Le Hong, James Word, Germain Fenger, Alexander Tritchkov, George Lippincott, Rachit Gupta, Neal Lafferty, Yuan He, Joost Bekaert, and Geert Vanderberghe. Directed self-assembly (dsa) grapho-epitaxy template generation with immersion lithography. In *Proc. SPIE*, volume 9423, 2015.

[6] Azat Latypov, Tamer H. Coskun, Grant Garner, Moshe Preil, Gerard Schmid, Ji Xu, and Yi Zou. Simulations of spatial DSA morphology, DSA-aware assist features and block copolymer-homopolymer blends. In *Proc. SPIE*, volume 9049, 2014.

[7] Sander Wuister, Tamara Druzhinina, Davide Ambesi, Bart Laenens, Linda He Yi, and Jo Finders. Influence of litho patterning on DSA placement errors. In *Proc. SPIE*, volume 9049, 2014.

[8] Yuansheng Ma, J. Andres Torres, Germain Fenger, Yuri Granik, Julien Ryckaert, Geert Vanderberghe, Joost Bekaert, and James Word. Challenges and opportunities in applying grapho-epitaxy DSA lithography to metal cut and contact/via applications. In *Proc. SPIE*, volume 9231, 2014.

[9] He Yi, Xin-Yu Bao, Jie Zhang, Richard Tiberio, James Conway, Li-Wen Chang, Subhasish Mitra, and H.-S. Philip Wong. Contact-hole patterning for random logic circuit using block copolymer directed self-assembly. In *Proc. SPIE*, volume 8323, 2012.

[10] Yuelin Du, Zigang Xiao, Martin D.F. Wong, He Yi, and H.-S. Philip Wong. DSA-aware detailed routing for via layer optimization. In *Proc. SPIE*, volume 9049, 2014.

[11] Zigang Xiao, Yuelin Du, Haitong Tian, Martin D. F. Wong, He Yi, H-S Philip Wong, and Hongbo Zhang. Directed self-assembly (DSA) template pattern verification. In *Proc. DAC*, pages 55:1–55:6, 2014.

[12] Yuelin Du, Daifeng Guo, Martin D. F. Wong, He Yi, H.-S. Philip Wong, Hongbo Zhang, and Qiang Ma. Block copolymer directed self-assembly (DSA) aware contact layer optimization for 10 nm 1D standard cell library. In *Proc. ICCAD*, pages 186–193, 2013.

[13] Zigang Xiao, Yuelin Du, Martin D.F. Wong, and Hongbo Zhang. DSA template mask determination and cut redistribution for advanced 1D gridded design. In *Proc. SPIE*, volume 8880, 2013.

[14] Jiaojiao Ou, Bei Yu, Jhih-Rong Gao, and David Z. Pan. Directed self-assembly cut mask assignment for unidirectional design. *JM3*, 14(3), 2015.

[15] Yasmine Badr, Andres Torres, and Puneet Gupta. Mask assignment and synthesis of DSA-MP hybrid lithography for sub-7nm contacts/vias. In *Proc. DAC*, pages 70:1–70:6, 2015.

[16] Yasmine Badr, Juan Andres Torres, Yuansheng Ma, Joydeep Mitra, and Puneet Gupta. Incorporating DSA in multipatterning semiconductor manufacturing technologies. In *Proc. SPIE*, volume 9427, 2015.

[17] Kuang-Yao Lee and Ting-Chi Wang. Post-routing redundant via insertion for yield/reliability improvement. In *Proc. ASPDAC*, pages 303–308, 2006.

[18] Kuang-Yao Lee, Cheng-Kok Koh, Ting-Chi Wang, and Kai-Yuan Chao. Fast and optimal redundant via insertion. *IEEE TCAD*, 27(12):2197–2208, 2008.

[19] Gang Xu, Li-Da Huang, David Z Pan, and Martin DF Wong. Redundant-via enhanced maze routing for yield improvement. In *Proc. ASPDAC*, pages 1148–1151, 2005.

[20] Huang-Yu Chen, Mei-Fang Chiang, Yao-Wen Chang, Lumdo Chen, and Brian Han. Full-chip routing considering double-via insertion. *IEEE TCAD*, 27(5):844–857, 2008.

[21] Kuang-Yao Lee, Cheng-Kok Koh, Ting-Chi Wang, and Kai-Yuan Chao. Optimal post-routing redundant via insertion. In *Proc. ISPD*, pages 111–117, 2008.

[22] Jiwoo Pak, Bei Yu, and David Z. Pan. Electromigration-aware redundant via insertion. In *Proc. ASPDAC*, pages 544–549, 2015.

[23] Monaldo Mastrolili and Georgios Stamoulis. Constrained matching problems in bipartite graphs. In *Proc. ISCO*, pages 344–355, 2014.

[24] Jan Plesnik. Constrained weighted matchings and edge coverings in graphs. *Discrete Applied Mathematics*, 92(2-3):229–241, Jun. 1999.

[25] CBC. http://www.coin-or.org/projects/Cbc.xml.

[26] OpenSPARC T1. http://www.oracle.com/technetwork/systems/opensparc/index.html.

[27] Synopsys Design Compiler. http://www.synopsys.com.

[28] NanGate FreePDK45 Generic Open Cell Library. http://www.si2.org/openeda.si2.org/projects/nangatelib, 2008.

[29] Cadence SOC Encounter. http://www.cadence.com.

Double-Patterning Aware DSA Template Guided Cut Redistribution for Advanced 1-D Gridded Designs *

Zhi-Wen Lin
Graduate Institute of Electronics Engineering
National Taiwan University
Taipei 10617, Taiwan
lzw@eda.ee.ntu.edu.tw

Yao-Wen Chang
Department of Electrical Engineering
National Taiwan University
Taipei 10617, Taiwan
ywchang@ntu.edu.tw

ABSTRACT

Directed self-assembly (DSA) technology has emerged as a promising candidate for cut printing in advanced 1-D gridded layouts, where cuts might need to be redistributed such that they can be patterned by specific DSA guiding templates. The cut redistribution significantly affects the performance and manufacturability of a circuit. In this paper, we propose an algorithm incorporating DSA with double patterning for a template guided cut redistribution problem. We first develop a linear-time optimal algorithm for a special case of the template guided cut redistribution problem, with contiguous rows. For the general problem, a linear-time double-patterning aware partitioning method is developed to select a set of subproblem candidates to generate a template distribution to minimize the impact on circuit performance and manufacturing. Consequently, we decompose a general problem into a set of subproblems conforming to the aforementioned special case, solve each subproblem optimally, and merge the solutions to the subproblems to obtain an overall solution to the general one. Experimental results show that our algorithm can resolve all spacing rule violations, with even smaller extended wire costs and running times, compared with the state-of-the-art works on a set of common benchmarks.

Keywords

Directed-self-assembly; double patterning; one-dimensional gridded design; design for manufacturability

1. INTRODUCTION

One-dimensional (1-D) layouts have been shown to be more suitable than 2-D ones for advanced nanometer circuit design, mainly due to their regularity and thus better yield [10, 16, 17]. In a 1-D layout, *cuts* are used for patterning designs. For advanced nanometer designs, however, cuts may be too dense to be printed by traditional 193nm immersion (193i) lithography [19]. As a result, researchers proposed to use hybrid lithography of multiple patterning, such as self-aligned double patterning (SADP), together with high-resolution e-beam lithography [4, 5, 6]. However, e-beam lithography is still very costly due to its low throughput.

---

*This work was partially supported by Genesys Logic, IBM, MediaTek, TSMC, Academia Sinica, MOST of Taiwan under Grant NSC 102-2221-E-002-235-MY3, NSC 102-2923-E-002-006-MY3, MOST 103-2221-E-002-259-MY3, MOST 103-2812-8-002-003, MOST 104-2221-E-002-132-MY3, NTU under Grant NTU-ERP-104R8951, and NTU under Grant NTU-ERP-105R8951

ISPD'16, April 03-06, 2016, Santa Rosa, CA, USA

© 2016 ACM. ISBN 978-1-4503-4039-7/16/04. . . $15.00

DOI: http://dx.doi.org/10.1145/2872334.2872350

On the other hand, The *directed self-assembly* (*DSA*) technology has emerged as a promising candidate for advanced sub-10 nm design [18]. Specialized polymer molecules, called *block copolymers*, can be directed by some guiding topographical templates to form self-assembled features required for layout designs. Self-assembled features guided by templates can have higher resolution than the templates and thus can satisfy desired placement accuracy. DSA has been used for contact holes patterning [1, 2, 7, 12, 18] and has been applied to cut printing in 1-D gridded designs [3, 12, 19].

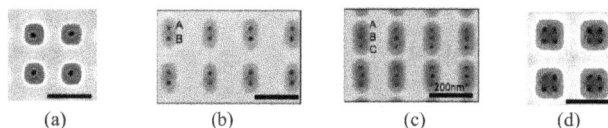

Figure 1: The template library used in [19]. (a) Single-cut template. (b) 2-cut template. (c) 3-cut template. (d) 4-cut template.

However, there are some issues for cut printing with DSA [19]. First, the overlay accuracy of self-assembled features and the printability of templates may vary with different topologies of templates [7]. Consequently, the size of the library consisting of feasible templates is typically small. Fig. 1 shows the template library used in [19]. Ma et al. showed in [12] that two close templates might interfere with each other such that they cannot pattern desired cuts. To handle this cut interference problem, we could redistribute cuts to resolve spacing conflicts between cuts to pattern them well. Meanwhile, the total length of extended wires for fitting the given cut locations should be minimized to mitigate the negative impact on circuit performance [19]. However, optimizing DSA template guided cut distribution is more complicated than that for traditional cut redistribution problems [5, 6], with the limited size of the DSA template library.

Xiao et al. presented pioneering work to match cuts to templates and then placed these templates [19] for a DSA template guided cut distribution problem. Nevertheless, we observe several insufficiencies in this work: (1) template matching significantly affects the subsequent template placement, but their measurement for conflicts and wire costs during template matching may not be sufficiently accurate; (2) this greedy-like method tends to match too many cuts to a template in order to reduce conflict costs; (3) this greedy-like method does not consider all possible matches, and thus their solution quality cannot be guaranteed. Fig. 2 compares the results of the greedy-like method and our algorithm. As shown in Fig. 2(b), the greedy-like method tries to find a template matching the maximum number of cuts. As a result, a template with four cuts (see Fig. 1(d)) is applied on the wires of the top two tracks; moving a cut (say, cut 1) far from its original location would increase its wire cost, measured by the length of its extended wire. Fig. 2(b) show the conflicting cut pairs $(1, 4), (2, 4), (3, 4), (3, 5), (3, 6)$ and $(7, 8)$ induced from the method used in [19], while our algorithm leads to zero conflict as illustrated in Fig. 2(c).

To our best knowledge, the DSA cut redistribution problem is so complicated that no existing work can generate optimal solutions efficiently. Although Ou et al. in [13, 14] proposed an ILP formulation to get an optimal solution of the DSA cut redis-

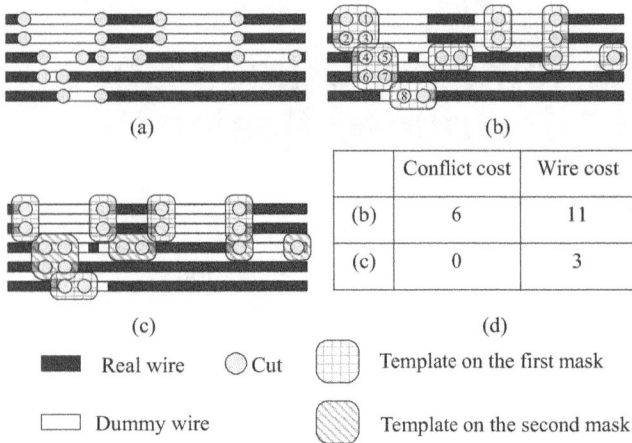

	Conflict cost	Wire cost
(b)	6	11
(c)	0	3

(c)   (d)

■ Real wire   ○ Cut   ▦ Template on the first mask

☐ Dummy wire   ▨ Template on the second mask

Figure 2: Comparison of a greedy-like method and our algorithm. (a) Original cut distribution. (b) The result of the greedy-like method. (c) The result of our algorithm. (d) Comparison of (b) and (c). The conflict cost is the number of the cut pairs with spacing conflicts, where two templates patterned by different masks have no conflict. The wire cost is the total length of extended wires (each of which is the distance between a cut and its original position).

tribution problem, the efficiency of their works is not good due to the computationally expensive ILP. A speedup heuristic was proposed for their ILP-based method, but their solutions are not optimal and the heuristic is not efficient. In contrast, existing non-ILP methods [14, 19] incur significantly worse quality than the ILP-based methods, with non-linear running times.

As suggested in the work [12], it is hard to achieve proper image fidelity with a single 193i patterning step. Consequently, it is desirable to incorporate double patterning to achieve high-quality solutions. Note that contact/via fabrication with DSA multiple-patterning hybrid lithography has been studied in [1, 2]. In this paper, we integrate DSA cut redistribution with double patterning such that cuts are well patterned with minimized mask costs. With double patterning, templates can be patterned by two different masks to resolve conflicts and also to reduce wire costs to mitigate the negative impact on circuit performance.

We summarize our main contributions below:

1. We identify a special case of the DSA template guiding cut redistribution problem with contiguous rows, and present a linear-time optimal algorithm for this problem.

2. With double patterning, we explore the criterion for different subproblems not interfering with each other.

3. We develop a linear-time algorithm to decompose a general problem into multiple subproblems conforming to the special case to achieve better performance considering the above criterion with double patterning.

4. Our algorithm can achieve a provably good performance bound, with the total wire cost of a template distribution only linear to the number of cuts.

5. Experimental results show that our algorithm can resolve all cut conflicts, with even smaller extended wire costs and running times, compared with the state-of-the-art works [2, 14, 19] on a set of benchmarks provided by the authors of [19].

The rest of this paper is organized as follows: Section 2 gives some preliminaries and the problem formulation. Section 3 shows the overall flow of our algorithm. Section 4 presents our algorithm for the special case with contiguous rows. Section 5 solves the general problem. Section 6 proposes a bottom-up clustering framework to enhance our algorithm. Experimental results are reported in Section 7. Finally, we conclude our work in Section 8.

2. PRELIMINARIES

In this section, we first introduce 1-D layout design with double-patterning aware DSA template guided cuts. We then define some

terminologies used in this paper and give the problem formulation.

2.1 1-D Layouts with Double-Patterning Assisted DSA Template Guided Cuts

We first introduce the manufacturing process of a 1-D layout with double-patterning guiding templates. First, dense parallel lines are patterned by the DSA or SADP technology [12]. Then the original lines are cut into segments of *real wires* and *dummy wires* by metal cuts. The segments of real wires are 1-D patterns realizing the functionality of the target circuit, and the other segments are dummy wires. For example, the yellow cuts in Fig. 2(c) chop up the dense lines into the blue (real wires) and white (dummy wires) segments. Note that the length of a dummy wire can be zero.

In this paper, guiding templates are used to form cuts with the DSA technology. A template can pattern one or more cuts within it, and thus we can group cuts into a template for better manufacturability. For example, the cuts 4, 5, 6 and 7 can be patterned by a 4-cut template shown in Fig. 2(b). Moreover, double patterning is used to pattern these templates to avoid some templates from interfering with each other. Fig. 2(c) shows two sets of guiding templates patterned by two different masks.

Due to issues of manufacturability, as mentioned in Section 1, a template library consisting of feasible templates is used to form metal cuts. In this paper, we use the guiding template library presented in [19], shown in Fig. 1, where the 2- and 3-cut templates in Fig. 1 can also be rotated by 90°.

However, for a layout design with DSA template guided cuts, every cut is patterned by exactly one template. Moreover, the cuts may need to be relocated [19] because two close templates might interfere with each other, and thus they cannot pattern desired cuts [12]. Figs. 2(b) and (c) show relocated cuts to be printed by DSA templates. Note that, as shown in Fig. 2(c), two templates can be placed close to each other without interference if they are in different masks. Such a property will be exploited by our algorithm to find desired solutions.

To describe the distribution of templates forming cuts, we define a template distribution as follows:

DEFINITION 1. *A template distribution is a set of templates, where every template is specified with its two-dimensional (2-D) positions on the layout and the mask used to pattern this template.*

With the position of a template, the positions of cuts in this template can thus be derived. To address the manufacturability issues, we consider the concept of *cut conflicts* [19] as follows:

DEFINITION 2. *A conflict (x, y) in a template distribution is a pair of two cuts x and y that violates the minimum spacing δ of the given design rule and are allocated in different templates of the same mask.*

With the minimum spacing δ, two cuts can have a conflict only when their vertical distance is smaller than or equal to r_M rows away.

When cuts are redistributed, the lengths of real wires may change. To preserve the functionality of a layout, every cut can only move within the dummy wire it originally cuts; i.e., we only allow the extension of a real wire as that in [19]. To mitigate the negative impact on circuit performance, we should minimize the total extended wire of a layout, same as that in [19]. Therefore, we should consider the conflict cost (for better manufacturability) and the wire cost (for better circuit performance) together while redistributing cuts.

2.2 Definitions

To consider the constraints of dummy wires and cut patterning, we use the following definitions:

DEFINITION 3. *A gap g_i of a dummy wire is denoted by (y_i, b_i^l, b_i^r), where y_i is the vertical location of gap i, and b_i^l (b_i^r) is the horizontal location of the original left (right) cut (i.e., the left (right) end of the dummy wire).*

Fig. 3 shows an example. The new locations of cuts in gap g_i are required to be within $[b_i^l, b_i^r]$. Let l_i (r_i) be the horizontal location of the redistributed left (right) cut in gap g_i. The wire cost of gap i is $(l_i - b_i^l) + (b_i^r - r_i)$ if there are two real wires abutting the two sides of the dummy wire segment; the cost is $b_i^r - r_i$ ($l_i - b_i^l$) if no real wire abuts the left (right) end of the dummy wire segment

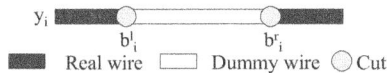

Figure 3: Notations for a gap g_i, where y_i is the vertical location of g_i, b_i^l (b_i^r) is the left (right) end of the dummy wire, and l_i (r_i) is the location of the redistributed left (right) cut in gap g_i. Cuts are allowed to be within $[b_i^l, b_i^r]$,

(thus the left (right) cut at l_i (r_i) is not necessary). However, it does not construct a gap for a track with no cut.

To further reduce the conflict cost, we also allows the merging of cuts in a gap as in [19], meaning that $b_i^l \leq l_i = r_i \leq b_i^r$ is feasible.

To satisfy the above constraints, we define the feasibility condition of a template distribution as follows:

DEFINITION 4. *We say a template distribution D to be* feasible *if every cut in a layout can be patterned by exactly one template in D and the locations of all cuts are within their own dummy wire segments.*

To evaluate a template distribution, we use a cost metric based on the conflicts and extended wires.

DEFINITION 5. *The* conflict cost *of a template distribution is the number of conflicts in this distribution.*

DEFINITION 6. *The* wire cost *of a template distribution is the sum of the wire cost of gaps in the layout in this distribution.*

Because the conflict cost is highly related to manufacturability and yield loss, we should prioritize minimizing the conflict cost over the wire one for a better design. To consider this issue, the objective function can be set as either a combined conflict and wire cost with a smaller weight for the wire one, or an ordered optimization on the conflict cost first and then the wire one. In ordered optimization, for two number pairs (c_1, w_1) and (c_2, w_2), where c/w means the conflict/wire cost, (c_1, w_1) is better than (c_2, w_2) if one of the conditions is satisfied: (1) $c_1 < c_2$; (2) $c_1 = c_2$ and $w_1 < w_2$. (Note that simultaneously optimizing two independent costs is typically difficult, often leading to an NP-complete problem like that in [8].)

2.3 Problem Formulation

We formally define the double-patterning-DSA-template guided cut redistribution (DPDSA-TCR) problem as follows:

PROBLEM 1. *Given a layout, two masks, a library of templates, distribution of cuts, and a design rule, find a template distribution with minimized conflict and wire costs, while every template is assigned to either mask.*

Our algorithm aims at minimizing the conflict cost first, and then the wire cost without increasing the conflict one.

3. OVERALL ALGORITHM FLOW

In this paper, we propose an algorithm, denoted by DPDSA-Core, incorporating DSA with double pattering for a template guided cut redistribution problem. We first develop a linear-time optimal algorithm for a special case of the template guided cut redistribution problem with contiguous rows. For the general problem, a linear-time double-patterning aware partitioning method is developed to select a set of subproblem candidates to generate a template distribution such that the impact on circuit performance and manufacturing is minimized. Consequently, we decompose a general problem into a set of subproblems conforming to the aforementioned special case, solve each subproblem optimally, and merge the solutions to the subproblems to obtain an overall solution to the general one.

To develop the special case, we first investigate the properties of design rules. If the difference of the vertical locations of two cuts is larger than r_M, there is no conflict between these two cuts. Further, there is no conflicts between two cuts if they are patterned by templates with different masks.

We divide a layout into subproblems such that: (1) each subproblem consists of contiguous rows; (2) templates in a subproblem are patterned by the same mask; (3) we pattern adjacent subproblems by different masks, and thus there is no conflict between two adjacent subproblems.

With the above three rules for subproblem extraction, if the number of rows in every subproblem is larger than or equal to r_M, there is no conflict between every two subproblems patterned by a same mask. Thus we can solve the subproblems independently without interference. However, the wire and conflict costs in a subproblem may be large if the number of rows in a subproblem is large. A redistributed cut may be far away from its original location because the number of rows in a subproblem is large, which may result in a large number of potential conflicts in a subproblem and thus the wire cost needs to be sacrificed. However, we should also try to reduce the wire cost; so we consider the subproblems with fewer rows to further improve the wire cost if the number of conflicts across these subproblems are small enough.

We identify the following special case of the original problem for a given design rule by the following constraints: (1) the problem consists of continuous rows in the original problem; (2) the number of rows is less than or equal to r_M; (3) every template in a template distribution of this special case should be patterned by a same mask. Every subproblem conforming to the above constraints is called a *subproblem candidate*. For every subproblem candidate, r_s is the number of rows in a subproblem candidate.

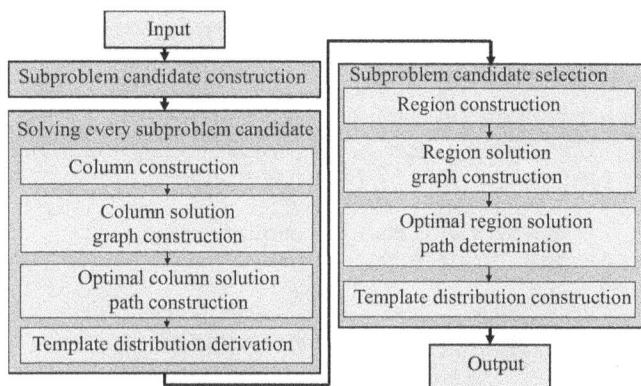

Figure 4: The DPDSA-Core flow.

Fig. 4 shows our algorithm flow. First, we solve each subproblem candidate. Then we decompose the problem into multiple subproblem candidates to construct a good solution of the whole problem.

Fig. 5 illustrates the subproblem candidates of the layout in Fig. 2. The blue boxes indicate rows of the layout. Every dashed box in Fig. 5 represents a subproblem candidate. For example, the dashed box including rows 1 and 2 represents the subproblem candidate containing rows 1 and 2. The black arrows in Fig. 5 are derived to construct a partition of the layout. For each partition, we construct a template distribution for the whole problem by constructing the templates derived in the subproblem candidates connected to the arrows. We pattern adjacent subproblems by different masks. For example, we pattern the middle subproblem candidate with rows 3 and 4 by mask 2 (instead of mask 1), and the template distribution in Fig. 2(c) is constructed. As a result, the wire cost of the template distribution is the sum of the wire costs of the selected subproblems, and the conflict cost of the template distribution is the sum of the conflict costs of the selected subproblems plus the number of conflicts between templates in different subproblems in a same mask.

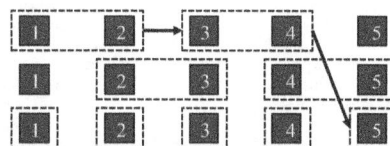

Figure 5: Subproblem candidates for the layout in Fig. 2. The blue boxes indicate rows of the layout. The black arrows give a partition of the layout. Every dashed box represents a subproblem candidate.

4. ALGORITHM FOR THE SPECIAL CASE

Given a number of rows in a subproblem, denoted by r_s, a template library, and a design rule, we can solve the special case defined in Section 3 optimally in $O(n)$ time, where n is the number of gaps in the subproblem. Our algorithm for the special case is described as follows.

We divide the layout of a subproblem into multiple *columns* such that every cut must be placed in a column. A column, denoted by $\hat{c}_h$, consists of a horizontal location h associated with the real/dummy wire segments containing h. For example, Fig. 6 shows a column with the horizontal location h, associated with g_1 and g_2. In this figure, the blue segments are real wire segments. For every column, our algorithm generates all feasible column solutions (feasible distribution of templates and cuts around the column), and introduce a graph to represent the column solutions. Fig. 7 illustrates some columns (the red boxes) with feasible column solutions (the purple ellipses).

In a column solution graph, we define column solutions and edges between the solutions such that we can construct every feasible template distribution of a subproblem by a path from the leftmost column to the rightmost one. Then for every column solution, its best predecessor is determined in order to construct an optimal path. A predecessor of a column solution $v_{h,j}$ is a column solution $\pi_{v_{h,j}}$ with an edge directing to $v_{h,j}$. For example, $v_{h,j}$ is a predecessor of $v_{h+1,j}$ in Fig. 7. We find the best predecessor of every column solution from the leftmost column to the rightmost one. At last, we trace back the column solutions from the rightmost column to the leftmost one to construct the path. To improve the efficiency, we construct columns with a column reduction technique such that the number of columns is in the order of $O(n)$.

Figure 6: An example column.

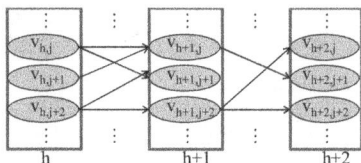

Figure 7: Column solution graph. Every column (red box) has some feasible solutions. If there is an edge between two column solutions, the two solutions can be simultaneously used to construct a template distribution.

In the following subsections, we first describe how we construct columns with a column reduction technique. Then we define a column solution and a column solution graph. Next, an optimization scheme to find the best column solution path is introduced. In addition, we describe how to derive a template distribution from the constructed path. At last, we analyze the running time of our algorithm for the special case.

4.1 Column Construction

Intuitively, we can construct a column at every possible horizontal location h with a cut. However, this method would result in a large number of generated columns, especially when the length of a gap is large. Instead, we propose a column reduction technique where the horizontal range of possible cut locations is reduced, while an optimal template distribution is still preserved.

Because δ is usually small, we could prune redundant solutions by removing the template distribution with a cut too far away from its original position. Fig. 8 illustrate this technique. In the left side of Fig. 8, the cut in the upper gap is too far away from the left boundary of the gap, and thus there must be a position closer to the original position such that the wire cost is reduced and the conflict cost is not increased, such as the right side of Fig. 8.

We apply this idea to restrict the horizontal ranges of possible cut locations. Before computing the restricted ranges, for every gap g_i, we define $m(g_i)$ as the number of gaps that could have conflicts with g_i. We show that the sum of $m(g_i)$ is linear to the number of gaps for a fixed minimum spacing δ and a fixed

Figure 8: Illustration of the reduction technique. For the cut of the upper gap, there is a position closer to the original position such that the wire cost is reduced and the conflict cost is not increased.

template library. Given a gap $g_i = (y_i, b^l_i, b^r_i)$, for every gap $g'_i = (y'_i, b^{l'}_i, b^{r'}_i)$ that may have a conflict with g_i, $|y'_i - y_i| \le r_M$. Also, the number of g'_is with the interval $[b^{l'}_i, b^{r'}_i] \subseteq [b^l_i, b^r_i]$ is amortized constant; i.e., the sum of the numbers over all g_i's is linear to the number of gaps. The main reason is that for every gap $g_j = (y_j, b^l_j, b^r_j)$ and every integer dy, there is at most one gap $g''_j = (y_j + dy, b^{l''}_j, b^{r''}_j)$ such that $[b^l_j, b^r_j] \subseteq [b^{l''}_j, b^{r''}_j]$. For example, g_2 in Fig. 6 is the only such gap of g_1 when $dy = -1$. Moreover, r_M is fixed for a fixed minimum spacing δ. In addition, the number of other g'_i's of g_i is bounded by a constant because of the small fixed minimum spacing δ. Therefore, the sum of $m(g_i)$ is linear to the number of gaps.

Using the above result, the maximum number $\gamma_{n_t,i,l}$ ($\gamma_{n_t,i,r}$) of templates conflicting with a template which tempts to move left (right) to reduce the wire cost, with template type n_t containing a left (right) cut of g_i, is amortized constant because of the following two reasons:

1. The sum of $m(g_i)$ is linear to the number of gaps.

2. The maximum height of a template is bounded by a constant because of the small size of template library.

Then, $M_{n_t,i,l} = 1 + \gamma_{n_t,i,l}(2\lceil\delta\rceil + L + W_t - 1)$ is the maximum distance from the left boundary for the template, containing a left cut of g_i, of type n_t, where W_t is the width of the template of type n_t, defined as the maximum distance of two cuts of the same row in a template ($W_t = 0$ if there is only one cut in the track), and L is the maximum width of all template types. Without loss of generality, $M_{n_t,i,r} = 1 + \gamma_{n_t,i,r}(2\lceil\delta\rceil + L + W_t - 1)$ is the maximum distance from the right boundary for the template, containing a right cut of g_i, of type n_t. Any template exceeding the above mentioned distance can be moved more closely to the left or right boundary of the template to reduce its wire cost without increasing the conflict cost.

$M_{n_t,i,l}$ ($M_{n_t,i,r}$) is amortized constant because δ and L are both constants for a fixed template library and a fixed design rule and $\gamma_{n_t,i,l}$ ($\gamma_{n_t,i,r}$) is amortized constant. Therefore, the sum of the restricted horizontal ranges is in the order of $O(n)$, where n is the number of gaps. With such a property, we have the following theorem:

THEOREM 1. *The total wire cost of the derived template distribution is $O(n)$, where n is the number of gaps.*

Using the restricted horizontal ranges, we can generate columns such that the number of columns is in the order $O(n)$. Fig. 9 shows an example. The green boxes in Fig. 9 are the restricted horizontal ranges, and the red boxes in Fig. 9 are the generated columns.

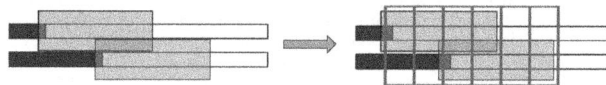

Figure 9: Columns(red boxes) generated from the restricted horizontal ranges(green boxes).

4.2 Column Solution Graph Construction

In this subsection, we first define the column solution and then the column solution graph.

4.2.1 Column Solution

A column solution not only defines cut distribution in a column, but also restricts the template distribution of the subproblems outside the column.

DEFINITION 7. *A column solution $v_{h,j}$ of a column $\hat{c}_h$ consists of $t_{h,j}$, $d_{h,j}$, and $s_{h,j}$, where $t_{h,j}$ is the template specifier of $v_{h,j}$, $d_{h,j}$ is the distribution specifier of $v_{h,j}$, and $s_{h,j}$ is the cut specifier of $v_{h,j}$.*

$v_{h,j}$ specifies the template topology, cut occupation, and properties of cuts (left/right cut) around a column. Fig. 10 shows an example.

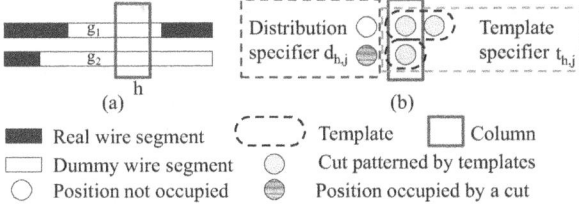

Figure 10: (a) An example of a column and (b) the topology of one of its column solutions. $r_s = 2$ **in this case. (b) shows the template specifier** $t_{h,j}$ **and distribution specifier** $d_{h,j}$ **of a column solution** $v_{h,j}$, **specifying the topology of a template distribution.**

The template specifier $t_{h,j}$ restricts the topology of every template t crossing h. A template t crosses h if $r_t \geq h \geq l_t$, where $r_t(l_t)$ is the horizontal location of the rightmost (leftmost) cut in t. Given a template t crossing h, for every 2-D position (x, y) occupied by a cut of t with $x \geq h$, the following conditions are satisfied: (1) (x, y) is also occupied in $t_{h,j}$; (2) for every 2-D position (x', y') occupied in $t_{h,j}$, (x', y') and (x, y) are restricted to be in a template in $t_{h,j}$ if and only if (x', y') is also occupied by a cut of t. For example, in Fig. 10(b), for every template patterning a cut of g_1 at h, it must also pattern a cut of g_1 at $h + 1$. Moreover, the template patterning a cut of g_2 at h is prohibited to pattern any other cut with a horizontal location larger than or equal to h. Furthermore, template specifiers are used to derive templates properly, to be elaborated in Subsection 4.4.

The distribution specifier $d_{h,j}$ restricts the cut occupation of every 2-D position (x, y) with $h > x > (h - (\lceil \delta \rceil - 1))$ to be the same as $d_{h,j}$. For example, in Fig. 10(b), $\lceil \delta \rceil = 3$ in this case. Fig. 10(b) suggests that there must be a cut of g_2 at $h - 1$, and no cut of g_1 at $h - 1$. Such a setting about the horizontal range is used to consider all conflicts with cuts in a column, to be explained in Subsection 4.3.

The cut specifier $s_{h,j}$ specifies whether the left/right cut is left to h for every gap associated with the column. $s_{h,j}$ can restrict $t_{h,j}$ and $d_{h,j}$ by checking the requirements for templates to pattern cuts. For example, there should be no template patterning a cut in $\hat{c}_h$ for a gap containing h if both the left and right cuts of the gap are left to h. Moreover, cut specifiers are used in the calculation of wire costs.

4.2.2 Column Solution Graph

To construct a column solution graph, we first define the *compatible* binary relation for column solution pairs.

DEFINITION 8. *For every pair of h and h' such that $h > h'$ and there is no column between h and h', a column solution $v_{h,j}$ of a column $\hat{c}_h$ is compatible with another column solution $v_{h',j'}$ of a column $\hat{c}_{h'}$ if the specifiers of $v_{h,j}$ do not contradict the ones of $v_{h',j'}$.*

The checking process includes the consistency of template topologies right to h', cut distribution left to h, and the properties of cuts. For the properties of cuts, a cut patterned at h' is the left/right cut of a gap if the left/right cut of a gap is specified as non-passed in $v_{h',j'}$ and is specified as passed in $v_{h,j}$. Note that if a cut of a gap is simultaneously specified as the left and the right cut of the gap by column solutions, it is a merged cut.

Then we can construct the column solution graph $G_c(V_c, E_c)$, where V_c is the set of vertices and E_c is the set of edges in G_c. In G_c, each vertex $v_{h,j}$ represents a column solution of a column $\hat{c}_h$. The established edges are the column solution pairs satisfying the above binary relation. In the following, we use the terminology of a column solution and a vertex interchangeably. Fig. 7 shows an example column solution graph.

4.3 Optimal Column Solution Path Construction

To find an optimal path on G_c, we first find the best predecessor of every column solution in the order of horizontal locations. Then we trace back the column solutions from the rightmost column to the leftmost one to construct a path.

To define the best predecessor for every column solution, we must define a metric to evaluate predecessors. Let $v_{h,k}$ represent the k-th column solution of $\hat{c}_h$. Let $v_{h',k'}$ represent the k'-th column solution of $\hat{c}_{h'}$, the previous column left to $\hat{c}_h$; i.e., there is no column between $\hat{c}_h$ and $\hat{c}_{h'}$. Without loss of generality, there is an edge e' connected to $v_{h,k}$ and $v_{h',k'}$ in G_c.

Given the edge e', we can calculate the wire cost and the conflict cost associated with $v_{h,k}$ and $v_{h',k'}$. The wire costs can be calculated by $t_{h,k}$, $s_{h,k}$, and $t_{h',k'}$. $t_{h,k}$ and $t_{h',k'}$ determine if there are cuts placed in $\hat{c}_h$ and $\hat{c}_{h'}$. And $s_{h,k}$ can be used to determine if the placed cuts are left/right cuts. We first initialize the edge wire cost (e_w) as zero, and perform the following operation for e': (1) if the left cut of a gap $g_i = (y_i, b_i^l, b_i^r)$ is placed in $\hat{c}_h$, the edge wire cost is increased by $h - b_i^l$; (2) if the right cut of a gap $g_i = (y_i, b_i^l, b_i^r)$ is placed in $\hat{c}_{h'}$, the edge wire cost is increased by $b_i^r - h$.

For the conflict costs, we first calculate the number of conflicts (positive conflict cost) with their right endpoints in $\hat{c}_h$. This calculation can be done with $t_{h,k}$, $t_{h',k'}$, $d_{h,k}$, and $d_{h',k'}$. Note that $t_{h,k}$ defines the placement of cuts in $\hat{c}_h$. Moreover, $t_{h',k'}$, $d_{h,k}$, and $d_{h',k'}$ define the placement of all cuts left to $\hat{c}_h$ such that these cuts may violate the spacing rule with cuts in $\hat{c}_h$ due to the definition of distribution specifiers. However, distribution specifiers do not include the information of templates, which may resolve the conflicts. Therefore, the number of conflicts (negative conflict cost) that can be resolved by $t_{h',k'}$ is calculated. Finally, we calculate the conflict cost (e_c) of edge e' by the positive conflict cost minus the negative conflict cost.

For a path in G_c, its wire cost (conflict cost) is equal to the sum of edge wire costs (edge conflict costs) over all edges in this path. The reasons are illustrated as follows. For the wire cost case, every line-end extension cost is calculated in exactly one edge. For the conflict cost case, the conflicts of positive (negative) conflict costs are calculated in the column solutions in which their right (left) endpoints are. Therefore, the total wire (conflict) cost $w(v_{h,k})$ ($c(v_{h,k})$) of $v_{h,k}$ in V_c is defined as the wire (conflict) cost of the optimal path among all paths with $v_{h,k}$ being the rightmost vertex. To calculate $w(v_{h,k})$ ($c(v_{h,k})$) of $v_{h,k}$, we calculate $d_w(e') = w(v_{h',k'}) + e_w(e')$ ($d_c(e') = c(v_{h',k'}) + e_c(e')$) for each e' and select the edge with the best (d_c, d_w) pair in the view of ordered optimization. Note that $w(v_{h,k})$ and $c(v_{h,k})$ are set to be very large numbers if no predecessor is found. Because the wire cost (conflict cost) of a path is equal to the sum of edge wire costs (edge conflict costs) over all edges in this path, the subpath of an optimal path must be also optimal. Therefore, such method for the best predecessor determination is optimal:

THEOREM 2. *Our algorithm for the special case is optimal.*

Note that there is no calculation of right-end wire extension costs and positive conflict costs when we traverse to the leftmost column because there is no predecessor of the leftmost column. The total wire (conflict) costs of vertices in the left column are derived by left-end wire extension costs and negative conflict costs.

4.4 Template Distribution Derivation

Given a path derived by the best predecessor determination, we construct the corresponding template distribution from the leftmost column to the rightmost one. When traversing to a column solution $v_{h,k}$ in the path, if there exists a 2-D position occupied by a cut in the template specifier $t_{h,k}$ of $v_{h,k}$, we check if there exists a cut at the 2-D position. If there is no cut at this 2-D position, we construct new templates by $t_{h,k}$. Every newly derived template t, with its $l_t = h$, consists of a maximal set of cuts specified to be in a same template in $t_{h,k}$. For example, the two dashed templates in Fig. 10 are derived if we construct new templates by the template specifier in Fig. 10. After t is constructed, we pattern all the cuts in t at corresponding positions, implying that the columns crossed by t would be placed with a cut. Note that we can determine if a cut placed in column $\hat{c}$ is the left/right cut in a gap by the cut specifiers of the current column solutions in $\hat{c}$ and the column next to $\hat{c}$.

4.5 Time Complexity

We already illustrate the optimality in Subsection 4.3. In the following, we analyze the time complexity of our algorithm. Because the number of generated columns is in the order $O(n)$ for a fixed design rule and a fixed template library, we check the number of column solutions in a column. Moreover, the number of column solutions in a column is bounded by a constant for a fixed design rule, a fixed template library, because the number of rows in the subproblem is bounded by r_M.

THEOREM 3. *Our algorithm for the special case runs in $O(n)$ time, where n is the number of gaps in the subproblem.*

5. SUBPROBLEM CANDIDATE SELECTION

This section details subproblem candidate selection for solving general layouts. Let r_L be the number of rows in a layout. To deal with general layouts, we divide a layout into $\lceil \frac{r_L}{r_M} \rceil$ regions for conflict cost calculation. Except for the last region, each region has r_M contiguous rows. Fig. 11(a) shows an example of regions. Note that the bottom red box is the region containing only the bottom row, and there is no row below the bottom row. The red boxes in Fig. 11(a) denote the regions for the layout. Every conflict occurs either within a single region or between two adjacent regions.

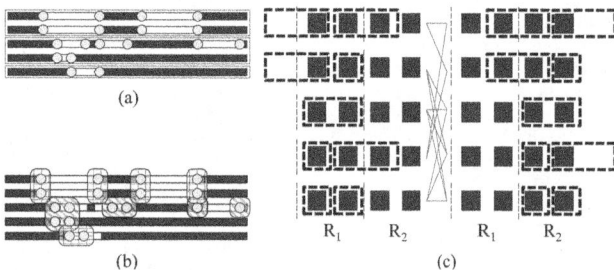

Figure 11: $r_M = 2$ in these examples. (a) Regions(red boxes) of a layout. (b) A template distribution constructed by the selected region solutions. (c) An example of region solutions of region R_1 and region R_2. The blue boxes represent rows in R_1 and R_2. The dashed boxes represent subproblem candidates. A red edge between two region solutions denotes that a feasible template distribution can be generated from the two solutions.

To select subproblem candidates, we define a region solution S_R of a region R as follows: (1) S_R is a set of subproblem candidates; (2) every subproblem candidate of S_R contains at least one row in R; (3) every row in R is contained in exactly one subproblem candidate of S_R.

Fig. 11(c) illustrates an example of region solutions. The dashed boxes represent subproblem candidates, and the blue boxes represent rows. All the five region solutions for region R_1 (R_2) are in the left (right) side of Fig. 11(c). For example, we can see that every region solution of region R_1 could cover all rows in R_1 (the blue boxes in R_1).

Then we define a graph $G_R(V_R, E_R)$ for region solutions of a layout. Each vertex v_i^R in V_R represents a region solution of the target layout. For every two vertices v_1^R and v_2^R in V_R, (v_1^R, v_2^R) is in E_R if the region solutions S_{R1} (represented by v_1^R) and S_{R2} (represented by v_2^R) satisfy the following conditions: (1) let R_1 be the region to which S_{R1} belongs, and R_2 the region to which S_{R2} belongs. The bottom row of R_1 is above the top row of R_2, and there is no other row between R_1 and R_2; (2) if there is any subproblem candidate in S_{R1} or S_{R2} with at least one row in each of R_1 and R_2, this subproblem candidate should be in both S_{R1} and S_{R2}. We use the notion of a vertex in V_R or a region solution interchangeably in the rest of this paper. Fig. 11(c) shows an example of edges between region solutions. Note that there is no edge between the top region solution of R_1 and the bottom region solution of R_2 in Fig. 11(c). The reason is that there is a subproblem candidate containing a row in R_1 and a row in R_2 in the top region solution of R_1, while there is no such a subproblem candidate in the bottom region solution of R_2.

To select subproblem candidates, we first construct region solutions for every region. Then we construct the region solution graph. We also determine the best predecessor of every region solution in order to construct a region solution path on G_R such that there is a region solution selected to this path in every region. Because the definition of G_R, the subproblem candidates associated with this path is a partition of the target layout into subproblems. Therefore, we can construct a good template distribution as mentioned in Section 3. The best predecessor determination is similar to that in Section 4, with the only difference in its cost evaluation.

5.1 Cost Evaluation

For the evaluation of the wire cost of an edge (v_1^R, v_2^R) in E_R, the wire cost of (v_1^R, v_2^R) is the sum of wire costs of the subproblem candidates in v_2^R and not in v_1^R. (The wire cost of a subproblem candidate is the wire cost of the template distribution derived by the algorithm in Section 4 for the subproblem candidate.) The conflict cost of an edge (v_1^R, v_2^R) is the sum of conflict costs of the derived template distributions of the subproblem candidates in v_2^R and not in v_1^R plus the number of conflicts between any two subproblem candidates (one of the two candidates is in v_2^R and not in v_1^R). Note that there is no conflict between templates patterned by different masks. For a region solution v_1^R in the top region (no predecessor), we check the template distribution D with its templates derived from the subproblem candidates of v_1^R. The total wire (conflict) cost of v_1^R is the wire (conflict) cost of D. For double patterning, we can easily determine if two subproblem candidates are patterned by a same mask by checking the number of subproblem candidates between them in a layout.

5.2 Quality and Efficiency

Under the layout-partition scheme in Section 3, the subproblem candidate selection procedure can find the best partition among the partitions conforming to this scheme. The reason is that every conflict occurs either within a single region or between adjacent regions and thus the evaluation of costs in Subsection 5.1 can consider all possible conflicts.

For running time, the sum of $m(g_i)$'s, mentioned in Subsection 4.1, over gaps in the layout is linear to the number of gaps in the layout with a fixed design rule and a fixed template library. Moreover, the number of region solutions in a region is bounded by a constant with a fixed design rule because r_M is bounded. In addition, for every gap g_i in a layout, the number of subproblem candidates including g_i is bounded by a constant with similar reasons. Therefore, the running time grows linearly to the number of gaps in a layout.

6. EXTENSION

To further reduce the wire costs, we propose a framework to utilize DPDSA-Core. Fig. 12 shows the framework. The basic idea is to relax the constraint of DPDSA-Core (cuts in a same row share the same color) by clustering cuts into multiple sets (components) in a bottom-up framework.

First, we construct a cut graph G, where each vertex represents a cut and two vertices form an edge if the corresponding two cuts are too close (violation of the spacing rule) to their initial positions. Then we define *connected components* for our framework. An undirected graph is called *connected* if for every pair of nodes u and v, there is a path between u and v. The connected components of an undirected graph are its maximal connected subgraphs. We derive connected components of G by depth first search (DFS). A connected component is *conflicting* if there exists a currently derived conflict with at least an endpoint in the connected component. Initially, we group every cut by a 1-cut template.

Two cuts might not violate the spacing rule if they are not in the same connected component. Therefore, for each conflicting connected component, we then apply DPDSA-Core on it independently. After performing DPDSA-Core, we reassign the colors of derived templates to solve conflicts, where DFS is applied for double patterning. After the double patterning processing, we determine if the currently derived template distribution satisfies the termination condition. If there is no conflict in the current template distribution, the template distribution is the final solution; otherwise, we check if the wire and conflict costs converge, and terminate the program if they converge or the number of components decreases to one. If the termination condition is not satisfied, we enter the conflicting component selection and merging stage to select and merge new conflicting components and then proceed with the next iteration.

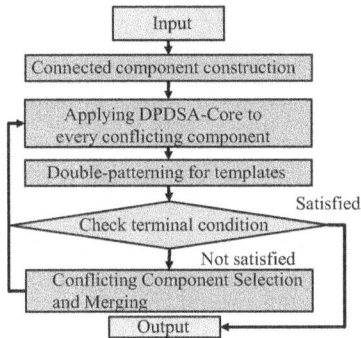

Figure 12: The extended framework.

The conflicting component selection and merging stage has two phases: the phase with only component selection and the other phase with component selection and merging.

In the first phase, every component with at least one conflict will be selected as an input to DPDSA-Core in the next iteration. The reason is that the double-patterning stage may introduce new conflicts when the template distributions of some components are changed after performing DPDSA-Core. Moreover, we try to resolve conflicts while keeping wire costs small by not merging components in this phase. However, if the selected components are the same as those in the previous iteration, it enters the second phase in the following iterations.

In the second phase, if there is no conflict within a single component, two components are merged if and only if there is a conflict crossing the two components. In addition, two components are also merged in the following situation: (1) there is a conflict within one of the two components, and (2) there is a cut-pair with one cut in one of the two components and the other cut in the other component such that the current positions of the two cuts violate the spacing rule; i.e. the double-patterning effect is ignored. The reason is illustrated as follows. When there is a conflict within a single component which has been applied DPDSA-Core more than once, it shows that there may exist an another component with cuts close to it disturbing the coloring during the double patterning stage.

To merge components in G, we introduce a graph G_p for current components in G. Every vertex in G_p represents a component in G. Two vertices in G_p form an edge if the two components are required to be merged during conflicting component selection and merging. We run DFS on G_p to get the connected components in G_p. Then for every connected component P in G_p, a new component of G will be derived by collecting the vertices in P.

Due to the fixed spacing, the time complexity of DFS is linear to the number of gaps. The reason is that the DFS-traversed edges are based on cut conflicts, and the number of conflicts is bounded with the fixed spacing as mentioned in Subsection 4.1.

7. EXPERIMENTAL RESULTS

Our algorithm was implemented in the C++ programming language on a 2.13 GHz Linux workstation with 16 GB memory. We applied the LEDA package [11] for our algorithm implementation. We compared our algorithm with the state-of-the-art works [13, 14, 19] based on a set of benchmarks provided by the authors of [19]. (Nevertheless, we were told that our benchmarks are slightly different from those used in [19] because the original data were lost.) For scalability test, we further randomly generated a set of benchmarks with 5000 to 100000 cuts. Because the binaries used in [14, 19] are not available to us, we carefully implemented their algorithms by ourselves, which is the best we can do. We refer to the implementation of the ILP algorithm and its speedup heuristic of the work [14], which were published in SPIE'15, as S15 and S15sp, respectively, that of the set-cover-based heuristic [14] as SC, and that of the work in [19], which was published in SPIE'13, as S13. Note that [14] is the journal version of [13].

We used CPLEX [9] to solve ILP. In our experiments, we adopted an ordered optimization of the conflict cost first and then the wire one. (Note that our algorithm can readily extend for optimizing the combined cost of conflicts and wires.)

Based on the information provided by the authors of [12], we set the metal pitch to be 32nm, the wire width 16nm, the spacing of a tip-tip metal cut 50nm, and the width/height of a cut 16nm,

which is intended for sub-7nm technology [15]. Consequently, the minimum spacing of the design rule for cut conflict in our experiments is 2.0625 grids away, resulting in $r_M = 2$.

Because the works [13, 14, 19] for DSA-template guided cut redistribution do not consider double patterning, we implemented the method in [2], a general high-level framework for DSA-multiple patterning hybrid lithography, which consists of the two stages GP-MP and MP-GP; GP-MP groups cuts into templates first and then assigns templates to different masks, while MP-GP assigns cuts to different masks first and then groups cuts in a same mask into templates. Nevertheless, the methods used for grouping cuts and multiple patterning are not mentioned in [2]. In this paper, S13, S15, S15sp, and SC were adopted in the GP stage for DSA cut redistribution, while depth-first search (DFS) was adopted in the MP stage for double patterning. We denote the GP-MP (MP-GP) binary as GM (MG).

Table 1: Comparison of the conflict cost under $r_M = 2$.
- : Running time $\geq$ 3 hours.

Number of cuts	Initial conflicts	GM				MG				Ours
		S13	S15sp	S15	SC	S13	S15sp	S15	SC	
50	12	0	0	0	0	0	0	0	1	0
100	46	0	0	0	0	0	1	0	0	0
200	83	0	0	0	0	3	0	0	4	0
500	223	0	0	-	0	4	0	0	5	0
1000	421	2	0	-	1	7	3	0	8	0
2000	855	0	0	-	2	17	2	0	11	0
5000	4025	33	4	-	48	156	41	-	124	0
10000	8476	63	1	-	116	343	112	-	270	0
20000	16852	117	14	-	196	684	211	-	544	0
50000	42496	337	27	-	513	1696	579	-	1400	0
100000	84553	632	93	-	1061	3425	1108	-	2789	0

Table 2: Comparison of the wire cost under $r_M = 2$. - : Running time $\geq$ 3 hours.

Number of cuts	GM				MG				Ours
	S13	S15sp	S15	SC	S13	S15sp	S15	SC	
50	48	8	6	3	13	1	1	0	1
100	109	29	24	30	48	5	2	6	6
200	272	58	48	63	150	27	11	23	10
500	665	153	-	166	235	33	14	29	27
1000	1466	307	-	289	542	48	32	45	49
2000	2647	593	-	576	1055	89	65	76	96
5000	7045	2669	-	2402	2304	666	-	611	687
10000	14690	5381	-	5159	5003	1405	-	1264	1464
20000	28485	10974	-	9964	10075	2864	-	2503	2924
50000	72730	27455	-	25612	24641	7173	-	6355	7330
100000	146060	55279	-	51629	49374	14473	-	12727	14691

Table 3: Comparison of running times (second) under $r_M = 2$. - : Running time $\geq$ 3 hours.

Number of cuts	GM				MG				Ours
	S13	S15sp	S15	SC	S13	S15sp	S15	SC	
50	0.01	0.09	0.22	0.01	0.01	0.08	0.04	0.01	0.01
100	0.02	0.45	9.78	0.03	0.02	0.16	0.07	0.03	0.02
200	0.04	0.53	609	0.09	0.04	0.33	0.45	0.07	0.03
500	0.12	1.95	-	0.34	0.12	0.84	1.06	0.20	0.08
1000	0.31	3.33	-	1.22	0.32	1.84	6.12	0.64	0.15
2000	0.91	7.99	-	4.38	0.92	4.49	55.1	2.45	0.30
5000	4.61	125	-	28.3	4.83	17.6	-	16.4	1.52
10000	16.4	342	-	117	17.9	55.2	-	69.9	1.47
20000	63.9	977	-	448	66.7	239	-	283	3.01
50000	397	2570	-	2800	413	1420	-	1800	8.19
100000	1580	7470	-	11600	1590	6370	-	7100	16.6

Tables 1, 2, and 3 show the comparisons of the conflict and wire costs and the running times based on the design rule. Note that the speedup heuristics in [14] sacrifice significant solution quality to improve their efficiency. The work [14] divides a layout into multiple groups and applies ILP for each group without considering the interferences from other groups during ILP solving. The problem size of solving a single ILP is reduced, and thus its efficiency is better. However, the post-processing stage, which resolves conflicts by merging templates, of the speedup heuristics cannot resolve all remaining conflicts well, resulting in either large conflicts or large wire costs in large benchmarks. In Table 1, we can reduce the number of conflict edges to zero for every benchmark, while most of the other works still incur non-zero conflicts under $r_M = 2$. Although the pure ILP methods (S15-GM and S15-MG) can achieve zero conflicts, their scalability is much worse than other methods. In addition to double pattering, the optimality property of our algorithm described in Section 4 also helps to resolve the conflicts well. For S13 and SC, they group cuts into templates first and then place and merge templates for the derived templates. However, the information about the conflict costs during template-grouping stages is not accurate, thus introducing either a significant number of conflicts (SC) or a large wire cost (S13). The main difference is that we can easily apply ordered optimization on S13, but not on SC. SC calculates a single weight (the estimated wire cost divided by the reduced number of uncut line-ends) for each template to select templates, thus incurring significant conflict costs in large benchmarks.

Table 2 shows the comparison of wire costs. For wire costs, our algorithm can achieve zero-conflict solutions with significantly smaller wire costs (more than 3X smaller) than S15sp-GM. In addition to the nice optimality property of the algorithm shown in Section 4, another reason is that the partitioning method introduced in Section 5 can select subproblem candidates with a small wire cost increase at a given conflict cost. Furthermore, the framework in Section 6 can further reduce wire costs, while S15sp-GM and S15-GM spend too much effort in solving conflicts due to ignoring the double-patterning effect at first. Note that for those with the same numbers of conflicts, our wire costs are consistently smaller than those of the previous works, say comparing with S15sp-MG. For S15sp-MG, it does not consider DSA-grouping information during multiple patterning. As a result, S15sp-MG might not resolve all conflicts in its post-processing stage. For S13 and SC, they perturb the locations of derived templates to solve conflicts; consequently, their final wire costs might differ significantly from their estimation during template-grouping stages, incurring large wire costs with the inaccurate estimation.

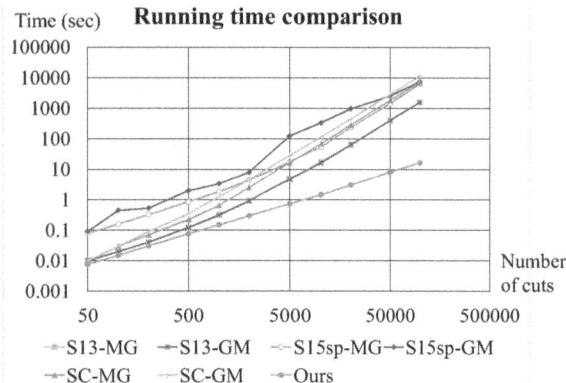

Figure 13: Comparison of running times in the log scale.

From Table 3, our algorithm is much more efficient than others. In Fig. 13, the running time of each work is plotted as a function of the number of cuts, except the two pure ILP works, S15-GM and S15-MG, which have prohibitively large running times. Applying regression analysis to evaluate the empirical time complexity of each work, we can find that our running time approaches to $0.0001x^{1.0073}$, where x is the number of cuts. In contrast, other works resulted in the exponents between 1.4 and 1.8. So the empirical time complexity of our algorithm is approximately linear, while the others are all superlinear. The difference is mainly due to the effectiveness and the efficiency of our DPDSA-Core, and thus the empirical number of loops of the framework in Section 6 is less than 5 to achieve zero conflicts for every benchmark, which also justifies our earlier theoretical analysis for the linear-time complexity for the special case presented in Section 4 and the linear-time complexity to partition a layout into multiple subproblem candidates presented in Section 5. For SC, its running time grows superlinearly because it enumerates all possible templates first and then re-calculates the weight of every remaining template when a template is selected to construct template distribution. For S13, the detailed placement stage in S13 iteratively perturbs modules until the result converges, which is time-consuming.

8. CONCLUSIONS

This paper has proposed a scheme incorporating DSA with double pattering for the template guided cut redistribution problem. A linear-time optimal algorithm is first proposed for a special case of the template guided cut redistribution problem with contiguous rows. Then a linear-time double-patterning aware partitioning method is proposed to select a set of subproblem candidates conforming to the special case to construct a low-cost template distribution for a general problem. Moreover, our algorithm can achieve a provably good performance bound, with the total wire cost of a template distribution only linear to the number of cuts. Experimental results have shown that our algorithm can resolve all spacing rule violations, with even smaller wire costs and running times, compared with the state-of-the-art works on a set of common benchmarks.

9. REFERENCES

[1] Y. Badr, J. A. Torres, and P. Gupta, "Mask assignment and synthesis of DSA-MP hybrid lithography for sub-7nm contacts/vias," in *Proc. ACM/IEEE Design Automation Conf.*, 2015

[2] Y. Badr, J. A. Torres, Y.-S. Ma, J. Mitra, and P. Gupta, "Incorporating DSA in multipatterning semiconductor manufacturing technologies," in *Proc. of SPIE*, Vol. 9427, pp. 94270P, 2015.

[3] Y. Borodovsky, "Complementary lithography at insertion and beyond," in *Proc. of Semicon West*, 2012.

[4] Y.-W. Chang, R.G. Liu, and S.-Y. Fang, "EUV and e-beam manufacturability: challenges and solutions," in *Proc. of ACM/IEEE Design Automation Conf.*, 2015.

[5] Y. Ding, C. Chu, and W.-K. Mak, "Throughput optimization for SADP and e-beam based manufacturing of 1D layout," in *Proc. of ACM/IEEE Design Automation Conf.*, 2014.

[6] Y. Du, H. Zhang, M. D. F. Wong, and K.-Y. Chao, "Hybrid lithography optimization with e-beam and immersion processes for 16nm 1D gridded design," in *Proc. of Asia and South Pacific Design Automation Conf.*, pp. 775–780, 2012.

[7] Y. Du, D. Guo, M. D. F. Wong, H. Yi, H.-S. Philip Wong, H. Zhang, and Q. Ma, "Block copolymer directed self-assembly (DSA) aware contact layer optimization for 10 nm 1D standard cell library," in *Proc. of IEEE/ACM International Conf. on Computer-Aided Design*, 2013.

[8] J.-M. Ho, D. T. Lee, C.-H. Chang, and C. K. Wong, "Minimum diameter spanning trees and related problems," *SIAM J. Computing*, Vol. 20, No. 5, pp. 987–997, 1991.

[9] IBM ILOG CPLEX Optimizer. http://www-01.ibm.com/software/integration/optimization/cplex-optimizer/

[10] D. K. Lam, E. D. Liu, M. C. Smayling and T. Prescop, "E-beam to complement optical lithography for 1D layouts," in *Proc. of SPIE*, Vol. 7970, pp. 797011, 2011.

[11] The LEDA package. http://www.algorithmic-solutions.com/leda

[12] Y. Ma, J. A. Torres, G. Fenger, Y. Granik, J. Ryckaert, G. Vanderberghe, J. Bekaert, and J. Word, "Challenges and opportunities in applying grapho-epitaxy DSA lithography to metal cut and contact/via applications," in *Proc. of SPIE*, Vol. 9231, pp. 92310T, 2014.

[13] J. Ou, B. Yu, J.-R. Gao, M. Preil, A. Latypov, and D. Z. Pan, "Directed self-assembly based cut mask optimization for unidirectional design," in *Proc. of Great Lakes Symposium on VLSI.*, pp. 83–86, 2015.

[14] J. Ou, B. Yu, and D. Z. Pan, "Directed self-assembly cut mask assignment for unidirectional design," in *J. Micro/Nanolith. MEMS MOEMS.*, Vol. 14(3), 2015.

[15] J. A. Torres, Personal communication, 2015.

[16] M. C. Smayling, H. Y. Liu, and L. Cai, "Low k1 logic design using gridded design rules," in *Proc. of SPIE*, Vol. 6925, pp. 69250B, 2008.

[17] M. C. Smayling, "1D design style implications for mask making and CEBL," in *Proc. of SPIE*, Vol. 8880, pp. 888012, 2013.

[18] H.-S. Philip Wong, C. Bencher, H. Yi, X.-Y. Bao, and L.-W Chang, "Block copolymer directed self-assembly enables sublithographic patterning for device fabrication," in *Proc. of SPIE*, Vol. 8323, pp. 832303, 2012.

[19] Z. Xiao, Y. Du, M. D. F. Wong, and H. Zhang, "DSA template mask determination and cut redistribution for advanced 1D gridded design," in *Proc. of SPIE*, Vol. 8880, pp. 888017, 2013.

Technology Inflection Points

Victor Moroz

Synopsys, Inc.

victorm@synopsys.com

ABSTRACT

Transistor design is becoming exciting again. FinFETs will take us to 7nm technology node. Beyond that, we tailor semiconductor bandstructure to optimize transistor behavior. Quantum transport analysis of transistors scaled from 10nm to 2nm design rules shows that the last node where materials with high mobility like Ge and III-V can be used is the 7nm node. At 5nm design rules and beyond, the high mobility materials exhibit unacceptable direct source-to-drain leakage and therefore become uncompetitive to silicon. Even silicon will require a careful choice of crystal orientation or a stress engineering to slow down the electrons and holes. In terms of transistor architecture, at 5nm, either a switch to nanowires or SiGe channel cladding can be used to extend the FinFET lifespan. One other key point is that Design-Technology Co-Optimization (DTCO) suggests that perfecting a single transistor is not enough to get a good Power-Performance-Area (PPA) trade-off. We employ standard library cells as a vehicle for benchmarking transistor and interconnect architectures. At 5nm design rules, several new trade-off choices come into play and enable further gains in terms of the PPA optimization.

Keywords

DTCO, PPA, TCAD, 5nm, 3nm, 2nm, transistor, MOL, material engineering, Si, Ge, III-V, InGaAs, InGaSb

SHORT BIO

Victor Moroz grew up as a hunter-gatherer in Siberia and received M.S. degree in Electrical Engineering from Novosibirsk Technical University and Ph.D. degree in Applied Physics from the University of Nizhny Novgorod. After engaging in technology development at several semiconductor manufacturing companies and teaching semiconductor physics at the University of Nizhny Novgorod, Dr. Moroz joined a Stanford spin-off Technology Modeling Associates in 1995. After IPO in 1997, the TMA TCAD team became part of Avanti in 1998, and in 2002 it became a key part of Synopsys, connecting a synthesis company to the manufacturing.

Currently Dr. Moroz is a Synopsys Scientist, engaged in a variety of projects on modeling FinFETs, gate-all-around nano-wires, stress engineering, 3D ICs, transistor scaling, Middle-Of-Line and Back-End-Of-Line RC, solar cell design, innovative patterning, random and systematic variability, junction leakage, non-Si transistors, and atomistic effects in layer growth and doping.

Several facets of this activity are reflected in three book chapters and over 100 technical papers and invited presentations. There are 65 granted patents, including fundamental FinFET manufacturing patents, and 37 pending US patents.

ISPD'16, April 3–6, 2016, Santa Rosa, California, USA.
ACM 978-1-4503-4039-7/16/04.
DOI: http://dx.doi.org/10.1145/2872334.2872337

Challenges and Opportunities with Place and Route of Modern FPGA Designs

Raymond Nijssen

Achronix Semiconductor Corp
2953 Bunker Hill Lane, Santa Clara, CA 95054, USA
raymond@achronix.com

ABSTRACT

In the last decade place and route algorithms used for large high performance FPGA designs have been successfully adapted from those used in ASIC design flows. All major FPGA tool sets now use advanced analytical global placement algorithms with sophisticated cell clustering. Thanks to this, fast runtimes and predictable performance on designs with millions of placeable objects empower designers to quickly and often evaluate their decisions. Fast design flow turnaround times and predictability are of tremendous value to help designers improve timing closure problems in their designs, and accommodate them to floorplanning constraints and congestion bottlenecks.

Although many P&R related aspects are common between ASIC and FPGA technologies, many are unique to FPGAs. For example, the many tight, rigid constraints, as well as aggressive runtime requirements and the heterogeneity of the problems. As these unique challenges have received relatively little coverage in literature this presentation focuses on the entailing opportunities.

In particular, unlike ASICs in which different types of cell instances can be moved between and within rows freely, FPGAs have discrete, fixed heterogeneous resource locations onto which the user design must be fitted: a flip-flop instance in the user netlist can only be placed onto a flip-flop site of the FPGA fabric. Carry chains in FPGA fabrics are very fast, but run only vertically, typically only in one direction. And the routing fabric of an FPGA must impose countless routing restrictions, like one-way routing and input sharing, without which the size of the chip would become prohibitively large.

These essential restrictions must be well understood and taken into account in algorithms targeting FPGAs. In its first part, this presentation will cover several examples of such aspects and will suggest approaches.

The second part covers incremental compilation, various forms of parallel processing are other must-have features for a competitive FPGA P&R flow. Such techniques present

challenges that demand a more algorithmical approach to take these to the next level.

Third, modern FPGAs have evolved far from the original textbook LUT-flop logic building blocks. They feature a hybrid between much more complex logic blocks and a rich variety of ASIC blocks implementing various commonly used IP like PCIe controllers, feature-rich IOs and dedicated function blocks in the FPGA core. FPGA P&R flows offering a more seamless integration between these environments must also automate the process of configuring such diverse components and all the connections related to it.

Finally, next generations of FPGAs and their EDA systems are facing peripheral interfaces whose bandwidths increase very rapidly while the processing logic's propagation delays are not expected to reduce significantly in upcoming fabrication technology nodes. Several existing and new techniques to deal with this widening discrepancy will need to be applied more aggressively, calling for new features in FPGA P&R algorithms in the near future.

AUTHOR BIOGRAPHY

Raymond Nijssen is VP of Systems Engineering at Achronix Semiconductor in Santa Clara. His responsibilities include deployment of complex IP and integration of programmable cores in customer environments. He joined Achronix in 2006 as its Chief Software Architect in charge of the creation from scratch of Achronix's EDA system to implement user designs with Achronix's unique very high performance FPGAs based on asynchronous technologies.

He has architected many key parts of the programmable cores and hardware-software integration of a later generation of products in which Achronix pioneered and productized the world's first hybrid FPGA combining a large programmable FPGA core with several large ASIC IP blocks.

Prior to Achronix he was with Tabula where his responsibilities included placement and timing analysis of a novel time-multiplexed FPGA technology.

In 1997 he joined Magma Design Automation where he covered a wide variety of areas in EDA ranging from detailed routing and placement to data models. He was in charge from conception to successful customer deployment of Magma's Blast Plan Pro hierarchical virtual prototyping and floorplanning products for very large ASIC designs.

He received his MSEE from Eindhoven University of Technology in The Netherlands, and became a postgraduate student at the same university to study electronic design automation. He holds several patents related to P&R and asynchronous circuit technologies.

ISPD'16 April 03-06, 2016, Santa Rosa, CA, USA

© 2016 Copyright held by the owner/author(s).

ACM ISBN 978-1-4503-4039-7/16/04.

DOI: http://dx.doi.org/10.1145/2872334.2872336

Challenges and Opportunities with Place and Route of Modern FPGA Designs

Devanand Nijssen
Semiconductor Corp.
Santa Clara, CA 95054, USA

Design and Tool Flow of IBM's TrueNorth:
An Ultra-Low Power Programmable Neurosynaptic Chip with 1 Million Neurons

Filipp A. Akopyan
IBM

Abstract

Developing scalable real-time systems that can simultaneously process massive amounts of noisy multi-sensory data, while being energy efficient, is a dominant challenge in the new era of cognitive computing. Low-power, flexible neurosynaptic architectures offer tremendous promise in this area. To this end, we developed TrueNorth, a 65mW brain-inspired processor that implements a non-von Neumann, parallel, distributed, event-driven, modular, scalable, defect-tolerant architecture. With 4096 neurosynaptic cores, the TrueNorth chip contains 1 million digital neurons and 256 million synapses tightly interconnected by an event-driven routing infrastructure. The fully digital 5.4 billion transistor implementation leverages existing CMOS scaling trends, while ensuring one-to-one correspondence between hardware and software.

Given that the TrueNorth architecture breaks path with prevailing architectures, conventional tool flows could not be used for the design. Therefore, we developed a novel design methodology that includes mixed asynchronous-synchronous circuits, interfaces, and a complete tool flow for building an event-driven, low-power neurosynaptic chip. Further, we have adapted existing VLSI CAD placement tools for mapping logical neural networks to the physical core locations on the TrueNorth chip to reduce the network's communication energy.

The TrueNorth chip's low power consumption is ideal for use not only in large-scale computationally intensive applications, but also for embedded battery-powered mobile applications. The chip is fully configurable in terms of connectivity and neural parameters to allow custom configurations for a wide range of cognitive and sensory perception applications. We have successfully demonstrated the use of TrueNorth chips in multiple applications, including visual object recognition, with higher performance and orders of magnitude lower power than the same algorithms run on von Neumann architectures.

ISPD'16, April 3–6, 2016, Santa Rosa, California, USA.
ACM 978-1-4503-4039-7/16/04.
DOI: http://dx.doi.org/10.1145/2872334.2878629

CCS Concepts

- **Computing methodologies - Computer vision**
- **Computer systems organization - Real-time systems**
- **Hardware - Asynchronous circuits**
- **Hardware - Application-specific VLSI designs**
- **Hardware - Methodologies for EDA**
- **Hardware - Emerging architectures**
- **Hardware - Neural systems**

Keywords

Asynchronous circuits, asynchronous communication, design automation, design methodology, image recognition, logic design, low-power electronics, neural networks, neural network hardware, neuromorphics, parallel architectures, real-time systems, synchronous circuits, very large-scale integration, custom tool flow.

Short Bio

Dr. Filipp Akopyan was born in Moscow, Russia, where he grew up and completed middle school. He became a permanent resident of the United States in 1995 and attended high school at Spring Valley, NY. He joined Rensselaer Polytechnic Institute (in Troy, NY) in September of 2001 and graduated with a Bachelor's Degree in Electrical Engineering in May of 2004. Filipp was ranked number 1 in the School of Engineering. His concentrations at RPI included electronic circuit design and signal processing.

Filipp began a joint M.S. / Ph.D. program at Cornell University in September of 2004. At Cornell, he excelled at the Asynchronous VLSI (AVLSI) research group led by Professor Rajit Manohar. Filipp has authored several highly cited publications (over 600 total citations[1]) in the areas of asynchronous design, signal processing, neuromorphic computing and low-power chip design. Filipp is a recipient of numerous awards and honors in the fields of electrical and computer engineering.

After receiving his Ph.D. in Electrical and Computer Engineering (with a minor in Applied Mathematics) from Cornell University in 2011, Dr. Akopyan joined the IBM Brain-Inspired Computing Group led by Dharmendra Modha. During his IBM tenure, Filipp was one of the lead engineers, who created the world's most advance neuromorphic chip, TrueNorth, as part of the DARPA SyNAPSE program funded by DSO; and he is a key contributor on the DARPA Cortical Processor program funded by MTO. One of Filipp's main contributions was leading the complex task of designing, simulating and verifying mixed Synchronous-Asynchronous circuits to implement the TrueNorth chip correctly and efficiently.

This novel methodology has a potential of revolutionizing future state-of-the-art designs by making them extremely flexible and energy efficient. At IBM Filipp has also been designing low-power cognitive systems and advancing neural algorithm development for various multi-sensory applications.

Filipp's main interests are in high-speed VLSI circuits (including 3-D integrated circuits and neuromorphic systems) that operate under extreme conditions and withstand process variations. He is also developing novel algorithms and low-power asynchronous systems for signal-processing and neural networks.

[1] **Google Scholar:**
http://scholar.google.com/citations?user=XkNtWmUAAAAJ&hl=en

Some Observations on the Physical Design of the Next Decade

Dr. Antun Domic

Synopsys, Inc.

Abstract

While physical design continues to fight the traditional data capacity and runtime challenges, it has also become critically important to overcome many drawbacks of the silicon technology roadmap.

At the emerging technology nodes, namely 10, 7 and 5 nanometers, sheer complexity hits unprecedented levels. Integration capacity in terms of number of transistors already exceeds 100 billion of transistors per die, with 1 trillion within our reach. Standard-cell complex abutment and multi-VTH design rules pose new placement challenge. Non-planar transistors get smaller and taller, but contacted metal pitch doesn't scale accordingly, thus making pins accessibility harder and introducing new routing congestion issues. Lithography transition to EUV is still unclear, which translates into triple, quadruple, and even octuple patterning cannot be ruled out. Interconnect RC delay not only has by far the lion's share of total delay, but its variation across the stack has reached over one order of magnitude between the lowest (Mx) and the highest (Mz) layers, while the R contribution of vias increases dramatically. Finally, the modelling, characterization, and computing of near-threshold – ultra-low voltage – design effects and their impact on timing and power bring design closure up to a much higher level of complexity.

At the established technology nodes, unlike in the past, the oldest nodes are not discontinued. On the contrary, not only the number of active technology nodes in volume production is increasing, but more than 90% of designs in 2016 will be at 45/40 nanometers and above, accounting for more than 60% of wafer production by area. However, today 180 nm designs are radically different from their late 1990s distant relatives. Physical design is increasingly being relied upon to achieve lower area and power, as well as to reduce the required silicon resources in the interest of a better performance and power envelope at a lower cost. Sophisticated physical design methodologies, originally devised for survival at the emerging technology nodes, are more and more frequently used to improve the metrics of the established technology nodes, and to extend their useful lifespan for a very long time.

Production volumes dictate which applications rush to the newest emerging technology nodes and which ones continue to hold at the established nodes. However, it is increasingly difficult to integrate digital computing with analog interfaces, to say nothing about sensors and actuators, energy harvesting or silicon photonics. It is hard to think of digital and true analog & mixed-signal blocks co-existing on the same die at 7 or 5 nanometers. 2.5D-IC and perhaps eventually 3D-IC integration will be required whenever digital computing won't be sufficient.

For all these reasons, the scope of physical design is expanding. On the one hand, all the diverse requirements of a broadening set of technology nodes have to be taken into consideration because our industry cannot afford to develop and maintain different tools for different technology nodes. On the other hand, floorplanners, placers, and routers have to deal with objects and structure beyond the classical digital P&R: as an example, analog placement and routing demand automation that co-exists with interactivity; silicon interposers require "board-level" types of I/O planning and interconnect untangling, along with non-Manhattan routing for re-distribution layers (RDL) among through-silicon vias (TSV) and micro-bumps/pillars. The physical design infrastructure must deal concurrently with multiple dies, implemented using different technology nodes, or for radically different operating conditions.

Physical design in the next decade demands a new wave of innovation to support the needed "revolutionary evolutions", and to continue to deliver the best quality-of-results within acceptable time-to-results.

Biography

Antun Domic is Executive Vice President at Synopsys, Inc. He is responsible for EDA tools ranging from Synthesis to Custom Layout. He joined Synopsys in 1997, having worked at Cadence Design, Digital Equipment Corp. and MIT Lincoln Laboratory. He holds a PhD in Mathematics from MIT and a BS from the Univ. of Chile.

ISPD'16, April 3–6, 2016, Santa Rosa, California, USA.
ACM 978-1-4503-4039-7/16/04.
DOI: http://dx.doi.org/10.1145/2872334.2878630

A Designer's Perspective on Timing Closure

Greg Ford
GlobalFoundries
Santa Clara, CA, United States
greg.ford@globalfoundries.com

ABSTRACT

As technology nodes advance and designs become more complex, EDA developers strive to provide new and better solutions to the traditional problems encountered in back-end implementation. The usefulness of these EDA solutions is dependent on acceptance by designers, who often have different goals than developers. This presentation will offer a designer's perspective on current EDA solutions, with a focus on timing closure. Topics will include automated floorplanning goals, clock tree structure tradeoffs, data net repowering challenges and hold padding strategies. Examples from design experience will be used to illustrate where current EDA solutions work well, and what the obstacles are in cases where they do not.

Keywords: Physical Design; Timing Closure

BIO

Greg Ford is a member of the GLOBALFOUNDRIES San Jose ASIC Design Center and has focused on physical design for the past 8 years. Over this time, Greg has been involved in both physical design and methodology development on a multitude of ASICs ranging from 130nm to 14nm process nodes. Greg holds a Master of Science and Bachelor of Science in Computer Engineering from Case Western Reserve University.

ISPD'16, April 3–6, 2016, Santa Rosa, California, USA.
ACM 978-1-4503-4039-7/16/04.
DOI: http://dx.doi.org/10.1145/2872334.2872339

Cell Selection for High-Performance Designs in an Industrial Design Flow

Tiago J. Reimann
PGMicro
Universidade Federal do Rio
Grande do Sul
Porto Alegre, RS - Brazil
tjreimann@inf.ufrgs.br

Cliff C. N. Sze
IBM Research
Austin, TX
csze@us.ibm.com

Ricardo Reis
PGMicro/PPGC
Universidade Federal do Rio
Grande do Sul
Porto Alegre, RS - Brazil
reis@inf.ufrgs.br

ABSTRACT

In recent years, an increasing number of papers have focused on the cell selection problem. However, previous papers fail to consider the actual problems of performing cell selection in the after placement and CTS optimization stages of industrial designs. This paper discusses the obstacles found when applying state-of-the-art Lagrangian relaxation-based cell selection in a real industrial flow. Solutions to such obstacles are presented, filling the gap in previous literature.

We propose a new method to find a suitable set of initial Lagrange multipliers based on the initial gates sizes in the netlist. Fast convergence in the presence of small timing violations is achieved by a novel Lagrange multiplier update method. Our new timing-constrained formulation incorporates and balances both power and area as optimization objectives. We also present a *ranking* method to reduce sign-off timer calls that gives a 10x speed up in the cell selection process. Experimental results show quality improvements on a set of already deeply timing, power and area-optimized high-performance industrial microprocessor blocks with very tight constraints. Leakage power reduction of up to 18.2% is achieved (10.8% total and 7.2% on average), while timing, area and dynamic power are also improved.

Keywords

EDA, Power Optimization, Gate Sizing, V_{th} Assignment

Categories and Subject Descriptors

B.7.2 [**Integrated Circuits**]: Design Aids

1. INTRODUCTION

The growing importance of low power designs for portable devices and the challenges imposed by the power density of new technology nodes is making both industry and academia target on power-optimization algorithms.

ISPD'16, April 03-06, 2016, Santa Rosa, CA, USA

© 2016 ACM. ISBN 978-1-4503-4039-7/16/04. . . $15.00

DOI: http://dx.doi.org/10.1145/2872334.2872358

One way to achieve this objective is through gate sizing and threshold voltage (V_{th}) assignment (here referred to as cell selection). Such methods can be applied in several stages of the design flow, from logic synthesis to post-route optimization, with increasing accuracy in timing analysis as a result of more accurate physical information along the flow.

The discrete gate sizing is a known NP-hard combinatorial optimization problem [9] and has been the subject of many works in the literature. Several techniques are proposed based on: Lagrangian relaxation (LR) [1, 18, 3, 10], dynamic programming (DP)[10], linear programming [2, 7], stochastic optimization[6], network-flow [16] and sensitivity-based methods [17, 6].

Compared to many other techniques applied to this problem, Lagrangian relaxation algorithms have shown the best results in the literature. The first work to prove convergence and to guarantee optimality for the continuous gate sizing problem using a LR-based method is [1]. An algorithm applying "one-gate/one-wire-at-a-time" local optimization is presented. The timing constraints are defined on the gates rather than on the signal paths. This produces a linear number of constraints with respect to the number of gates, allowing linear runtime complexity.

The ISPD 2012 Discrete Gate Sizing Contest [12] brought attention back to the discrete gate sizing problem. Contestant teams applied many different techniques [14]. The results could be improved by a considerable margin, as exposed in later publications [8, 5, 3]. The ISPD 2013 Contest presented more challenging benchmarks and more realistic parasitics data. Interconnections are represented as RC trees and effective capacitance calculation is introduced. This delay model imposes more challenges to the correct assessment of timing and electrical violations in algorithms that rely on internal timing engines.

Following the formulation for the contest, reference [6] presents a multi-threaded, stochastic optimization tool for cell selection to minimize leakage power. The work also discusses the impact of timing accuracy on leakage power results, showing that frequent timing calibration (more accuracy) provides the best leakage power results when compared to results with less frequent calibration.

Reference [4] presents a Lagrangian relaxation-based flow that relies on internal timing analysis with sign-off timing accuracy. It is an extension of the winning tool of ISPD 2013 Contest. The described method presents the best results in the ISPD 2013 benchmarks with around 10% leakage power improvement over the best results in the contest.

Similar to the contest formulation, most recent works focus only on the leakage power optimization. However, it is important to also ensure that dynamic power and area are not badly affected by this optimization process. A consistent formulation must enable an appropriate balance between those parameters in order to further improve the solution provided by the physical design flow and after extensive timing optimization.

Despite the substantial number of publications and advances related to the cell selection problem, few papers focus on the practical application of these techniques in a real industrial design flow [11, 13, 15].

[15] presents several reasons for applying LR-based methods for cell selection in post-routing stages. Authors adapt the flow in [4] using a new Langrange multiplier update method to handle negative slacks. The method shows promising results. However, the following problems are not addressed: (1) runtime scalability, (2) preserving timing quality of results, and (3) incremental optimization. Moreover, many design objectives like area and placement changes are just ignored. Also, there are missing details of how the multi-objective optimization should be applied.

In this context, this work presents solutions for the challenges imposed by the insertion of a state-of-the-art Lagrangian relaxation-based cell selection algorithm in the optimization stage after placement and clock tree synthesis (CTS) in an industrial design flow. The main contributions presented here are:

- A new multi-objective LR formulation balancing power and area using scaling factors calculated based on the cell options from the standard cell library.

- A method to find a suitable set of initial Lagrange multipliers to prevent increase in timing violations and improve convergence, emulating an incremental optimization process.

- We incorporate a sign-off timer into the flow to ensure timing quality and the correct assessment of electrical violations.

- A *ranking* method to greatly reduce sign-off timer calls and speed up 10x the cell selection process by filtering solutions based on a simpler delay model.

- A novel Lagrange multiplier update method for fast convergence in the presence of small (but undesired) timing violations.

- Improvements in post-LR solution refinement, which also incorporates gate-by-gate incremental placement.

The remainder of this paper is organized as follows. Section 2 discusses the challenges of applying cell selection algorithms in real designs. Section 3 presents the proposed flow and the necessary changes to perform cell selection in an industrial design flow. Section 4 shows the experimental results obtained with the described method, followed by the conclusions in Section 5.

2. INDUSTRIAL DESIGN FLOW

Different from the aforementioned contests, the initial solution provided by the industrial flow (i.e. the solution after placement, several timing optimization steps, clock tree

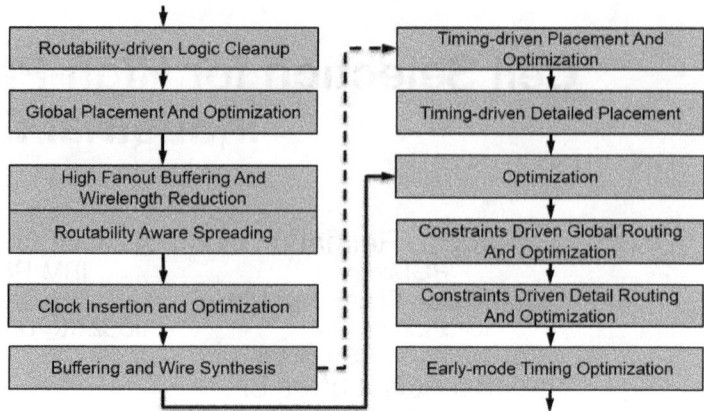

Figure 1: Physical synthesis flow.

synthesis, global routing, power optimization) is expected to have a good quality in area, timing and power. Therefore, applying cell selection in an industrial flow requires that such quality is kept or further improved. This is different than finding a good power/delay tradeoff – a common formulation in cell selection literature. In a pure power/area optimization stage of an industrial flow, the input timing quality must be considered as a hard constraint in the LR algorithm [15].

As introduced and exemplified in [15], true total negative slack ($TTNS$) is a better metric to quantify timing quality of results in the presence of negative slacks. This metric accounts for non-critical paths with negative slacks that do not reach timing endpoints. In an industrial design flow, other techniques are expected to be used in order to solve timing violations. After solving timing violations for critical paths, the non-critical paths become exposed and then have to be timing optimized too. If the cell selection algorithm degrades timing in such paths to reduce power, this power savings will later be lost again to recover timing. This makes the power savings achieved by cell selection misleading and power improvements reported are not actually feasible. In this work we also address the $TTNS$ metric in the results, maintaining or improving overall timing quality.

Following the same principles presented in [15], we insert our cell selection algorithm after the "Optimization" step in the industrial flow shown in Figure 1. Although the algorithm does not rely on any specific flow, the issues here addressed are a direct consequence of where the cell selection algorithm is placed in the flow.

One of the major challenges for cell selection algorithms is the complex timing models needed for accuracy in modern technologies and designs. Several characteristics make the sign-off timing engines too slow to be used throughout the optimization flow: (1) complexity of delay models, (2) existence of multiple clock domains and multiple corners, and (3) use of accurate interconnection models for delay and slew propagation. Faster timing estimation techniques are needed to enable the successful integration of a global cell selection method in an industrial design flow.

Another challenge is the change in overall gate placement (legalization). Significant changes in sizes (area) will directly affect interconnection parasitics and thus timing. Testing every placement change, even in a simple way, i.e. the change required only by the cell option being tested, would be prohibitive in terms of runtime. Also, just limiting the

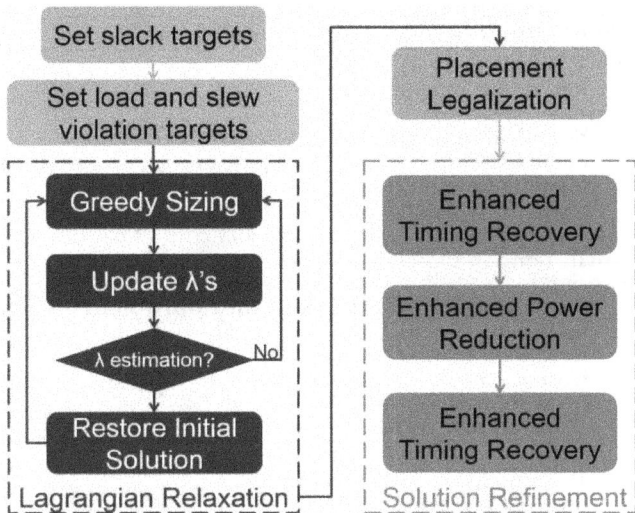

Figure 2: The proposed cell selection flow.

maximum footprint of a cell to its current area will excessively restrict gate sizing. However, an overall increase in area is not desirable and should be avoided. Thus, the algorithm also needs to take into account the area of the gates. Keeping a good balance between area, power, and timing will prevent unnecessary upsizing on critical gates. Excessive area increase will create overlap between cells, requiring further placement legalization that will degrade timing in interconnections and lengthen wires.

Our flow incorporates the area into the objective minimization function, so that the timing-constrained optimization will balance area and power. The multi-objective function requires scaling factors to set the correct proportion between the power, area, and timing objectives. Such units are library dependent. Therefore, a library- or design-based calculation method must be used.

Another placement related feature introduced in our flow is the legalization test during the post-LR solution refinement. This legalization test ensures that the new solution will have the desired effect after the final placement legalization. More details are discussed in Section 3.5.

3. PROPOSED FLOW AND TECHNIQUES

The new proposed flow is shown in Figure 2 and the details of each step are discussed below. Table 1 shows notation used in this paper.

The two initial steps set the timing and electrical violation targets for each pin in the design. The sizing algorithm will consider the existing electrical violation as the violation limit for each pin, not allowing an increase in electrical violations. The third step implements the iterative LR-based cell selection algorithm described in Section 3.1. Sections 3.2 to 3.4 discuss the initial Lagrange multiplier estimation method, the new multiplier update and the *ranking* algorithm, respectively. After that, a placement legalization is performed to fix any placement overlaps created.

In the *Solution Refinement* step, *Enhanced Timing Recovery* works to improve solutions with slack degradation. Next, *Enhanced Power Reduction* further reduces leakage power and area by a greedy method. The last step is a second run of *Enhanced Timing Recovery*. Both refinement methods are discussed in Section 3.5.

Table 1: Notation.

T	clock period
WNS	Worst Negative Slack
TNS	Total Negative Slack
$TTNS$	True Total Negative Slack [15]
$d_{i \to j}$	delay of timing arc $i \to j$
a_i, q_i	arrival and required time at node i
λ	Lagrange multiplier
$D(c)$	worst delay for all timing arcs in gate c
$G(c)$	set of options in the cell library for gate c
$N(c)$	number of cell options in $G(c)$
$F(c)$	$G(c)$ after *ranking*
$P(c), A(c)$	total power and area of gate c
$P_l(c), P_d(c)$	leakage and dynamic power of gate c
$C(c)$	sum of input pin capacitances of gate c

3.1 The Lagrangian Relaxation Algorithm

The cell selection optimization problem, the Primal Problem (PP), can be formulated as:

PP:

$$
\begin{aligned}
\textbf{minimize} \quad & \beta \times power + \theta \times area \\
\textbf{subject to} \quad & a_i + d_{i \to j} \leq a_j \ , \forall \text{ timing arc } i \to j \\
& a_o \leq T \qquad\qquad , \forall \text{ timing endpoint } o
\end{aligned} \tag{1}
$$

where β and θ are the scaling factors for each optimization objective in order to scale the different units. Both scaling factors are calculated based on the standard cell library as follows. They reflect the average power or area change between cell options in the library for a reference gate c_{REF}. This formulation allows the Lagrangian multipliers to span over all options in the library balancing the different objectives properly. For example, if the leakage power difference between the most leaky option and the less leaky option is big, but the area difference is not so big, the scaling factors will reflect that and adequately balance both units.

$$
\beta = \frac{N_{c_{REF}}}{P_l(c_n) - P_l(c_0)}, \quad \theta = \frac{N_{C_{REF}}}{A(c_n) - A(c_0)} \tag{2}
$$

where c_n and c_0 are the largest (lowest V_{th}) and smallest (highest V_{th}) cell in the standard cell library and $N_{C_{REF}}$ represents the number of options available in the library for a reference cell C_{REF}. Since dynamic and leakage power share the same unit, the power scaling factor β calculated based only on leakage power is applied to both metrics. The θ calculation involves only a single V_{th} level. Applying the scaling factors makes the optimization free of power and area units, which helps as such units may change between standard cell libraries and technologies. In our experiments C_{REF} is an inverter.

The library-based weighting parameters may also be replaced by design-dependent parameters like average power and average area for all cells in the design. Both methods lead to similar results in our experience.

Applying the Lagrangian relaxation method we obtain the Lagrangian Relaxation Sub-problem (LRS) in (3).

Algorithm 1: SolveLangrangianRelaxationSubproblem

```
1  foreach gate c ∈ Design do
2  │   best_option ← option(c)
   │   best_cost ← α × lambda-delay(c)
3  │              + β × (Pₗ(c) + P_d(c))
   │              + θ × A(c)
4  │   foreach gate option g ∈ F(c) do
5  │   │   option(c) ← g
6  │   │   if electrical violations bigger than initial then
7  │   │   │   go to the next option
8  │   │   end
9  │   │   local timing update
10 │   │   if new_slack < γ * original_slack then
11 │   │   │   go to the next option
12 │   │   end
   │   │   cost ← α × ∑ λ_{i→j}d_{i→j}
13 │   │            + β × (Pₗ(c) + P_d(c))
   │   │            + θ × A(c)
14 │   │   if cost < best_cost then
15 │   │   │   best_option ← g
16 │   │   │   best_cost ← cost
17 │   │   end
18 │   end
19 │   option(c) ← best_option
20 │   local timing update
21 end
```

Algorithm 2: SolveLagrangianDualProblem

```
1  store initial solution
2  set initial multipliers
3  repeat
4  │   SolveLangrangianRelaxationSubproblem
5  │   update timing
6  │   UpdateLagrangeMultipliers
7  │   restore initial solution
8  │   update timing
9  until iteration limit;
10 repeat
11 │   SolveLangrangianRelaxationSubproblem
12 │   update timing
13 │   UpdateLagrangeMultipliers
14 │   if new_score > best_score then
15 │   │   store solution
16 │   │   best_score ← new_score
17 │   end
18 until converged or iteration limit;
19 restore best solution found
```

LRS:

$$\textbf{minimize} \quad \beta \times power + \theta \times area + $$
$$\sum \lambda_{i \to j}(a_i + d_{i \to j} - a_j) + \qquad (3)$$
$$\sum \lambda_o(a_o - T)$$

Further simplification can be achieved by applying Karush-Kuhn-Tucker (KKT) conditions for optimality ($\lambda \in \Omega_\lambda$ as defined in [1]). Then, (3) is simplified resulting in the form in (4).

LRS ($\lambda \in \Omega_\lambda$):

$$\textbf{minimize} \quad \beta \times power + \theta \times area + \alpha \times \sum \lambda_{i \to j}d_{i \to j} \qquad (4)$$

Here, another scaling factor α is introduced to remove the timing unit. It is defined as:

$$\alpha = \frac{N_{C_{REF}}}{D(c_n) - D(c_0)} \qquad (5)$$

where delays $D(c_n)$ and $D(c_0)$ are calculated based on the standard cell library with the same reference output load.

We apply a method similar to [4] to solve the LRS. Algorithm 1 shows the pseudo-code for the LRS solver. In the algorithm, $option(c)$ represents the library option currently assigned to gate c.

Then, the new problem is to find the optimal set of lambdas that solve the PP. Thus, the Lagrangian Dual Problem (LDP) is simply the maximization of LRS where λ is the variable.

Algorithm 2 shows the new proposed method to solve the

LDP problem. The first loop (lines 3-9) performs initial lambda estimation (details in Section 3.2). Second loop (lines 10-18) is the main LR flow that is limited by a maximum number of iterations or by convergence metrics. Notice that the *iteration limit* in the two loops is not the same.

The overall solution quality is measured by a score function. The score function penalizes timing degradation exponentially:

$$score = - \left(\Delta Power + \Delta Area + 2^{-(\Delta TV + \Delta WNS)} - 1 \right) \qquad (6)$$

where ΔTV represents the percentage of change in timing violation and ΔWNS is the degradation in worst negative slack. All Δs are calculated with respect to the input solution. Positive scores represent improved solutions while negative scores show undesired solution degradation. The exponential score relation to timing violations is chosen in order to penalize the increase in violations without setting a hard limit to it. This relation allows a small window of compromise between the objectives and timing violations. It is important to remember here that no significant timing degradation is to be accepted in order to improve power or area. Although, minimal degradation in timing (few or fractions of picoseconds) must be ignored if power and/or area improvements are achieved. The use of this score function allows the algorithm to ignore solutions with significant timing (TNS and WNS) degradation.

3.2 Initial Lagrange Multiplier Estimation

A well known issue in Lagrangian relaxation-based methods is what to set the initial values to for the Lagrange multipliers. The initial set of multipliers plays a significant role in convergence and final quality of results, as shown in reference [18].

Reference [15] highlights the need for incremental algorithms for cell selection in industrial design flows. However, finding a set of multipliers for a given input set of gate sizes with their respective delays is a problem with a similar difficulty to the cell selection problem. Moreover, considering the KKT conditions, it may be impossible to find such a set of multipliers that meet those flow conditions.

We propose a simple and straightforward method to overcome the lack of a good set of initial multipliers. The method consists of running a few LR iterations where we solve the *LRS* problem, update the multipliers and restore the initial solution. The new set of multipliers represents a *LRS* solution with delays closer to the delays present in the input solution. This estimation method provides a set of initial multipliers to the main LR flow simulating an incremental approach and avoiding quality disruption when performing incremental sizing, rather then starting with all cells at minimum sizing. A disruption may prevent LR to converge to an improved solution, as discussed in Section 4.

In order to avoid excessive runtime due to sign-off timer calls, only the *ranking* method (Section 3.4) is used to solve the *LRS*, i.e., $F(c)$ has only one option that is always chosen in *SolveLRS*, with no need to update timing.

3.3 Lagrange Multiplier Update

In the post-placement optimization problem in industrial flows, designs may have timing violations that are expected to not be solved by any means. As a consequence, the standard academic LR formulation would lead to an increase in power/area in an attempt to fix all timing violations, which is not the desired effect of such an optimization process. The main goal must be to keep the same timing quality of results (or improve it) and to improve power and area of the design. To accomplish that, a change in the LR formulation is required.

Reference [15] presents a new lambda update method that enables LR-based algorithms to handle designs with negative slacks which are not expected to be solved by cell selection. New lambda values are calculated to target the initial timing arc slack S_{init}. In this work, we apply a similar but more aggressive method for the Lagrange multiplier update.

In order to achieve fast convergence to avoid excessive runtimes, and to achieve better timing quality of results, the timing reference for the multiplier increase (T) is replaced by the worst slack degradation in the current solution with respect to the initial state – called ΔWNS.

Also, two step factors (ρ) are included to smooth convergence based on the number of LR iterations performed (*iter*) (see Algorithm 3). These factors are similar to step sizes in the subgradient method. Without step factors, the solution quality has large variations along iterations (due to discreteness of the problem) that lead to a slower convergence and degradation in quality of results. The choice for ρ parameters is done empirically. In our experiments we set ρ_{init} to 0.05. Our experience shows that a smaller step size for multiplier decreasing (bigger ρ_{dec}) produces a more stable convergence.

Algorithm 3 presents the proposed Lagrange multiplier update method. S_{curr} is the current worst slack obtained from the sign-off timer. The control variable k is set to determine the convergence priority: timing constraints or the optimization objective. For $k < 1$, multipliers will increase faster, resulting in delay reduction in next *SolveLRS* run. On the other hand, $k > 1$ results in faster multiplier decrease, allowing more power/area savings while increasing delay in non-violating paths. The ranges for k are empirically defined according to the quality of the previous LR iteration, as shown in (7). The settings are determined based on experience. Different choices for k do not significantly affect the final quality of results, but allow faster convergence, reducing the number of iterations required.

Algorithm 3: UpdateLagrangeMultipliers

1 $\rho_{inc} = \rho_{init} \times (1 + iter)$
2 $\rho_{dec} = \rho_{init} \times (15 + iter)$
3 foreach *timing arc* $i \to j$ **do**
4

$$\lambda_i \leftarrow \lambda_i \times \begin{cases} \left(1 - \frac{S_{curr} - S_{init}}{\Delta WNS \times \rho_{inc}}\right)^{1/k} & a_j \geq q_j - S_{init} \\ \left(1 + \frac{S_{curr} - S_{init}}{T \times \rho_{dec}}\right)^{-k} & a_j < q_j - S_{init} \end{cases}$$

5 end
6 KKT projection ($\lambda \in \Omega_\lambda$)

Algorithm 4: OptionRanking

1 foreach *gate option* $g \in G(c)$ **do**
2 estimate local delays for g
3 $cost \leftarrow \alpha \times \sum \lambda_{i \to j} d_{i \to j} + \beta \times P_l(c) + \theta \times A(c)$
   $+ \zeta \times C(c)$
4 insert g in *cost*-ordered vector $F(c)$
5 end

$$k = \begin{cases} 5 & \text{for } \lambda \text{ estimation step} \\ k < 1 & \text{if timing degraded} \\ k > 1 & \text{if solution improved} \\ 1 & \text{otherwise} \end{cases} \tag{7}$$

This method makes the presence of multiple clock domains transparent to the LR engine, as derived in [11].

3.4 Filtering Cell Options

The use of a high accuracy timer to evaluate all cell options is very slow. A less accurate timing model can be used instead. However, the less accurate timer may not only evaluate (rank) the options differently but also make any electrical violation (max input slew and max output load) control ineffective.

We propose the use of a less accurate timing model to rank all gate options using the same cost function as the *SolveLRS* algorithm. The less accurate timer ignores the delay and slew rate changes in the interconnect parasitics. It also ignores effective capacitance calculations. Timing arc delays and output slews are calculated using the lookup tables in the standard cell library. After that, the sign-off timer only evaluates the top t ranked gate options, skipping several high accuracy timing updates.

The *ranking* method is presented in Algorithm 4. Since there is no timing update when ranking the options, the accurate dynamic power calculation is not available. For fast estimation, dynamic power is replaced by the input pin capacitance of the new gate option. The input pin capacitance must also be properly scaled to eliminate its unit. The input pin capacitance scaling factor ζ is calculated as follows.

$$\zeta = \frac{N_{C_{REF}}}{C(c_n) - C(c_0)} \tag{8}$$

As for the other scaling factors, ζ can also be calculated using design statistics like average input pin capacitance, without considerable difference in results.

69

Table 2: Designs used for experimental validation.

Design	# Gates	Worst Slack	TNS	$TTNS$	Leakage Power	Dynamic Power	Total Power	Area
ibm2014uP_01	95057	-78.3	-144167	-910468	80.6	13.5	94.1	809.1
ibm2014uP_02	9260	-135.1	-2973	-22778	1.1	1.3	2.4	58.5
ibm2014uP_03	8827	8.9	-14	-30	2.8	51.4	54.1	67.3
ibm2014uP_04	7293	-8.4	-552	-560	1.6	1.3	2.9	72.7
ibm2014uP_05	15777	-82.1	-43263	-76068	19.1	45.3	64.4	134.9
ibm2014uP_06	75148	-142.6	-36833	-62323	37.7	112.0	149.7	777.0
ibm2014uP_07	70331	-39.4	-54401	-392551	61.0	12.6	73.6	637.2
ibm2014uP_08	17942	-72.9	-37290	-195777	16.7	68.4	85.1	148.5
ibm2014uP_09	17510	-32.7	-14491	-71828	14.7	33.0	47.7	150.9
ibm2014uP_10	124670	-34.2	-70737	-322544	86.2	304.5	390.7	990.4
ibm2014uP_11	24425	-165.3	-195168	-1054130	35.3	21.5	56.8	235.7
ibm2014uP_12	17480	-421.9	-359981	-777205	4.3	20.5	24.7	161.1
ibm2014uP_13	20167	-49.8	-26647	-133504	20.3	61.2	81.5	196.4
ibm2014uP_14	12941	-61.9	-6526	-11213	8.2	9.7	17.9	251.9

3.5 Solution Refinement

The fast and highly constrained convergence adopted during LR iterations generates solutions that can be further improved by local optimization schemes.

In some cases, timing must be improved to better resemble the timing quality of the initial state. The algorithm used for that is described next. Also, power can be locally optimized by a greedy algorithm as exposed hereafter.

3.5.1 Enhanced Timing Recovery

The Timing Recovery algorithm [4] is here adapted to handle placement legalization for each gate size/V_{th} change. Also, a new ordering for the search is set. Instead of ordering the gates as in the original work, we order the gates by their worst slack, processing the most critical gates first.

For each new gate option under test, the algorithm checks if the gate needs to be moved from the current location to fit the new option size. In the cases where the gate has its footprint increased and there is no free space to fit it, a new placement location[1] with available space is found. Thereby, the timer takes into account the routing parasitics changes during the timing update.

The second run takes advantage of capacitance and area reduction obtained in the *Enhanced Power Reduction* step. Only paths violating the initial worst slack are searched in both runs.

3.5.2 Enhanced Power Reduction

The Power Reduction algorithm [4] can further improve the solution after LR, reducing power and area of cells. Since it only performs downsizing and V_{th} increase, placement legalization is usually not required. Nevertheless, the algorithm is also placement-aware and can find new cell placement locations if overlaps occur.

The algorithm is here adapted to prioritize downsizing of non-critical gates in the fanout of critical paths, reducing the output load of critical gates and allowing more improvements in next run of *Enhanced Timing Recovery*.

---
[1]The closest possible free location from current gate placement that can accommodate the new footprint.

We also change the algorithm to prevent $TTNS$ degradation [15]. The original implementation would take advantage of worst slack propagation, powering down gates in paths dominated by a another negative slack. Since $TTNS$ calculation includes the slacks of side paths, degradation occurs when any slack gets more negative. Our enhanced algorithm checks for slack degradation in the output pin of all changed gates and rejects solutions with slack degradation.

4. EXPERIMENTAL RESULTS

We evaluate the proposed method in the post-routing optimization stage of an industrial design flow with the fourteen high-performance industrial microprocessor blocks with 5GHz clock frequency presented and 22nm library in reference [15]. Considering that the input solution to our algorithm is already optimized (i.e. the best solution found by the industrial flow), all designs are challenging in terms of timing, area and power.

Table 2 shows the characteristics for the designs used in this work. Timing values are shown in picoseconds (*ps*) while power and area units are normalized. The characteristics may change in results because experiments are performed with a complete flow run, that includes placement, CTS and optimization. Nevertheless, the comparisons are done with results reported before and after executing the algorithms proposed in this work.

This set of benchmarks comprises designs with different timing, leakage/dynamic power ratio, area and number of gates. This variety of characteristics is desired in order to evaluate the algorithms under real conditions.

As proposed in [15], we also include $TTNS$ measurements to show all timing changes in the design including side paths, not only the worst timing paths that reach the timing endpoints. Table 4 briefly shows the results without applying the new enhancements to prevent $TTNS$ degradation in the *Enhanced Power Reduction* algorithm. Total values are obtained using the sum (absolute values) of all designs. It is clear that ignoring degradation of slacks in side paths results in an unacceptable timing quality degradation in $TTNS$ for industrial design flows. Such results show that the method is unsuitable for industrial design flows.

Table 3: Experiments applying the proposed flow that prevents $TTNS$ degradation.

Design	CPU (min)	Worst Slack before	Worst Slack after	TNS before	TNS after	$TTNS$ before	$TTNS$ after	Power Leakage	Power Dynamic	Power Total	Area
ibm2014uP_01	377	-75.8	-75.1	-141471	-137744	-906301	-897859	−18.2%	−0.4%	−15.7%	−2.3%
ibm2014uP_02	40	-141.0	-140.3	-3030	-2752	-23004	-21656	−6.5%	−3.9%	−5.1%	−6.0%
ibm2014uP_03	53	8.9	8.9	-14	-6	-30	-10	6.2%	−3.3%	−2.8%	−0.4%
ibm2014uP_04	14	-8.4	-7.4	-552	-516	-560	-519	−0.3%	−0.5%	−0.4%	−0.1%
ibm2014uP_05	32	-82.1	-82.1	-43263	-42763	-76068	-75175	−3.6%	−0.2%	−1.2%	0.2%
ibm2014uP_06	260	-133.4	-133.4	-31798	-30242	-52800	-49614	−2.7%	0.0%	−0.7%	0.0%
ibm2014uP_07	310	-37.9	-37.9	-52108	-50126	-376012	-357385	−9.4%	0.0%	−7.8%	−0.6%
ibm2014uP_08	110	-80.4	-80.4	-39823	-36858	-211734	-201734	−11.4%	−0.7%	−2.8%	−2.3%
ibm2014uP_09	75	-33.8	-33.1	-14110	-13724	-72869	-71636	−15.7%	0.6%	−4.4%	−1.8%
ibm2014uP_10	788	-35.1	-36.3	-67145	-64510	-305053	-290806	−11.6%	−2.4%	−4.5%	−2.5%
ibm2014uP_11	104	-165.3	-165.3	-191527	-188435	-1034800	-1022700	−10.2%	0.0%	−6.3%	1.3%
ibm2014uP_12	69	-421.7	-421.5	-359783	-350035	-787596	-764491	−7.8%	−2.1%	−3.0%	−6.8%
ibm2014uP_13	55	-53.0	-53.2	-27185	-24680	-134543	-128356	−9.3%	−0.5%	−2.7%	−1.9%
ibm2014uP_14	12	-59.0	-59.0	-6419	-6425	-10950	-10986	−0.5%	0.0%	−0.2%	−0.1%
Average								−7.2%	−1.0%	−4.1%	−1.7%
Total								−10.8%	−1.4%	−4.6%	−1.5%

Table 4: Results not avoiding $TTNS$ degradation in *Enhanced Power Reduction* algorithm.

Design	TNS (change)	$TTNS$ (change)	Power Leakage	Power Dynamic	Area
ibm2014uP_01	11691	-10236	-20.0%	-0.4%	-2.6%
ibm2014uP_02	386	-4139	-8.3%	-4.0%	-6.3%
ibm2014uP_03	8	20	5.2%	-2.9%	-0.3%
ibm2014uP_04	37	39	-0.4%	-0.5%	-0.1%
ibm2014uP_05	753	-726	-6.1%	-0.5%	-0.2%
ibm2014uP_06	1294	-4712	-4.0%	0.0%	-0.2%
ibm2014uP_07	1541	-21700	-16.8%	0.0%	-1.9%
ibm2014uP_08	2785	-18585	-19.8%	-1.0%	-2.7%
ibm2014uP_09	1248	-16244	-21.8%	0.1%	-2.7%
ibm2014uP_10	1862	-37498	-20.7%	-3.3%	-3.5%
ibm2014uP_11	5521	-21750	-18.0%	0.0%	-0.5%
ibm2014uP_12	11012	90	-11.3%	-2.3%	-7.5%
ibm2014uP_13	1060	-4192	-15.5%	-0.5%	-2.0%
ibm2014uP_14	143	144	-0.5%	0.0%	-0.1%
Average	2810	-9963	-11.3%	-1.1%	-2.2%
Total	39341	-139489	-16.3%	-1.8%	-2.1%

Table 5: Results without initializing Lagrange multipliers to reflect input solution.

Design	CPU (min)	TNS (change)	TTNS (change)	Leakage Power	LR Cvg
ibm2014uP_01	511	4891	-121689	-16.9%	**N**
ibm2014uP_02	39	50	-3882	-2.2%	Y
ibm2014uP_03	54	-13	11	-0.8%	**N**
ibm2014uP_04	29	9	8	-0.1%	**N**
ibm2014uP_05	41	316	-2994	-4.0%	**N**
ibm2014uP_06	270	410	-2003	-1.7%	**N**
ibm2014uP_07	488	1097	-2926	-4.3%	Y
ibm2014uP_08	87	1060	-42852	-16.7%	**N**
ibm2014uP_09	65	1807	2205	-12.8%	Y
ibm2014uP_10	824	1689	-46259	-10.7%	**N**
ibm2014uP_11	85	5288	-6610	-16.8%	Y
ibm2014uP_12	78	11009	-2241	-8.5%	Y
ibm2014uP_13	62	2988	-6428	-17.9%	Y
ibm2014uP_14	15	146	3	-0.1%	Y
Average		2196	-16833	-8.1%	
Total		30747	-235658	-10.7%	

The contribution of the initial multiplier estimation method is also analyzed. Table 5 shows power results without the initial multiplier estimation iterations. Column "LR Cvg" indicates when LR is able to converge to an improved solution ("Y") or does not provide a solution better than the input solution ("N" – bold), based on the *score* function from Equation 6. Comparing to Table 4, we see a major quality degradation mainly due to lack of convergence of the LR method. LR is not able to converge for half of the designs, where all power improvement is given by the Power Reduction algorithm. This implementation resembles Table 4, where PR implementation can find a large space for improvements by degrading $TTNS$. The resulting $TTNS$ degradation for this set of results is more than 50% greater than results using initial lambda estimation.

Table 3 shows results and total runtime when applying the new *Enhanced Power Reduction* method that prevents slack degradation for every pin in the design, avoiding $TTNS$ degradation. This implementation will keep (or improve) the timing quality obtained in the Lagrangian relaxation stage, for all metrics.

As mentioned before, design information varies between results due to the adopted test methodology, where all results are generated running the whole physical synthesis flow. Thus, timing, power, area are slightly different in the results in Tables 2, 4, 5, and 3.

Although power reduction is less, the method still gives very good leakage power reduction. It is important to remember that such improvements are for designs already power-optimized by other methods at several stages of the industrial design flow. We achieve 10.4% average (12.1% total, and up to 18.2%) leakage power reduction with similar or better timing quality for all designs tested. Total power is reduced by 4.1% in average and cell area is also reduced by 1.9% in average.

Due to runtime limitations, we have set an expected number of iterations for LR to converge. This limit is set to 20 iterations in our experiments. The effectiveness of the initial multiplier estimation clearly affects convergence. LR converges within 12 iterations on average, while 15 iterations on average are necessary to converge without initial multiplier estimation (not considering the 7 designs in which LR cannot converge within the 20 iterations limit).

The experiments also show 10x average runtime speedup due to *ranking* method with less than 2% difference in leakage power improvement. More speedup is expected when more cells are available in the library. In our experiments, the average number of cell options for each gate varies from 20 to 30 options. Results presented in this work are obtained with $t = 2$, i.e. only the top two ranked cell options are evaluated using the sign-off timer. These results show the effectiveness of the proposed *ranking* method that enables the use of a sign-off timer for the proposed cell selection algorithm.

5. CONCLUSION

This paper addresses and presents solutions to the challenges imposed by the use of a cell selection algorithm in a real industrial physical design flow. We present the required adjustments to incorporate a state-of-the-art LR-based cell selection tool in an industrial design flow. The results show a good opportunity for power improvement in current industrial power-driven design flows.

We show the effectiveness of the proposed methods in several industrial designs, with up to 18.2% leakage power reduction with no timing quality degradation. Nevertheless, runtime still poses a challenge in cell selection with sign-off timing analysis.

6. ACKNOWLEDGEMENTS

We would like to thank Dr. David Chinnery, for his many helpful comments and the several insightful discussions about the contents of this work.

7. REFERENCES

[1] C. P. Chen, C. C.-N. Chu, and D. F. Wong. Fast and exact simultaneous gate and wire sizing by lagrangian relaxation. *IEEE TCAD*, 18(7):1014–1025, 1999.

[2] D. Chinnery and K. Keutzer. Linear programming for sizing, Vth and Vdd assignment. In *ISLPED 2005*, pages 149–154, 2005.

[3] G. Flach, T. Reimann, G. Posser, M. Johann, and R. Reis. Simultaneous Gate Sizing and V_{th} Assignment using Lagrangian Relaxation and Delay Sensitivities. In *IEEE Computer Society Annual Symposium on VLSI, ISVLSI 2013*, pages 84–89, 2013.

[4] G. Flach, T. Reimann, G. Posser, M. Johann, and R. Reis. Effective Method for Simultaneous Gate Sizing and V_{th} Assignment Using Lagrangian Relaxation. *IEEE TCAD*, 33(4):546–557, April 2014.

[5] J. Hu, A. B. Kahng, S. Kang, M.-C. Kim, and I. L. Markov. Sensitivity-guided metaheuristics for accurate discrete gate sizing. In *Proceedings of the Int'l. Conf. on Computer-Aided Design*, ICCAD '12, pages 233–239, New York, NY, USA, 2012. ACM.

[6] A. Kahng, S. Kang, H. Lee, I. Markov, and P. Thapar. High-performance gate sizing with a signoff timer. In *Computer-Aided Design (ICCAD), 2013 IEEE/ACM Int'l. Conf. on*, pages 450–457, Nov 2013.

[7] J. Lee and P. Gupta. Incremental gate sizing for late process changes. In *Computer Design (ICCD), 2010 IEEE Int'l. Conf. on*, pages 215–221, Oct 2010.

[8] L. Li, P. Kang, Y. Lu, and H. Zhou. An efficient algorithm for library-based cell-type selection in high-performance low-power designs. In *Proceedings of the Int'l. Conf. on Computer-Aided Design*, ICCAD '12, pages 226–232, New York, NY, USA, 2012. ACM.

[9] W. Li. Strongly NP-hard discrete gate sizing problems. In *Computer Design: VLSI in Computers and Processors, 1993. ICCD '93. Proceedings., 1993 IEEE Int'l. Conf. on*, pages 468–471, Oct 1993.

[10] M. Ozdal, S. Burns, and J. Hu. Gate sizing and device technology selection algorithms for high-performance industrial designs. In *Computer-Aided Design (ICCAD), 2011 IEEE/ACM Int'l. Conf. on*, pages 724–731, Nov 2011.

[11] M. Ozdal, S. Burns, and J. Hu. Algorithms for gate sizing and device parameter selection for high-performance designs. *IEEE TCAD*, 31(10):1558–1571, Oct 2012.

[12] M. M. Ozdal, C. Amin, A. Ayupov, S. Burns, G. Wilke, and C. Zhuo. The ISPD-2012 Discrete Cell Sizing Contest and Benchmark Suite. In *ISPD 2012*, pages 161–164, Napa, CA, EUA, 2012.

[13] H. Qian and E. Acar. Timing-aware power minimization via extended timing graph methods. *ASP Journal of Low Power Electronics*, pages 318–326, 2007.

[14] T. Reimann, G. Posser, G. Flach, M. Johann, and R. Reis. Simultaneous Gate Sizing and Vt Assignment Using Fanin/Fanout Ratio and Simulated Annealing. In *IEEE International Symposium on Circuits and Systems, ISCAS 2013*, Beijing, China, 2013.

[15] T. Reimann, C. C. N. Sze, and R. Reis. Gate Sizing and Threshold Voltage Assignment for High Performance Microprocessor Designs. In *20th ASP-DAC*, jan 2015.

[16] H. Ren and S. Dutt. A network-flow based cell sizing algorithm. In *The International Workshop on Logic Synthesis*, pages 7–14, 2008.

[17] A. Srivastava, D. Sylvester, and D. Blaauw. Power minimization using simultaneous gate sizing, dual-vdd and dual-vth assignment. In *Design Automation Conference, 2004.*, pages 783–787, July 2004.

[18] H. Tennakoon and C. Sechen. Efficient and accurate gate sizing with piecewise convex delay models. In *42nd annual conference on Design automation*, pages 807–812, Anaheim, California, USA, 2005.

Drive Strength Aware Cell Movement Techniques for Timing Driven Placement

Guilherme Flach, Mateus Fogaça, Jucemar Monteiro, Marcelo Johann and Ricardo Reis

Universidade Federal do Rio Grande do Sul (UFRGS) - Instituto de Informática - PGMicro/PPGC

{gaflach, mpfogaca, jucemar.monteiro, johann, reis}@inf.ufrgs.br

ABSTRACT

As the interconnections dominate the circuit delay in nanometer technologies, placement plays a major role to achieve timing closure since it is a main step that defines the interconnection lengths. In initial stages of the physical design flow, the placement goal is to reduce the total wirelength, however total wirelength minimization only roughly addresses timing. A timing-driven placement incorporates timing information to remove or alleviate timing violations. In this work, we present an incremental Timing-Driven Placement (TDP) flow to further optimize timing violations via single-cell movements. For late violations, we developed techniques to reduce the load capacitance on critical nets and to obtain load capacitance balancing using drive strength. For early violations, we present techniques that rely on clock skew optimization, register swap and interconnection increase. Our flow is experimentally evaluated using the International Conference on Computer-Aided Design (ICCAD) 2015 Incremental Timing-Driven Contest infrastructure. Experimental results show that our flow can significantly reduce timing violations. On average, for long maximum displacement, the quality of results is improved by 67.8% with late Worst Negative Slack (WNS) and Total Negative Slack (TNS) being improved by 2.31% and 10.84%, respectively, early WNS and TNS improved by 68.92% and 76.42%, respectively and congestion metric Average Bin Utilization (ABU) improved by 74.9% compared to the 1st place in the contest. The impact on Steiner Tree Wirelength (STWL) is less than 2.5%.

Keywords

Microelectronics, EDA, Timing-Driven Placement, Timing Closure

ISPD'16, April 03 - 06, 2016, Santa Rosa, CA, USA

© 2016 Copyright held by the owner/author(s). Publication rights licensed to ACM.
ISBN 978-1-4503-4039-7/16/04... $15.00

DOI: http://dx.doi.org/10.1145/2872334.2872359

1. INTRODUCTION

Timing-driven placement incorporates timing information to reduce timing violations which are only roughly addressed by total wirelength minimization. A detailed timing-driven placement works on a globally optimized and legalized solution trying to further improve timing while keeping the solution legalized. Typically a detailed placement will process only a fraction of the total cells of a design, preserving the global properties of the initial solution.

A pure placement flow can only improve timing by changing cell positions and hence the length of the wires that connect them. As the interconnection dominates the circuit delay in nanometer technologies, placement plays a major role to achieve timing closure.

Although the length minimization of a single wire typically improves the local delay, the minimization of total wirelength does not guarantee the best global delay. The reason is that the minimization of the sum of wirelength completely ignores the fact that some wires are more important than others in defining the circuit performance. Therefore a timing-driven placement prioritizes critical interconnections and typically trades-off increase on non-critical interconnection lengths with decrease on critical interconnection lengths.

In this work, we develop a detailed timing-driven flow that can incrementally improve the timing of a legalized placement solution. Our flow is composed by several single-cell movements aiming both early (hold) and late (setup) timing violations. For late violations, we apply load reduction and load balancing to accomplish the wirelength trade-offs. For early violations, we devise methods to increase delay by moving cells away and by skew optimization.

The main contributions of this work can be summarized as follows:

- a set of single-cell movement techniques to mitigate both early and late timing violations;

- load balancing via an analytical formulation to find the optimal position of a cell w.r.t. its driver and sink considering drive strengths;

- clock skew exploration to reduce early (hold) violations;

- a flow for incremental timing-driven placement validated with ICCAD 2015 contest infrastructure.

Our experimental results show that there is expressive room for mitigation of timing violations using incremental local search techniques. The Timing-Driven Placement

(TDP) flow was experimentally evaluated using an state-of-the-art set of circuits provided by International Conference on Computer-Aided Design (ICCAD) 2015 Contest.

This paper is organized as follows. Section 2 reviews the state-of-the-art algorithms for TDP optimization. Some definitions are provided on Section 3. The proposed algorithms are discussed in Sections 4, 5 and 6 while in Section 7 we show our incremental TDP flow. The experimental results are discussed in Section 8 and the concluding remarks are made in Section 9.

2. RELATED WORKS

Most of the timing-driven placement techniques are divided into 2 groups: net-based [9, 13, 3] and path-based approaches [11, 15, 16].

The former group prioritizes nets with timing violations by assigning them higher weights during global wirelength-driven placement or by assigning a max wirelength constraint. These techniques can deal with a lot of violations at the same time, keeping a global view of the problem. However, while these nets are optimized, other violations may show up and, thereby, the weights need to be updated and new constraints created. At the end, the problem may be over constrained, and the solution may be a local minima. Over constrained solutions also may lead to congestion and can affect routability.

On the other hand, path-based approaches focus on fixing a set of critical or near critical paths. The idea is to straighten the critical paths in order to reduce their length. The procedure can be done by heuristic local search or linear programing techniques.

ITOP [14] proposes various techniques in order to achieve timing closure. The first one is a netlist transformation in which virtual 2-pin nets are created linking cells in critical paths to raise attraction between them in global placement. Furthermore, an incremental path smoothing algorithm locally moves critical modules trying to achieve local improvements. Unlike most algorithms, after changing the solution, small movements are performed to mitigate congestion and to ensure routability. Finally, the authors combine other techniques, like buffering and sizing (repowering), to further improve the solution quality.

A set of local search algorithms was proposed by [2]. Their work rely on two strategies: path straightening and clustering. The goals of clustered movement are to speed up the execution time and to escape from suboptimal solutions. The idea is to minimize the euclidean distance between the most critical upstream and downstream pins of a cluster. A formulation using Lagrangian Relaxation to mitigate TDP timing violations was proposed by [5]. The proposed technique updates dynamically net's weights according to Lagrange multipliers.

3. DEFINITIONS

In this section, some concepts used throughout this paper are presented.

An *early timing violation* occurs whenever a signal propagates too fast reaching a registers before the previous signal had been captured. An early violation is also referred to as a *late timing violation* occurs whenever the signal takes too long to propagate reaching a register after the time-frame necessary to store the signal. A late timing

violation is also referred to as a setup violation. In this work both early and late timing violations are handled.

3.1 Drive Strength

To obtain a measure of the drive strength of cells, more specifically of timing arcs, we compute a representative driver resistance R for each timing arc. The delay of a timing arc is estimated as in Equation (1),

$$d = RC + p \qquad (1)$$

where C is the load capacitance being driven and p is the parasitic delay. The drive resistance is then computed via least square approximation of the delay values for several different loads.

3.2 Criticality and Centrality

The **criticality** $\{criticality \in \mathbb{R} \mid 0 \leq criticality \leq 1\}$ of a pin is the negative slack of the pin divided by the worst negative slack found in the design. The normalized **centrality** $\{centrality \in \mathbb{R} \mid 0 \leq centrality \leq 1\}$ of a pin is a rough measure of how many critical endpoints are affected by the pin. It can be seen as the importance of such pin to the Total Negative Slack (TNS).

The centralities are computed by traversing the design in the reverse topological order. By definition, the centrality at endpoints is set as the endpoint's criticality. The centrality of a driver pin is simply the sum of centralities of its sink pins. The centrality of the output (driver) pin is then proportionally distributed among the input pins of the respective cell according to the input pin criticalities. Centrality values can be seen as the endpoint criticalities flowing through the circuit, which is a standard technique used by timing driven optimization methods based on Lagrangian Relaxation [1] to obey the flow conservation as implied by the KKT optimally conditions.

4. LATE OPTIMIZATION

In this section, we present a set of techniques that targets to decrease wire load capacitance and resistance of the critical nets. We also propose an analytical formulation to explore driver strength in critical nets to reduce late violations. We devise an analytical formulation to obtain the position where the late timing violation is locally minimized.

4.1 Clustered Movement

As demonstrated by [2], moving one cell at a time may lead to suboptimal solutions. To avoid this problem we implemented an algorithm that performs a Breadth-First Search (BFS) finding topological neighbor cells with timing violations within a given range. For each cluster, we find an ideal position and shift all cells toward that position. These two operations are described below.

4.1.1 Cell Clustering

Algorithm 1 presents the proposed clustering algorithm. Two inputs must be specified: *initialCell* and *maxDistance*. The former refers to the cell with which the algorithm will begin the BFS and the latter is the maximum Manhattan distance a cell can be from *initialCell* in order to be clustered. At the beginning, the *cluster* is empty (Line 2) and the queue that controls the BFS, called *neighbors*, is initialized with *initialCell* (Line 3).

Lines 4-11 show the algorithm's main loop. In each iteration, the first element from the queue is stored in *current* variable and then removed (Line 5). If the current element is critical, i.e., has negative slack, it is clustered (Line 9) and its topological neighbors are added to the queue (Line 10). The loop continues until *neighbors queue* is empty (Line 11).

Algorithm 1: Cell clustering

input : initialCell, maxDistance
output: cluster

1 **begin**
2   cluster = ∅
3   neighbors.push(initialCell)
4   **repeat**
5   current ← neighbors.pop()
6   **if** *minSlack ≥ 0* **or**
7   *dist(current, intialCell) > maxDistance* **then**
8   continue
9   cluster.insert(current)
10   neighbors.pushAll(current.neighbors())
11   **until** *neighbors.empty();*

4.1.2 Clustered Movement

Once a cluster is formed, we must decide in which direction to move it. In this work, we opted to shift the cluster towards the center of mass of critical neighbor pins weighted by their negative slack, as shown in Figure 1.

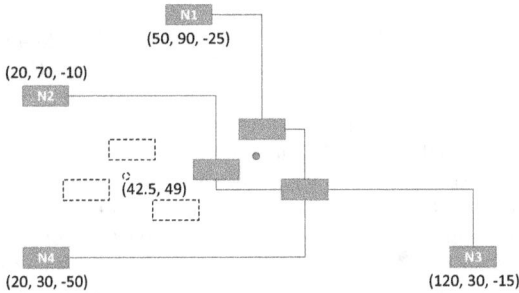

(50, 90, -25)
(20, 70, -10)
N2
N1
(42.5, 49)
N4
(20, 30, -50)
N3
(120, 30, -15)

Figure 1: The target position for a cluster according to Equation (2). For each neighbor node N a tuple (x, y, slack) is specified.

So, the target position of cluster cells is computed as:

$$target\_pos(cluster) = \frac{\sum_{i=1}^{n} pos(N_i) \times slack(N_i)}{\sum_{i=1}^{n} slack(N_i)} \quad (2)$$

where n is the number of critical neighbor pins of the cluster, $pos(N_i)$ and $slack(N_i)$ are the position and the slack of the pin associated to the neighbor cell i. Then, for each cell in the cluster we obtain a new position as:

$$new\_pos(cell) = pos(cell) + [target\_pos(cluster) - center(cluster)] \quad (3)$$

where $pos(cell)$ is the current cell position, $target\_pos(cluster)$ is the cluster center target position computed in Equation

(2) and $center(cluster)$ is the current central position of the cluster.

4.2 Buffer Balancing

After buffer insertion, the circuit may contain several buffer chains. However placement is not always aware of the different drive strengths of cells that compose the chain, which may degrade timing. The general idea of buffer balancing is shown in Figure 2 where the delay of the path segment is reduced if the buffer is placed closer to its sink.

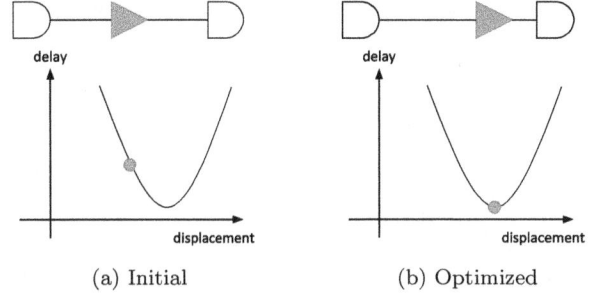

(a) Initial   (b) Optimized

Figure 2: Buffer balancing technique finds the buffer position that minimizes the segment path delay.

To find the displacement where the delay is minimum, an analytical formula is devised. This formula takes into account the cell strengths assuming that the interconnection is modeled as an RC tree and its delay is computed via Elmore delay [4]. We assume the buffer's driver and its sink are fixed while the buffer can freely move between them. Moreover the driver is assumed to drive only the buffer and the buffer to drive only one sink. This idea can be applied iteratively so that buffer chains with arbitrary number of buffers can be handled. In our experiments, only a few iterations are necessary to align all the buffers in the design.

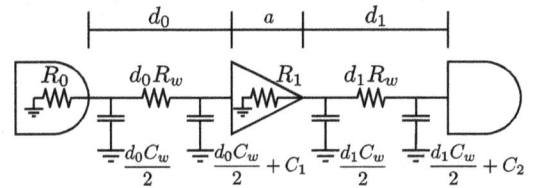

Figure 3: Buffer balancing modeling.

Figure 3 shows a single buffer chain, whose delay, D can be described as in Equation (4) using the Elmore delay model.

$$D = R_0 \left(C_1 + d_0 C_w\right) + d_0 R_w \left(C1 + \frac{d_0 C_w}{2}\right) + p_0$$
$$+ R_1 \left(C_2 + d_1 C_w\right) + d_1 R_w \left(C2 + \frac{d_1 C_w}{2}\right) + p_1 \quad (4)$$

where R_0 is the resistance of the buffer's driver, C_1 is the input pin load capacitance of the buffer, d_0 is the wirelength from driver to buffer, R_w is the wire resistance per unit-length, C_w is the wire capacitance per unit-length, R_1 is the buffer resistance, d_1 is the wire length from the buffer to its sink, C_2 is the load capacitance on the input sink pin, p_0 and p_1 are parasitic delays of the driver and buffer, respectively.

Considering that $d = d_0 + a + d_1$ where a is the distance of input and output buffer pins, the minimum delay is obtained by setting $\frac{\partial D}{\partial d_0} = 0$ as described by Equation (5), which for practical purposes is clamped in the range $[0, d]$.

$$d_0 = \frac{C_w(R_1 - R_0) + R_w[C_2 - C_1 + C_w(d-a)]}{2C_w R_w} \quad (5)$$

Equation (6) defines the optimal position of the buffer w.r.t. its driver. As Manhattan routing is used, this may lead to multiple optimal positions. However by placing the buffer on the straight line connecting the driver and sink may help straightening the path which is a very common way to improve delay. Therefore, the buffer is placed on the straight line by setting its position to

$$P_b = P_d + \frac{d_0}{d} \times (P_s - P_d) \quad (6)$$

where P_b is the new buffer position, P_d is the driver position and P_s is the sink position.

4.3 Cell Balancing

In this section, we extend the formulation of buffer balancing to handle more general cases, i.e, non-buffers cells with multiple input pins and multiple sinks. To do so, we first compute the cell position for each timing arc individually and then combine the results to obtain the best cell position.

We restrict the region of a cell movement between the point it connects to its driving tree, here called driver point, and the point it connects to its sink tree, sink point, as shown in Figure 4.

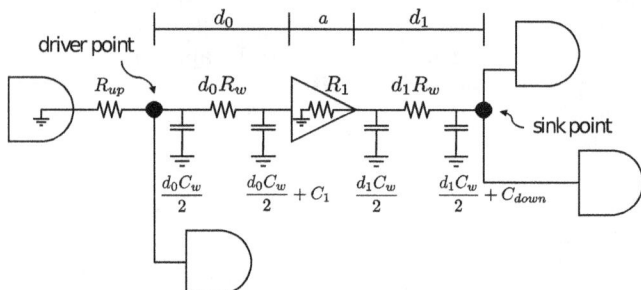

Figure 4: Cell balancing modeling.

Let R_{up} be the upstream resistance of the driver point (i.e. the sum of the resistance from the driver point up to the root of the tree, which includes the driver resistance). Let D_{up} be the delay at the driver point when the branch from the driver point to the cell is removed. Let C_{down} be the downstream capacitance of the sink point excluding any capacitance added by the branch connecting the cell to the sink point (i.e. sum of all capacitances from the sink point down to all leaf points including pin capacitances). Then the delay, D, from the driver cell and the sink point is given by Equation (7)

$$D = D_0 + D_1 \quad (7)$$

where

$$\begin{aligned} D_0 = & D_{up} + R_{up}(C_1 + C_w d_0) \\ & + d_0 R_w \left(C_1 + \frac{d_0 C_w}{2} \right) + p_0 \end{aligned} \quad (8)$$

is the delay from the driver cell to the input of the current cell and

$$D_1 = R_1[C_{down} + d_1 C_w] + d_1 R_w \left[C_{down} + \frac{d_1 C_w}{2} \right] + p_1 \quad (9)$$

is the delay from the current cell to the sink point, C_1 is cell input pin capacitance, d_0 is the wirelength between the driver point and the cell, d_1 is wirelength from the cell to the sink point, R_1 is the cell resistance and p_0 and p_1 are the driver and cell parasitic delay, respectively.

To a reason that will be apparent later D_0 and D_1 are weighted by w_0 and w_1 respectively so that the weighted delay is given by Equation (10).

$$D = w_0 D_0 + w_1 D_1 \quad (10)$$

Considering that $d = d_0 + a + d_1$ where a is the distance of input and output cell pins, the minimum delay is obtained by setting $\frac{\partial D}{\partial d_0} = 0$ as described by Equation (11) which for practical purposes is also clamped in the range $[0, d]$.

$$\begin{aligned} d_0 = & \frac{w_1 C_w R_1 - w_0 R_w C_1 + w_1 R_w[C_w(d-a) + C_{down}]}{R_w C_w(w_0 + w_1)} \\ & - \frac{w_0 R_{up} C_w}{R_w C_w(w_0 + w_1)} \end{aligned}$$
$$(11)$$

Note that Equation (11) reduces to Equation (5) for a single buffer chain. The final position is obtained in the same way as in the buffer alignment technique.

Since we may have several target positions, one for each input pin, they are combined by their weighted average. Where the weight of each position is the importance of the input pin, which is set to $2 \times centrality + criticality$ in this work.

The reason to weight the partial delays is due to the effect on the delay of side cells. By minimizing the delay of a tuple driver-cell-sink we may degrade the delay of other cells nearby. For instance, if the critical sink of the driver is not the cell we are handling and if the cell moves away from the driver it will probably increase the delay on the critical cell due to the increased load capacitance. Here we use the driver's output pin importance as w_0 and the cell's output pin importance as w_1. Note that if the driver is more critical than the sink, the cell will likely get close to the driver, reducing its load capacitance and hence improving its delay.

4.4 Load Optimization

For critical nets with more than two cells, the sink cells with no late violations (i.e. positive slack) are moved closer to their driver cells in order to improve timing as shown in Figure 5. The main idea behind this approach is to reduce the interconnection load capacitance of critical nets and therefore improve the delay of the driver cell. Note that, by moving non-critical sinks closer to the root of the tree, besides reducing the total tree capacitance, we also are reducing the cumulative impact of the sink capacitance in the downstream nodes of the routing tree. Since the sinks moved are non-critical, the paths passing through them are likely to not generate new violations.

Nevertheless the movements are accepted only if they actually are likely to reduce timing violations in critical nets and do not cause timing violation in the sink cells. Otherwise, non-critical sink cells are kept in their initial position.

To accomplish that, after routing trees are re-built, the timing is updated locally.

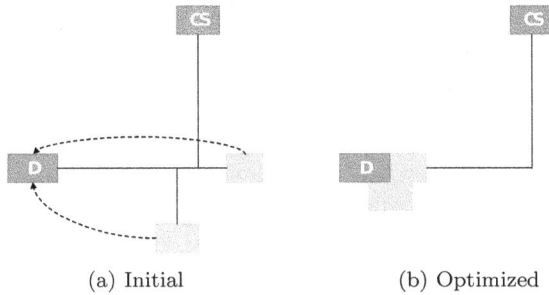

(a) Initial   (b) Optimized

Figure 5: Load Reduction applied to a critical net. Non-critical sinks (lighter cells) are moved closer to their driver cell (D).

5. EARLY OPTIMIZATION

In this section, techniques for early violation mitigation during the placement are also presented. We present four algorithms targeted to minimize early violations. The proposed algorithms explore wire load capacitance and resistance of the critical nets and useful clock skew to minimize early timing violations.

Let us consider a timing path between two registers. The register at the beginning of the path is called input register and the register at the end, output register. The early slack in a register-to-register path is defined by Equation (12)

$$
\begin{aligned}
slack_D^{early} &= at_D^{early} - rat_D^{early} \\
slack_D^{early} &= l_i^{early} + d_{path}^{early} - l_o^{late} - t_{hold}
\end{aligned}
\tag{12}
$$

where at_D^{early} and rat_D^{early} are the early arrival and required time respectively at the data input pin of the output register, l_i^{early} and l_o^{late} are the early and late clock latency at the clock pin of input and output registers respectively, d_{path}^{early} is the early delay among the registers and t_{hold} is the hold time of the output register.

According to Equation (12), the early slack can be improved by (i) increasing the path delay, (ii) increasing the clock latency at the input register, (iii) decreasing the clock latency on the output register and (iv) decreasing hold time. In this work, hold time is considered constant. The difference among the clock latencies is called clock skew.

5.1 Skew Optimization

The early slack can be improved by decreasing the clock latency on the output register. One way to achieve that is by moving the register closer to the clock source (e.g. a local clock buffer) as depicted in Figure 6.

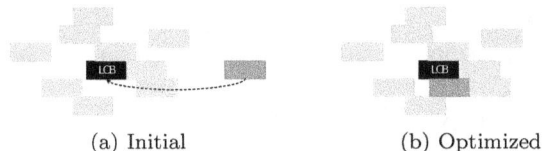

(a) Initial   (b) Optimized

Figure 6: Clock skew optimization by moving registers closer to LCBs.

Although the latency on the moved register is typically reduced, there might be side effects as latency changes on other registers and on other data path delay. Also a register can be both the start and end point of different paths. So a reduction on the latency may improve the slack on the incoming path, but may worsen the slack on the outgoing path. However, our experimental results showed that this technique is effective to improve early slack, on average.

5.2 Iterative Spreading

The iterative cell spreading tentatively moves all cells with early timing violation to north, south, east and west. The displacement from current position is set initially to 10% of a maximum displacement. If a better position is not found, the search area is gradually increased. The cost of a position is calculated updating timing locally and checking if the arrival time in the involved pins have increased.

5.3 Register Swap

Register swap tries to avoid the side effect on clock latency present in clock skew optimization (Section 5.1). Assuming that the registers are all the same (e.g. same size, V_{th}), by swapping the registers driven by a same clock source, the clock tree and its timing characteristics will not change. Hence the latency on each tree endpoint can be seen as constant.

The register swap is modeled as an assignment problem similar to [6], which can be optimally solved in polynomial time by the Hungarian algorithm [10]. The current register positions are seen as the slots to where the register should be assigned as illustrated by Figure 7. The goal is to minimize the total cost of the assignment.

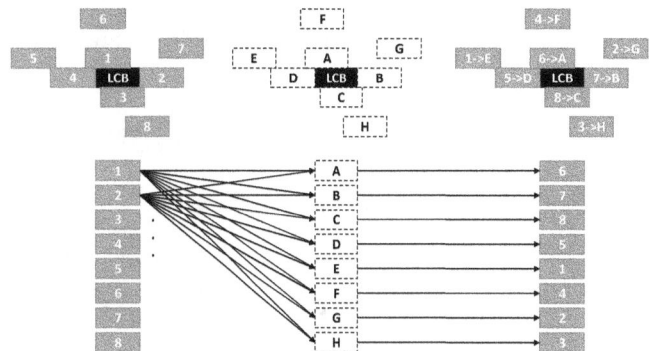

Figure 7: Register swap by optimal assignment.

The cost to assign a register i to a slot k is set as in Equation (13) where $criticality_D^{early}$ and $criticality_{CK}^{early}$ are the criticality of the data and clock pins of the register, respectively. The maximum displacement constraint can be modeled by setting an infinity cost whenever an assignment violates the maximum allowed displacement.

$$
cost(i,k) = l^{late} criticality_D^{early} - l^{early} criticality_{CK}^{early} \tag{13}
$$

The idea behind this cost function is as follows. When the register acts as the output register (path ends at the data pin), according to Equation (12), its clock latency should be decreased to improve slack. In terms of assignment cost, a larger latency should imply a larger cost $(+l^{late} criticality_D^{early})$. Similarly, when the register acts as the input register (path starts at the clock pin), its clock latency should be increased. From an assignment cost point of view, a larger latency should imply a smaller cost $(-l^{early} criticality_{CK}^{early})$. The latencies are weighted by pin criticalities to optimize latency based on the influence of registers on timing violations.

5.4 Register-to-Register Path Fix

A common source of hold violations is a path connecting directly two registers, i.e. no combinational logical cells between them, as show Figure 8.

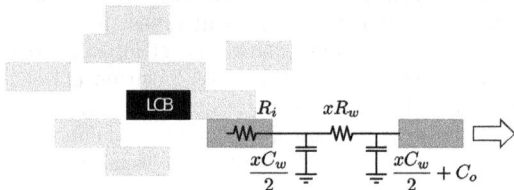

Figure 8: Register-to-register early violation path fix.

Besides skew optimization, early (hold) violations can be fixed by increasing the timing path delay. By setting the early slack to zero in Equation (12), the path delay that eliminates the violation is given by Equation (14).

$$d_{path}^{early} = l_o^{late} + t_{hold} - l_i^{early} \qquad (14)$$

In the case of a direct path between registers, the timing path delay is simply composed by the input register delay plus the wire delay and it can be increased by moving the registers apart. Assuming that the cell delay is modeled via its driver resistance and the wire via Elmore delay, Equation (14) can be rewritten as in Equation (15) where x is the distance between the input and output registers and $K = l_o^{late} + t_{hold} - l_i^{early}$.

$$K = R_i \left(xC_w + C_o \right) + xR_w \left(\frac{xC_w}{2} + C_o \right) \qquad (15)$$

Assuming that the latencies do not change as the registers are moved apart and that the hold time is also constant (i.e. K is constant), Equation (15) can be solved w.r.t. x as in Equation (16).

$$x = \frac{\sqrt{2C_w R_w K + C_o{}^2 R_w{}^2 + C_w{}^2 R_i{}^2} - C_o R_w - C_w R_i}{C_w R_w} \qquad (16)$$

Once the optimum wirelength, x, is calculated, the input register is moved away from the output register following the straight line formed by the two registers.

6. ABU REDUCTION

We implemented an algorithm to minimize Average Bin Utilization (ABU) area violation. All cells with positive slack inside of bins with ABU violation are ranked. The cells with highest positive slack are moved first to the nearest bin with enough room. The source and target bin utilization are update incrementally after each cell movement. After each cell is moved, the routing trees are rebuilt and the timing updated locally. We only accept a cell movement if its estimated slack is still positive and the target bin utilization is lower than the maximum area utilization allowed. The

process continues until all bins reach their target density or no more cell can be moved.

7. FLOW

The techniques presented in this work are combined in an incremental flow for timing-driven detailed placement, as shown in Figure 9. The diamond shape indicates that the steps are run until the quality of the result is not improved. The circle shape indicates that the quality of the result can degrade a certain number of times before exiting. The best solution found is restored.

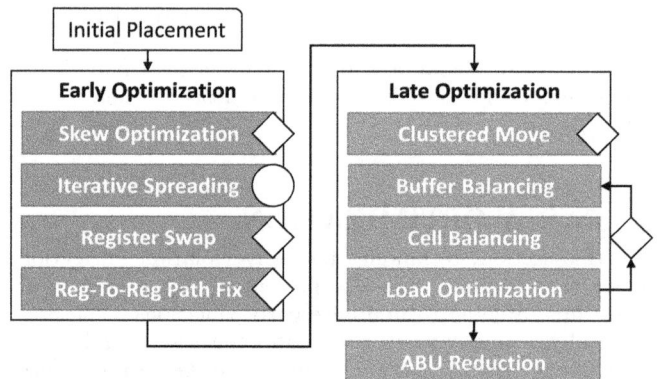

Figure 9: Our incremental timing-driven detailed placement flow.

The flow is divided into three main phases: early optimization, late optimization and ABU reduction. Early and late phases are divided into several steps.

In the early optimization phase, all early critical registers are tentatively moved closer to their local clock buffers in the Skew Optimization step. Registers are processed in increasing order of criticality. Next the Iterative Spreading is performed on all early critical cells. This is the only step allowed to degrade the quality of result. The rationale is that the clock skew has a large influence on early violations which may introduce a large noise in the estimated timing changes. Experiments show that it is better to allow degradation and to keep track of the best solution than to stop immediately when a degradation occurs. If the Iterative Spreading is not able to remove all the early violations, the Register Swap and Register-to-Register Path Fix are executed.

The late optimization phase begins by applying the Clustered Movement on top most late critical cells in increasing order of criticality. Once a cell is moved, it is not moved again in the same iteration. Next a loop composed of one iteration of Buffer Balancing, Cell Balancing and Load Optimization is executed. Buffer and Cell Balancing are applied for all late critical cells in increasing order of criticality. Load Optimization is performed for all non-critical sinks of critical nets. Cells are processed in increasing order of their driver cell's criticallity.

Finally, the ABU Reduction is performed to spread non-critical cells and hence to reduce the number of regions with high cell density.

7.1 Legalization

After a move is executed, the cell is likely to overlap other cells and a legalization needs to be performed. Current designs have a lot of free space intentionally added to improve routablity and to make easier to perform incremental changes such as sizing and detailed placement. Therefore, to avoid disturbing the position of other cells, the legalization, in this work, is performed by searching for the nearest whitespace available around the intended target position. Our legalization relies on Jezz [12] legalizer.

7.2 Filtering out Bad Moves

A cell movement may cause the routing trees connected to the cell to change drastically and hence huge timing variation may occur, which misleads some optimization methods. To avoid timing degradation caused by such changes and also by legalization noise, local timing is evaluated and the move is optionally committed only if the local timing violation is reduced.

The degradation is computed as $\Delta cost$ where the cost is the sum of the weighted arrival times of the neighboring pins of the moved cell. In this work, the weight is set to $2 \times centrality + criticality$, which gives more importance to TNS-critical pins. This weighting function also helps to avoid focusing too much on Worst Negative Slack (WNS) improvement which may cause side effect degradation on TNS.

8. EXPERIMENTAL RESULTS

Our flow is implemented in C++11 and executed on an Intel® Core™ i7-4790K CPU @ 4.00GHz × 8 CPU with 32GB running Ubuntu 14.04 LTS (64-bit). Our flow relies on a built-in timer.

It is empirically validated using the ICCAD 2015 Incremental Timing-Driven Placement Contest infrastructure [7]. Eight mixed-size benchmarks are available ranging from approximately $700k$ to $2M$ elements. Initial placement solutions are provided for all benchmarks and they are optimized using two configurations for the maximum cell displacement: *short* and *long*. The quality of results is measured using *quality score* [8], which takes into account the early and late slack improvement and the ABU change.

Table 1 presents the benchmark characteristics and the results of our flow along with the initial solution and the results from the 1st place in the ICCAD 2015 Contest. The timing information, Steiner Tree Wirelength (STWL) and ABU are reported by the evaluation script provided by the contest organizers. Runtimes were measured in different machines and they are mostly shown for reference. However it is worth pointing out that our flow is about 4.6× faster, on average, than the 1st place.

For *long maximum cell displacement*, compared to the 1st place, our flow provides improved quality score results for all benchmarks. Considering metrics individually, with the exception of STWL, our flow also provides improved results in almost all cases. The exceptions are early violations in superblue7 and late violations in superblue5. Our flow is also able to achieve zero early violations in 5 out of 8 benchmarks.

For *short maximum cell displacement*, our flow provides improved quality score results on average. However results are mixed for both circuits and metrics. Results from the 1st place are particularly better on early WNS. This probably comes from the fact that they perform Local Clock Buffer (LCB) reallocation where registers can be connected to a different LCB. Note that for short maximum displacement

the exploration space is reduced, which tends to flatten the improvements obtained among different approaches.

8.1 Move Gains

Table 2 shows the average impact of each move over all ICCAD 2015 benchmarks for short and long displacement. The results were obtained by applying only one pass of each technique directly to the initial solution. Note that the improvements of some moves may be better if they are combined with other moves. Also some moves may benefit more than others when multiple passes are performed.

As it can be seen the most effective method for early timing violation reduction is the Iterative Spreading. For late timing violation reduction, the Cell Balancing technique is the most effective one. The benefit of the Cell Balancing over other moves is particularly prominent in the short displacement.

Although very simple, the Load Reduction can achieve a significant improvement on quality score for this set of benchmarks. This comes at cost of increased density as measured by ABU, however such an increase is easily mitigated by the ABU Reduction step. The step ABU Reduction does not present quality score gains, in spite of its large gains in the ABU penalty as the ABU improvement works as a scaling factor in the quality score metric.

9. CONCLUSIONS

In this paper, we presented an incremental TDP flow composed by several single-cell move techniques able to reduce early and late timing violations.

Our results show that our drive strength aware load balancing technique is very effective to reduce late timing violations. Although load balancing can also be achieved via cell sizing, by finding a more balanced cell position during placement, one can reduce delay with no or minor impact on power. Moreover, our techniques for early slack improvement are able to remove violations for almost every benchmark.

Our TDP flow was empirically validated using the ICCAD 2015 contest infrastructure. It achieves, on average, best timing closure compared to the 1st place team on the contest particularly when cells are allowed to move greater distances.

10. ACKNOWLEDGMENT

This work is partially supported by Brazilian Coordination for the Improvement of Higher Education Personnel (CAPES) and by the National Council for Scientific and Technological Development (CNPq).

11. REFERENCES

[1] R. K. Ahuja, T. L. Magnanti, and J. B. Orlin. *Network Flows: Theory, Algorithms, and Applications.* Prentice-Hall, Inc., Upper Saddle River, NJ, USA, 1993.

[2] A. Bock, S. Held, N. Kämmerling, and U. Schorr. Local search algorithms for timing-driven placement under arbitrary delay models. In *DAC*, pages 29:1–29:6. ACM, 2015.

[3] M. Burstein and M. Youssef. Timing influenced layout design. In *DAC*, pages 124–130, June 1985.

Table 1: Experimental results of our incremental timing-driven placement flow on ICCAD 2015 contest benchmarks.

Benchmark Cells / Macros Max Disp.	Solution	Short								Long							
		ABU	StWL (μm) ×10^7	Early (ps)		Late (ps)		Run-time (min)	Quality Score	ABU	StWL (μm) ×10^7	Early (ps)		Late (ps)		Run-time (min)	Quality Score
				WNS ×10^0	TNS ×10^0	WNS ×10^3	TNS ×10^5					WNS ×10^0	TNS ×10^0	WNS ×10^3	TNS ×10^5		
superblue1	Initial	0.054	9.59	-9.34	-317	-4.98	-4.6	-	-	0.054	9.59	-9.34	-317	-4.98	-4.6	-	-
1.21M / 3787	1st Place	0.058	9.6	-3.83	-41.6	-4.67	-3.74	40.5	447.59	0.056	9.61	-16.7	-80.9	-4.57	-3.51	37.4	346.64
40μm / 400μm	Ours	0.008	9.72	-9.25	-50.6	-4.61	-3.82	6.5	391.65	0.011	9.9	-9.25	-36.7	-4.46	-3.41	5.4	508.41
superblue3	Initial	0.029	11.4	-78.4	-1460	-10.1	-15	-	-	0.029	11.4	-78.4	-1460	-10.1	-15	-	-
1.21M / 2074	1st Place	0.031	11.4	-65.7	-684	-9.44	-13.7	19.4	243.18	0.031	11.5	-13.1	-214	-8.71	-11.6	22.4	551.74
40μm / 400μm	Ours	0.007	11.5	-30.3	-434	-9.4	-13.4	7.8	351.05	0.008	11.6	-10.7	-91	-8.38	-9.33	7.6	755.54
superblue4	Initial	0.044	7.15	-12.6	-519	-6.22	-34.8	-	-	0.044	7.15	-12.6	-519	-6.22	-34.8	-	-
796k / 3471	1st Place	0.045	7.15	-6.08	-174	-5.94	-32	16.7	287.55	0.048	7.16	-12.3	-53.8	-5.76	-24.6	18.6	507.31
20μm / 400μm	Ours	0.032	7.21	-11.8	-145	-5.98	-31.2	5.2	276.19	0.040	7.55	0	0	-5.68	-23.6	5.7	665.55
superblue5	Initial	0.021	10.8	-36.8	-591	-25.7	-69.7	-	-	0.021	10.8	-36.8	-591	-25.7	-69.7	-	-
1.09M / 1872	1st Place	0.022	10.8	-36.8	-586	-25.1	-67.8	14.7	40.67	0.021	10.8	-36.8	-618	-24.3	-58.4	15.9	179.53
30μm / 400μm	Ours	0.000	10.8	-35.8	-291	-25.3	-67.2	6.3	149.11	0.000	10.9	0	0	-24.6	-59.9	3.2	469.52
superblue7	Initial	0.030	14	-7.65	-1990	-15.2	-18.6	-	-	0.030	14	-7.65	-1990	-15.2	-18.6	-	-
1.93M / 4910	1st Place	0.031	14	-6.75	-1940	-15.2	-17	42.8	98.48	0.031	14	-6.75	-1960	-15.2	-15.1	53.1	200.72
50μm / 500μm	Ours	0.007	14.2	-7.53	-1970	-15.2	-16.1	8.1	141.32	0.007	14.2	-7.53	-1970	-15.2	-13.8	7.8	264.42
superblue10	Initial	0.042	20.5	-8.62	-621	-16.5	-332	-	-	0.042	20.5	-8.62	-621	-16.5	-332	-	-
1.88M / 1696	1st Place	0.043	20.5	-8.62	-361	-16.2	-325	22.5	111.87	0.043	20.6	-5.15	-374	-16.1	-315	25.3	181.33
20μm / 500μm	Ours	0.020	20.6	-6.8	-383	-16.3	-319	11.8	142.67	0.012	21.1	0	0	-15.7	-280	9.3	492.91
superblue16	Initial	0.033	9.33	-10.7	-114	-4.58	-7.76	-	-	0.033	9.33	-10.7	-114	-4.58	-7.76	-	-
982k / 419	1st Place	0.041	9.36	-8.38	-30.7	-4.36	-5.14	22.8	524.72	0.040	9.37	-7.55	-37.6	-3.85	-2.66	32.0	894.76
30μm / 400μm	Ours	0.000	9.4	-0.548	-0.9	-4.34	-4.72	6.5	735.00	0.000	9.54	0	0	-3.46	-1.96	3.8	1,209.42
superblue18	Initial	0.040	5.77	-19	-283	-4.55	-10.3	-	-	0.040	5.77	-19	-283	-4.55	-10.3	-	-
768k / 653	1st Place	0.043	5.77	-3.81	-69.4	-4.12	-9.44	22.8	365.26	0.045	5.78	-1.95	-6.86	-3.82	-7.76	27.0	613.07
20μm / 400μm	Ours	0.013	5.83	-14.7	-81.9	-4.14	-9.48	4.5	302.28	0.010	5.9	0	0	-3.81	-6.45	3.6	780.90
Avg Change (%)	Initial	-72.82	0.89	-26.41	-60.80	-4.43	-13.24	-	-	-72.92	2.64	-73.60	-85.36	-10.75	-32.90	-	-
	1st Place	-74.00	0.79	45.25	-19.13	0.08	-2.31	-	48.55	-74.90	2.43	-68.92	-76.42	-2.31	-10.84	-	67.80

Table 2: Average impact of each technique over all ICCAD 2015 contest benchmarks for short and long maximum displacement.

Move	Goal	Short								Long							
		Quality Score	Run-time (s)	ABU	StWL	Early		Late		Quality Score	Run-time (s)	ABU	StWL	Early		Late	
						WNS	TNS	WNS	TNS					WNS	TNS	WNS	TNS
Iterative Spreading	Early	56.31	0.52	0.0%	0.4%	-6.7%	-24.8%	0.0%	0.0%	128.71	0.62	0.0%	0.5%	-26.2%	-51.3%	0.0%	0.0%
Clock Skew Opto	Early	43.32	0.03	0.0%	0.4%	5.9%	-24.7%	0.0%	0.0%	125.57	0.03	-0.1%	0.5%	-27.9%	-48.8%	0.0%	0.0%
Register Swap	Early	54.32	0.41	0.0%	0.5%	-10.3%	-22.0%	0.0%	0.0%	71.27	0.41	0.0%	0.5%	-14.1%	-28.6%	0.0%	0.0%
Reg-to-Reg Path Fix	Early	5.13	0.03	0.0%	0.4%	1.6%	-3.4%	0.0%	0.0%	29.86	0.04	0.0%	0.5%	0.6%	-15.2%	0.0%	0.0%
Clustered Movement	Late	15.90	9.29	0.1%	0.4%	0.0%	0.0%	-0.7%	-1.2%	52.87	9.33	0.1%	0.4%	0.0%	0.0%	-2.8%	-3.9%
Buffer Balancing	Late	44.26	0.58	0.8%	0.5%	0.0%	0.0%	-1.8%	-3.6%	89.32	0.81	0.0%	0.5%	0.0%	0.0%	-3.9%	-7.0%
Cell Balancing	Late	98.65	8.15	0.6%	0.5%	0.0%	0.0%	-3.2%	-8.2%	194.86	8.76	-0.2%	0.6%	0.0%	0.0%	-6.3%	-16.4%
Load Reduction	Late	42.65	7.60	2.1%	0.6%	0.0%	-0.1%	-0.9%	-3.8%	116.81	7.65	6.6%	1.8%	0.0%	-0.3%	-2.3%	-10.5%
ABU Reduction	ABU	-0.03	8.67	-52.4%	0.6%	0.0%	0.0%	0.0%	0.0%	-0.02	8.27	-58.5%	0.8%	0.0%	0.0%	0.0%	0.0%

[4] W. C. Elmore. The Transient Response of Damped Linear Networks with Particular Regard to Wideband Amplifiers. *Journal of Applied Physics*, 19(1):55–63, Jan. 1948.

[5] C. Guth, V. Livramento, R. Netto, R. Fonseca, J. L. Güntzel, and L. Santos. Timing-driven placement based on dynamic net-weighting for efficient slack histogram compression. In *ISPD*, pages 141–148. ACM, 2015.

[6] S. Held and U. Schorr. Post-routing latch optimization for timing closure. In *DAC*, pages 7:1–7:6. ACM, 2014.

[7] M.-C. Kim, J. Hu, J. Li, and N. Viswanathan. Iccad-2015 cad contest in incremental timing-driven placement and benchmark suite. In *ICCAD*, pages 921–926, Nov 2015.

[8] M.-C. Kim, J. Huj, and N. Viswanathan. Iccad-2014 cad contest in incremental timing-driven placement and benchmark suite: Special session paper: Cad contest. In *ICCAD*, pages 361–366, Nov 2014.

[9] T. Kong. A novel net weighting algorithm for timing-driven placement. In *ICCAD*, pages 172–176, Nov 2002.

[10] H. W. Kuhn. The hungarian method for the assignment problem. *Naval Research Logistics Quarterly*, 2(1-2):83–97, 1955.

[11] D. Papa, T. Luo, M. Moffitt, C. Sze, Z. Li, G.-J. Nam, C. Alpert, and I. Markov. Rumble: An incremental timing-driven physical-synthesis optimization algorithm. *TCAD*, 27(12):2156–2168, Dec 2008.

[12] J. Puget, G. Flach, M. Johann, and R. Reis. Jezz: An effective legalization algorithm forminimum displacement. In *SBCCI*, Sept 2015.

[13] R.-S. Tsay and J. Koehl. An analytic net weighting approach for performance optimization in circuit placement. In *DAC*, pages 620–625, June 1991.

[14] N. Viswanathan, G.-J. Nam, J. A. Roy, Z. Li, C. J. Alpert, S. Ramji, and C. Chu. Itop: Integrating timing optimization within placement. In *ISPD*, pages 83–90. ACM, 2010.

[15] Q. B. Wang, J. Lillis, and S. Sanyal. An lp-based methodology for improved timing-driven placement. In *ASP-DAC*, volume 2, pages 1139–1143 Vol. 2, Jan 2005.

[16] C. S. William Swartz. Timing driven placement for large standard cell circuits. In *DAC*, pages 211–215, 1995.

Construction of Latency-Bounded Clock Trees[*]

Rickard Ewetz, Chuan Yean Tan, Cheng-Kok Koh
School of Electrical and Computer Engineering
Purdue University
West Lafayette, IN 47907-2035
rewetz,tan56,chengkok@purdue.edu

ABSTRACT

Clock trees must be constructed to function even under the influence of on-chip variations (OCV). Bounding the latency of a clock tree, i.e., the maximum delay from the tree root to any sequential element, is important because the latency correlates with the maximum magnitude of the skews caused by OCV. In this paper, a latency constraint graph (LCG) that captures the latencies of a set of subtrees and the skew constraints between the subtrees is introduced. The minimum latency of a clock tree that can be constructed from the corresponding subtrees is equal to the (negative of the) length of a shortest path in the LCG, which can be computed in $O(VE)$. Based on the LCG, we propose a framework that consists of a latency-aware clock tree synthesis (CTS) phase and a clock tree optimization (CTO) phase to construct latency-bounded clock trees. When applied to a set of synthesized circuits, the framework is capable of constructing latency-bounded clock trees that have higher yield compared to clock trees constructed in previous studies.

Keywords

useful skew; latency; CTS; CTO

1. INTRODUCTION

With increasing impacts of on-chip variations (OCV), it is crucial to consider both timing constraints and latency when constructing clock trees for sequential circuits. Clock skew is the difference in the arrival time of the clock signal between a pair of sequential elements (or clock sinks). A clock tree must be constructed such that the clock signal is delivered meeting skew constraints even when the clock tree is under the influence of OCV. Earlier studies have focused on satisfying the skew constraints by providing guardbands to OCV by inserting safety margins in the skew constraints [15, 8]. However, by inserting safety margins in the skew constraints,

---

[*]This research was supported by NSF awards CFF-1065318 and CFF-1527562.

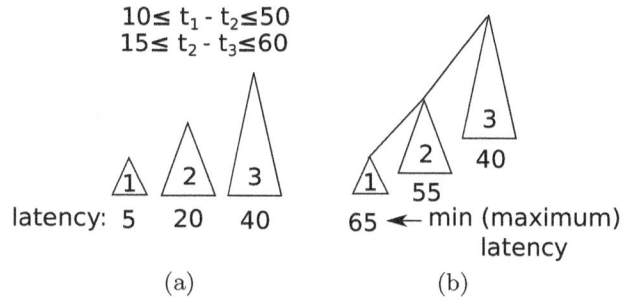

Figure 1: (a) Three subtrees, the respective latencies to the clock sinks, and the skew constraints between the clock sinks. (b) The minimum (maximum) latency to the clock sinks is 65.

the construction process becomes more constrained and the maximum delay from the root of the clock tree to any clock sink (maximum latency or simply latency in this paper) may become longer. This makes the constructed clock tree more susceptible to OCV. Typically, the propagation delay of a path in the clock tree correlates with the delay variations along the path. Therefore, by bounding the latency, the maximum magnitude of the skews caused by OCV is also bounded. Consequently, it is important to consider both safety margins and latency bounds when constructing clock trees.

In [15], a clock tree meeting arbitrary skew constraints (with safety margins inserted) was constructed by iteratively joining two smaller subtrees to form a larger subtree. The skew constraints were satisfied by joining each pair of subtrees within a feasible skew range (FSR). In [8], the Greedy-UST/DME algorithm in [15] was extended to enable larger safety margins to be inserted in the skew constraints. However, latency optimization was not considered in [15, 8]. Latency optimization has been considered indirectly during the construction of a clock tree in [3, 5, 11] and directly during clock tree optimization (CTO) in [12, 13].

The limitation of [12, 13] is that the potential latency reductions may be limited because of the structure of the initial clock tree. The drawback of [15, 8, 3, 5, 11] is that latency is not considered explicitly in the tree construction process. It is important to realize that the minimum latency of a clock tree, constructed from a set of subtrees, is dependent on both the latencies of the subtrees and the skew constraints between the subtrees, as illustrated in Figure 1.

Ideally, clock trees with an optimal latency and safety margin should be constructed. In this paper, we propose a framework to synthesize clock trees meeting a user-specified latency bound L_{user} while providing a user-specified safety margin M_{user} in the skew constraints. A main contribution is the introduction of a latency constraint graph (LCG). An LCG captures the latencies to the sequential elements, the skew constraints, and the skews committed in a tree construction process. The minimum (maximum) latency of a clock tree that is constructed from the sinks captured in the LCG is equal to the negative value of the length of the shortest path from a virtual source to a virtual sink in an LCG, which we refer to as the *latency path*. Both the latency path and the length of the latency path can be computed using the Bellman-Ford algorithm in $O(VE)$ [6].

The proposed framework consists of a latency-aware clock tree synthesis (CTS) phase and a CTO phase. In the latency-aware CTS phase, the construction of a clock tree is viewed as performing a series of delay insertions and skew commitments. By performing delay insertions and skew commitments within feasible delay insertion ranges (FDIRs) and feasible latency ranges (FLRs), respectively, it is ensured that the length of the *latency path* is bounded, which in turn bounds the latency of the clock tree. After the CTS phase is complete, CTO is performed to remove any remaining timing violations by realizing delay adjustments.

To the best of our knowledge, this is the first work that performs latency minimization while providing safety margin in the skew constraints. Moreover, by committing skews within the intersections of FSRs [15] and an FLRs, both arbitrary skew constraints and the latency bound are satisfied. Therefore, compared to [15, 8], our framework is also capable of constructing clock trees with given latency bounds. Furthermore, we observe that CTO is more effective when applied to clock trees with shorter latencies. Hence, we say that our latency-aware CTS phase constructs clock trees that are amenable to CTO. On a set of synthesized circuits with up to $13,216$ sequential elements, we improve the yield to 100%.

2. PRELIMINARIES

2.1 Skew constraints

The clock signal delivered to the sequential elements must meet both setup and hold time constraints. The setup and hold time constraints between a launching flip flop FF_i and a capturing flip flop FF_j are formulated as follows:

$$t_i + t_i^{CQ} + t_{ij}^{max} + t_j^S \leq t_j + T, \qquad (1)$$

$$t_i + t_i^{CQ} + t_{ij}^{min} \geq t_j + t_j^H, \qquad (2)$$

where t_i and t_j are the arrival times of the clock signal at FF_i and FF_j; t_i^{CQ} is the clock to output delay of FF_i; T is the clock period; t_j^H and t_j^S are the hold time and setup time of FF_j, respectively; t_{ij}^{max} and t_{ij}^{min} are the maximum and minimum propagation delays through the combinational logic from FF_i to FF_j, respectively. Using $skew_{ij} = t_i - t_j$, and $l_{ij} = t_j - t_i^{CQ} - t_{ij}^{min}$ and $u_{ij} = T - t_i^{CQ} - t_{ij}^{max} - t_j^S$, Eq (1) and Eq (2) are reformulated as follows, and referred to as skew constraints:

$$l_{ij} \leq skew_{ij} \leq u_{ij}. \qquad (3)$$

To satisfy the skew constraints under variations, the constraints are tightened with a uniform safety margin M_{user} as follows:

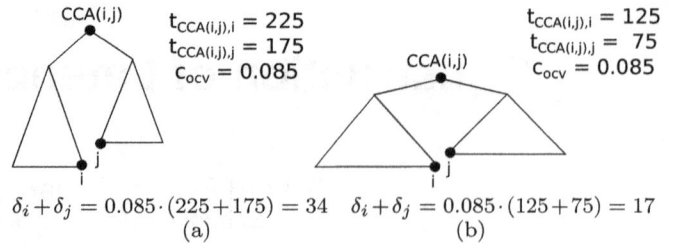

Figure 2: (a) A clock tree with long latency. (b) A clock tree with short latency. The delay variations in the setup and hold time constraint between FF_i and FF_j are estimated to be 34 ps and 17 ps in (a) and (b), respectively.

$$l_{ij} + M_{user} \leq skew_{ij} \leq u_{ij} - M_{user}. \qquad (4)$$

The skew constraints are tightened with a uniform safety margin because it is hard to estimate the impact of OCV before an initial clock tree has been constructed in CTS. The skew constraints with safety margins in Eq (4) can be captured in a skew constraint graph (SCG). In an SCG $G = (V, E)$, the vertices V represent the sequential elements and the edges E represent the skew constraints. The skew constraints with safety margins in Eq (4) are represented with an edge e_{ij} from vertex i to vertex j, with the weight $w_{ij} = -(l_{ij} + M_{user})$ and with an edge e_{ji} from vertex j to vertex i with a weight of $w_{ji} = u_{ij} - M_{user}$. The SCG of the skew constraints in Figure 1(a) is shown with red dashed lines and circles in the middle part of Figure 3.

2.2 On-chip variations

After CTS has been performed, the negative effects of the OCV can be estimated using the timing and topology of the initial clock tree. Next, the estimates are used to evaluate performance and to guide CTO. The constraints in Eq (1) and Eq (2) are extended to include OCV as follows:

$$t_i + t_i^{CQ} + t_{ij}^{max} + t_j^S + \delta_i \leq t_j + T - \delta_j, \qquad (5)$$

$$t_i + t_i^{CQ} + t_{ij}^{min} - \delta_i \geq t_j + t_j^H + \delta_j, \qquad (6)$$

where δ_i and δ_j are the delay variations caused by OCV. Let the closest common ancestor (CCA) of FF_i and FF_j be denoted as $CCA(i,j)$. The delay variations δ_i and δ_j are only accumulated on the paths from $CCA(i,j)$ to FF_i and FF_j, respectively.

By assuming that the delay variations on a path are proportional to the propagation delay of the path, the delay variations δ_i and δ_j are estimates as follows:

$$\delta_i = c_{ocv} \cdot t_{CCA(i,j),i}, \qquad (7)$$

$$\delta_j = c_{ocv} \cdot t_{CCA(i,j),j}, \qquad (8)$$

where $t_{CCA(i,j),i}$ and $t_{CCA(i,j),j}$ are the propagation delays from $CCA(i,j)$ to FF_i and FF_j, respectively; c_{ocv} is a user-specified parameter. Consequently, a clock tree with a long latency is more susceptible to OCV variations compared with a clock tree with short latency, as illustrated in Figure 2.

Using the estimates, the total negative slack (TNS) and the worst negative slack (WNS) in the constraints in Eq (5) and Eq (6) can be computed. Note that if the latency of the clock tree L is less than or equal to a latency bound $L \leq \frac{M_{user}}{2 \cdot c_{ocv}}$, it is ensured that $\delta_i + \delta_j \leq M_{user}$ is satisfied for each pair of flip flops FF_i and FF_j, i.e., TNS = 0 and WNS = 0. This holds because the delay variations $\delta_i + \delta_j$ can be estimated with $c_{ocv} \cdot t_{CCA(i,j),i} + c_{ocv} \cdot t_{CCA(i,j),j}$ and bounded by $2 \cdot c_{ocv} \cdot L$ because $t_{CCA(i,j),i} \leq L$, and $t_{CCA(i,j),j} \leq L$.

However, it is typically impossible, or very costly, to construct a clock tree meeting such stringent latency bounds. Therefore, we set the user-specified latency bound L_{user} to be a fraction of the latency of a clock tree constructed with no latency bound.

2.3 Problem definition

This paper considers a clock tree synthesis problem, i.e., constructing a clock trees that deliver synchronizing clock signals to sequential elements while satisfying skew constraints and transition time constraints under the influence of OCV, in order to obtain high yield. The objective is to minimize the power consumption of these clock trees.

Two key factors that influence yield are latency and safety margins. Large safety margins implies tighter skew constraints, which restrict the tree construction process and typically results in clock trees that have longer latencies; such clock trees are more susceptible to OCV. Therefore, we approach the synthesis problem by constructing latency-bounded clock trees with uniform safety margin provided in the skew constraints. This problem has two inter-related components: (1) Determining the optimal values for the latency bound and the uniform safety margin, which are denoted as L_{opt} and M_{opt}, respectively. (2) Constructing a clock tree for some L_{opt} and M_{opt}.

We limit the scope of this paper to component (2) of this problem, i.e., constructing a clock tree for some given user-specified latency bounds L_{user} and uniform safety margins M_{user}. We rely on the user to provide appropriate values of L_{user} and M_{user}. In our future work, we will also investigate component (1) of the problem, i.e., how to determine M_{opt} and L_{opt}, and the problem as a whole.

2.4 The Greedy-UST/DME algorithm

Using the Greedy-UST/DME algorithm [15], a clock tree can be constructed meeting the constraints captured in an SCG, i.e., the skew constraints with safety margins in Eq (4). The algorithm constructs a clock tree meeting arbitrary skew constraints by iteratively merging a pair of smaller subtrees to form a larger subtree. In [15], it was shown that if two subtrees were merged within a feasible skew range (FSR), all the skew constraints would be satisfied. An FSR is computed by finding two shortest path in an SCG. Specifically, the FSR between two subtrees i and j is:

$$FSR_{ij} = [-d_{ij}, d_{ji}], \qquad (9)$$

where, d_{ij} and d_{ji} are the shortest paths from vertex i to vertex j and the shortest path from vertex j to vertex i in the SCG, respectively. Later, when the merging location is decided and the two subtrees are joined physically, the FSR is narrowed to a specific skew value, committing the skew. The skew commitment requires two edges to be added to the SCG, an edge e_{ij} with a weight of $w_{ij} = -a$ and an edge e_{ji} with a edge weight of $w_{ji} = a$, are added.

3. LATENCY CONSTRAINT GRAPH

We introduce the concept of a latency constraint graph (LCG) as follows. First, we define the term *sink latency*.

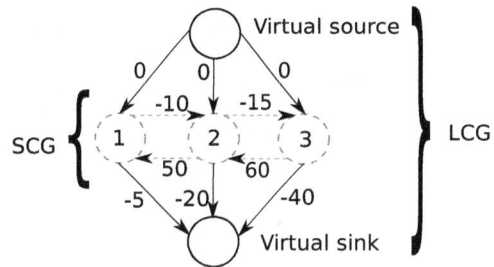

Figure 3: The latency path, i.e., the shortest path from the virtual source to the virtual sink has a length of $0 + (-10) + (-15) + (-40) = -65$.

For each respective sink, the *sink latency* is equal to the delay from the root of a subtree where the sink resides to the respective sink. An LCG $G = (V, E)$, is an extension of an SCG. An LCG consists of the vertices and edges of an SCG with the addition of a virtual source and a virtual sink. An LCG for the subtrees in Figure 1(a) is shown in Figure 3. We refer to the original vertices of an SCG as sink vertices. As illustrated in Figure 3, the virtual source is connected to each of the sink vertices with a directed edge with a weight of 0. Moreover, each sink vertex is connected to the virtual sink with an directed edge with a weight equal to the negative value of the respective *sink latency*.

Latency path: We call the shortest path from the virtual source to the virtual sink the *latency path* and the length of the latency path is denoted as s^p. The minimum (maximum) latency of a clock tree that is constructed from the sinks captured in the LCG is equal to $-s^p$. Both the latency path and the length of the latency path can be found in $O(VE)$ using the Bellman-Ford algorithm [6]. Consequently, the subtrees in Figure 1 can be joined to a clock tree with a latency of 65 because $-s^p = 65$ in Figure 3.

To find a clock tree with the latency of $-s^p$, we introduce the reversed graph $\bar{G}$ of the LCG G. In the reversed graph $\bar{G}$, all the edges in G are reversed, i.e., an edge from vertex i to vertex j in G is equivalent to an edge from vertex j to vertex i in $\bar{G}$. Moreover, the top-down shortest path from the virtual source to a vertex i in G is denoted s_i^t and the bottom-up shortest path from the virtual sink to a vertex i in $\bar{G}$ is denoted s_i^b. Interestingly, a clock tree constructed such that the latency to each sink is equal to the bottom-up shortest path to the respective sink vertex satisfies both the latency requirement and the skew constraints. Consequently, in the example, the latency to the sequential elements in such a clock tree would be $[-s_1^b, -s_2^b, -s_3^b] = [65, 55, 40]$.

3.1 Updating edge weights in LCG

The construction of a clock tree can be viewed as a series of delay insertion and skew commitment operations that correspond to both physical commitments in a tree construction process and an equivalent modifications of edge weights in the LCG and its reversed graph. The two operations are outlined as follows:

Delay insertion: This is the process of inserting a piece of wire or a buffer at the root of a subtree. In the LCG, the delay insertion increases the latency to all the sinks of residing in the subtree, which necessitates a reduction of the corresponding latency edge weights. (Without loss of generality, every subtree can be captured using a single representative sink. Therefore, a delay insertion is equivalent to the reduction of a single edge weight.)

Skew commitment: This is the process of joining two subtrees i and j to a single subtree. As in an SCG, if a $skew_{ij} = a$ is committed, two edges are required to be added to the LCG, an edge e_{ij} with a weight of $w_{ij} = -a$ and an edge e_{ji} with a edge weight of $w_{ji} = a$. Again, the added edge weights always correspond to a reduction of the edge weights.

In summary, both the delay insertion and skew commitment operations result in reductions of edge weights in the LCG. Moreover, the reductions may reduce the length of the latency path. To ensure that all subtrees can be joined to clock tree meeting a user-specified latency bound L_{user}, we introduce a feasible delay insertion range (FDIR) and a feasible latency range (FLR). If each delay insertion or skew commitment is performed within an FDIR or an FLR, respectively, $-s^p \leq L_{user}$ is ensured, and consequently the latency bound is satisfied.

3.2 Derivation of FDIRs and FLRs

Consider a delay insertion or a skew commitment operation that reduces the edge weight w_{ij} to $\widehat{w}_{ij}$. Assume that before the operation, $-s^p \leq L_{user}$ is satisfied. By reducing the edge weight w_{ij}, the latency path can only be reduced if the edge e_{ij} is part of the latency path. The shortest path from the virtual source to the virtual sink using the edge e_{ij} is denoted s_{ij}^p and equal to $s_{ij}^p = s_i^t + w_{ij} + s_j^b$. To meet the latency bound constraint, after the edge weight reduction, $-s_i^t - \widehat{w}_{ij} - s_j^b \leq L_{user}$ is required to be satisfied. This implies a constraint on $\widehat{w}_{ij}$, which is:

$$-\widehat{w}_{ij} \leq L_{user} + s_i^t + s_j^b. \tag{10}$$

The maximum delay insertion Δ_i at the root of a subtree i is equal to the slack in Eq (10) before the edge weight reduction, i.e., $L_{user} + s_i^t + s_j^b + w_{ij}$. Consequently, the $FDIR_i$ for a delay insertion Δ_i is formulated as follows:

$$FDIR_i = [0, \ L_{user} + s_i^t + w_{i,vsink}], \tag{11}$$

where $w_{i,vsink}$ is the weight of the edge from the sink vertex i to the virtual sink before the delay insertion, and s_i^t is the top-down shortest path to the sink vertex i and $s_j^b = 0$ since vertex j corresponds to the virtual sink.

Next, we formulate the FLR_{ij} for a skew commitment $skew_{ij}$. Recall that a skew commitment results in the addition of two edges e_{ij} and e_{ji} with weights $\widehat{w}_{ij} = -skew_{ij}$ and $\widehat{w}_{ji} = skew_{ij}$, respectively. Using the constraints in Eq (10), FLR_{ij} is obtained as follows:

$$FLR_{ij} = [-L_{user} - s_j^t - s_i^b, \ L_{user} + s_i^t + s_j^b]. \tag{12}$$

In Eq (12) s_i^t and s_j^b are the shortest paths to the sink vertices i and j with the edges e_{ij} and e_{ji} removed from G and $\bar{G}$. This modification is required because both edge weights w_{ij} and w_{ji} are reduced with the same skew commitment.

Finally, to satisfy both skew constraints and latency bound, a concept of a feasible skew-latency range (FSLR) is introduced, which is the intersection of an FSR in Eq (9) and an FLR in Eq (12) as follows:

$$FSLR_{ij} = FSR_{ij} \cap FLR_{ij}. \tag{13}$$

It can be proved that if both FSR and FLR are non-empty, FSLR is also non-empty. In short, the statement holds be-

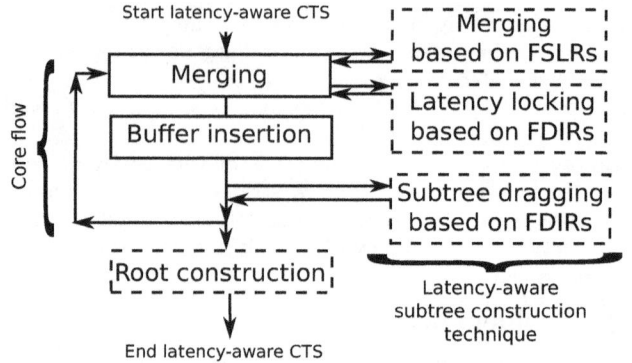

Figure 4: Flow for latency-aware CTS.

cause the bottom-up shortest path to each sink vertex defines a latency assignment to the sinks that is by definition a part of both the FLR and FSR.

Note that the use of FDIRs and FLRs is orthogonal to the use of FSR in [15]. Consequently, if the latency bound is loose, our proposed approach is equivalent to the Greedy-UST/DME algorithm [15].

4. PROPOSED SYNTHESIS FLOW

In this section, we present the proposed framework for synthesizing latency-bounded clock trees. The framework consists of a latency-aware CTS phase and a CTO phase. The innovations proposed in the paper focus on the latency-aware CTS phase. The CTO phase an adaptation of algorithms proposed in previous studies.

4.1 Latency-aware CTS phase

The latency-aware CTS is based on a traditional bottom-up tree construction flow that constructs a clock tree buffer stage by buffer stage, alternating between merging subtrees [15] and inserting buffers [4, 2, 8]. This "core flow" is illustrated with solid boxes in Figure 4 and consists of "merging" and "buffer insertion".

Merging: The process is based on the Greedy-UST/DME algorithm [15] using a nearest neighbour graph (NNG). In an NNG, each subtree is represented with a vertex and each edge represents the wiring cost of merging two subtrees. Iteratively the two subtrees connected with the least cost edge are attempted to be merged within an FSR. If the two subtrees connected with the least cost edge can be merged within an FSR while meeting a transition time constraint, the two subtrees are replaced by a larger subtree, which is reinserted into the NNG. Otherwise, the two subtrees are locked from further merging. After all subtrees are locked from further merging, a buffer is inserted at the root of each of the subtrees in the buffer insertion step.

Buffer insertion: A minimally sized buffer that can drive each respective locked subtree while meeting the transition time constraint is inserted at the root of the respective subtree, as in [4, 2, 8].

Assume that a set of subtrees has been constructed from the "merging" and "buffer insertion" processes. In addition, assume that the roots of these subtrees are located at the same spatial location. In such a situation, the LCG can be utilized to merge subtrees into a clock tree with a latency of $-s^p$ and the latency to each of the sequential elements would be equal to (the negative of) the bottom-up shortest path to each respective sink vertex in the LCG. Consider subtrees in Figure 1(a) with the LCG in Figure 3, one way to construct such a clock tree would be to insert the delay difference between the final latencies [65, 55, 40] and the current latencies [5, 20, 40], i.e., [65, 55, 40] − [5, 20, 40] = [60, 35, 0], at the root of the respective subtrees. Note the required delay insertions can be shared among the subtrees as illustrated in Figure 1(b). This method of joining the subtrees, based on the LCG, is referred to as *root construction*; it is labeled as "root construction" in Figure 4 and is further explained in Section 4.1.1.

However, to utilize the root construction, all subtrees are required to be located at the same spatial location. To satisfy this requirement, a root container is introduced. (In our implementation, the root container is located at the center of the circuit.) After the "buffer insertion" step in the core flow, it is checked, for every subtree, whether the subtree can reach the root container by inserting a stem wire below the newly inserted buffer. (A stem wire is a wire that is connected between the root of a subtree and the respective driving buffer [4]). If so, the subtree is routed to and placed in the root container and removed from the core flow. Otherwise, the subtree continues to be part of the iterative merging and buffer insertion process. After all subtrees in the core flow are located in the root container, the proposed root construction is applied.

Next, we propose to supplement the core flow with a latency-aware subtree construction technique. This technique is to overcome the limitation that $-s^p \leq L_{user}$ may not be satisfied at the beginning of the root construction. Therefore, to ensure that $-s^p \leq L_{user}$ holds at the beginning of the root construction, we propose to incorporate techniques called "Merging based on FSLRs", "Latency locking based on FDIRs", and "Subtree dragging based on FDIRs", which are illustrated in Figure 4 and explained in Section 4.1.2.

4.1.1 Root construction

The input to the root construction is a set of subtrees located at the same spatial location (in a root container). The output is a clock tree with the latency to each sequential element equal to the (negative value of) the bottom-up shortest path to each sink vertex. We explain the root construction in Figure 5, by illustrating how the subtrees in Figure 1(a), with the LCG in Figure 3, are joined to form a clock tree in Figure 1(b), with a latency of $-s^p = 65$.

In Figure 3, the (negative of the) bottom-up shortest paths are [65, 55, 40]. To realize these latencies from the current latencies [5, 20, 40] of the subtrees, delay insertions $\Delta =$ [65, 55, 40] − [5, 20, 40] = [60, 35, 0] are required. A naive solution would be to realize each of the delay insertions separately, i.e., a delay $\Delta_1 = 60$ and $\Delta_2 = 35$ could be added to the subtrees 1 and 2 respectively, before joining the three subtrees at the root.

Instead, we propose a method of maximal sharing of the required delay insertions. The delay insertions Δ are sorted in a decreasing order, i.e., [60, 35, 0]. This sorted order defines both the merging order and the sharing of the delay insertions. The subtrees are merged from left to right corresponding to the sorted order of the delay insertion, i.e., subtree 1 is merged with subtree 2 and the resulting subtree is merged with subtree 3. The delay insertions are shared with all subtrees located to the left in the sorted delay inser-

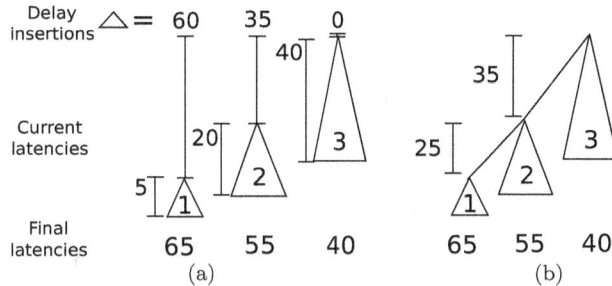

Figure 5: Maximal sharing of delay insertions.

tion array, i.e., the delay 35 is shared among both subtree 1 and 2. By using the maximal sharing of the delay insertions, we expect the cost to be reduced compared with the case when root construction is not applied. Moreover, yield may also improve since the sinks will be closer in the tree topology.

Furthermore, the delay insertions Δ are realized *imperfectly* to simplify root construction process. We restrict the delay realization to be performed by buffer insertion. Therefore, the delay insertion granularity is limited by the buffer library. Here, instead of realizing each delay insertion precisely, we attempt to realize each delay insertion as close to but less than or equal to, the specified delay insertion as possible. The motivation to realizing delays imperfectly is that the CTO process can realize more precise delay adjustments after CTS is complete. Since the timing and the topology of the initial clock tree is available during CTO, delay adjustments can be realized with a finer granularity while considering more accurate OCV estimates.

It is expected that the imperfect root construction may affect the yield after CTS. If inadequate safety margins are provided in a single skew constraint, the constructed clock tree may suffer substantial yield loss. However, after CTO, the yield should be recovered.

4.1.2 Latency-aware subtree construction

The root construction step is capable of joining the subtrees to a clock tree with a latency of $-s^p$. The techniques in this section are designed to ensure that $-s^p \leq L_{user}$ is satisfied at the beginning of the root construction.

It is straightforward to only allow subtrees to be merged within FSLRs introduced in Eq (13), ensuring that $-s^p \leq L_{user}$ is satisfied after two subtrees are merged. However, with only that extension of the core construction flow, subtrees with long latencies that are spatially distant from the root container may be created. Moreover, when these subtrees are routed to the root container, the constraint $-s^p \leq L_{user}$ may be violated.

To account for the spatial location of a subtree, the concept of *virtual subtree latency* is introduced. The virtual sink latency of a subtree is equal to the delay that is inserted if a subtree is routed (or dragged) to the root container by connecting a wire from the root of the subtree to the location of the root container (with buffers inserted on the wire to control the transition time). Next, the latency edge weights are modified to be the negative value of the sum of the sink latency and the virtual subtree latency.

With the inclusion of virtual latencies, a clock tree with a latency of L_{user} can be constructed by dragging each subtree to the root container and then joining them at the root container. When dragging the subtrees to the location of the root container, the virtual latency would be replaced with "real" latency and the weight of each latency edge would remain the same. Consequently, the length of the latency path s^p would also remain the same, and a clock tree with a latency of $-s^p \leq L_{user}$ can be constructed. However, routing each of the subtrees (or sinks) to the location of the root container directly would be very costly, in terms of wire and buffer resources. Therefore, we do not drag subtrees to the root container directly but instead continue to merge subtrees while ensuring that $-s^p \leq L_{user}$. Only after a subtree has grown beyond a threshold, it is dragged to the root container. The core flow is modified as follows:

Merging based on FSLRs: The "Merging" in the core flow is modified to merge subtrees within FSLRs in Eq (13) instead of FSRs. By merging subtrees within FSLRs it is ensured that both skew constraints and the latency bound are satisfied.

Subtree locking based on FDIRs: If a subtree has long latency or is distant from the root container, it may be costly to merge it with another subtree. Therefore, we lock such subtrees from further merging and drag them towards the root container in the subtree dragging step. A subtree is locked if the upper bound of its FDIR (see Eq (11)) is less than a parameter $p_{lock} = 20$ ps. This condition is checked in the merging process after each new subtree is formed.

Subtree dragging based on FDIRs: The subtree dragging is applied after the buffer insertion step. It is applied to every subtree whose upper bound of its FDIR (see Eq (11)) is less than a parameter $p_{drag} = 20$ ps. The driving buffer is sized up to the next driver size and a piece of stem wire is inserted between the buffer and the subtree. The stem wire is elongated to the maximum length while satisfying a transition time constraint. Next, the buffer is dragged as close to the root container as possible using the stem wire, transferring virtual latency to real latency.

4.2 Clock tree optimization (CTO) phase

The CTO phase is based on the techniques proposed in [9]. The optimization aims to remove timing violations (or negative slacks, i.e., TNS and WNS) in a clock tree by realizing non-negative delay adjustments. The location and the magnitude of the delay adjustments are determined by solving an LP formulation. Next, the delay adjustments are realized by inserting buffers and detouring wires [10].

Note that delay insertions that are realized imperfectly during the root construction can be realized as delay adjustments during CTO process, if required. Moreover, it is important to observe that if the latency of the initial clock tree is long, large delay variations are present in many skew constraints and there may be little room for CTO to improve performance. Therefore, we say that by bounding the latency of a clock tree during latency-aware CTS, the clock tree is more amenable to CTO.

5. EXPERIMENTAL EVALUATION

The proposed algorithms are implemented in C++ and the experiments are performed on a quad core 3.10 GHz Linux machine with 7.7 GB of memory.

To evaluate our proposed framework, the extension [8] of the problem formulation in the ISPD 2010 contest [14] is used. A summary of the properties of the synthesized circuits that are used in the evaluation are shown in Table 1 [7].

Table 1: Properties of synthesized circuits.

Name	Clock period (ns)	Number of nets	Number of cells	Number of sequential elements	Number of skew constraints
scaled_s15850	0.32	-	-	597	318
ecg	1.00	62164	61491	7674	63440
aes	1.00	262884	262497	13216	53382

In [8], a Monte Carlo framework is used to evaluate the robustness of a clock tree subject to voltage (15%), wire width (10%), temperature (30%), and channel length variations (10%). The variations are generated using a quad-tree model [1] to exhibit spatial correlation. The robustness of a clock tree is measured by simulating it with 500 Monte Carlo simulations. In each simulation, it is checked whether all the skew constraints (see Eq (5) and Eq (6)) and a transition time constraint are satisfied. The transition time states that the 10% to 90% rise or fall time of the clock signal at any point in the clock tree must be below 100 ps. The quality of a clock tree is measured in terms of yield. The yield is defined to be the number of simulations with no constraint violations divided by the total number of simulations. The power consumption is estimated with capacitive cost.

To clearly demonstrate the impact of each optimization step we show the performance and cost of the constructed clock trees after both CTS and CTO. Even though the evaluation is performed in terms of yield, we show the TNS and WNS estimates that are used to guide the CTO process. It is expected that if the TNS and WNS are zero, or small, the yield of the clock tree will be high when evaluated by the Monte Carlo framework. However, there is no guarantee that a clock tree with zero TNS and WNS will have 100% yield or that a clock tree with non-zero TNS and WNS will suffer yield loss. The parameter $c_{ocv} = 0.085$ is used based on statistics obtained through circuit simulations.

We construct and evaluate several different tree structures to show the impact of our proposed optimization techniques. The structure "Tree" is a clock tree constructed using only the traditional core flow, i.e., using merging and buffer insertion. The structure "R-Tree" is the core flow with the addition of the root construction. The structure "L-R-Tree", is the structure obtained by the complete flow, i.e., the core flow with the latency-aware subtree construction techniques and the root construction. After the different tree constructions have been performed, CTO is performed. We also report the results of the most competitive clock trees constructed in [8]. The construction process of clock trees in [8] is similar to that of our "Tree" structure. However, CTO is not performed in [8]. To enable a more fair comparison, we perform CTO on the "Tree" structures in [8].

5.1 Evaluation of root construction

Table 2 shows the experimental results on the circuits scaled_s15850, ecg, and aes. We construct the "Tree" structures and "R-Tree" structures with different safety margins M_{user} and compare the performance after CTS and after CTO. We have also included relevant results from [8].

We observe the same trends as in [15, 8] for the "Tree" structures constructed with different safety margins M_{user} after CTS. The performance in TNS, WNS, and yield is improved when larger safety margins are inserted in the skew constraints. For example, on ecg, a yield of 92.8% (97.4% and 99.6%) is obtained when a safety margin of 20 ps (30 ps and 40 ps) is inserted. However, as larger safety margins are

Table 2: Evaluation of root construction after CTS and after CTO.

Circuit	Structure	M_{user} (ps)	After CTS						After CTO					
			Latency (ps)	Cap (pF)	TNS (ps)	WNS (ps)	Yield (%)	Run time (min)	Latency (ps)	Cap (pF)	TNS (ps)	WNS (ps)	Yield (%)	Run time (min)
scaled_s15850	Tree	20	299	16.3	-196	-20	95.0	1	324	16.7	-156	-20	95.0	1
	R-Tree	20	273	16.1	-262	-26	97.2	4	311	16.5	-218	-29	63.4	10
	Tree	25	424	17.7	-329	-25	96.4	4	424	18.4	-239	-25	34.0	13
	R-Tree	25	303	17.3	-291	-30	80.4	1	313	17.7	-212	-19	97.6	1
	Tree in [8]	27	405	20.2	-150	-19	96.6	5	425	20.7	-72	-13	99.4	13
	Tree	27	328	19.0	-329	-18	99.8	5	376	20.2	-187	-17	99.6	20
	R-Tree	27	291	18.1	-200	-21	94.0	5	329	19.0	-93	-13	100.0	17
ecg	Tree in [8]	20	420	57.0	-4577	-24	82.6	29	427	57.6	-9342	-46	0.0	272
	Tree	20	344	32.4	-7061	-24	92.8	18	392	36.4	-9443	-31	23.2	201
	R-Tree	20	317	30.9	-1983	-16	75.6	28	348	33.4	-3085	-18	63.0	119
	Tree in [8]	30	417	66.8	-1569	-19	98.8	39	474	75.7	-1874	-20	91.6	341
	Tree	30	454	40.2	-2849	-21	97.4	15	447	44.8	-4122	-37	86.0	233
	R-Tree	30	382	35.8	-205	-6	99.4	20	401	36.3	-24	-3	99.4	33
	Tree in [8]	40	716	96.8	-245	-15	96.2	106	742	98.8	-158	-10	98.6	109
	Tree	40	850	62.4	-1890	-18	99.6	33	862	68.2	-2140	-26	99.0	293
	R-Tree	40	811	58.2	-419	-16	94.2	69	854	58.4	-3	-2	99.8	45
aes	Tree	40	1954	180.4	-24073	-57	93.4	139	2003	212.1	-52775	-56	0.0	895
	R-Tree	40	1756	160.8	-5116	-29	75.4	116	1880	164.0	-561	-12	96.2	254
	Tree	50	2468	228.8	-2036	-43	91.4	189	2474	264.2	-15317	-38	78.2	883
	R-Tree	50	2207	207.5	-2877	-27	82.8	245	2320	208.3	-13	-3	97.6	180
	Tree	60	2706	270.2	-823	-20	96.4	193	2708	273.1	-117	-7	97.6	137
	R-Tree	60	2397	245.9	-1779	-32	71.4	220	2482	246.3	0	0	98.0	199
Norm.	Tree in [8]		1.17	1.62	2.83	1.68	1.03	1.40	1.14	1.65	46.58	5.03	0.73	3.96
	Tree		1.15	1.07	3.49	1.44	**1.13**	1.44	1.11	1.14	243.52	5.56	0.76	4.81
	R-Tree		**1.00**	**1.00**	**1.00**	**1.00**	1.00	**1.00**	**1.00**	**1.00**	**1.00**	**1.00**	**1.00**	**1.00**

inserted, the construction process becomes more constrained and it can be observed that the capacitive cost and latency increase from 32.4 pF and 344 ps to 62.4 pF and 850 ps, respectively.

Next, to demonstrate the importance of considering latency during CTS, we discuss the difference in performance between the "Tree" and the "R-Tree" structures. Both structures are constructed based on a user-specified safety margin M_{user}. However, the "R-Tree" structures also try to minimize latency (although no latency bound is required).

After CTS, it can be observed that the "R-Tree" structures have 15% shorter latency and 7% lower capacitive cost compared with the "Tree" structures on the average. The latency improvements are a consequence of using the LCG to join the subtrees in the root container to a single clock tree. Moreover, it is likely that the reductions in capacitive cost mostly stem from the the sharing of delay insertions during root construction, and because of the imperfect root construction.

The "R-Tree" structures also outperform the "Tree" structures in terms of TNS and WNS. This is expected because the delay variations introduced by OCV are smaller in clock trees with shorter latencies. However, on a few circuits, the "R-Tree" structures obtain worse TNS and WNS; we believe this is because of the imperfect delay insertion during root construction. For example, on circuit aes, with $M_{user} = 60$ ps, the "R-Tree" structure has worse TNS and WNS.

Even though the "Tree" structures have worse performance in TNS and WNS, it is expected that the yield in the Monte Carlo evaluation is better compared with the "R-Tree" structures. This is because if a single skew constraint is violated as a result of the imperfect root construction for the "R-Tree" structures, yield loss is suffered. (However, we expect this yield loss to be recovered after CTO.)

Next, we focus our attention on the experimental results obtained after CTO. For the "Tree" structures, it can be observed that on many circuits, CTO is unable to improve the performance in TNS and WNS. As mentioned, this may be because the "Tree" structures have long latencies and there is no room for further optimization. On circuits where CTO is unable to improve or close timing in terms of TNS and WNS, it can be understood that the yield may be worse after CTO because the safety margins in the skew constraints may have been redistributed unevenly, and inadequate safety margins in a single skew constraint may result in substantial yield loss.

On the other hand, the CTO process is capable of removing or reducing TNS and WNS when applied to the "R-Tree" structures. Therefore, we say that our framework constructs clock trees that are more amenable to CTO. Moreover, the capacitive overhead of performing CTO is small on the average; only an 2.4% increase in capacitive cost is observed. Since significant reductions in TNS and WNS are obtained, it is not surprising that the yield of the "R-Tree" structures is higher after CTO compared with after CTS. Moreover, we also note that the "R-Tree" structures have higher yield after CTO compared with the "Tree" structures after both CTS and CTO. This confirms the importance of considering both latency and safety margins during CTS. Nevertheless, if the initial clock tree is constructed with a too small safety margin M_{user}, CTO may not be able to achieve timing closure, and the yield may be inadequate (See $M_{user} = 20$ ps and 20 ps for scaled_s15850 and ecg, respectively.)

5.2 Evaluation of latency-bounded clock trees

We are interested in improving yield on the circuits, ecg, aes, and scaled_s15850. As observed in Table 2, the "R-Tree" structures performed better compared with the "Tree" structures mainly because of their shorter latencies. There-

Table 3: Evaluation of latency-bounded clock trees after CTS and CTO.

Circuit	Structure	L_{user} (ps)	After CTS						After CTO					
			Latency (ps)	Cap (pF)	TNS (ps)	WNS (ps)	Yield (%)	Run time (min)	Latency (ps)	Cap (pF)	TNS (ps)	WNS (ps)	Yield (%)	Run time (min)
scaled_ s15850 $M_{user} = 25$ ps	R-Tree	∞	303	17.3	-291	-30	80.4	4	321	17.9	-182	-20	81.4	14
	L-R-Tree	270	248	17.7	-96	-15	99.2	5	267	18.1	-45	-6	**100.0**	11
	L-R-Tree	250	214	18.3	-78	-10	**100.0**	3	229	18.8	-30	-7	**100.0**	14
	L-R-Tree	230	194	22.3	-85	-13	99.8	6	227	22.7	-48	-10	**100.0**	12
ecg $M_{user} = 30$ ps	R-Tree	∞	382	35.8	-205	-6	99.4	20	401	36.3	-24	-3	99.4	33
	L-R-Tree	380	318	35.0	-345	-16	94.6	29	345	35.2	-4	-1	**100.0**	51
	L-R-Tree	360	325	39.1	-823	-12	99.8	26	343	40.4	-260	-10	**100.0**	67
	L-R-Tree	340	265	39.3	-741	-16	**100.0**	34	303	40.7	-245	-12	**100.0**	64
aes $M_{user} = 50$ ps	R-Tree	∞	2207	207.5	-2877	-27	82.8	245	2320	208.3	-13	-3	97.6	180
	L-R-Tree	2000	1863	233.9	-1492	-18	**100.0**	133	1933	234.7	-13	-2	99.0	152
	L-R-Tree	1800	1638	234.1	-2064	-29	**100.0**	281	1706	236.6	-119	-4	98.2	294
	L-R-Tree	1600	1483	237.5	-1347	-18	**100.0**	129	1513	240.0	-187	-5	99.6	175

fore, we speculate that we may be able to improve performance by combining the use of safety margins and latency bounds. Moreover, potentially, by imposing a latency bound, a smaller safety margin M_{user} can be used, which may translate into savings in capacitive cost. In Table 3, we construct three versions of the "L-R-Tree" structure on each circuit, each with the same safety margin M_{user} but a different latency bound L_{user}. The safety margin M_{user} is set to 25 ps, 30 ps, and 50 ps because these safety margins seem to provide a reasonable starting point in yield and capacitive cost (see the relevant results for "R-Tree" in Table 2, which are repeated in Table 3).

In Table 3, we observe that the framework is capable of constructing clock trees meeting specified latency bounds. For example, on ecg and aes, the "R-Tree" structures have latencies of 382 ps and 2207 ps, respectively; the "L-R-Tree" structures have latency ranges of 265 ps to 318 ps and 1483 ps to 1863 ps, respectively. Moreover, it is observed that it is not too costly to reduce the latency quite substantially. The capacitive overheads are at most 15%.

We observe that the performance in TNS and WNS after CTS is inconclusive. On some circuits and for certain latency bounds, the performance of the "R-Tree" structures is better and for others, "L-R-Tree" structures have better performance. This may be because of the imperfect root construction that is applied in the construction of both the "R-Tree" and the "L-R-Tree". However, after CTO, the "L-R-Tree" structures seem to obtain better performance in TNS and WNS, if a L_{user} is set to an appropriate value.

Moreover, the yield of the "L-R-Tree" structures is better compared with the "R-Tree" structures. On scaled_s15850 and ecg, the yield is better after CTO compared with after CTS, as expected. However, on aes, it is observed that the yield is actually better after CTS compared with CTO, even though the performance is better in TNS and WNS after CTO. We believe that this may be because the performance in TNS and WNS does not correlate perfectly with yield performance. However, we still believe that TNS and WNS are useful metrics for optimization.

Based on the results in Table 2 and Table 3, it seems essential to combine the use of safety margins and latency bounds to be able to construct clock trees with high yield. Only the "L-R-Tree" is capable of obtaining a yield of 100% (after CTS or CTO) on all the circuits. Moreover, the "L-R-Tree" structures are cheaper in terms of capacitance compared to the clock trees constructed with larger safety margins M_{user} in Table 2.

6. SUMMARY AND FUTURE WORK

We have introduced the concept of an LCG that captures, skew constraints, latencies, and skews committed in a synthesis process. Based on the LCG we have proposed a framework that constructs latency-bounded clock trees given a user-specified latency bound L_{user} and a user specified uniform safety margin M_{user}. In the future, we will solve component (1) of the problem defined in Section 2.3, i.e., determining appropriate M_{user} and L_{user}, and the problem as a whole.

7. REFERENCES

[1] A. Agarwal, D. Blaauw, and V. Zolotov. Statistical timing analysis for intra-die process variations with spatial correlations. ICCAD'03, pages 900–907, 2003.

[2] S. Bujimalla and C.-K. Koh. Synthesis of low power clock trees for handling power-supply variations. ISPD '11, pages 37–44, 2011.

[3] R. Chaturvedi and J. Hu. Buffered clock tree for high quality ic design. In *Quality Electronic Design, 2004. Proceedings. 5th International Symposium on*, pages 381–386, 2004.

[4] Y. P. Chen and D. F. Wong. An algorithm for zero-skew clock tree routing with buffer insertion. EDTC'96, pages 230–237, 1996.

[5] Y.-Y. Chen, C. Dong, and D. Chen. Clock tree synthesis under aggressive buffer insertion. DAC'10, pages 86–89, June 2010.

[6] T. H. Cormen, C. Stein, R. L. Rivest, and C. E. Leiserson. *Introduction to Algorithms*. McGraw-Hill Higher Ed., 2001.

[7] R. Ewetz, S. Janarthanan, and C.-K. Koh. Benchmark circuits for clock scheduling and synthesis. https://purr.purdue.edu/publications/1759, 2015.

[8] R. Ewetz and C.-K. Koh. A useful skew framework for inserting large safety margins. ISPD'15, pages 85–92, 2015.

[9] R. Ewetz and C.-K. Koh. MCMM clock tree optimization based on slack redistribution using a reduced slack graph. ASP-DAC'16, pages 366–371, 2016.

[10] D.-J. Lee, M.-C. Kim, and I. L. Markov. Low-power clock trees for cpus. ICCAD'10, 2010.

[11] A. Rajaram and D. Z. Pan. Variation tolerant buffered clock network synthesis with cross links. ISPD'06, pages 157–164, 2006.

[12] V. Ramachandran. Construction of minimal functional skew clock trees. ISPD'12, pages 119–120, 2012.

[13] S. Roy, P. M. Mattheakis, L. Masse-Navette, and D. Z. Pan. Clock tree resynthesis for multi-corner multi-mode timing closure. *CAD of IC and Sys.*, pages 589–602, 2015.

[14] C. N. Sze. ISPD 2010 high performance clock network synthesis contest: Benchmark suite and results. ISPD'10, pages 143–143, 2010.

[15] C.-W. A. Tsao and C.-K. Koh. UST/DME: a clock tree router for general skew constraints. *(TODAES)*, pages 359–379, 2002.

Scaling Beyond 7nm: Design-Technology Co-optimization at the Rescue

Julien Ryckaert

IMEC

Abstract

At 7nm and beyond, designers need to support scaling by identifying the most optimal patterning schemes for their designs. Moreover, designers can actively help by exploring scaling options that do not necessarily require aggressive pitch scaling. In this talk we will illustrate how design technology co-optimization can help achieving the expected Moore's law scaling; how optimizing device performance can lead to smaller standard cells; how the metal interconnect stack needs to be adjusted for unidirectional metals and how a vertical transistor can shift design paradigms. This paper demonstrates that scaling has become a joint design-technology co-optimization effort between process technology and design specialists, that expands way beyond just patterning enabled dimensional scaling.

Keywords

Design-technology co-optimization; Technology scaling

Short Bio

Julien Ryckaert received the M.Sc. degree in Electrical Engineering from the University of Brussels (ULB), Belgium, in 2000 and the PhD degree from the Vrije Universiteit Brussel (VUB) in 2007. He joined IMEC (Leuven, Belgium) first as an RF designer for WLAN transceivers. From 2003 on, he worked as system architect for low-power low data rate ultra-wideband transceivers in which he completed his PhD. In 2010 he joined the process technology division of imec coordinating the design of test chips for 3D system integration and high-speed photonics interconnects. He is now managing the design enablement team for Logic Technology and is in charge of imec's Design-Technology Co-Optimization task force for advanced technology nodes. Julien Ryckaert was member of the Asian Solid-State Circuits Conference technical program committee.

ISPD'16, April 3–6, 2016, Santa Rosa, California, USA.

ACM 978-1-4503-4039-7/16/04.

DOI: http://dx.doi.org/10.1145/2872334.2878629

Proximity Optimization for Adaptive Circuit Design

Ang Lu
Department of ECE
Texas A&M University
College Station, TX 77843
lvang90822@gmail.com

Hao He
Department of ECE
Texas A&M University
College Station, TX 77843
haohe2012fall@tamu.edu

Jiang Hu
Department of ECE
Texas A&M University
College Station, TX 77843
jianghu@tamu.edu

ABSTRACT

The performance growth of conventional VLSI circuits is seriously hampered by various variation effects and the fundamental limit of chip power density. Adaptive circuit design is recognized as a power-efficient approach to tackling the variation challenge. However, it tends to entail large area overhead if not carefully designed. This work studies how to reduce the overhead by forming adaptivity blocks considering both timing and spatial proximity among logic cells. The proximity optimization consists of timing and location aware cell clustering and incremental placement enforcing the clusters. Experiments are performed on the ICCAD 2014 benchmark circuits, which include case of near one million cells. Compared to alternative methods, our approach achieves $\frac{1}{4}$ to $\frac{3}{4}$ area overhead reduction with an average of 0.6% wirelength overhead, while retains about the same timing yield and power.

CCS Concepts

•Hardware → Physical design (EDA);

Keywords

Adaptive circuit design; incremental placement; cell clustering

1. INTRODUCTION

Variability, such as process variations and device aging, and power are notorious barriers to the progress of VLSI technology. Their compound effect is even more difficult to deal with. Variations demand extra power for timing margins and therefore exacerbate power dissipation. On the other hand, increasingly tight power budget seriously hinders design techniques for variation tolerance. Adaptive circuit design is an approach to getting out of this difficult situation.

An adaptive circuit contains sensors that detect timing variations. Broadly speaking, there are two kinds of sen-

sors: critical path replica [1, 2] and canary flip-flop [3, 4]. Sensor outputs control certain tuning knobs, such as body bias [1] and supply voltage change [5, 6], such that timing variations are compensated. Unlike conventional methods, which allocate extra power and timing margins according to the worst case variations, an adaptive circuit spends additional power only when timing variation is actually observed. Adaptive design is conceptually more power-efficient than conventional designs, however, it entails area overhead on sensors, tuning circuits and control wires. If not carefully designed, the overhead can be quite significant. For example, a naïve implementation of the voltage interpolation technique [5] can double chip power grid. In [6], over 20% area overhead is observed for adaptive designs. Indeed, the overhead issue is a key reason that prevents wide application of adaptive design techniques.

The efficiency of an adaptive design highly depends on how its adaptivity blocks are formed. The circuit cells within one block share the same sensors, control and tuning knobs. Ideally, one prefers to put cells that need similar tuning actions into the same block. As such, a small number of sensors and knobs can cover a large circuit and the amortized overhead is relatively low. At the same time, cells in a block need to be spatially close to each other or form a contiguous region. Separating cells of the same block far apart would at least cause unnecessarily large control wire overhead. Overall, adaptivity blocks should be formed according to both timing proximity and spatial proximity among cells.

The adaptivity block generation problem is studied in [7] for adaptive body bias. It estimates timing proximity among cells by Monte Carlo simulation of body bias assignment. The assignment assumes that body voltage of each cell can be individually controlled and is implemented by quadratic programming. After the simulation, the probability distribution of body bias tuning for each cell is obtained. Then, cells with similar distributions and high correlations are clustered to form a block. It is observed that spatial correlation among tuning actions of different cells is similar as physical proximity among them. To ensure that cells in the same block are located in a contiguous region, incremental placement change is performed using the Capo placer [8]. This is a pioneer work that demonstrates the importance of adaptivity clustering. However, it has a few drawbacks. First, Monte Carlo simulation of quadratic programming is immensely time consuming and very difficult, if not impossible, to scale to large cases. For example, a 32K-cell case, which is fairly small from the point of view of modern IC design, costs nearly four and half hours runtime in [7]. Second, it

ISPD'16, April 03-06, 2016, Santa Rosa, CA, USA

© 2016 ACM. ISBN 978-1-4503-4039-7/16/04...$15.00

DOI: http://dx.doi.org/10.1145/2872334.2872354

is not described how Capo [8] enforces spatial continuity among cells in a cluster. Third, although timing and spatial proximity are correlated, the difference between them cannot be neglected. In fact, the timing-only clustering [7] results in 3% wirelength overhead, which is not trivial.

In this work, we propose a balanced approach: cell clustering with consideration of both timing and spatial proximity. To make the clustering more scalable, the consideration of timing is based on timing analysis result instead of Monte Carlo simulation of quadratic programming. The clustering is followed by an incremental placement that enforces the spatial continuity of cells in a cluster. The placement is formulated and solved by min-cost network flow model that minimizes total cell movement. Experiments are performed on the ICCAD 2014 incremental timing-driven placement contest benchmark suites, which include circuit of near one million cells. Compared to timing-only and location-only clustering, our approach achieves $\frac{1}{4}$ to $\frac{3}{4}$ area overhead reduction. Its average wirelength overhead is 0.6%, which is 95% less than that from the timing-only clustering. At the same time, it retains about the same timing yield and power consumption.

The rest of this paper is organized as follows. An overview of our method and design flow background will be given in Section 2. The cell clustering will be described in Section 3. Section 4 will be focused on the incremental placement. Experimental results will be shown in Section 5. Finally, conclusions will be provided in Section 6.

2. OVERVIEW

The input to our method is a circuit, for which cell placement (including detailed placement) and timing analysis have been performed. It is represented by a graph $G = (V, E)$, where the node set V indicates cells and edges E imply fanin/fanout among cells. Our method is a two-phase approach: phase I cell clustering and phase II incremental placement. The clustering partitions cells into blocks, where cells in a block have similar timing characteristics and are close to each other. The incremental placement further forces cells of each cluster to form a contiguous region. The clustering method uses a few weighting coefficients to balance timing and spatial proximity. If a large wirelength overhead is observed after incremental placement, the weight for spatial proximity is increased and the two phases are performed again. The result of our method is fed to the adaptive circuit optimization [9], which decides if to assign adaptivity to each block and simultaneously performs gate sizing. An overview of entire design flow is sketched in Figure 1, where our main contributions are highlighted with the orange dashed rectangle.

The proposed methodology allows flexibility of changes. For example, one can start with merely global placement at the beginning and perform detailed placement with legalization after the clustering. Also, the clustering and incremental placement can be repeated after gate sizing to form another layer of iterations.

3. TIMING AND LOCATION AWARE CELL CLUSTERING

We start with an example in Figure 2 to illustrate that considering only timing in clustering like [7] is insufficient. The argument in [7] is that timing correlations highly depend on spatial correlations. As such, spatial proximity is largely addressed by considering only timing proximity. This statement is often true, however, it is not difficult to find counter examples that easily happen in practice. In Figure 2, there are two timing critical paths: one from gate $A1$ to $A2$ and the other from $B1$ to $B2$. Along path A (B), forward body bias (FBB) of either gate $A1$ ($B1$) or $A2$ ($B2$) can fix timing error. If FBB of NAND gates is slightly more efficient than FBB of NOR gates, the quadratic programming in [7] may mostly choose FBB for $A1$ and $B2$ at the same time. Then, the clustering of [7] would put $A1$ and $B2$ into the same cluster although they are spatially far apart. The subsequent incremental placement must move those cells for a long distance to bring them together. Consequently, wirelength is significantly increased. Moreover, the large cell moves may invalidate the original timing analysis result. It is not difficult to find that a better solution is to cluster $A1$ ($A2$) with $B1$ ($B2$).

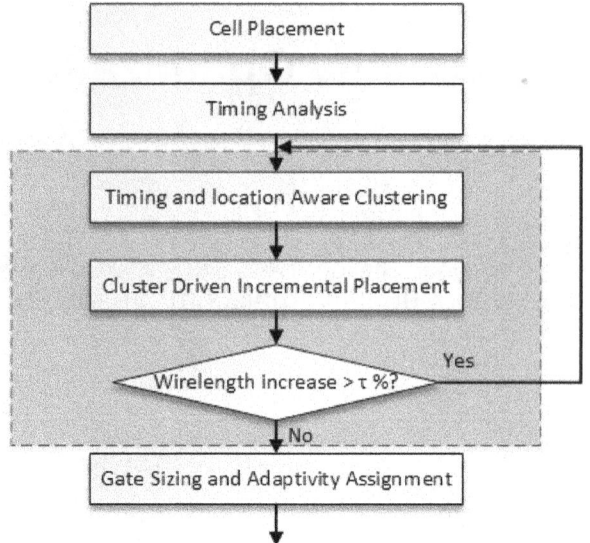

Figure 1: Overview of proposed design flow.

Figure 2: An example for clustering.

In our clustering, both timing and spatial proximity are considered. Straightforwardly, spatial proximity between two cells are estimated by the Manhattan distance between them.

Timing proximity is remarkably more complex. Ideally, it should indicate the probability that two cells take the same tuning actions. Monte Carlo simulation of quadratic programming like [7] serves this purpose well, but is too expensive to use. Therefore, we resort to a simple surrogate metric that include two factors. The first factor is timing slacks at cells. If two cells have similar slack, then it is more likely that they would take the same tuning actions. Otherwise, they tend to take different tuning actions. However, when slacks are extremely large or extremely negative, the corresponding cells may still take the same actions. For example, two cells with hugely negative slacks would both take the maximum FBB level regardless their slack difference. Hence, a cell g_i is characterized by *capped slack* defined as

$$\hat{s}_i = \max(\min(slack_i, \theta_{max}), \theta_{min}) \qquad (1)$$

where $slack_i$ is the original slack at cell g_i, and θ_{max} and θ_{min} are constant thresholds. To further account for timing variability, the $slack_i$ here is based on nominal delay plus scaled σ (standard deviation) of the delay. It is conceivable that a cell with large σ is more likely to be tuned when it has the same nominal delay as others.

The second factor in the surrogate timing proximity is sensitivity, which is defined as ratio of slack increase by tuning a cell versus the tuning cost, i.e.,

$$\psi = \frac{Critical\_Path\_Slack\_Increase}{Tuning\_Cost} \qquad (2)$$

where the tuning cost can be power increase or area overhead of adaptivity. When two cells have similar timing slack, the sensitivity may make a difference on if to take tuning action. Indeed, it makes sense for tuning policies to favor change on cells with relatively large sensitivities.

Overall, the distance between g_i at (x_i, y_i) and g_j at (x_j, y_j) in the clustering is defined as

$$d_{i,j} = \alpha \cdot |\hat{s}_i - \hat{s}_j| + \beta \cdot |\psi_i - \psi_j| + \gamma \cdot (|x_i - x_j| + |y_i - y_j|) \quad (3)$$

where α, β and γ are constant parameters. Usually, the value of β is much smaller than α. These parameters are not necessarily static. If a large wirelength overhead is observed after the subsequent incremental placement, the value of γ is increased and the clustering is performed again.

Note that we handle timing proximity in a much simpler way than [7]. One may argue that this simple approach has a drawback. That is, only one or a few cells along the same critical path need to be tuned while our approach sees the same slack/sensitivity among all cells along the path and may cluster them all together. Actually, this problem is addressed by simultaneously considering spatial proximity. It is rare that all cells along one path are crowded together. It is quite likely these cells are separated into different clusters due to spatial distance.

Based on the distance defined by Equation (3), we adopt Lloyd's K-means algorithm for the clustering. To make the description complete, we summarize the main steps of this algorithm. It starts with K arbitrary means or centers. Then, each cell is assigned to the cluster with nearest center. After assigning all cells, the centers are updated with the centroids of the newly formed clusters. This assignment and center update procedure is repeated till the within-cluster sum of distance (WCSD) converges to the minimum. WCSD is defined by

$$\sum_{i=1}^{K} \sum_{\vec{x} \in C_i} |\vec{x} - \vec{\mu}_i| \qquad (4)$$

where C_i is a cluster, $\vec{x}$ is the vector characterizing a cell and $\vec{\mu}_i$ is the mean or center for cluster C_i. Unlike the original Lloyd's algorithm, which is based on Euclidean distance, we use Manhattan distance to match the layout convention in VLSI circuits. The value of K is decided empirically [9]. Moreover, we allow K to be changed according to clustering results. If two clusters are very near to each other, they are merged and K is therefore decreased.

4. CLUSTER DRIVEN INCREMENTAL PLACEMENT

After the clustering, a small number of cells are often located away from the majority cells of their own clusters. For example, in Figure 3, where clusters are indicated by colors, two blue cells and one orange cell are away from their clusters. We call them *alien cells*. Due to alien cells, control wires for a cluster must span a relatively large region. Moreover, tuning overhead, such as extra power lines in voltage interpolation [5], is also increased by the spreading out of clusters.

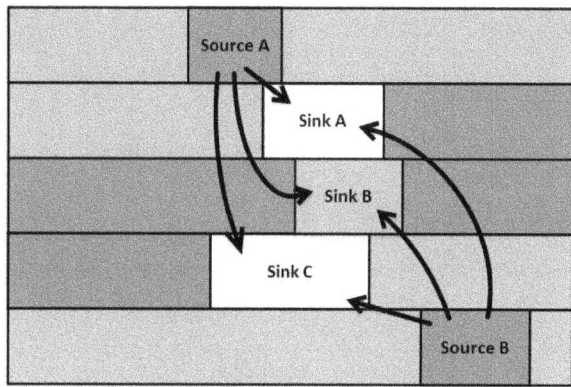

Figure 3: An example of cell placement after clustering. The white regions are empty.

The purpose of incremental placement is to move alien cells back to their clusters such that each cluster forms a compact and contiguous region. An alien cell g_i^k belonging to cluster C_k can be moved to an empty space among majority cells of C_k. Alternatively, it can be moved to the position of another alien cell g_j^l that belongs to another cluster C_l but sits within cluster C_k, as g_j^l will be moved out of cluster C_k sooner or later. For example, the blue cell in top row of Figure 3 can be moved to the location of the orange cell in the middle row. Of course, these moves are allowed only if the size of empty space or g_j^l is no less than that of g_i^k. In order to retain the original design as much as possible, the total cell movement needs to be minimized at the same time.

In essence, the incremental placement is a min-cost assignment problem – assigning alien cells to empty or potentially empty space. In general, an assignment problem can be solved through min-cost network flow model. However, there is a pitfall. That is, if one attempts to move all alien cells simultaneously in a network flow model, it is difficult to ensure that an alien cell is moved to its own cluster, not other clusters. In fact, this is a multi-commodity network flow problem, which is NP-complete. On the other hand, this issue is not difficult to circumvent, simply by processing only one cluster at a time. Specifically, alien cells belonging to one cluster are collected back using min-cost network flow model.

Since the clusters are processed one at a time, we need to find the order for processing them. The order is based on cluster porosity, i.e., the percentage of space can be used by its alien cells. A cluster with low porosity is processed first. White space between two clusters can be claimed by either cluster. Processing low porosity (high density) clusters first would allow them to have high priority for taking white space between clusters. Evidently, if the overall placement density is not high, this order does not matter.

Now we describe the network flow model for moving alien cells belonging to cluster C_k back to C_k. The network is a directed graph $G' = (V', E')$. The node set V' is composed by the following types of nodes:

- *Source node*: Each source node corresponds to an alien cell g_i^k that needs to be moved to cluster C_k.

- *Sink node*: Each sink node indicates (1) a contiguous empty space inside or adjacent with cluster C_k, or (2) an alien cell g_j^l that sits inside C_k.

- *Super source S*: This is a virtual node and there is an edge from S to every source node.

- *Super sink T*: This is a virtual node and there is an edge from every sink node to T.

There are three types of edges in E'.

- *From S to source nodes*: Each such edge has capacity equal to the size of corresponding alien cell, and cost of 0.

- *From source to sink node*: There is an edge between every pair of source and sink nodes. Its capacity is infinity and its cost is equal to the distance of moving the corresponding alien cell to C_k.

- *From sink node to T*: Each such edge has capacity equal to the size of corresponding empty space or alien cell that does not belong to C_k. The edge cost is 0.

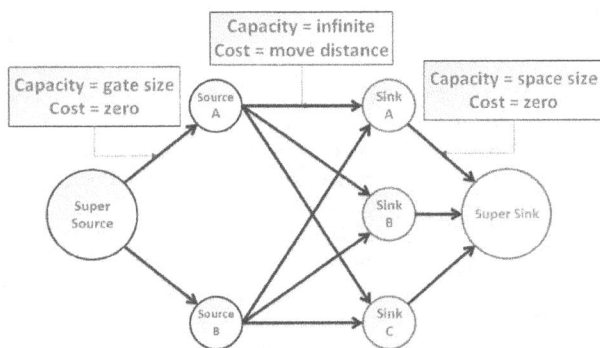

Figure 4: Network flow model for consolidating the blue cluster in Figure 3.

Figure 4 shows the network flow model for moving the two blue alien cells in Figure 3. The flow constraint is equal to the total size of alien cells to be moved. In practice, placement density is rarely near 100% and the percentage of alien cells is small. Hence, there is usually plenty of white space

accommodating the moves. After the model is formulated, the Edmonds-Karp algorithm [10] is performed to obtain min-cost flow solution. The algorithm can guarantee to find the optimal solution in polynomial time. In the solution, the flow on each edge from source to sink node tells how to move an alien cell. The incremental placement algorithm flow is outlined in the pseudo code below.

Algorithm 1 Incremental Placement

---

input : cell placement and clusters $\mathcal{C} = \{C_1, C_2, ...\}$
output : cell placement where each cluster forms contiguous region

---

Sweep each cell row to identify alien cells and empty space
for Each cluster $C_i \in \mathcal{C}$ **do**
  1. Find alien cells belonging to C_i and usable space in/around C_i
  2. Build min-cost network flow model for moving the alien cells back to C_i
  3. Solve the min-cost network flow problem using the Edmonds-Karp algorithm
end for

In implementation, we need to identify alien cells, the clusters they belong to and the empty space within (or adjacent with) clusters. Since circuit designs mostly use standard cells and cells are placed in rows, the identification is done by scanning individual rows. By checking if a consecutive set of cells belong to the same cluster, one can detect potential alien cell. If a cell does not have left or right neighbors from the same cluster, the rows right above and below it are also examined to see if it has neighbor above/below that belongs to the same cluster.

5. EXPERIMENTS

5.1 Experiment Design and Setup

The entire flow of Figure 1 is evaluated in the experiments. The initial placement (including detailed placement) is done using the Capo placer [8]. All the other steps in Figure 1 are implemented by C++ language. The timing analysis after the initial placement follows the method of PCA-based statistical static timing analysis [11]. The wirelength is evaluated according to half-perimeter of net bounding boxes. The last step gate sizing and adaptivity assignment uses the method of [9]. The timing yield of adaptive designs is estimated by the technique of [12]. All the implementations run on an AMD Opteron processor with 2.2GHz frequency, 4GB memory and Linux operating system.

The experiments are performed on ICCAD 2014 Incremental Timing-Driven Placement Contest benchmark suites [13]. Adaptive body bias is employed as platform of adaptive circuit design. Please note that our method can be applied to other types of adaptive design, such as voltage interpolation [5]. We assume canary flip-flop [3] based delay variation sensors. The control signals incur only several dozens of nets, whose wirelength is negligible in circuits with hundreds of thousands of nets. We did routing for a few cases and found that the control wirelength accounts for less than 0.1% of total wirelength. The tiny increase in wirelength makes sure despite cell placement is perturbed during incremental placement, the timing disturbance is very small. In the experiments, we only focus on the wirelength overhead arising from the clustering and incremental placement. The area overhead from adaptive circuits mostly includes sensor area and gate area increase due to triple-well process for body bias. The number of clusters is empirically chosen in a range from 10 to 25. Please note our clustering algorithm can autonomously adjust the number of clusters. Because the nature of K-means clustering algorithm, the cluster size differ from each other. The difference in size can be quite dramatic in some extreme cases. Hence, there is no obvious pattern between the final result changes with number of clusters and the clustering solution. The timing is estimated according to RC switch model and the Elmore model. The power model is the same as that in [7]. Gate length variations with standard deviation of 5% nominal value are considered.

The following approaches are compared in the experiments.

- *Over-design*: This is the conventional non-adaptive circuit design. It does not have sensors, control or tuning circuits, and therefore cannot adapt to variations. It applies identical amount of power among all chips according to the worst case variation.
- *Location-aware clustering*: This is an implementation of the flow in Figure 1, but only spatial proximity is considered in the clustering step. As such, each cluster forms a contiguous region without the need of incremental placement.
- *Timing-aware clustering*: This is an implementation of the flow in Figure 1, but only timing proximity is considered in the clustering step, i.e., $\gamma = 0$ for the clustering distance defined in Equation (3). This implementation tries to emulate the approach of [7] in a broad sense, but in a simpler manner.
- *Ours*: This is our complete flow in Figure 1 based on timing and location aware clustering.

5.2 Experimental Results

All methods are tested under several different timing constraints and the average results are shown in Table 1 and 2. The results in Table 1 are from experiments with only forward body bias (FBB). One can see that all methods achieve about the same timing yield and adaptive design can save about 26% power compared to over-design. Our method results in 26% less area overhead than the location-aware clustering method. Compared to the timing-aware clustering, our method not only reduces area overhead by 31% but also incurs much less wirelength overhead. The average wirelength overhead from our method is only 0.6%, which is about 95% less than that from the timing-aware clustering.

Table 2 summarizes results from experiments with both FBB and RBB (Reverse Body Bias). The observation is similar to Table 1 except that area overhead reduction from our method is 78% on average compared to location-aware clustering. For circuit *mgc_matrix_mult*, the adaptive design leads to area decrease. This is because the optimization in the last step of Figure 1 may downsize cells.

Flow computing runtime data for different methods with FBB are outlined in Table 3. Even for the largest case *netcard*, which has near one million cells, our complete flow takes about 3 hours. This is much faster than the approach of [7], which spends near 4.5 hours to process a small circuit with 32K cells. The over-design flow has only the initial

placement and timing analysis part of Figure 1. By comparing with the runtime of our complete flow, one can tell that the initial placement and timing analysis account for about 1/3 of total runtime. The location-aware clustering method does not include incremental placement. A simple calculation tells that the incremental placement causes about 1/3 of entire runtime, and the clustering plus adaptivity optimization also costs about 1/3 of total runtime.

Table 3: Runtime of an entire flow for FBB.

Circuit	Over-design	Location-aware clustering	Ours
	Rutime(s)	Rutime(s)	Rutime(s)
mgc_edit_dist	693	1698	2197
mgc_matrix_mult	1020	1794	2318
vga_lcd	609	1381	3615
b19	1419	3111	3882
leon3mp	2544	4369	7880
leon2	3133	4953	8477
netcard	3729	7363	11307
Average	1878	3524	5754

Table 4: Impact of weight factors in clustering distance (Equation (3))for circuit *mgc_matrix_mult* with FBB. Adaptive power is denoted by AP.

α	β	γ	# clusters	AP	ΔArea	ΔWire
0	1	1	23	3707	4111	0%
5	1	1	24	3500	1851	0.61%
6.5	1	1	22	7764	8538	0.76%
7.2	1	1	22	9582	10585	0.82%
15	1	1	12	10376	10903	6.7%
20	1	1	12	6686	8423	8.5%
1	1	0	20	3771	2533	9.5%
5	0	1	24	3500	1851	0.61%
5	2	1	24	3377	1653	0.60%
5	4	1	24	4330	3673	0.55%

Experiment is performed to investigated the impact of weight factors α, β and γ in Equation (3), which defines the distance for clustering. The experiment is conducted on circuit *mgc_matrix_mult* with FBB, and the result is shown in Table 4. In this Table, the column of AP is for adaptive power, which is the average power increase due to the tuning from zero body bias to forward body bias. The minimum area overhead ΔArea is 1653, which is significantly lower than that in Table 1. This is because the timing constraint for Table 4 is relatively loose while the area overhead in Table 1 is an average from multiple experiments including those with tight timing constraints. The wirelength overhead ΔWire is mostly decided by the ratio between α and

Table 1: Experimental results with only forward body bias (FBB). Area and wirelength overhead are denoted by ΔArea ΔWire, respectively.

Circuit	#gates	Over-design		Location-aware Clustering			Timing-aware Clustering				Ours			
		Yield	Power	Yield	ΔArea	Power	Yield	ΔArea	Power	ΔWire	Yield	ΔArea	Power	ΔWire
mgc_edit_dist	130674	99.9%	806862	99.0%	13200	677812	99.1%	6416	679502	8%	99.2%	5279	678047	0.0%
mgc_matrix_mult	155341	99.9%	1280460	99.4%	12534	954764	99.7%	13982	952605	8%	99.4%	7603	949890	0.6%
vga_lcd	164891	99.9%	1025100	99.1%	7048	821001	99.6%	8639	820743	11%	99.3%	4776	820007	0.6%
b19	219268	99.9%	1994560	99.2%	12793	1501780	99.1%	7343	1493885	9%	98.8%	6695	1493931	0.6%
leon3mp	649191	99.9%	5206540	98.9%	25356	3730190	99.3%	27124	3732427	14%	98.5%	21401	3727880	0.9%
leon2	794286	99.9%	6063358	98.6%	33516	4351986	99.2%	29367	4349844	13%	98.2%	25998	4347273	0.7%
netcard	958792	99.9%	7026287	99.1%	56990	5376300	99.7%	79730	5385104	14%	99.3%	46900	5369778	0.9%
Average	438920	99.9%	3343310	99.0%	23062	2487691	99.4%	24657	2487330	11%	99.0%	16950	2483829	0.6%
Normalized			1		1.36	0.744		1.45	0.744	1		1	0.743	0.05

Table 2: Experimental results with Adaptive Body bias (ABB). Area and wire-length overhead are denoted by ΔArea and ΔWire, respectively.

Circuit	#gates	Over-design		Location-aware Clustering			Timing-aware Clustering				Ours			
		Yield	Power	Yield	ΔArea	Power	Yield	ΔArea	Power	ΔWire	Yield	ΔArea	Power	ΔWire
mgc_edit_dist	130674	99.9%	806862	98.9%	10485	674719	98.8%	7207	674920	8%	98.9%	6004	674593	0.0%
mgc_matrix_mult	155341	99.9%	1280460	99.2%	-1532	941004	99.7%	1476	942688	8%	99.2%	-1982	940700	0.6%
vga_lcd	164891	99.9%	1025100	99.0%	24379	817091	99.5%	4674	819654	11%	99.3%	3492	816888	0.6%
b19	219268	99.9%	1994560	99.4%	30641	1476531	97.6%	7720	1480902	9%	99.4%	5319	1479105	0.6%
leon3mp	649191	99.9%	5206540	98.1%	55381	3635033	98.9%	25343	3644075	14%	98.1%	19509	3625009	0.9%
leon2	794286	99.9%	6063358	98.6%	149873	4267482	98.3%	26735	4243923	13%	98.6%	23986	4264651	0.7%
netcard	958792	99.9%	7026287	98.2%	174698	5287475	99.7%	58021	5292620	14%	99.0%	40056	5274198	0.9%
Average	438920	99.9%	3343310	98.8%	63418	2442762	98.9%	18739	2442683	11%	98.9%	13769	2435021	0.6%
Normalized			1		4.61	0.731		1.36	0.731	1		1	0.728	0.05

γ. Not surprisingly, wirelength overhead is quite remarkable when this ratio is large. The timing yield results for these different weight factors are very similar.

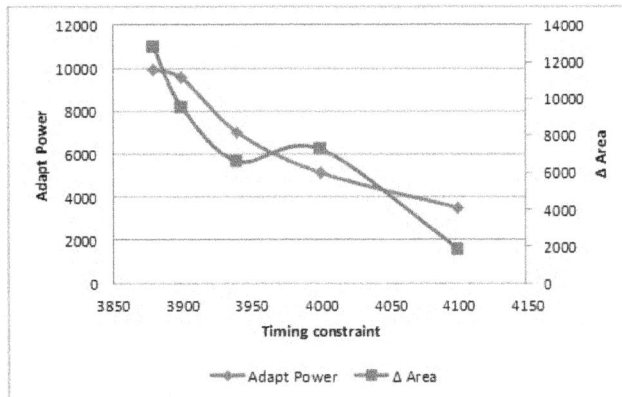

Figure 5: Power/area - timing tradeoff for *mgc_matrix_mult* with FBB.

In another experiment, timing constraint is varied to observe the effect on power and area overhead for circuit *mgc_matrix_mult* with FBB. The timing constraint is the target critical path delay we set for the circuit to meet. The power here only includes the adaptive power, which is incurred due to body bias change. The tradeoff curves are depicted in Figure 5. It is as expected that power/area increases as timing constraint is tightened. The optimization and adaptivity tuning are carried out in a way to obtain similar timing yield.

Table 5 provides data related with design perturbation due to the clustering and incremental placement. The third

column lists the percentage of cells being moved in the incremental placement, i.e., alien cells. One can see that this percentage is usually small. The rightmost column displays the average cell move distance in term of the minimum NAND2 cell width. The move distance is typically a few dozens of NAND2 cell width, which is fairly small in chip layout area. These data indicate that the perturbation from the clustering and incremental placement is limited.

Table 5: Perturbation by the incremental placement. The cell move distance is in term of min NAND2 cell width.

Circuit	#gates	#cells moved	Avg cell move distance
mgc_edit_dist	130674	5.1%	7
mgc_matrix_mult	155341	5.7%	8
vga_lcd	164891	8.1%	27
b19	219268	8.3%	12
leon3mp	649191	3.9%	89
leon2	794286	8.3%	50
netcard	958792	5.5%	90

6. CONCLUSIONS

In this work, a new approach is proposed to reduce overhead of adaptive circuit design. It is composed by cell clustering and incremental placement. The clustering considers both timing and spatial proximity, and is much faster than its previous work. The incremental placement is realized by iterative min-cost network flow algorithm. Experimental results from benchmark circuits show that our approach significantly reduces area overhead while maintains the same power and timing performance. It incurs 95% less wirelength overhead than the approach of timing-only clustering.

7. ACKNOWLEDGMENTS

This work is partially supported by NSF (CCF-1255193) and SRC (2013-TJ-2421).

8. REFERENCES

[1] J. W. Tschanz, J. T. Kao, S. G. Narendra, R. Nair, D. A. Antoniadis, A. P. Chandrakasan, and V. De. Adaptive body bias for reducing impacts of die-to-die and within-die parameter variations on microprocessor frequency and leakage. *IEEE Journal of Solid-State Circuits*, 37(11):1396–1402, November 2002.

[2] Q. Liu and S. S. Sapatnekar. Capturing post-silicon variations using a representative critical path. *IEEE Transactions on Computer-Aided Design*, 29(2):211–222, February 2010.

[3] T. Sato and Y. Kunitake. A simple flip-flop circuit for typical-case designs for DFM. In *Proceedings of the IEEE International Symposium on Quality Electronic Design*, pages 539–544, 2007.

[4] M. Agarwal, B. C. Paul, M. Zhang, and S. Mitra. Circuit failure prediction and its application to transistor aging. In *Proceedings of the IEEE VLSI Test Symposium*, pages 277–286, 2007.

[5] X. Liang, G.-Y. Wei, and D. Brooks. Revival: a variation-tolerant architecture using voltage interpolation and variable latency. *IEEE Micro*, 29(1):127–138, January 2009.

[6] K.-N. Shim, J. Hu, and J. Silva-Martinez. Dual-level adaptive supply voltage system for variation resilience. *IEEE Transactions on VLSI Systems*, 21(6):1041–1052, June 2013.

[7] S. H. Kulkarni, D. M. Sylvester, and D. T. Blaauw. Design-time optimization of post-silicon tuned circuits using adaptive body bias. *IEEE Transactions on Computer-Aided Design*, 27(3):481–494, March 2008.

[8] J. A. Roy and I. L. Markov. ECO-system: embracing the change in placement. *IEEE Transactions on Computer-Aided Design*, 26(12):2173–2185, December 2007.

[9] H. He, J. Wang, and J. Hu. Collaborative gate implementation selection and adaptivity assignment for robust combinational circuits. In *Proceedings of the ACM/IEEE International Symposium on Low Power Electronics and Design*, pages 122–127, 2015.

[10] R. K. Ahuja, T. L. Magnanti, and J. B. Orlin. *Network flows: theory, algorithms, and applications*. Prentice Hall, Upper Saddle River, NJ, 1993.

[11] H. Chang and S. S. Sapatnekar. Statistical timing analysis under spatial correlations. *IEEE Transactions on Computer-Aided Design*, 24(9):1467–1482, September 2005.

[12] R. Kumar, B. Li, Y. Shen, U. Schlichtmann, and J. Hu. Timing verification for adaptive integrated circuits. In *Proceedings of Design, Automation and Test in Europe Conference*, pages 1587–1590, 2015.

[13] M.-C. Kim, J. Hu, and N. Viswanathan. ICCAD-2014 CAD contest in incremental timing-driven placement and benchmark suite. In *Proceedings of the IEEE/ACM International Conference on Computer-Aided Design*, pages 361–366, 2014.

Load-Aware Redundant Via Insertion for Electromigration Avoidance

Steve Bigalke
Institute of Electromechanical and Electronic
Design (IFTE)
Dresden University of Technology
01062 Dresden, Germany
✉ steve.bigalke@outlook.com

Jens Lienig
Institute of Electromechanical and Electronic
Design (IFTE)
Dresden University of Technology
01062 Dresden, Germany
✉ jens@ieee.org

ABSTRACT

The ongoing shrinking of interconnects in integrated circuits (ICs) induces reliability issues caused by electromigration (EM), including void-induced failure mechanisms in IC vias. We propose a new post-routing approach to insert redundant vias specially targeted for EM avoidance. Our algorithm compares all possible insertions and utilizes the configuration with the highest reliability gain. This is achieved by considering the connecting segment loads. These loads are an estimation of the risk involved in creating EM-induced voids as a continuous function of current density, segment length and stress development over time. Inserting vias in those segments with highest loads, our approach efficiently increases circuit reliability by reducing EM effects. We were able to reduce the total, average and maximum via load for the MCNC benchmark suite on average by 6.6%, 4% and 13.9%, respectively. The increase in via reliability was confirmed by subsequent modeling of EM-inducing factors.

Keywords

Electronic design automation; physical design; reliability; redundancy; electromigration; post-routing redundant via insertion; layout

1. INTRODUCTION

As the downscaling of integrated circuits (ICs) continuously decreases IC structures, reliability issues due to interconnect and via failures gain more and more influence. Particularly, vias are critical elements in a design [18]. This is due to the influence of material transport caused by electromigration (EM) which is higher in via regions than in interconnects due to the smaller cross-sectional area.

Via failures can also be introduced by the manufacturing process or by thermally induced stress. Nevertheless, EM is the primary cause of via failure during an IC lifetime, since manufacturing defects can be detected by design-for-

ISPD'16, April 03-06, 2016, Santa Rosa, CA, USA

© 2016 Copyright held by the owner/author(s).

ACM ISBN 978-1-4503-4039-7/16/04.

DOI: http://dx.doi.org/10.1145/2872334.2872355

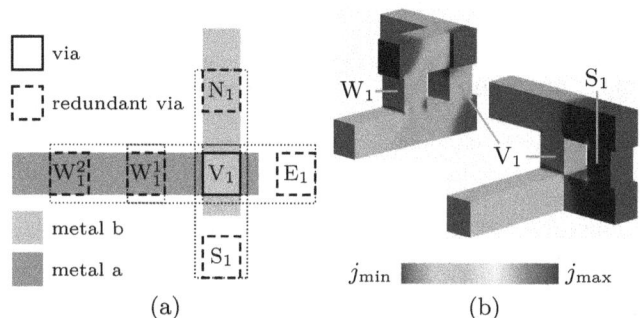

Figure 1: (a) Candidate positions for redundant vias to the north (N_1), south (S_1), east (E_1) and west (W_1, W_2) of the (original) via (V_1). (b) Two different via insertions with on-track via W_1 distributing the current density (j) better than off-track via S_1.

test structures and thermally introduced stress has been mainly identified on bigger structures such as through silicon vias (TSVs) or packaging elements.

EM is a material dislocation caused by the momentum transfer of moving electrons to steady lattice metal ions at the moment of collision. Therefore, one of the main factors of influence is the current density (j). The International Technology Roadmap for Semiconductors (ITRS) [9] predicts a rise in current density, since interconnects and vias are shrinking at a higher rate than the reduction in current consumption in active silicon elements [9]. Hence, in the near future almost every net, including signal nets, will be affected by EM. The IC industry is facing a lack of EM solutions from, and including, 5 nm technology nodes and beyond [9][18].

Redundant vias, as shown in Fig. 1, not only increase yield but also extend chip lifetime [1]. The manufacturing process introduces voids between metal and via layers, which can be starting points for a via failure induced by EM. Figure 2a shows that voids in via areas predominantly occur at the interface of via trenches and interconnects. These defects can also grow through the entire interconnect (Fig. 2b). If a redundant via is inserted next to a failing via, then chip lifetime is extended since EM must deplete two or more via areas before this net segment fails. Here (as in other papers), a *segment* is defined as a single part of a net, which is located only in one metal layer and enclosed by a diffusion barrier.

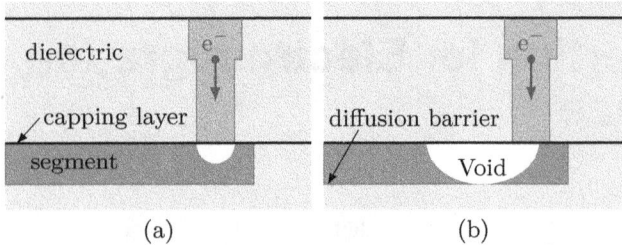

Figure 2: A void formation directly underneath the via trench is shown in (a), while (b) depicts a void growth through the entire interconnect.

This paper presents a novel, post-routing redundant via insertion process. It is based on combining EM-inducing factors into a *load* metric. Here, a *segment load* represents the risk of void creation in a particular segment based on current density, segment length and resulting time-dependent stress development. A *load per via* is defined as the highest segment load of the via-connected segments divided by the number of vias used to establish this particular connection. In our opinion, these parameters determine the reliability gain with each redundant via.

To the best of our knowledge, this is the first algorithm that optimizes the (local) redundant via insertion in order to minimize the (global) sum of all "loads per via" in the design (*total via load*).

Our paper is structured as follows. After outlining the current via insertion algorithms in Sec. II, we demonstrate the necessity for their extension in Sec. III. Section IV describes such a comprehensive via insertion procedure and Sec. V presents our experimental results.

2. PREVIOUS WORKS

Redundant via insertion can be applied as part of the routing step or as an additional post-routing optimization with the latter being the main focus in physical design. Nevertheless, redundant via insertion while routing has been investigated as well, such as in [5][19][24].

Post-routing redundant via insertion was first presented and utilized in EYE/PEYE [1]. In general, the redundant via insertion subject can be formulated as maximum bipartite matching (MBM) or maximum independent set (MIS).

The MBM approach was investigated in [26] and adapted to timing constraints in [25] and [22]. Lei et al. extended the MBM problem in [16] to a maximum-weighted bipartite matching (MWBM) (includes candidate dependencies and weights) and solved it by using an efficient heuristic minimum weighted matching algorithm. In [15] the MWBM approach is particularly used to insert aligned stacked vias in a grid-based layout with up to three metal layers. Later on, Chang et al. [4] introduced a new rectangle via candidate, which occupies a smaller footprint than a two via compound while it still prolongs via lifetime.

MBM is generally less time consuming than MIS but it cannot always determine the optimal solution [13]. Therefore, our algorithm is based on MIS.

MIS was first applied to the redundant via insertion problem in [13]. Here, all feasible redundant via candidates are simultaneously examined which improves the solution quality. In [14] the same author introduced a zero-one integer linear programing (0-1 ILP) algorithm to solve the MIS problem. Since finding the solution of this can be NP-complete,

Lee et al. proposed in [11] speed-up techniques to reduce the problem size and enabled the consideration of via density constraints. In [12] the approach has been extended by weights to consider on-track vias or non-wire bending redundant via candidates.

Pak et al. in [21] were the first to apply the MIS approach for EM-aware redundant via insertion. The authors presented a two-phase algorithm, which first determines only feasible redundant vias based on current density, before inserting as many as possible additional vias. However, their approach lacks the consideration of segment length and time-dependent stress, which greatly influence EM-induced via failures.

3. PROBLEM DEFINITION

3.1 Electromigration

EM is a material transport caused by the momentum transfer of moving electrons to metal ions. The metal ions break out of their lattice and begin to move towards the anode. The amount of dislocated material over time depends on the current density and therefore also on current and cross sections of each net segment. Not only does the cross-section geometry matter but also the length of a segment. Next to current density and segment geometry, EM also depends on the temperature, the material and the manufacturing process [17]. These three factors are excluded from our study, since they are given parameters for physical design.

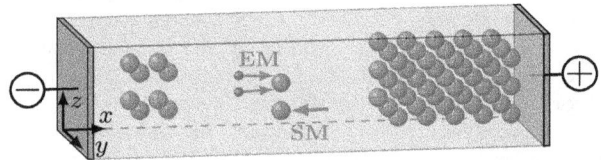

Figure 3: Metal ion transportation from cathode towards anode due to EM, resulting in tensile stress at the cathode and compressive stress at the anode. The stress gradient causes SM which compensates EM and results in a balanced state [8].

The current density and segment geometry essentially influence the build up of the time-dependent stress along a segment. As Fig. 3 depicts, the dislocated metal ions build up tensile stress at the cathode and comprehensive stress at the anode. This is mathematically expressed by:

$$\frac{\partial \sigma}{\partial t} = \frac{\partial}{\partial x}\left[\frac{D_a B \Omega}{kT}\left(\frac{\partial \sigma}{\partial x} - \frac{|Z^*|e\rho j}{\Omega}\right)\right], \quad (1)$$

where σ is the stress, D_a the self-diffusion coefficient, B the applicable modulus, Ω the atomic volumes, kT the thermal energy, $|Z^*|$ the effective charge number, e the elementary charge, ρ the electrical resistivity and j the current density [10].

The exemplary one-dimensional solution of Eq. (1) along the x-axis is plotted in Fig. 4 for a 50 μm long segment and a current density of $1\,\mathrm{MA\,m^{-2}}$. The plot shows the stress increase over time until EM is compensated by stress migration (SM, red straight line). From this moment on, the absolute maximal stress (σ_{max}) is reached on both segments ends. We should point out that the tensile stress at the cathode is more critical than the comprehensive stress at the anode because the critical stress (σ_{crit}) for void creation is usually lower than the threshold for hillock building.

100

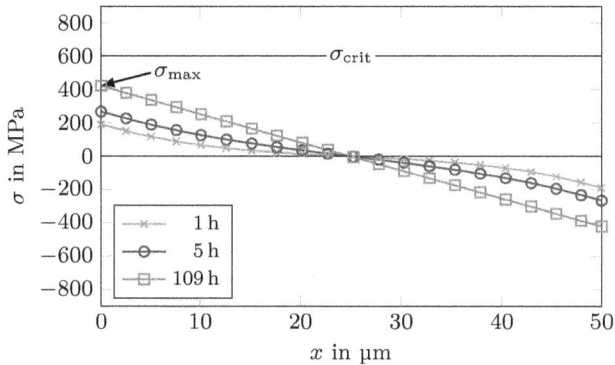

Figure 4: One-dimensional stress development over time, based on a current density of $1\,\mathrm{MA\,m^{-2}}$ and a segment length of $50\,\mu m$.

The void formation starts with the depletion process until the stress oversteps the critical stress. Equation 1 must be solved to determine the void depletion time (when the stress reaches the critical stress). From this point on, the void starts to grow and the interconnect resistance starts to significantly increase till a chip failure is detected due to a voltage drop that is too great, or an open circuit.

If the stress development is stable over time, the steady state is reached and EM is balanced by SM. In 1975 *Blech* found that an interconnect segment is immortal to EM if the maximal stress is lower than the critical stress [2]. The so called Blech-length effect connects current density and segment length to the time-dependent stress:

$$jl \leq (jl)_{\mathrm{crit}} = \frac{\Omega \sigma_{\mathrm{crit}}}{|Z^*| e\rho}. \qquad (2)$$

Equation (2) shows that the higher the product of current density and segment length, the higher the risk of EM failure.

As a consequence, an EM-robust redundant via insertion process should not only consider current density, but also segment length. The following sections explain in detail why current density, segment length and time-dependent stress must be considered in order to prevent EM-induced via failures.

3.2 Influence of Current Density

A segment's current density is the main driving force behind EM. As shown in [12], on-track vias facilitate a more balanced current distribution and enable a shorter wire length than off-track vias. Even though the approach in [21] states that off-track triple via configurations can have a 2% longer lifetime than on-track configurations, we recommend balancing and reducing current densities per via.

A reason to prefer on-track to off-track vias is shown in Fig. 5. An unbalanced current density per via can easily lead to a void, which grows through the segment (compare Fig. 2b). The reason for this is the increase in current density under void V_1. While the void is growing underneath the via trench, the current density is rising in the region underneath the void (red zone). Therefore, EM is continuously increasing to move material out of this area until the increase in resistance leads to a chip failure. This might happen even before the redundant via fails.

As mentioned, the higher the current density, the more stress builds up and therefore the more likely the segment is to fail (Fig. 6).

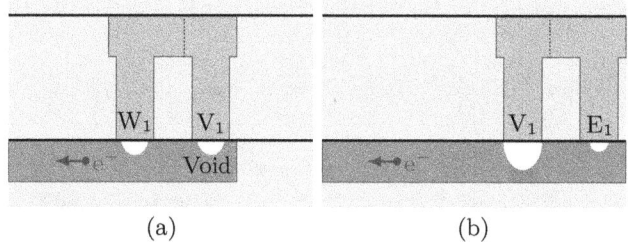

Figure 5: Systematic void growth in on- and off-track vias. Figure (a) depicts uniform void growth under the via and the redundant via. Figure (b) shows the increased current density in the red area underneath the via (V), which continues to grow until an interconnect failure occurs.

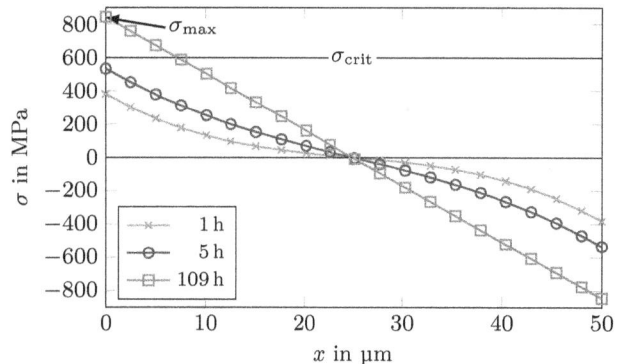

Figure 6: One-dimensional stress development over time, based on a current density of $2\,\mathrm{MA\,m^{-2}}$ and a segment length of $50\,\mu m$ (compare with Fig. 4).

Comparing Figs. 4 and 6, we can see that while the time to reach steady state does not depend on the current density, the time to reach a certain level of stress does. The general rule is that the higher the current density, the faster the stress builds up.

Current density thus impacts the segment load and should be considered when evaluating the importance of a redundant via in a segment. To the best of our knowledge, current densities have never been used to directly rank redundant via candidates.

To lend credence to our recommendation to compare current densities in different segments, we constructed the "academic example" in Fig. 7a. Here, there is only one redundant via location for an insertion in either net 1 or net 2. (By definition, a *via location* is a connection of two metal segments on different layers at a single position in the design.) In Fig. 7a, the net of via 2 carries twice as much current as the net of via 1. Again, as far as we are aware, all published redundant via insertion algorithms solve this conflict randomly if both segments are EM critical or EM stable.

If we compare the current density distribution of both vias without insertion (Fig. 7b), we can clearly see that via 2 carries a higher current density than via 1. Therefore, the redundant via W_2 (Fig. 7d) balances the current density distribution per via better than a redundant via E_1 (Fig. 7c). This example illustrates that the commonly applied goal of "as many as possible" redundant vias is not detailed enough for an EM-robust redundant via insertion process.

101

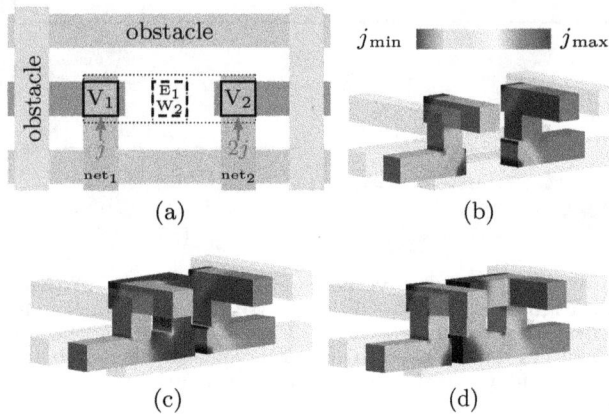

Figure 7: (a) Layout with only one redundant via location which qualifies for a insertion in either net 1 or net 2. Figure (b) shows the current density distribution without insertions. Figures (c) and (d) depict the current density distribution after a insertion in net 1 and net 2, respectively. Here, configuration (d) balances the current density best and therefore gains reliability.

3.3 Influence of Segment Length

In this section we show that not only current density but also segment length should be considered. Therefore, we expand our previous example in Fig. 7a to the example in Fig. 8. Here, the segment lengths are added to show their influence.

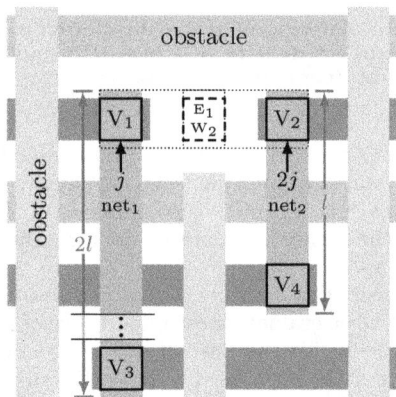

Figure 8: Extended layout example of Fig. 7 to illustrate the influence of segment length on EM. Please note that the distance between via 1 and 3 is twice as long as the distance between via 2 and 4. However, the current density between via 1 and 3 is only half the value of that between via 2 and 4.

The subsequently derived stress development in Fig. 9 demonstrates that the product of current density and segment length is not sufficient to fully describe the influence of stress induced by EM. This product is the same in both segments. Therefore, the maximum stress is also the same after it reaches the steady state condition for EM and SM. Nevertheless, in this configuration the redundant via should be inserted next to V_2 since Fig. 9 shows that the critical stress is reached about five times faster at this via than it is at the other one. This means that a void underneath via 2 depletes about five times faster than a void under via 1.

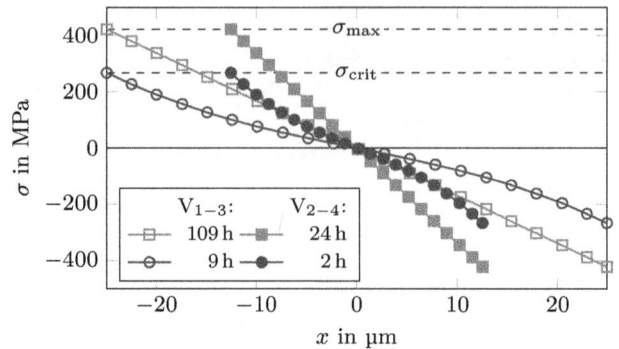

Figure 9: Comparison of one dimensional stress development over time, based on a $j_{1,3} = 1 \, \mathrm{MA \, m^{-2}}$, $l_{1,3} = 50 \, \mathrm{\mu m}$, $j_{2,4} = 2 \, \mathrm{MA \, m^{-2}}$ and $l_{2,4} = 25 \, \mathrm{\mu m}$.

3.4 Segment Load

We recommend that an EM-aware redundant via insertion process should consider: (1) current density, (2) segment length, and (3) time-dependent development of stress. These three EM-inducing factors are subsequently labeled as segment load. (Please refer to Eq. (3) for their mutual relationship). With these factors, we can not only estimate whether a segment is EM critical or EM stable but we can also estimate and compare the reliability gain of each via insertion.

The term "EM critical" means that the segment stress exceeds the critical stress. EM stable segments are (in theory) immortal against EM because the segment stress is lower than the critical stress. In reality, however, the manufacturing process induces defects, which are starting points for void creation. Therefore, we should also insert redundant vias in EM stable segments but only if there are no other redundant via candidates with higher segment loads that could also use this location. In summary, the insertion of redundant vias must be based on the connecting segment loads.

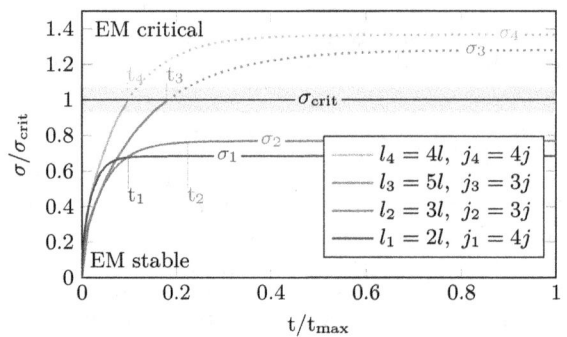

Figure 10: Time dependent stress development for different current densities and segment length combinations ($j = 1 \, \mathrm{MA \, cm^{-2}}$ and $l = 1 \, \mathrm{\mu m}$). Segments 1 and 2 are EM stable since their maximum segment stresses are lower than the critical stress. Consequently, segments 3 and 4 are EM critical.

Figure 10 plots four different combinations of current densities and segment lengths. Please note that the critical stress threshold is blurred by manufacturing variances. Two of the segments are EM stable and two are EM critical. The plot shows that we have to calculate all load factors for each current density and length combination because void depletion time and maximum stress do not correlate.

4. LOAD-AWARE VIA INSERTION PROCEDURE

4.1 Flow Sequence

This section describes the main steps in our approach. Net capacities and currents, both determining the segment loads, are input values of our algorithm. Furthermore, technology information is needed as a constraint while searching for redundant via locations. The latter are represented in a conflict graph including geometric dependencies between the redundant via candidates. Finally, these conflicts are transformed into a 0-1 ILP problem which allows us to find the *optimal* redundant via insertions with regard to EM effects.

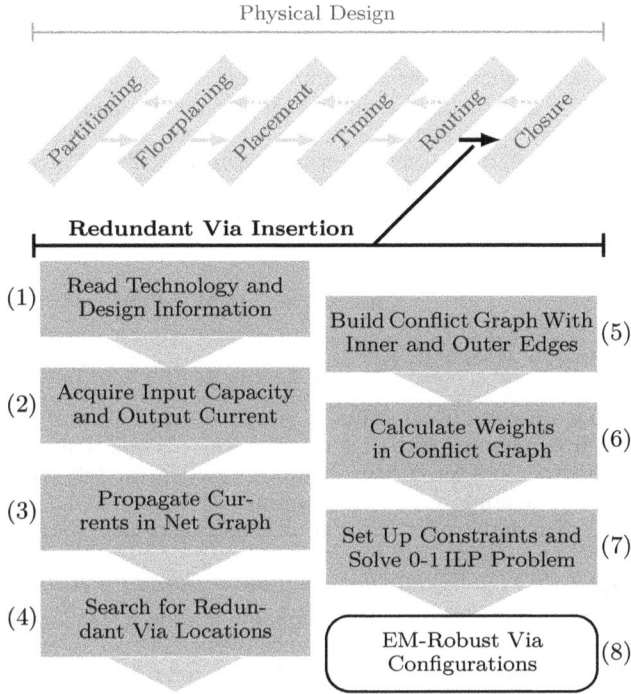

Figure 11: Main steps in our algorithm for load-aware redundant via insertion. These steps are fleshed out in Sec. 4.1 (Step 1) to (Step 8).

Step 1: Read Technology and Design Information

The first step is to read the technology and design information which are commonly provided in the Layout and Design Exchange Format (LEF/DEF). Our approach requires technology information such as interconnect space, width and height in each layer. The design information include the routing result and possible via configurations.

Step 2: Acquire Input Capacity and Output Current

Next, the net currents, based on net topology and input pin capacitances, are determined. Pins in standard cells are usually characterized in a look-up library file (*.lib*) which contains the information about current characteristic and pin capacitance. Our approach assigns to each input net pin the appropriate capacitance and determines the current values based on the waveform and switching activity.

Step 3: Propagate Currents in Net Graph

We model the current flow starting from the net output pin and heading towards the input pins. Therefore, we transform the interconnect segments for each net into a current flow graph. This graph representation contains a vertex for each net segment and edges between connecting segments as shown in Fig. 12.

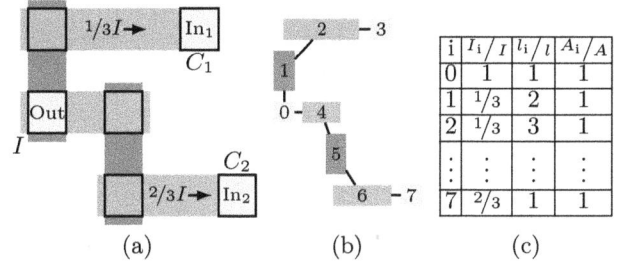

Figure 12: (a) Net transformation into a graph representation. (b) Propagation of currents along segment connections. (c) Vertex properties including segment length (l), current (I) and cross section (A).

Circuit analyses have shown that, in a first approximation, the current in each path between output and input pins can be divided as per the ratios of the different path capacitances to the total net capacitance. To determine the shortest path between output and input pins in the current flow graph, we execute the Dijkstra algorithm [6] starting at the output. After that, the different paths are obtained by backtracking from the inputs pins. The currents for all identified segments on each path are added up to the total segment current. From now on, each segment contains its current, length and cross-section information, so that the current density value can be calculated.

All previous steps must be finished before executing the next step, searching for redundant via locations.

Step 4: Search for Redundant Via Locations

This step detects all possible locations in the design which can serve as redundant via locations (Fig. 13).

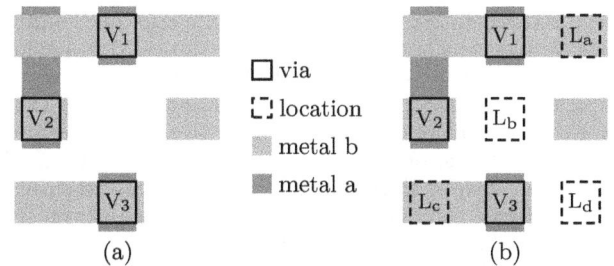

Figure 13: (a) Design example with vacant space after routing. (b) Redundant via locations in accordance with the design rules.

The following conditions must be fulfilled to ensure a location is suitable for a redundant via:

- Inserting a redundant via must not violate any spacing rules to existing interconnects, and
- the redundant via candidate can only intersect with its own net.

Step 5: Build Conflict Graph With Inner & Outer Edges

Each via location, identified in the previous step, is tested by the adjacent vias to check if it can serve as a redundant via location. If one or more redundant vias can be inserted, candidates are found and a vertex is added for each candidate to a conflict graph (Fig. 14). Various redundant via candidates which occupy the same location are defined as "in conflict".

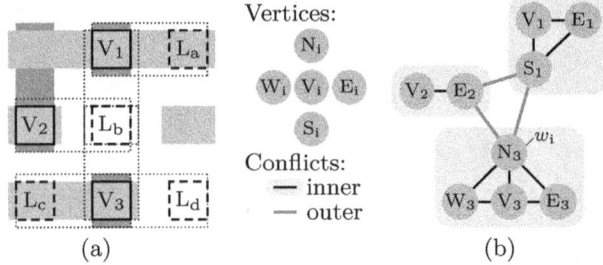

Figure 14: (a) Geometric intersections of redundant via candidates. (b) Transformation of geometry information into a conflict graph with internal and external edges. Internal edges link redundant via candidates of the same via location. External edges represent conflicts of redundant via candidates from different via locations.

The geometric intersections of these candidates are transferred into edges in the conflict graph. We distinguish between inner and outer conflicts (edges), as it was done in [21]. Inner edges are added between all possible redundant via candidates of the same via location. Outer edges are inserted to the conflict graph between redundant via candidates from different via locations.

Step 6: Calculate Weights in Conflict Graph

A very essential step in our approach is to assign weights to every vertex in the conflict graph. These values are crucial for rating the conflicting via candidates and inserting the most fitting candidate. In our approach, a *weight* is the previously defined load per via. As mentioned, the sum of all load per vias (weights) in a design is called total via load (z). The global objective is to minimize the total via load in the design.

As discussed in Sec. 3.4, current density, segment length, maximal stress and the time to reach the critical stress influence the segment load. The first two parameters are input values; the time-dependent stress is determined by Eq. (1).

A segment load consists of two main load factors representing void depletion ($t_{\min}/t_i$) and void growth ($jl_i/jl_{\max}$) phases, respectively. Both ranges are standardized to ensure a value between zero and one. Additionally, these values are adjusted by the linear scaling factors: α and β.

The factor of void depletion is a measure of time t_i at which the segment resistance starts to increase considerably. The longer it takes, the more robust the segment is. Therefore, the individual depletion time of the investigated segment is reciprocal standardized to the minimal depletion time of all segments in the design.

The factor of void growth is represented by the product of current density (j) and segment length (l). The higher the product, the faster the void grows. This product is also proportional to the maximum segment stress and standardized by the maximum occurring value.

The sum of both scaled segment load factors is finally divided by the number of vias each vertex utilizes. This means that a segment load is divided by one for a single via, by two for a double via, and so on. The load per via is based on the highest segment load of the connecting segments. The equation to calculate a weight (w_i) is formulated as follows:

$$w_i = \frac{\left(\alpha \frac{t_{\min}}{t_i} + \beta \frac{(jl)_i}{(jl)_{\max}}\right)}{n_i} \Rightarrow \frac{\text{load}}{\#\text{via}}, \qquad (3)$$

where α was determined empirically to be 1 and β to be 2. (We value the influence of void growth speed more than depletion time). This assumption holds for today's copper interconnects manufactured by the dual-damascene process.

Additionally, we adjust t_i for EM stable and EM critical segments depending on the maximum segment stress. In an EM stable segment, the maximum stress does not exceed the critical void stress and therefore the depletion time is set to infinity and the depletion factor becomes zero. Note that the void growth factor for an EM critical segment is always higher than the factor for an EM stable segment. Consequently, our algorithm focuses on redundant via insertion in EM critical segments.

$$t_i = \begin{cases} \infty & \sigma_{\max} < \sigma_{\text{crit}} \quad \text{(EM stable)} \\ t_{i,\,\text{crit}} & \sigma_{\max} \geq \sigma_{\text{crit}} \quad \text{(EM critical)} \end{cases} \qquad (4)$$

Since our weight function is length dependent, our approach prefers on-track vias to off-track vias and non-wire bending candidates to wire bending candidates. Off-track and wire bending candidates prolong the segment length which is directly reflected in an increase in segment load.

Step 7: Set Up Constraints and Solve 0-1 ILP Problem

Having created the conflict graph, our approach transforms the vertex weights and edges into a 0-1 ILP problem to determine the optimal solution. (Our weight function can also be used in a MWBM problem formulation, because it is generally applicable.) As mentioned before, the objective function is to minimize the total via load (sum of all weights) in the design which can be expressed as:

$$\text{minimize: } z = \sum_{i \in V} w_i v_i, \quad v_i \in \{0, 1\}, \qquad (5)$$

where V, IE and OE represent vertices, and inner and outer edges in the conflict graph ($G = (V, IE, OE)$), respectively. It should be noted that v_i can only be one or zero, which means this vertex is or is not taken, respectively.

The conflict graph edges are transformed as constraints which must be fulfilled. Inner edges represent a minimum of candidates to be taken and can be modeled as:

$$\sum_{j \in IE} v_j \geq 1, \qquad (6)$$

which ensures that at least one configuration is included in the final design.

Outer edges represent vertex intersections. This means that only one vertex can be chosen in the final solution:

$$v_i + v_j \leq 1, \quad \forall i, j \in OE. \qquad (7)$$

4.2 EM-Robust Via Configurations

Our approach reduces the total, average and maximum via load in the design because we utilize redundant via candidates with the lowest load per via if multiple choices exist. The general principle is: the higher the segment load, the more important it is to insert redundant vias in order to lower the load per via.

Illustrating this principle in Fig. 8 means that the location is taken by a redundant via in the west of via 2 belonging to net 2. The load of via 2 is higher than the load of via 1, because the segment load of net 2 is higher than the segment load of net 1 and the number of vias are the same. The segment load in net 2 is higher than the segment load in net 1, because segment 2 depletes faster than segment 1. In order to minimize the total via load, the optimal EM-robust solution is to divide the high segment load of net 2 by two vias and to retain the single via in net 1.

5. EXPERIMENTAL RESULTS

To verify our load-aware redundant via insertion for EM avoidance, we implemented our approach in C++ and applied it on the MCNC benchmark from [5], which is widely used in this research field. The details are subsequently explained based on the flow sequence depicted in Fig. 11:

- Step (1) uses the LEF/DEF parser from *Si2* [23] to read in the benchmarks.
- Step (2) requires the standard cell characterization. Unfortunately, the benchmark suite does not provide these look-up tables for output current characteristics and capacitance values. To overcome this issue, we used the open cell library files provided by *NanGate* [20] and mapped these standard cell values randomly to the cell pins of the MCNC benchmark suite. Since the technology dimensions of the MCNC benchmark suite are bigger than the *NanGate* 45 nm dimensions, we reasonably scale these values to achieve a comparable result.
- Step (3) utilizes a *boost* adjacency list [3] to represent the undirected current flow net graph.
- Step (4) fills a *boost* r-tree [3] with all interconnect elements and queries around each via. The query box measures the bounding box of the redundant via candidate plus the minimum layer space.
- Step (5) also represents all via candidates in an undirected graph as *boost* adjacency list [3].
- Step (6) reads in pre-calculated look-up tables to determine the maximal stress and time to reach the critical stress from current density and segment length. These look-up tables are generated by a *Python* script which solves Eq. (1) for multiple current density and segment length combinations.
- Step (7) employs the *Gurobi* library [7] to formulate and solve the 0-1 ILP representation. We also use the independent component computation from [21] to speed up the process.
- Step (8) replaces the vias in the original input DEF file and creates a new output file of the configuration which utilizes a minimum total via load in the design.

For the MCNC benchmark suite, we limited our load-aware redundant via insertion to single and double vias because the original technology contains only these via configurations.

Table 1: MCNC benchmark suite characteristics

Name	#nets	#layers	#segments	#vias
mcc1	802	4	6513	5948
mcc2	7118	4	36773	34376
primary1	904	3	7362	5536
primary2	3029	3	30088	23154
s5378	1694	3	10082	6739
s9234	1486	3	8638	5365
s13207	3781	3	22391	13972
s15850	4472	3	26527	16922
s38417	11309	3	65836	40942
s38584	14754	3	88368	55381
struct	1920	3	11719	7598

Table 2: Reduction of total, average and maximum via load in our designs compared to the designs from [5]

Name	Total via load		Red.: $\frac{\Delta \text{ via load}}{[5] \text{ via load}}$ in %		
	Design [5]	Our design	Total	Average	Maximum
mcc1	1147.1	1050.8	8.4	4.1	31.1
mcc2	6710.7	5978.7	10.9	5.2	4.5
primary1	446.9	436.4	2.4	1.5	19.8
primary2	1284.6	1255.5	2.3	0.7	0.1
s5378	554.1	509.1	8.1	5.2	21.1
s9234	477.0	441.1	7.5	4.9	15.4
s13207	903.9	837.7	7.3	4.7	0.2
s15850	1271.7	1168.1	8.1	5.3	28.2
s38417	2383.7	2192.6	8.0	5.5	11.3
s38584	2958.7	2703.5	8.6	5.8	9.9
struct	598.4	590.2	1.4	1.1	0.2

Table 1 depicts the number of nets, layers, segments, and vias for each benchmark.

All experiments were performed on a 3.4 Ghz Intel i7 Linux workstation with 8 GB of memory. Our implementation utilizes only one core but solving the biggest benchmark takes less than 2 min and requires about 200 MB of RAM.

Our evaluation is based on the total, average and maximum via load in the design according to Eq. (3). We compared our values to the original designs from [5].

Table 2 contains the total, average and maximum via load values of our and the original designs from [5], both based on Eq. (3). As shown, we were able to reduce the total, average and maximum via load on average by 6.6%, 4% and 13.9%, respectively. It should be mentioned that we achieved similar runtime and insertion rates while inserting redundant vias with the highest reliability gain.

We also modeled current densities in some via configurations prior to and after via insertion. Figure 7(b,c,d) pictures an example where a marked reduction in peak current density within the vias can be observed. Our approach has also been evaluated by the reduction of via stress (Fig. 15).

6. SUMMARY AND CONCLUSIONS

We utilize the redundant via insertion process in order to make vias significantly more EM robust. This efficiently counteracts today's increasing reliability issues due to technology downscaling.

We have shown that a comprehensive consideration of EM during redundant via insertion should not only consider current densities but also the segment length and the related time-depended stress. We combined these EM-inducing factors into a "load per via" metric.

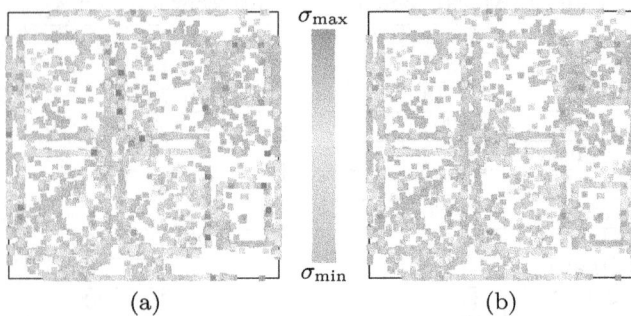

Figure 15: Via stress in the mcc1 benchmark before (a) and after (b) applying our approach. Numerical values range between 4.2% and 25% reduction in average and peak via stress, respectively.

To the best of our knowledge, this approach is the first that rates continuously all redundant via candidates based on their load per via. For this reason, we specially developed a weight function which determines the load per via representing the risk of void formation. This enables us to insert (local) redundant vias in order to minimize the (global) total via load in the design.

The verification of our approach on the MCNC benchmark suite showed a significant reduction in the total, maximum and average via load in a reasonable runtime. Subsequent modeling of current density and stress values within the vias verified this reduction. Our post-routing approach inserts load-aware redundant vias for EM avoidance during a single execution. It can also consider different kinds of vias, such as on- or off-track or multiple vias, as well as wire bending candidates.

7. REFERENCES

[1] G. A. Allan. Targeted layout modifications for semiconductor yield/reliability enhancement. *IEEE Transactions on Semiconductor Manufacturing*, 17(4):573–581, Nov. 2004. DOI: 10.1109/TSM.2004.835727.

[2] I. A. Blech. Electromigration in thin aluminum films on titanium nitride. *Journal of Applied Physics*, 47(4):1203–1208, Apr. 1976. DOI: 10.1063/1.322842.

[3] boost. *C++ libraries*, 2015.

[4] T.-F. Chang, T.-C. Kan, S.-H. Yang, and S.-J. Ruan. Enhanced redundant via insertion with multi-via mechanisms. In *Proc. of IEEE Computer Society Annual Symposium on VLSI (ISVLSI)*, pages 218–223, Jul. 2011. DOI: 10.1109/ISVLSI.2011.50.

[5] H.-Y. Chen, M.-F. Chiang, Y.-W. Chang, L. Chen, and B. Han. Full-chip routing considering double-via insertion. *IEEE Transactions on Computer-Aided Design of Integrated Circuits and Systems*, 27(5):844–857, May 2008. DOI: 10.1109/TCAD.2008.917597.

[6] E. W. Dijkstra. A note on two problems in connexion with graphs. *Numerische Mathematik*, 1(1):269–271, Jun. 1959. DOI: 10.1007/BF01386390.

[7] Gurobi. *Optimization 6.0*, 2015.

[8] C. S. Hau-Riege. An introduction to cu electromigration. *Microelectronics Reliability*, 44(2):195–205, Feb. 2004. DOI: 10.1016/j.microrel.2003.10.020.

[9] International Technology Roadmap for Semiconductors (ITRS). *Interconnect*, 2011 edition.

[10] M. A. Korhonen, P. Børgesen, K. N. Tu, and C.-Y. Li. Stress evolution due to electromigration in confined metal lines. *Journal of Applied Physics*, 73(8):3790–3799, Apr. 1993. DOI: 10.1063/1.354073.

[11] K.-Y. Lee, C.-K. Koh, T.-C. Wang, and K.-Y. Chao. Fast and optimal redundant via insertion. *IEEE Transactions on Computer-Aided Design of Integrated Circuits and Systems*, 27(12):2197–2208, Dec. 2008. DOI: 10.1109/TCAD.2008.2006151.

[12] K.-Y. Lee, S.-T. Lin, and T.-C. Wang. Enhanced double via insertion using wire bending. *IEEE Transactions on Computer-Aided Design of Integrated Circuits and Systems*, 29(2):171–184, Feb. 2010. DOI: 10.1109/TCAD.2009.2035559.

[13] K.-Y. Lee and T.-C. Wang. Post-routing redundant via insertion for yield/reliability improvement. In *Proc. of 11th Asia and South Pacific Design Automation Conference (ASP-DAC)*, pages 303–308, Jan. 2006. DOI: 10.1109/ASPDAC.2006.1594699.

[14] K.-Y. Lee, T.-C. Wang, and K.-Y. Chao. Post-routing redundant via insertion and line end extension with via density consideration. In *Proc. of IEEE/ACM International Conference on Computer-Aided Design (ICCAD)*, pages 633–640, Nov. 2006. DOI: 10.1109/ICCAD.2006.320027.

[15] K.-Y. Lee, T.-C. Wang, C.-K. Koh, and K.-Y. Chao. Optimal double via insertion with on-track preference. *IEEE Transactions on Computer-Aided Design of Integrated Circuits and Systems*, 29(2):318–323, Feb. 2010. DOI: 10.1109/TCAD.2009.2035581.

[16] C.-K. Lei, P.-Y. Chiang, and Y.-M. Lee. Post-routing redundant via insertion with wire spreading capability. In *Proc. of 14th Asia and South Pacific Design Automation Conference (ASP-DAC)*, pages 468–473, Jan. 2009. DOI: 10.1109/ASPDAC.2009.4796524.

[17] J. Lienig. Introduction to electromigration-aware physical design. In *Proc. of the 2006 ACM International Symposium on Physical Design (ISPD)*, pages 39–46, Apr. 2006. DOI: 10.1145/1123008.1123017.

[18] J. Lienig. Electromigration and its impact on physical design in future technologies. In *Proc. of the 2013 ACM International Symposium on Physical Design (ISPD)*, pages 33–40, Mar. 2013. DOI: 10.1145/2451916.2451925.

[19] Y.-H. Lin, Y.-H. Lin, G.-C. Su, and Y.-L. Li. Dead via minimization by simultaneous routing and redundant via insertion. In *Proc. of 15th Asia and South Pacific Design Automation Conference (ASP-DAC)*, pages 657–662, Jan. 2010. DOI: 10.1109/ASPDAC.2010.5419806.

[20] NanGate. *45nm Open Cell Library*, 2011.

[21] J. Pak, Y. Bei, and D. Pan. Electromigration-aware redundant via insertion. In *Proc. of 20th Asia and South Pacific Design Automation Conference (ASP-DAC)*, pages 544–549, Jan. 2015. DOI: 10.1109/ASPDAC.2015.7059063.

[22] C.-W. Pan and Y.-M. Lee. Redundant via insertion under timing constraints. In *Proc. of 12th International Symposium on Quality Electronic Design (ISQED)*, pages 1–7, Mar. 2011. DOI: 10.1109/ISQED.2011.5770794.

[23] Si2. *LEF/DEF Parser*, 2015.

[24] G. Xu, L.-D. Huang, D. Pan, and M. Wong. Redundant-via enhanced maze routing for yield improvement. In *Proc. of Asia and South Pacific Design Automation Conference (ASP-DAC)*, volume 2, pages 1148–1151, Jan. 2005. DOI: 10.1109/ASPDAC.2005.1466544.

[25] J.-T. Yan, B.-Y. Chiang, and Z.-W. Chen. Timing-constrained redundant via insertion for yield optimization. In *Proc. of IEEE Northeast Workshop on Circuits and Systems (NEWCAS)*, pages 1126–1129, Aug. 2007. DOI: 10.1109/NEWCAS.2007.4488005.

[26] H. Yao, Y. Cai, Q. Zhou, and X. Hong. Multilevel routing with redundant via insertion. *IEEE Transactions on Circuits and Systems II*, 53(10):1148–1152, Oct. 2006. DOI: 10.1109/TCSII.2006.881822.

Early Days of Automatic Floorplan Design

Martin D. F. Wong
Department of Electrical and Computer Engineering
University of Illinois at Urbana-Champaign

Abstract
In this talk, we will give a brief survey of automatic floorplan design techniques in the early days of EDA. We will focus on presenting the pioneering contributions of Prof. Ralph Otten in the field.

Keywords
Floorplan design; Electronic design automation.

Short Bio
Martin D. F. Wong received his Ph.D. in CS from the University of Illinois at Urbana-Champaign (UIUC) in 1987. From 1987-2002, he was a faculty member at UT-Austin. He is currently the Executive Associate Dean in the College of Engineering and the Edward C. Jordan Professor in Electrical and Computer Engineering at UIUC. His primary research area is Electronic Design Automation (EDA) focusing on physical design. He has published over 400 papers and graduated 46 Ph.D. students in EDA. He is a Fellow of IEEE.

Permission to make digital or hard copies of part or all of this work for personal or classroom use is granted without fee provided that copies are not made or distributed for profit or commercial advantage and that copies bear this notice and the full citation on the first page. Copyrights for third-party components of this work must be honored. For all other uses, contact the Owner/Author(s). Copyright is held by the owner/author(s).

ISPD'16, April 3–6, 2016, Santa Rosa, California, USA.
ACM 978-1-4503-4039-7/16/04.
DOI: http://dx.doi.org/10.1145/2872334.2872345

The Annealing Algorithm revisited

Lukas P.P.P. van Ginneken
DigiPen Institute of Technology
9931 Willows Road NE
Redmond, WA 98052
+1-425-629-5033
lukas.vanginneken@digipen.edu

ABSTRACT

This paper reviews theoretical advances to the field of simulated annealing optimization and applications to physical design contributed by Ralph Otten. At this year's ISPD, Ralph Otten receives the ISPD Lifetime Achievement award for outstanding contributions made to the field of physical design automation over multiple decades. For this occasion this paper highlights some of the research contributions by Ralph Otten in simulated annealing. It recounts how he moved from applications of simulated annealing to analyzing and understanding the method from a theoretical standpoint and how it was developed into a general purpose algorithm.

CCS Concepts

• **Mathematics of computing ~ Simulated annealing**
• *Hardware ~ Physical design (EDA)*

Keywords

Annealing schedule; annealing algorithm; illegal states; accessibility; stop criterion; weak control; strong control

1. INTRODUCTION

Shortly after the invention of the computer, computers were already used to simulate stochastic physical processes, such as cooling or annealing. [1]. While [1] described the simulation of a physical reality, it was not until the publication of [2] that the algorithm was applied to combinatorial optimization. This last paper also presents applications to a chip placement problem and the traveling salesman problem. Simulated annealing is a general technique for combinatorial optimization which has been applied to a wide range of problems. However, these applications share some of the same theoretical properties, which lend themselves to mathematical analysis.

Simulated annealing is a combinatorial optimization technique that is based on a simulation of a cooling process. In this simulation, each *state* is a potential solution to the optimization

ISPD'16, April 03-06, 2016, Santa Rosa, CA, USA

© 2016 ACM. ISBN 978-1-4503-4039-7/16/04…$15.00

DOI: http://dx.doi.org/10.1145/2872334.2872346

problem and the energy level of the state becomes their score, a measure for the quality or desirability of that state. The *score* is the object function of the optimization algorithm. *Moves* are transitions from states to similar states. A control parameter t, the *temperature*, controls the state move probabilities so that the probabilities of the states are distributed according to the Boltzmann distribution. By changing the move probabilities, it is possible to skew the entire state probability distribution. By reducing the temperature, the states with the lowest scores (the best solutions) become the most likely states. To actually converge to a solution state with a low score, it is important that sufficient moves are done to achieve and maintain a statistical equilibrium. To accomplish this an annealing *schedule* is used, which determines the starting temperature and controlled temperature decrements.

2. CHANNEL ROUTING

Just months after the publication of [2] in 1983, Ralph Otten had the idea to develop a channel routing algorithm using simulated annealing based on the vertical constraint graph of [7].

The channel routing problem was defined as follows: the channel is a rectangular area where the wiring is to be placed. The top and the bottom of the channel have a given set of pins with given pin positions, which have to be connected by nets. Two routing layers are available, and each layer must be used solely in one direction. Wires traveling in the same direction cannot use the same grid lines, but orthogonal wires can cross each other freely. For the purpose of this project, a routing grid was used. Pin positions on the top and bottom of the channel were on grid, and the horizontal grid lines were called tracks. Nets may connect to the left or right of the channel, but the exact track is not specified. This allows the number of tracks and hence the vertical width of the channel to be minimized and the object of the channel router was to connect all of the pins and to do so using the minimum number of tracks.

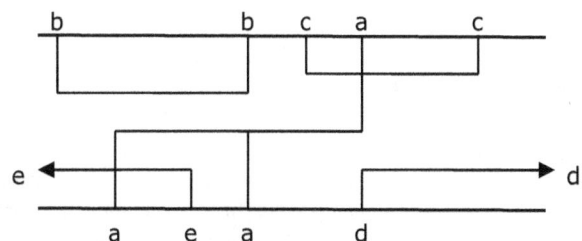

Fig. 1. Channel routing example. The letters indicate net connections to the sides of the channel. A horizontal constraint exists between for instance nets c and d, while vertical constraints exist between a and b and a and d.

For simplicity, each net is assigned to a single track, that is, no track changes or 'dog-legs' are permitted. Two constraint graphs are built, as described in [3]. Based on the known pin positions and a possible exit to the left or right of each net, each net has a given horizontal range or interval. Nets with overlapping intervals cannot be assigned to the same track. The horizontal constraint graph indicates if two intervals were overlapping.

The vertical constraint is based on the pin positions. A constraint in the vertical constraint graph is introduced between two nets with pins that have the same horizontal position. These two nets have to use the same vertical grid line to connect to the top and bottom of the channel. Therefore, the net connected to the top of the channel has to be located in a track higher than a net that is connected the bottom of the channel at the same horizontal location.

The straightforward encoding of the state space would be to assign each net to a track. However, the problem with this approach is that there are many illegal states. Moving a net to a different track is very likely to create overlaps with multiple other nets in that track. It is therefore difficult to move from one legal state to another legal state. That might require moving more than a few nets to different tracks.

To avoid this problem, the state space is defined as the order of the routing segments in the channel. To find the actual track assignment, a quick greedy algorithm places the nets into the tracks according to the order of the state space. A state change or move is implemented by exchanging the positions of two nets in the order. This way, the state space never contains states that are illegal due to horizontal constraints. Vertical constraints, however, can still introduce illegal states.

As an undergraduate student in EE at Eindhoven University in the Netherlands Design Automation group of Jochen Jess, I did the programming for this simulated annealing algorithm. The algorithm was implemented in Pascal, and ran on a Burroughs B7700 mainframe.

From this initial experiment in simulated annealing a number of things became clear. First, there was the problem of illegal states, that is, any order of nets that was prohibited by the vertical constraints. Two possible solutions were attempted: one was to allow illegal states, but to penalize them in the object function. The other solution was to prohibit the illegal states at all times.

The second problem that became apparent was the issue of tuning the parameters for the annealing schedule. In practice, it often took a lot of tweaking of these parameters to get the algorithm to perform well. This in itself begged for automation.

3. THE SCHEDULE

Ralph Otten had done important and groundbreaking work in automatic floor plan design for VLSI before. It was thus an obvious next step to see if simulated annealing could be applied to automatic floor plan design. In [5] he presented his proposal for applying simulated annealing to floor plan design.

Like the channel routing algorithm before, the floor plan design algorithm maintains the floor plan as ordered sequences, in this case of modules. Two sequences are maintained, one for each dimension. A move was simply exchanging two randomly chosen modules in one of the sequences. This formulation had the advantage that there are no illegal states. The object function is an estimate of the wire length between the modules.

While an actual software implementation of the algorithm of [5] had been developed, the paper contains no mention of it and presents no measured benchmark results. Instead the paper focuses to a large extent on the development of criteria for schedule control.

Ralph Otten insisted, that in order to be considered an algorithm, simulated annealing would have to automatically adapt to the problem instance at hand. That meant that the algorithm would have to determine it's schedule automatically. The paper proposes criteria for determining a start temperature, a stop criterion and a decrement, based on theoretical derivations.

For the starting value of the temperature t, it proposes that the Markov process first be observed with all moves accepted, that is with t=∞. This allows the standard deviation of the state distribution to be estimated. For higher temperatures the standard deviation σ is not affected by the temperature t. This is a consequence of the score distribution being very close to a normal distribution. A choice of t >> σ ensures that the state probabilities aren't severely affected by the choice of t.

Second, a stop criterion was proposed that the improvement that is still possible $E(t)-E_0$ compared to the improvement $E_\infty-E(t)$ that already has been achieved is small:

$$\frac{E(t)-E_0}{E_\infty-E(t)} \leq \frac{\sigma_t^2}{t(E_\infty-E(t))} \leq \theta$$

where θ is a small fraction, say 1%.

Third, it was proposed that a decrement in the temperature should not disturb the equilibrium distribution too much. This led in [7] to a decrement of

$$\Delta t = \gamma \frac{t^2}{\sigma(t)}$$

4. THE ANNEALING ALGORITHM

Shortly after the publication of [5] Ralph Otten worked on elaborating these ideas on schedule control into a more comprehensive and general form. In "Annealing: the Algorithm" [4] these ideas were formalized and the mathematical foundation was explored in detail. This research report became the backbone of the later book [7], even though the publication of the book had to wait four more years. Some of the results were published in [6].

"The Annealing Algorithm" [7] starts with a review of the mathematics needed to prove the chain limit theorem. The chain limit theorem states that under certain weak assumptions about the state space and the move set, the Markov chain has a unique equilibrium probability distribution.

The following chapter introduces aggregate functions for the average score E(t), the standard deviation of the score σ(t) and the *accessibility* of the state space H(t) also known as the entropy. Jaynes principle then says that the most likely equilibrium distribution is the distribution that maximizes H(t).

One of the important sections of the book discusses the behavior of the aggregates E(t), σ(t) and H(t) as a function of temperature. It distinguishes two different regions called *weak control* and *strong control* regions. The weak control region is the high temperature part of the schedule where t > T. In this region, the

standard deviation σ(t) does not depend on the temperature and the average score E(t) decreases proportionally with 1/t. In the strong control region, that is the lower temperature range, both E(t) and σ(t) decrease linearly.

Table 1. Aggregate functions E(t), σ(t) and H(t) for the weak (t > T) and strong (t < T) control regions.

	$t > T$	$t < T$
E(t)	$E_\infty - \dfrac{\sigma_\infty^2}{t}$	$E_\infty + \dfrac{\sigma_\infty^2}{T}(\dfrac{t}{T} - 2)$
σ(t)	σ_∞	$\sigma_\infty \dfrac{t}{T}$
H(t)	$H_\infty - \dfrac{\sigma_\infty^2}{2t^2}$	$H_\infty + \dfrac{\sigma_\infty^2}{T^2}(\ln\left(\dfrac{t}{T}\right) - \dfrac{1}{2})$

The behavior of the three important aggregate functions is tabulated in table 1. Experimentally, it has been confirmed with that actual annealing problems, including the placement problem and the traveling salesman problem accurately follow this behavior. The behavior in the weak control region is explained by assuming that the distribution of the scores of the states follows a normal distribution. When the temperature decreases, the center of the normal distribution changes, but it remains a normal distribution with the same standard deviation. In the strong control region, it becomes noticable that there is a minimum score, and that the tail of the distribution is not actually infinite. This leads to a Gamma distribution and the behavior that both E(t) and the standard deviation are linear with t.

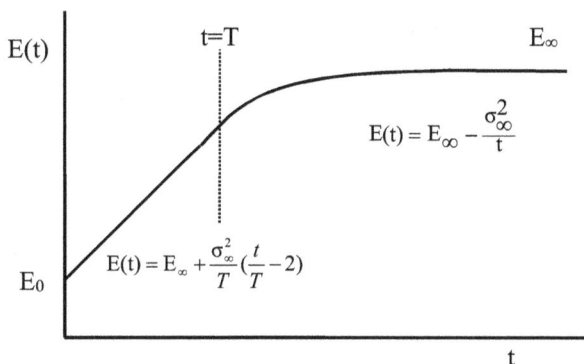

Fig. 2. Weak and strong control regions for E(t).

In addition to the criteria first proposed in [5] the book also proposes a criterion for the number of iterations needed to achieve equilibrium after a temperature step similar to the criterion of [8]. It is based on the concept of local accessibility $H(s_1 \mid s_0)$. The accessibility or entropy H(t) is a measure of how dispersed the distribution of the states is. $H(s_1 \mid s_0)$ is a measure of how much the states are spread out during one move.

The local accessibility can be calculated using the state transition probabilities, that is, the probabilities of the moves. A bound for the number of iterations needed to achieve equilibrium can be calculated by

$$n \geq \frac{H(t)}{H(s_1 \mid s_0)}$$

which may be interpreted as a comparison between the amount of dispersion that a single move does and the accessibility of the equilibrium distribution. In practice, it can be estimated by observing the move probabilities of the states actually taken.

5. CONCLUSIONS

Many of the contributions to the theory of simulated annealing by Ralph Otten were of a deep and theoretical nature. Unfortunately, as they were mostly published in the form of a book, they did not receive the same level of recognition that a more timely paper might have received. The contributions to schedule control that make a fully automated algorithm possible remain of direct practical value.

6. ACKNOWLEDGMENTS

I would like to thank Patrick Groeneveld, DigiPen Institute of Technology and the International Symposium on Physical Design. I would also like to express my appreciation for the inspiration, guidance and insight provided by Ralph Otten throughout my time as a student and beyond.

7. REFERENCES

[1] Metropolis, N., Rosenbluth, A.W., Rosenbluth, M.N., Teller, A.H. and Teller, E. 1953. Equation of state calculations by fast computer machines. *J. Chemical Physics,* 21, 1087-1092.

[2] Kirkpatrick, S., Gelatt, C.D. and Vecchi, M.P. 1983. Optimization by simulated annealing. *Science,* 220, 671-680.

[3] Yoshimura, T. and Kuh, E.S. 1982. Efficient algorithms for channel routing. *IEEE Trans. Computer-Aided Design of Integrated Circuits and Systems*, 1, 1, 25-35.

[4] Otten, R.H.J.M. and van Ginneken, L.P.P.P. 1984. *Annealing: the Algorithm.* Research Report RC 10861, IBM, Yorktown Heights, NY.

[5] Otten, R.H.J.M. and van Ginneken, L.P.P.P. 1984. Floorplan design using simulated annealing. In *Proc. IEEE Int. Conf. Computer-Aided Design.* (Santa Clara, Nov. 12-15, 1984) ICCAD '84. IEEE Computer Society, 96-98.

[6] Otten, R.H.J.M. and van Ginneken, L.P.P.P. Stop criteria in simulated annealing. *Proc.IEEE Int. Conf. Computer Design.* (Rye, Oct.2-6, 1988), ICCD '88. IEEE Computer Society, 549-552.

[7] Otten, R.H.J.M., and van Ginneken, L.P.P.P. 1989. *The Annealing Algorithm.* Kluwer Academic, Dordrecht.

[8] van Ginneken, L.P.P.P. and Otten, R.H.J.M. 1988. An inner loop criterion for simulated annealing. *Physics Letters A.* 130, 8–9 (July 1988), 429–435.

Trailblazing Physical Design Flows
Ralph Otten's Impact on Design Automation

Patrick R. Groeneveld
Synopsys Inc.
445 North Mary Avenue
Sunnyvale, CA 94085 United States
patrick.r.groeneveld@synopsys.com

ABSTRACT

Engineering is the science of converting theory into practice. It is also the 'art' of technical design. Among all engineering disciplines semiconductor electronic design has pushed the limits of true design automation far further than any other technical discipline. Armies of engineers were needed to design the Airbus A380, yet it is morphologically identical to a Boeing 747 designed using slide rulers 50 years ago. Contrast that to IC designers who build a billion-component chip from idea to hardware in just a few months. And they do that while the scale of the design reliably doubles every 2 years. Enabling this unprecedented degree of electronic design automation are a set of algorithms chained together as a flow that crosses several design abstractions down to a physical circuit mask pattern. During his illustrious career Ralph Otten's ideas and vision have shaped design automation in significant ways: by contributing algorithms and by defining methodologies to safely cross abstraction levels using automated tools. Ralph Otten's career parallels the development of circuit design flows from birth to mature flows. He developed the very first floorplan representations and worked on the very first logic synthesis flows (then called a 'silicon compiler'). As director of education Ralph has set new directions, celebrating the strong points of the broader Electrical Engineering discipline. This presentation will address the the impact he has putting putting EDA on the map as an engineering discipline with a solid theoretical foundation. As a result, visionary-yet-small university projects matured into a coherent industrial-strength tools flows.

ISPD'16, April 3–6, 2016, Santa Rosa, California, USA.
ACM 978-1-4503-4039-7/16/04.
DOI: http://dx.doi.org/10.1145/2872334.2872347

Complexity and Diversity in IC Layout Design

Ralph Otten
Technische Universiteit Eindhoven

Abstract

The paper is a concise survey as well as an exposition of ideas about automation of layout design. Central is a discussion of imperatives of a layout design system suitable for VLSI. Of course, such a system has to take account of the embedding into an integrated design system. However, layout design faces two major problems. One results from industry's ability to pack over 10000 gate equivalents into a single chip. Beside this increase in complexity today's micro-electronics technology made a variety of processes - each with its own set of design rules - available for integration. This diversity has been existing for a long time, but complexity raised the problem, since development of efficient systems for designing complex systems is costly and time-consuming.

Keywords

Layout design automation; Design complexity; Design diversity

Short Bio

Ralph Otten was born on February 26 1949, in the Dutch Indies, in a valley of five vulcanos, a village with the name Garut. He went through schools in the Netherlands, up to masters in Electrical Engineering at Eindhoven University of Technology. He worked on various topics in that field: a generalization of star-polygon transformation (which yielded his first IEEE publication), filters with constant group delay, propagation effects in earth-satellite communication and dual electromotors for usual traction and cogwheel tracks. His master thesis from 1971 was on algebraic decomposition of automata.

Next he developed a graph model for chips with a single wiring layer. That was the basis for a sequence of algorithms to provide the mask layout from electronic schematics. This sequence, implemented in cooperation with Rinus van Lier, led to a PhD thesis in 1976. It was the first result in what became the recurring theme in his design automation research: iteration free design.

After a postdoctoral study in floorplan design he went to the mathematics department of IBM Research in Yorktown Heights in 1981. There he provided the backend of the Yorktown Silicon Compiler, aiming at translating a functional description into the masks of an integrated circuit.

From 1987 he worked at Delft and Eindhoven University with research on closure problems in design automation. At both universities he also directed the developments in EE curricula.

ISPD'16, April 3–6, 2016, Santa Rosa, California, USA.
ACM 978-1-4503-4039-7/16/04.
DOI: http://dx.doi.org/10.1145/2872334.2878629

An Interactive Physical Synthesis Methodology for High-Frequency FPGA Designs

Sabya Das
Xilinx Inc.
San Jose, CA
sabyad@xilinx.com

Rajat Aggarwal
Xilinx Inc.
San Jose, CA
rajata@xilinx.com

Zhiyong Wang
Xilinx Inc.
San Jose, CA
mwa@xilinx.com

ABSTRACT

State-of-the-art FPGA design has become a very complex process primarily due to the aggressive timing requirements of the designs. Designers spend significant amount of time and effort trying to close the timing on their designs. In that timing closure methodology, Physical Synthesis plays a key role to boost the design performance. In traditional approaches, user performs placement followed by physical synthesis. With increasing design complexity, Physical Synthesis cannot perform all the optimization steps due to the physical constraints imposed by the placement operation.

In this work, we propose an interactive methodology to perform physical synthesis in the pre-placement stage of the FPGA timing closure flow. The approach will work in two iterations of the FPGA design flow. In the first iteration, the designer will perform the regular post-placement flavor of physical synthesis operation on the design. That phase will automatically write a replayable-file which will contain information about all the optimization actions. That file will also contain all the attempted optimization moves what physical synthesis deemed beneficial from QoR perspective, but was not able to accept due to the physical constraint. In the second iteration of the design flow, the designer will perform all those physical synthesis optimizations by importing the replayable file in the pre-placement stage. In addition to performing all the changes of the physical synthesis flow, it also performs the optimizations that were not possible in the traditional physical synthesis flow. After these changes are made in the logical stage of the design flow, the crucial placement step can adapt to the optimized/better netlist structure. As a result, this approach will greatly help the users reach their challenging timing closure goal.

We have evaluated the effectiveness and performance of our proposed approach on a large set of industrial designs. All these designs were targeted towards the latest Xilinx Ultrascale^{TM} devices [1]. Our experimental data indicates that the proposed approach improves the design performance by 4% to 5%, on an average.

ISPD'16, April 03-06, 2016, Santa Rosa, CA, USA

© 2016 ACM. ISBN 978-1-4503-4039-7/16/04... $15.00

DOI: http://dx.doi.org/10.1145/2872334.2872340

Keywords

Physical Synthesis; Timing Optimization; Electronic Design Automation (EDA) and Methodology; Field Programmable Gate Array (FPGA); EDA Tool Flow; Timing Optimization; CAD Tool; Timing Closure; Netlist Transformations; Integrated Circuit

1. INTRODUCTION

As we migrate toward ultra deep sub-micron era, designs are becoming increasingly complex, with very aggressive frequency goals. The design complexity and the performance requirements of computationally intensive operations implemented in systems-on-chips have increased considerably over the years. This is especially true for the designs used in the domain of communication network, multimedia and graphic applications, because such circuits typically have highly parallel implementations of digital signal processing (DSP) algorithms.

In recent times, many types of designs are moving towards a design methodology based on Field Programmable Gate Array (FPGA). The flexibility of FPGA and faster time to market makes it more appealing to the design community. As FPGA-based designs are advancing, the frequency requirements is also going in the upward direction. As a result, physical synthesis and other optimization techniques are increasingly becoming more important for closing timing.

Several techniques have been proposed to implement a powerful physical synthesis solution in the context of ASIC and FPGA designs. Three post-placement physical synthesis tools were described in [2]. These tools improve the performance and routability of high-end gate array ASICs. Ye et al. proposed a physical synthesis methodology for ASIC datapath modules that integrates physical planning with the synthesis process [3]. In the physical synthesis approach of [4], a linear timing model was used to optimize timing by simultaneously replacing multiple gates. In [5], a metric was introduced for predicting the accuracy of the interconnect delay model. Then, that metric was used in an efficient and fast timing driven physical synthesis flow. Chang et al. introduced a resynthesis algorithm to enhance circuit timing without detrimental effects on route length and congestion [6]. For the Variability-Aware FPGA Physical Synthesis Tools [7], a Fast and Accurate Interval-Based Timing Estimator was used. In [8], an FPGA physical synthesis algorithms was introduced that was leveraging statistical static timing analysis with process variation and prerouting interconnect delay uncertainty. In the domain of microprocessors, an integrated physical synthesis timing closure methodology was proposed in [9]. In [10], Singh et al. presented FPGA specific industrial physical synthesis CAD flow. Same authors described a retiming based incremental optimization flow in [11]. In [12], a post-placement physical synthesis algorithm was introduced that can apply multiple circuit synthesis and placement transforms on a placed circuit. Using that technique, the critical path delay under area constraints was improved by simultaneously considering the benefits and costs of all transforms. Two techniques were discussed for placement-based distributed physical synthesis in [13]. One was in timing-driven partitioner and and the other one was virtual physical synthesis based budgeter. An algorithm for rewiring a post-layout LUT-based FPGA design was introduced in [14]. That approach was used to reduce the overall criticality of the circuit, where criticality is the fraction of primary inputs that lead to observable errors at the primary outputs if an single event upset inverts a configuration bit. In [15], the authors analyzed the power and reliability optimization problems in FPGA physical synthesis.

All the above-mentioned research work focuses on performing physical synthesis either after the placement or during the placement. In our proposed approach, we bring in physical synthesis changes during the logical steps of the design flow, in a subsequent iteration of the design process.

We have organized the rest of the paper as follows: In Section 2, we present some preliminary information. In Section 3, we discuss our proposed approach in detail. The experimental setup is explained in Section 4. Section 5 presents the experimental results. Conclusions are drawn in Section 6.

2. PRELIMINARIES

In an FPGA device, different types of blocks are positioned in pre-defined locations. Some of the heavily used logic blocks are Look-Up Tables (LUTs), Flip Flops (FFs), Block RAMs (RAMBs), Shift Registers (SRLs), Carry Logic, Digital Signal Processing Blocks (DSPs) etc.

A typical CAD-flow is shown in the Fig 1. The flow works as follows:

- First, Synthesis tool reads in designer's input RTL along with timing constraints and synthesizes those to the relevant logic blocks that are available in the targeted FPGA device

- After that, Logic Optimization tool performs logical changes in the design to improve the performance of the design.

- Next, Placement tool puts each of the logical blocks into unique physical locations on the actual targeted FPGA device.

- Physical Synthesis tool analyzes the design and can perform both logical and physical changes to improve the design's frequency even further

- Finally, Routing tool performs the wire connection between all the physical blocks.

In modern designs, it has been observed that the frequency demand is very high. In addition, the designs are very congested with high utilization of the FPGA devices. These

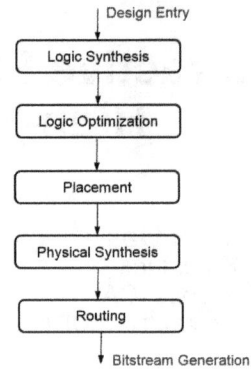

Figure 1: Simplified CAD flow for FPGA design

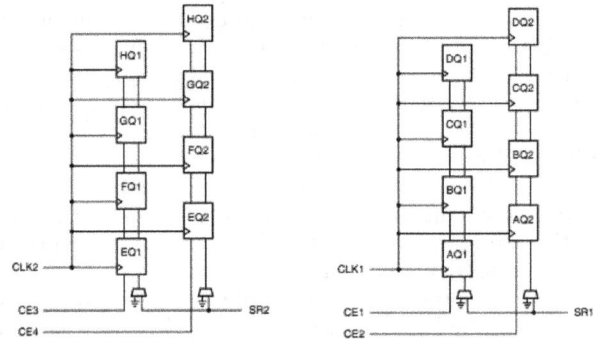

Figure 2: Control Signal Connections in a Slice

challenges exposed following couple of issues in the traditional Physical Synthesis centric flow.

Often times, Physical Synthesis is unable to perform the desired changes after the Placement step. Placement engine has to optimally position different logic blocks across all the physical blocks in the design. As a result, the new instances introduced by the Physical Synthesis step is not able to get the optimal location to improve design's timing situation. A good example of this problem is the Flip Flop placement. Even though a SLICE can accommodate many flip flops, all the flops have to conform to specific control set rules. Fig 2 shows the control set structure for a Configurable Logic Block SLICE in the Xilinx Ultrascale[TM] architecture [16]. As a result, Physical Synthesis often cannot perform flip-flop optimization in a high-frequency and highly-congested designs.

Placement step analyzes the whole design in a global context and makes both global and local decisions. The goal of the placer is to meet timing across all timing paths in all path-groups, as much as possible. In a typical design flow, since physical synthesis is done after Placement, the crucial Placement step has to work with a sub-optimal design. While that has been working well so far, but modern designs are showing that the Placement flow is getting stuck in local minima and the design is finding it hard to meet the timing by overcoming that local minima.

So, it almost indicates that Physical Synthesis changes need to be performed before the Placement step. On the other hand, Placement information is crucial for a Physical Synthesis tool to make the crucial optimization decision. Our proposed approach is developed to break this cyclic dependency.

3. OUR APPROACH

Since FPGA designs complexity is steadily increasing, all the modern designs go through several iterations before the timing convergence is accomplished. In the early part of this design cycle, significant portions of RTL gets changed between two iterations. Towards the later part of the design cycle, RTL change gets reduced and different timing-closure techniques get applied.

Our proposed methodology spans through two such iterations of the design cycle. The approach is shown in the Fig 3. In general, Our methodology applies to iteration i and iteration $i + j$, where j is any positive number. Due to the ease of explanation, throughout the rest of the paper, we would refer to these two iterations as the first iteration and the second iteration. The flow works as follows:

3.1 Steps in the First Iteration

In the first iteration, the designer follows the traditional approach of performing physical synthesis operations on a fully placed design. This physical synthesis step performs a detailed analysis of the overall design and timing situations. In that analysis, few factors to consider are the design structure, timing requirements, placement locations, congestion metrics, routing estimates etc. Based on the analysis, the actual logical and physical changes are committed to the design. These changes improve the overall Quality of Results for the design and helps Router produce a better result.

While performing these changes, all the details of these changes are written in a replayable file. The order of the changes in the file will exactly match the sequence in which the changes took place in the design database. This step of creation of replayable file in the first iteration is shown in the left-side of the Fig 3.

In any optimization flow, it is very likely that some optimization attempts will not be successful. In other words, few changes can be tried and then rejected when the attempted change produces worse QoR. In the FPGA-based design flow, this type of rejection rate is quite high due to the physical constraints imposed by the placement of the existing logic blocks. As a result, the new instances introduced by the Physical Synthesis step is not able to get the optimal location to improve design's timing situation. A good example of this problem is the Flip Flop placement. Even though a SLICE can accommodate many flip flops, all the flops have to conform to specific control set rules. Fig 2 shows the control set structure for a Configurable Logic Block SLICE in the Xilinx Ultrascale architecture [16]. This indicates the challenge faced in the flip-flops optimization during Physical Synthesis. As a result, Physical Synthesis often cannot perform flip-flop optimization in a high-frequency and highly-congested designs.

In our proposed approach, we evaluate all the failed moves. If we identify that the optimization step was rejected due to an invalid netlist change or timing constraint, we consider that as a valid rejection. On the other hand, if we identify that the rejection was caused by a sub-optimal placement due to non-availability of more-optimal physical locations, then we write that change in the replayable file as well.

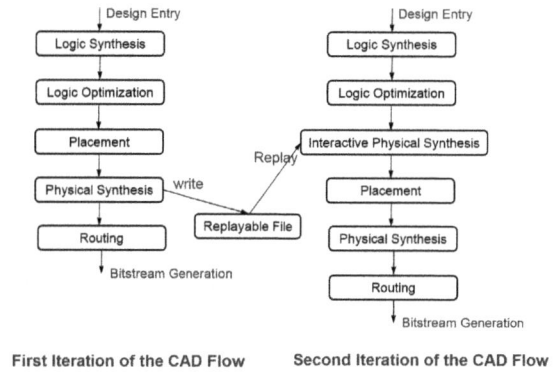

Figure 3: Proposed Interactive CAD flow for FPGA design

That is how we prepare our replayable file that stores information about more optimization moves than what could have been achieved in the regular physical synthesis flow. Our analysis indicate that by using this approach of analyzing and recording the unaccepted moves, we open up lot of opportunities in many parts of the design. This additional opportunity is very high in the timing paths related to the Macro blocks like Digital Signal Processing (DSP) or Block RAM (BRAM).

3.2 Steps in the Second Iteration

In the second iteration, the designer follows the traditional approach of performing logical steps like RTL synthesis and logic optimization. Before they perform placement step, our approach performs the new step of *Interactive Physical Synthesis*. In that step, the replayable file is *played*. In other words, those physical synthesis changes of the first iteration get performed during the logical implementation steps in the second iteration. Since the replay is getting performed in the logical step, it does not get impacted by the physical constraints imposed by the placement operation. In addition, replay file successfully performs all the moves that were unsuccessful in the first run. Combining all these, we achieve the physical synthesis effect in the logical stage of the design flow.

After this replay-based interactive physical synthesis step, the design flow enters the crucial placement stage. Now, the placement engine gets the opportunity to work with a more optimized netlist structure. As a result, Placer can adapt to the new structure and can produce an even better placement solution compared to that of the first iteration.

This step of performing the interactive physical synthesis by replaying the replayable file in the second iteration is shown in the right-side of the Fig 3.

In addition to performing the physical synthesis tasks in the logical stage of the design flow, our approach is also aware of the design changes that has happened between first iteration and the second iteration. During our replay mechanism, all the stored moves are analyzed to ensure that the moves are still valid. This validity analysis is performed by using a comprehensive signature-based approach. The signature for a specific optimization record consists of the relevant connectivity, logic blocks' functions and names of the instances and nets. In that process, our approach catches

Design Name	Number of LUTs	Number of Flips Flops	Number of Input/Outputs	Number of Block RAMs	Number of Carry Blocks	Number of DSP Blocks	Number of Control Sets
Industrial-1	406243	727628	3898	2172	42062	560	11470
Industrial-2	666305	851842	350	2755	23786	0	19872
Industrial-3	622310	969451	251	2283	17456	676	16352
Industrial-4	503014	675224	123	871	7936	1200	8163
Industrial-5	748962	733466	50	1724	19305	836	14628
Industrial-6	529903	979971	422	1463	14619	155	17938
Industrial-7	381506	598509	59	1823	12938	3236	15729
Industrial-8	242339	393180	154	730	9381	3298	13714
Industrial-9	567451	831593	406	1686	6738	0	8261
Industrial-10	282304	514592	326	1424	18456	2518	12831

Table 1: Characteristics of Different Industrial Designs

all the invalid situations and does not perform those stored moves. That is how we ensure that our approach always precedes legal and functionally correct netlist.

This methodology can be particularly useful in timing-critical and congested designs. Following are two specific examples where this approach can produce significantly better timing results.

- In many timing critical designs, users want to perform the macro-block (DSP, BRAM etc) placement in an ideal manner, because that placement can be used as a seed for the overall placement of the remaining millions of instance. In this methodology, the designer can obtain the replayable file and then selectively perform the transformations that are related to the macro blocks. Since these optimizations will happen before placement, the moves will always be accepted due to absence of the congestion situation. As a result, subsequent placement step will be able to successfully adapt to these changes.

- Similar logic holds for high-fanout nets that have larger impact on the design. In the proposed interactive physical synthesis flow, high fanout nets will be optimized before placement and that in turn will allow placement engine to perform a better placement, leading to overall QoR gain.

4. EXPERIMENTAL SETUP

We have implemented our proposed interactive approach in the Xilinx Vivado® Design Suite [17]. The experiments were performed with different types of industrial designs written in the Verilog hardware description language. For all our runs, we used Linux workstations containing 8-cores and 48GB memory.

To collect all the different data-points regarding the QoR (quality of results) of our proposed approach, we used the following variations:

- Multiple designs of industrial complexity: In the Table 1, we report different configurations of the designs that have been used in our experiments.

  - Name of the design is presented in the 1st column. We chose the names as Industrial-1, Industrial-2, Industrial-3 etc.

  - For each design, we report few key utilization aspects. These are number of Look-Up Tables

(LUTs), Flip Flops (FFs), Block RAMs (RAMBs), Digital Signal Processing Blocks (DSPs) and Carry Blocks.

  - We compute the number of unique control sets for each design and report that number. This control set greatly impacts the potential packing or placement density of Flip Flops into the SLICE logic.

  - Finally, we report the number of inputs and outputs present in the design.

- Two different FPGA devices in 20nm technology[1]:

  - Multiple parts in Xilinx Virtex® Ultrascale™

  - Multiple parts in Xilinx Kintex® Ultrascale™

- Realistically aggressive timing constraints: All these designs were in the high-speed category of the FPGA domain. Target frequency of these designs were between 250 MHz and 460 MHz. In the design suite, timing constraints were very realistic. Few key characteristics of timing situation were as follows:

  - All the designs had multiple clock-groups.

  - Just like today's state-of-the-art designs, timing requirement in few clock-groups were very aggressive. On the other hand, timing requirement in remaining clock-groups were not so aggressive.

5. EXPERIMENTAL RESULTS

A typical FPGA design flow starts from reading the RTL and ends in final bitstream generation. To measure the effectiveness and correctness of our algorithm, we use the following methodology.

This interactive flow requires two iterations. The baseline is the first iteration where user performs complete front-to-back flow that includes RTL Synthesis, Logic Optimization, Placement, Physical Synthesis, Routing and Bitstream Generation, as shown in the Fig 1.

Our new flow has the baseline iteration followed by the second iteration that includes the feedback-driven interactive physical synthesis optimization step, as shown in the Fig 3.

In our source code, we have two top-level routines. The code in routine-1 implements the technique to write the replayable physical synthesis file. That routine gets executed during the first iteration run (baseline run) of the flow. The

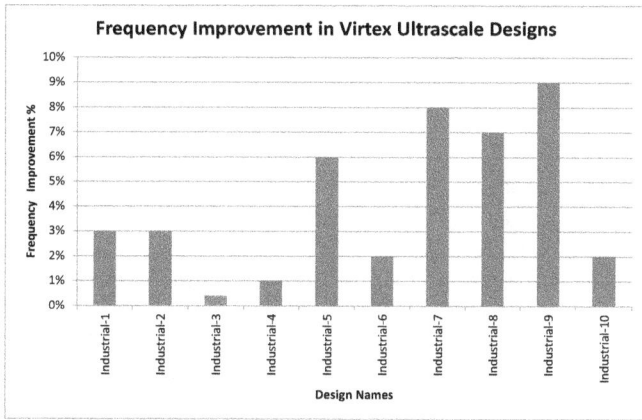

Figure 4: Frequency Improvement in Virtex Ultrascale Designs

Design Name	Device Architecture	Improvement in Frequency (%)
Industrial-1	Kintex Ultrascale	5%
Industrial-2	Kintex Ultrascale	1%
Industrial-3	Kintex Ultrascale	0%
Industrial-4	Kintex Ultrascale	4%
Industrial-5	Kintex Ultrascale	2%
Industrial-6	Kintex Ultrascale	5%
Industrial-7	Kintex Ultrascale	9%
Industrial-8	Kintex Ultrascale	4%
Industrial-9	Kintex Ultrascale	7%
Industrial-10	Kintex Ultrascale	2%
Average		3.9%

Table 3: Frequency Improvement in Kintex Ultrascale Designs

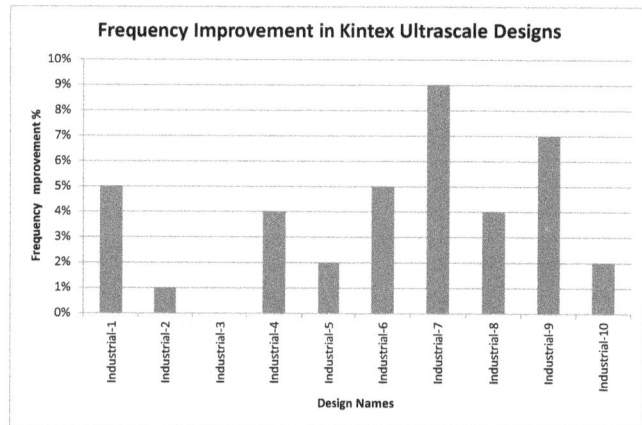

Figure 5: Frequency Improvement in Kintex Ultrascale Designs

code in routine-2 takes that replayable file and replays that during the pre-placement stage of the second iteration run of the design flow.

For different combinations of design, device architecture and timing constraint, we performed the above-mentioned runs. At the end, we measured the operating frequency of the baseline output bitstream and the interactive flow's output bitstream.

In Table 2, we report the frequency improvement achieved by our interactive physical synthesis flow over the baseline flow, when the designs were run on Xilinx Virtex Ultrascale devices. That data indicates that the designs' frequency improved by anywhere between 1% and 9%. The average gain was around 4.5%. The frequency improvement data is graphically displayed in the Fig 4.

Design Name	Device Architecture	Improvement in Frequency (%)
Industrial-1	Virtex Ultrascale	3%
Industrial-2	Virtex Ultrascale	3%
Industrial-3	Virtex Ultrascale	4%
Industrial-4	Virtex Ultrascale	1%
Industrial-5	Virtex Ultrascale	6%
Industrial-6	Virtex Ultrascale	2%
Industrial-7	Virtex Ultrascale	8%
Industrial-8	Virtex Ultrascale	7%
Industrial-9	Virtex Ultrascale	9%
Industrial-10	Virtex Ultrascale	2%
Average		4.5%

Table 2: Frequency Improvement in Virtex Ultrascale Designs

After running the flow on Xilinx Kintex Ultrascale devices, we obtained the frequency improvement data as shown in the Table 3. That data indicates that the designs' frequency improved by 3.9%, on an average. The frequency improvement data is graphically displayed in the Fig 5.

6. CONCLUSION

In this paper, we have presented an interactive physical synthesis methodology to perform physical synthesis in the pre-placement stage of the FPGA timing closure flow. This two-iteration approach will first record all the optimization moves in the first iteration and then will apply those moves in the second iteration. In addition to performing the physical synthesis flow's changes, it also perform the optimizations that were not possible in the traditional physical synthesis flow. By using this interactive approach, lot more physical synthesis moves get successfully executed. In addition, the crucial placement step can adapt to the better structural netlist produced by the early physical synthesis changes. We have evaluated the effectiveness and performance of our proposed approach on a large set of industrial designs. Our experimental data indicates that the proposed approach improves the design performance by 4% to 5%, on an average.

7. REFERENCES

[1] Ultrascale Architecture, Xilinx Inc. http://www.xilinx.com/products/technology/ultrascale.html, 2015. [Online; accessed 20-Jan-2016].

[2] R.P. Pokala, R.A. Feretich, and R.W. McGuffin. Physical synthesis for performance optimization. In *ASIC Conference and Exhibit, 1992., Proceedings of 5th Annual IEEE International*, Sep 1992.

[3] T.T. Ye, S. Chaudhuri, F. Huang, H. Savoj, and G. De Micheli. Physical synthesis for asic datapath circuits. In *Circuits and Systems, 2002. ISCAS 2002. IEEE International Symposium on*, volume 3, pages III–365–III–368 vol.3, 2002.

[4] D.A. Papa, Tao Luo, M.D. Moffitt, C.N. Sze, Zhuo Li, Gi-Joon Nam, C.J. Alpert, and I.L. Markov. Rumble: An incremental timing-driven physical-synthesis optimization algorithm. *Computer-Aided Design of Integrated Circuits and Systems, IEEE Transactions on*, 27(12):2156–2168, Dec 2008.

[5] V. Manohararajah, G.R. Chiu, D.P. Singh, and S.D. Brown. Predicting interconnect delay for physical synthesis in a fpga cad flow. *Very Large Scale Integration (VLSI) Systems, IEEE Transactions on*, 15(8):895–903, Aug 2007.

[6] Kai-Hui Chang, I.L. Markov, and V. Bertacco. Safe delay optimization for physical synthesis. In *Design Automation Conference, 2007. ASP-DAC '07. Asia and South Pacific*, pages 628–633, Jan 2007.

[7] Cliee Sing Lee, Wei Ting Loke, Wenjuan Zhang, and Yajun Ha. Fast and accurate interval-based timing estimator for variability-aware fpga physical synthesis tools. In *Field Programmable Logic and Applications, 2007. FPL 2007. International Conference on*, pages 279–284, Aug 2007.

[8] Yan Lin, Lei He, and M. Hutton. Stochastic physical synthesis considering prerouting interconnect uncertainty and process variation for fpgas. *Very Large Scale Integration (VLSI) Systems, IEEE Transactions on*, 16(2):124–133, Feb 2008.

[9] Yiu-Hing Chan, P. Kudva, L. Lacey, G. Northrop, and T. Rosser. Physical synthesis methodology for high performance microprocessors. In *Design Automation Conference, 2003. Proceedings*, pages 696–701, June 2003.

[10] D.P. Singh, V. Manohararajah, and S.D. Brown. Two-stage physical synthesis for fpgas. In *Custom Integrated Circuits Conference, 2005. Proceedings of the IEEE 2005*, pages 171–178, Sept 2005.

[11] D.P. Singh, V. Manohararajah, and S.D. Brown. Incremental retiming for fpga physical synthesis. In *Design Automation Conference, 2005. Proceedings. 42nd*, pages 433–438, June 2005.

[12] Huan Ren and S. Dutt. Algorithms for simultaneous consideration of multiple physical synthesis transforms for timing closure. In *Computer-Aided Design, 2008. ICCAD 2008. IEEE/ACM International Conference on*, pages 93–100, Nov 2008.

[13] F.Y.C. Mang, Wenting Hou, and Pei-Hsin Ho. Techniques for effective distributed physical synthesis. In *Design Automation Conference, 2007. DAC '07. 44th ACM/IEEE*, pages 859–864, June 2007.

[14] M. Jose, Yu Hu, R. Majumdar, and Lei He. Rewiring for robustness. In *Design Automation Conference (DAC), 2010 47th ACM/IEEE*, pages 469–474, June 2010.

[15] M. Jose, Yu Hu, and R. Majumdar. On power and fault-tolerance optimization in fpga physical synthesis. In *Computer-Aided Design (ICCAD), 2010 IEEE/ACM International Conference on*, pages 224–229, Nov 2010.

[16] Ultrascale Architecture Configurable Logic Block User Guide, Xilinx Inc. http://www.xilinx.com/support/documentation/user_guides/ug574-ultrascale-clb.pdf, 2015. [Online; accessed 04-Feb-2016].

[17] Vivado Design Suite, Xilinx Inc. http://www.xilinx.com/products/design-tools/vivado.html, 2015. [Online; accessed 03-Feb-2016].

Power Optimization of FPGA Interconnect Via Circuit and CAD Techniques

Safeen Huda and Jason H. Anderson
Dept. of Electrical and Computer Engineering
University of Toronto
Toronto, ON Canada
{safeen|janders}@ece.toronto.edu

ABSTRACT

We target power dissipation in field-programmable gate array (FPGA) interconnect and present three approaches that leverage a unique property of FPGAs, namely, the presence of *unused* routing conductors. A first technique attacks dynamic power by placing unused conductors, adjacent to used conductors, into a high-impedance state, reducing the effective capacitance seen by used conductors. A second technique, charge recycling, re-purposes unused conductors as charge reservoirs to reduce the supply current drawn for a positive transition on a used conductor. A third approach reduces leakage current in interconnect buffers by pulsed-signalling, allowing a driving buffer to be placed into a high-impedance stage after a logic transition. All three techniques require CAD support in the routing stage to encourage specific positionings of unused conductors relative to used conductors.

CCS Concepts

•Hardware → **Reconfigurable logic and FPGAs; Programmable interconnect;**

Keywords

FPGA, physical design, low-power, routing

1. INTRODUCTION

Field-programmable gate arrays (FPGAs), long used in communications and industrial applications, are gaining traction in the high-performance computing space, where they are used alongside traditional processors to implement accelerators that provide improved computational throughput and energy efficiency. The recent \$16B acquisition of Altera (a leading FPGA vendor) by Intel, and the use of FPGAs by Microsoft for Bing search acceleration [10] assure the presence of FPGAs in future datacenters. At the other end of the computing spectrum, however, in low-power/mobile/IoT, FPGAs have seen far less success, primarily because of their high power consumption, which recent work [6] has shown to be multiple times higher than fixed-function ASICs. In this paper, we present combined architecture, circuit, and

ISPD'16, April 03-06, 2016, Santa Rosa, CA, USA

© 2016 ACM. ISBN 978-1-4503-4039-7/16/04... \$15.00

DOI: http://dx.doi.org/10.1145/2872334.2872341

CAD techniques for reducing power consumption in FPGA interconnect, which accounts for the majority of dynamic and leakage power in FPGAs [13, 12].

We present three techniques for reducing FPGA interconnect power consumption, that hinge on a unique property of FPGAs – the property that a given application circuit implemented in an FPGA uses only a fraction of the FPGA's underlying interconnect resources, leaving many resources unused. The presented techniques leverage the unused resources in several different ways. Two of the techniques presented target dynamic power; the third targets leakage power. All three techniques are tied together in that they require very similiar CAD support in the routing stage of the flow. Specifically, the three techniques require that, to the extent possible, used conductors in the FPGA interconnect are physically adjacent to unused conductors.

The dynamic power consumed by a logic signal in a CMOS circuit is given by: $\alpha \cdot C \cdot V_{DD} \cdot V_{swing}$, where α represents the signal's toggle frequency, C is capacitance, V_{DD} and V_{swing} the supply and swing voltage, respectively. In a first approach [4], we attack the C term by reducing the intra-layer coupling capacitance a used conductor "sees" towards an unused neighbour. This is achieved by a lightweight switch buffer design that permits the unused neighbour to be placed into a high-impedance state, resulting in the coupling capacitance being *in series* with other capacitances, thereby lowering effective capacitance. In a second approach, we target V_{swing} by *charge recycling* to/from neighboring unused routing conductors [3]. The key idea is to pair together routing conductors in the FPGA routing architecture such that, when one of the pair is unused, it can serve as a charge reservoir for the used conductor. A portion of the charge normally dissipated to ground on a falling transition is instead stored in the reservoir, to be recycled to the used conductor on a rising transition, reducing V_{swing} and saving power.

We then present a new approach for reducing leakage power in the FPGA interconnect structures. We propose pulsed-signalling, wherein a driving interconnect buffer "pulses" its intended signal value to a receiving buffer for a short time interval, after which it enters a high-impedance (low-leakage state), instead of maintaining the value as in traditional CMOS signalling. To the extent possible, conductors adjacent to used conductors must be kept unused, to mitigate noise and ensure the logic value "captured" by the receiving buffer is not disrupted. Again, this approach relies on noise-reduction support in the routing stage of the FPGA CAD flow. To the authors' knowledge, this is the first work to propose pulsed-signalling in the FPGA context.

The remainder of this paper is organized as follows: Section 2 provides background material on FPGA interconnect architecture. Section 3 summarizes the charge recycling and capacitance reduction work for dynamic power reduction. Section 4 introduces the pulsed-signalling for leakage reduc-

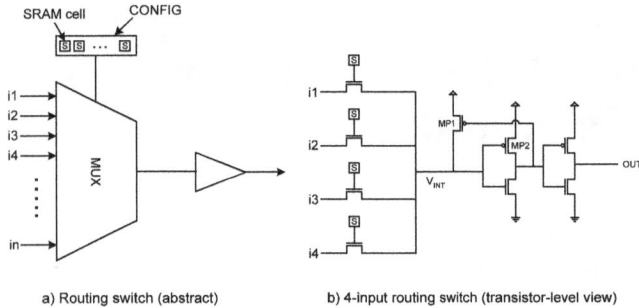

a) Routing switch (abstract)   b) 4-input routing switch (transistor-level view)

Figure 1: Interconnect switch.

tion. CAD support is discussed in Section 5. Experimental results appear in Section 6, followed by conclusions and future work.

2. BACKGROUND

FPGA interconnect consists of metal wire segments that may be programmably connected to logic block pins and to one another through interconnect switches. Fig. 1(a) shows an FPGA routing switch comprised on a multiplexer (MUX), buffer and SRAM configuration cells. The data inputs to the MUX attach to logic block output pins and/or other routing conductors. The SRAM cell contents select a particular input to drive to the switch output, which attaches to a logic block input or a routing conductor. The transistor-level view in Fig. 1(b) illustrates that the MUX is typically built with NMOS transistors and the buffer is "level-restoring" via transistor $MP1$, which serves to pull the buffer input to the supply rail when a logic-1 is passed through the NMOS-based MUX. State-of-the-art Xilinx and Altera FPGAs use such unidirectional buffered switches.

The two main commercial FPGA vendors use a variant of the PathFinder negotiated congestion routing algorithm [9]. In PathFinder, the device interconnect is represented as a directed graph, $G(V, E)$, where each $v \in V$ represents a conductor and each $e \in E$ represents a programmable connection between two conductors. Routing a signal from its driver to its loads is therefore translated into a minimum-cost search in G between the vertices corresponding to the driver/load pins. The PathFinder algorithm allows shorts between signals at intermediate stages of the routing process. Congestion removal is handled via cost adjustments based on node oversubscription, along with rip-up and re-route. Signal timing criticality information is used to encourage the routing of a design's timing-critical connections on low-delay paths through the FPGA fabric.

3. DYNAMIC POWER REDUCTION TECHNIQUES

3.1 Reducing Effective Interconnect Capacitance

We recently proposed a technique to reduce the effective capacitance loading a routing wire [4]. The approach is inspired by an analysis of the capacitance seen at the output of a routing buffer: this capacitance is mainly the parasitic capacitance of the driven metal interconnect wire. The different components of the total parasitic capacitance for a routing conductor are annotated in Fig. 2a.

The figure shows that the capacitance of a routing conductor is due to the coupling capacitance (C_C) between adjacent metal conductors on the same metal layer, and the plate capacitance (C_P), due to overlap with other conductors on adjacent layers (the adjacent layer is depicted as a ground

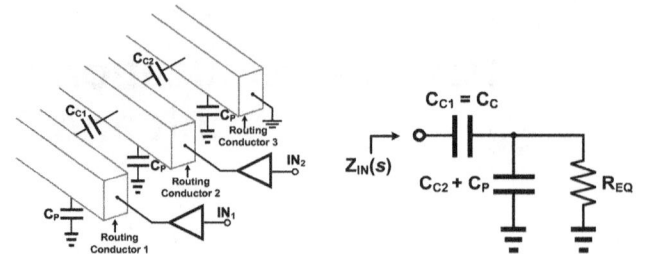

(a) Routing buffers and their respective loads.

(b) Simplified model of the impedance seen by a routing buffer looking towards an adjacent conductor

Figure 2: Interconnect impedance modeling

plane). Currently, C_C dominates the total interconnect capacitance: ITRS projections indicate C_C is approximately twice as large as C_P (and this ratio is projected to continue to increase) [5]. This fact is leveraged to reduce the effective capacitance of an interconnect conductor, since the total capacitance is equal to $C_{tot} \approx 2C_C + 2C_P$, if C_C is reduced it will result in a significant reduction in C_{tot}. Our technique to reduce C_C is based on an analysis of the capacitance a routing conductor "sees" when looking towards an adjacent routing conductor on the same metal layer.

Fig. 2a shows three routing conductors, with their respective driver circuits. Routing conductor 1 is coupled with conductor 2 through coupling capacitor C_{C1} and similarly, conductor 2 is coupled with conductor 3 through C_{C2}. From the perspective of conductor 1, conductor 2 and coupling capacitors C_{C1} and C_{C2} together form the equivalent, approximated circuit shown in Fig. 2b. In the figure, R_{eq} is the effective output resistance of the driver driving conductor 2, and it is assumed that the effective driver resistance for the buffer driving conductor 3 is near 0 (the conductor is grounded). The input impedance of this circuit has the following transfer function in the Laplace (s) domain:

$$Z_{in}(s) = \frac{R_{eq}(2 \cdot C_C + C_P)s + 1}{C_C s[R_{eq}(C_c + C_p)s + 1]} \qquad (1)$$

where it is assumed that $C_{C1} = C_{C2} = C_C$. We now note that if $R_{eq} >> 1/(C_C + C_P)$, $Z_{in}(s) \approx (2 \cdot C_C + C_P)/(C_C(C_C + C_P))$. This implies that if conductor 2 is unused, and its driver impedance can be set large, the effective impedance seen from conductor 1 looking towards conductor 2 is that of capacitor C_{C1} in *series* with the parallel combination of capacitors C_{C2} and C_P, which means that the effective parasitic loading on routing conductor 1 can therefore be *reduced*. A buffer with a reasonably small effective output resistance can be made to have a much larger output resistance if the buffer can be put into a tristate mode. Putting a buffer into tristate mode requires disconnecting all paths to either V_{DD} or GND, which ensures that there are no low-impedance paths to either rail.

In [4], we proposed to reduce power dissipated in active routing conductors by placing their adjacent unused conductors into tristate mode. Parasitic capacitance reduction is observed only when an active routing conductor is adjacent to one or more unused routing conductors. Since the proposed technique requires routing buffers to be tristateable, we also propose a tristate buffer topology with minimal area-overhead, specially tailored for FPGA interconnect drivers.

3.2 Charge Recycling

Another technique we proposed that exploits unused routing conductors is charge recycling [3]. The idea is to make use of the energy dissipated in previous transitions, and thus to actively recycle "used" charge. In conventional logic circuits, when a conductor makes a falling transition, the stored energy on the wire – equal to $CV_{DD}^2/2$ where C is the wire capacitance – is completely dissipated. In contrast, charge recycling stores some of that (normally) dissipated charge in secondary nodes (capacitors). This charge can then be delivered to a wire which is making a rising transition, reusing some of the energy that would have been otherwise lost. The overall principle behind the technique is shown in Figs. 3 and 4.

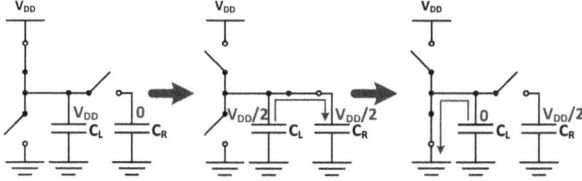

Figure 3: Charge recovery from a "1" to "0" transition

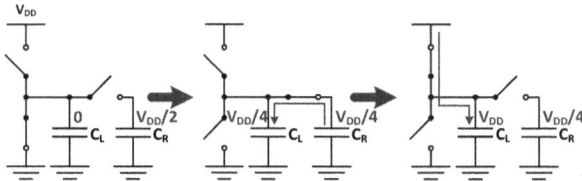

Figure 4: Charge recycling during a "0" to "1" transition

The figures show two capacitors, C_L, the load capacitor, and C_R, a reservoir capacitor used to store recovered charge. Switches connect C_L to either V_{DD} or GND, and a third switch can be used to connect the two capacitors together. In Fig. 3, we see that C_L is initially connected to V_{DD}, and there is no charge stored in C_R. During a falling transition at C_L, initially the circuit undergoes a *charge recovery phase*, where C_R and C_L are connected (both V_{DD} and GND are disconnected from C_R). Given that the two capacitors have equal capacitance, through charge sharing, half of the charge initially stored in C_L will be transferred to C_R, and thus the voltages of these capacitors will settle to $V_{DD}/2$. After the charge recovery phase, the two capacitors are disconnected, and C_L is connected to GND, and thus fully discharged.

In Fig. 4, C_L is initially connected to GND, and the voltage at C_R is equal to $V_{DD}/2$ as a consequence of the charge recovery phase of a preceding falling logic transition. In a rising transition, the circuit initially undergoes a *charge recycling phase* where C_R and C_L are connected to one another while both the V_{DD} and GND rails are disconnected. Through charge sharing, the voltage at C_L will rise (while the voltage at C_R will fall) to $V_{DD}/4$. After the voltage at C_L has settled, C_L and C_R are disconnected from one another, and the C_L is connected to V_{DD} to complete the full transition to logic-1. Note that in this example, the amount of charge actually drawn from the V_{DD} rail is equal to $0.75 \cdot C_L \cdot V_{DD}$ as opposed to $C_L \cdot V_{DD}$. That is, there is an immediate 25% reduction in energy.

To reduce power consumption in the routing network, we propose an FPGA architecture wherein unused routing conductors are re-purposed as charge reservoirs, where they store charge from falling transistors on the used routing conductors to which they are paired , and permit that charge to be recycled on rising transitions.

To implement the desired behavior, we designed the buffer circuit shown in Fig. 5, which includes an intermediate stage to apply the appropriate signals to the gates of $M1$ and $M2$ (which comprise the buffer's output stage), based on the operating mode of the buffer. For a full description of the

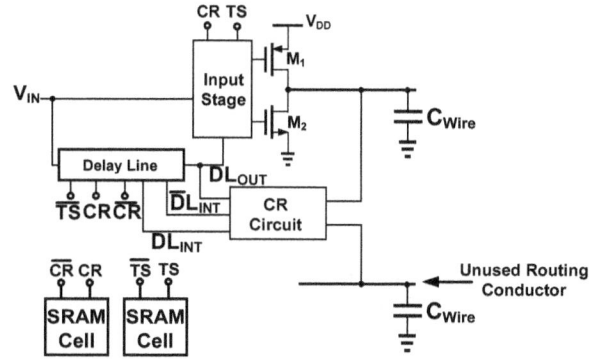

Figure 5: Charge recycling routing buffer.

circuit structures, the reader is referred to [3]. When operating in charge recycling mode, the technique allows dynamic power of the buffer to be reduced by ∼26% which compares favourably to a theoretical maximum power reduction of 33%.

4. PULSED-SIGNALLING FOR LEAKAGE POWER REDUCTION

Routing conductors in FPGAs are connected to a significant number of routing multiplexers which typically have a large number of inputs to ensure sufficient routing flexibility. For the sake of optimizing area-delay tradeoff, routing multiplexers are usually built with pass transistors in a two-stage topology [1]. However, these routing multiplexers contain multiple leakage paths, resulting in considerable leakage power being dissipated in FPGA interconnect. In the face of impending issues in the sub-10nm era, such as direct source-drain tunneling (DSDT), it has become critical to find means to reduce the leakage dissipated in FPGA interconenct without sacrificing routing flexibility.

To reduce leakage, we begin by observing that the output impedance of the routing buffers in the interconnect network plays a crucial role in the leakage currents which flow from/to routing MUXes. Conventional routing buffers provide low impedance paths (either from V_{DD} or to GND), and it is through these paths that leakage currents flow. If instead we are able to increase the impedance of these paths, leakage current may be reduced. Simply increasing the output impedance of routing buffers is not an acceptable solution, as this would lead to performance penalties. Note however that a buffer's output impedance only has to be low when the buffer is in the process of transmitting data (and its output is transitioning); if at all other times, the output impedance is kept high, leakage power will be reduced. To achieve this desired behaviour, we propose to replace conventional routing buffers in FPGAs (see Fig. 1)) with routing buffers which are tristated when they are not in the process of sending data, and dynamically activated following a transition at their inputs (when they need to send data). In the following sections, we detail the circuit-level modifications and CAD support necessary to implement the proposed leakage power reduction technique.

4.1 Pulsed-Signalling Circuit

Fig. 6 shows the proposed routing buffer, and as depicted, the buffer can loosely be divided into four stages: receiver stage, gating stage, output stage, and low-leakage keeper stage. Starting at the receiver stage, we note that in contrast to conventional FPGA routing buffers whose first stage consists of an inverter with a level-restoring PMOS transistor connected in feedback, the first stage of our buffer consists of

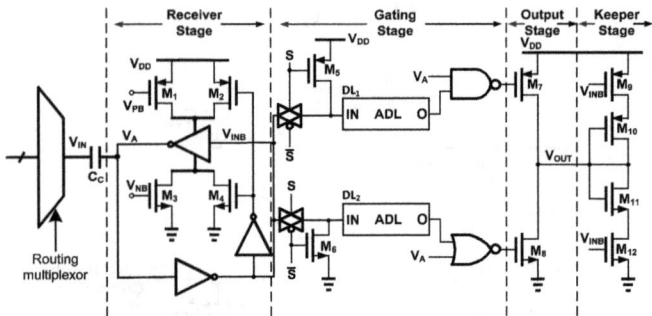

Figure 6: Pulsed-signalling buffer.

an asynchronous fully-regenerative receiver. A regenerative receiver (which is effectively a latch) is made necessary because routing conductors upstream from the routing buffer exist in a low-leakage mode after transmission of data transitions, and as will be made clear later on in this section, the voltage of the routing conductors will tend to drift away from V_{DD} or GND. As such, the burden of retaining state is on the receiver, thus the need for it to be fully regenerative. To eliminate leakage paths, we propose to capacitively couple the output of the routing multiplexer to the input of the reciever with a coupling capacitor C_C; this bears some resemblance to previously proposed AC-coupled on-chip interconnect [2], although previous techniques placed the coupling capacitor at the output of a routing driver in an effort to improve performance and reduce signal swing (and thus power). While many options exist for the implementation of C_C, we propose to use a metal-insulator-metal (MIM) capacitor due to its high capacitance density ($\sim$1-10 $fF/\mu m^2$), low series resistance, and the fact that additional active area is not generally required with this option. In a $65nm$ process, we believe a $5fF$ MIM cap will be able to fit within the footprint of each routing multiplexer, thus will not requiring any additional area, and can be accomodated with low impact to overall layout and cost.

While a $5fF$ capacitor is large enough to allow for sufficient signal swing when driving the parasitic capacitance at node V_A, we must ensure that the output impedance of the feedback path of the regenerative receiver is very high, otherwise, all of the charge injected into V_A by C_C will be immediately dissipated. On the other hand, the regeneration time (and thus delay) of the receiver will vary in an inverse manner to the output impedance of the feedback path. To balance these two requirements, a regenerative receiver with hysteresis is employed; we optimized the transistor sizing of this topology to allow for reliable data transmission assuming 6σ variation in transistor parameters (specifically V_T) and $\pm 10\%$ varation in the capacitance of C_C.

Immediately following a rising (or falling) transition at V_{INB}, the output stage is activated with $M8$ ($M7$) turning on while $M7$ ($M8$) remains off, allowing for the output V_{OUT} to fall (rise). Observe that immediately following a transition, the outputs of the (non-inverting) delay lines DL_1 and DL_2 hold the *previous* value of V_{INB}. Once the rising (falling) transition has made its way through DL_1 and DL_2, $M8$ ($M7$) is shut off, which leaves V_{OUT} tristated. As such, for the duration of time following an input transition when the output of DL_1/DL_2 holds its previous value, the output stage is activated and the input transition is allowed to propagate to the output of the buffer. However, once the outputs of both delay-lines have transitioned to their new states, the output stage is tristated. This therefore ensures a low-impedance path to either rail when data is being transmitted by the buffer, but a high effective output impedance when the buffer is in a quiescent state. One subtle point

to note is that DL_1 and DL_2 have assymetric delays: DL_1 has a fast rise delay of τ_f (which in our design was around $25ps$), and a slow fall delay of τ_s (in our design, this was set to 300 ps), while DL_2 has a slow rise delay of τ_s and a fast fall delay of τ_f. These two assymetric delay lines are needed to ensure proper functionality in the event of a glitch at the input, as it can be shown that having a single symmetric delay line with equal rise and fall delays τ_D can lead to improper function if a glitch of pulse-width less that τ_D were to appear at the input to the buffer. While very specific values have been indicated here, the routing buffer presented in this work is able to tolerate significant variation in τ_s and τ_f. All that is required is that τ_f is sufficiently smaller than the output transition time at V_{OUT}, which in our experiments was around 180 ps when the buffer is loaded by a length-4 wire, while τ_s must be sufficiently larger.

Transistors $M9$-$M12$ realize weak diode keepers which are needed to bound the DC wander at V_{OUT} when the buffer is dynamically tristated, as excessive DC wander can lead to errors when transmitting data. This is because downstream receivers are capacitively coupled, and as such, the input transitions that are seen by receivers is proportional to the difference between ($V_{DD} - GND$) and the DC wander. Excessive DC wander may diminish the amplitude of signal transitions seen by downstream receivers to the point where signal transisitons are no longer propagated. The diode keepers are sized to bound the maximum DC wander such that under 6σ parameter variation, the worst case signal transition seen at downstream receivers can still be reliably propagated. Moreover, the use of diode weak keepers ensures that leakage paths to either rail are still high impedance.

Finally, an SRAM cell (not shown) outputs signal S and $\overline{S}$ to set the state of the routing buffer; when S is logic-1, the routing buffer operates in pulsed-signalling mode, allowing us to reduce leakage power, while when the output of S is logic-0, the buffer operates in conventional mode. This SRAM cell is configured when the device is being programmed, and the mode of operation of each routing buffer is determined by an analsyis of the worst case injected noise at the buffer output at compile time. We discuss the impact of noise in the following section.

All circuits were designed and simulated with commercial $65nm$ STMicroelectronics models for functionality verification and power and timing characterization. The dynamic and leakage power overheads arising from the circuitry needed for pulsed-signalling were negligible compared to the leakage and dynamic power dissipated for a length-4 routing wire with the routing multiplexer fanout arising from a routing architecture consisting of fully populated, Wilton-style switch blocks [14]. On the other hand, there is a small delay penalty when a buffer is used in pulsed-signalling mode, since the inherent DC wander at the output of the buffer will degrade the signal swing seen by downstream routing buffers. Under worst-case conditions (a combination of worst case transistor variation resulting in degraded receiver sensitivity and worst-case DC wander), the delay penalty due to reduced signal swing is approximately $80ps$. When the buffer is not used in pulsed-signalling mode, the delay penalty is negligible. As such, in addition to noise considerations discussed below, only conductors on paths with sufficient slack may be used in pulsed-signalling mode.

4.2 Noise Considerations

One potential source of concern with the proposed routing buffer is the fact that since the output is tristated, the buffer is sensitive to crosstalk. With V_{OUT} tristated, capacitive coupling noise from adjacent routing conductors can lead to errors. If the noise exceeds a certain threshold, it may be interpretted as an actual signal transition by downstream routing buffers, since they too are capacitively coupled, and potentially have difficulty distinguishing between noise and actual data. Even if the noise injected into V_{OUT} does not lead to an erroneous data transition on downstream routing buffers, the noise is somewhat *residual*, since by design there are no low impedance paths to either rail, as such the injected noise will decay at a slow rate. This is a problem as it can lead to a degraded amplitude of valid data transitions at V_{OUT} seen at downstream receivers. In the worst case, the amplitude of such transition is proportional to $(V_{DD} - GND) - (|N_{INJ}^{(max)}| + |DCW^{(max)}|)$ where $N_{INJ}^{(max)}$ is the worst case noise injected onto V_{OUT} and DCW_{MAX} is the worst case DC wander. Therefore, for a given design, this power reduction technique cannot be applied to all routing conductors in the circuit in general, but rather only to those routing conductors whose injected noise can be bounded below some maximum threshold level, which in this paper we call N_S (which for the sake of simplicity is normalized to V_{DD}). Let $f_{MUX}(V)$ represent the voltage at the output of a routing multiplexer whose select input is at V volts. Let V_{RT} represent the minimum voltage amplitude that can be reliably detected by the proposed hysteretic regenerative receiver in the presence of 6σ parameter variation of its constituent transistors, and let V_{RR} represent the maximum voltage amplitude that can be reliably rejected by the receiver, again subject to transistor variation. We therefore require $f_{MUX}(N_S) < V_{RR}$ and $f_{MUX}(V_{DD} - GND - N_S - DCW^{(max)}) \geq V_{RT}$. Through transistor sizing optimization, we found that $N_S \approx 1/4$, given that the routing multiplexers use a boosted gate voltage, which is a commmon feature in commercial FPGAs [1]. For $65nm$, the maximum reliable gate voltage is 1.2 V.

Let $C(i, j)$ represent the coupling capacitance between conductors i and j, $C(i)$ the total (plate and coupling) capacitance of conductor i, and $Adj(i)$ the set conductors within the same metal layer and adjacent to i. Also, let $occ(i)$ be equal to 1 if i is a used conductor or 0 if i is unused. Therefore, for conductor i to operate in pulsed-signalling mode, the following condition must hold:

$$\sum_{j \in Adj(i)} \frac{C(i,j)}{C(i)} occ(j) \leq N_S \qquad (2)$$

In the following sections, we discuss how a conventional FPGA CAD flow may be modified to optimize leakage power by maximizing the number of used conductors which are to operate in pulsed-signalling mode, subject to the constraints described in this section.

5. CAD SUPPORT

As mentioned previously, all three power reduction techniques considered in this paper leverage the fact that FPGAs often have many unused routing conductors, and by ensuring specific routing conductors are unused, different power reduction opportunities are available for each of the power reduction techniques. For the remainder of this paper, we define $F(n)$ to be a set of "friend" conductors of n: routing conductors whose occupancies determine the power reduction opportunities for conductor n. For the charge recycling technique, $F(n)$ will always contain a single element, the paired routing conductor of conductor n. For the capacitance optimization and pulse-signalling techniques, $F(n)$ is the set of conductors adjacent to n within the same metal layer. The power reduction opportunities for each of the aforementioned techniques can then be expressed as follows: The effective capacitance of conductor n is proportional to

the number of conductors $j \in F(n)$ which are used (and their respective individual coupling capacitances with conductor n), thus we seek to minimize this quantity to reduce the dynamic power of conductor n when using the capacitance optimization technique described in Section 3.1. For the charge recycling technique described in Section 3.2, if n is a used routing conductor, we seek to ensure the sole member of $F(n)$ is unused so that it may be used as a charge reservoir. Finally, to minimize active leakage power of a routing conductor using the technique described in Section 4, we need to ensure that a *sufficient* number of conductors $j \in F(n)$ are unused, and thus can be used as shielding conductors to allow n to safely operate in pulsed-signalling mode, as described in Section 4.2.

As such for each technique, special effort must be made during the physical implementation of a circuit to ensure that while a signal is routed between source and sink pins, specific routing conductors along the path are unused in order to minimize power. Our proposed CAD flow builds on VTR (a conventional FPGA CAD flow) [11], where we have made modifications to the router and added a routing conductor mode selection phase which takes place after routing and timing analysis.These modifications are discussed in the following sections.

5.1 Power-Aware Router

The VPR router incorporates the PathFinder algorithm [9] which was discussed in Section 2. The cost function incorporates metrics of timing performance and *routability* (i.e. the ability to legally route all of the connections in the circuit) in order to yield a routed circuit with a favorable quality of results. The cost function implemented VPR is:

$$Cost_n = (1 - Crit_i) \cdot cong\_cost_n \\ + Crit_i \cdot delay\_cost_n \qquad (3)$$

where n is the routing resource (e.g. wire segment) being considered for addition to a partially-completed route, i is the driver/load connection being routed, $Crit_i$ is the timing criticality of the connection (equal to 1 for connections on the critical path, and decreasing to 0 as the slack of the connection increases), $cong\_cost_n$ is the congestion cost of routing resource n which gives an indication of the *demand* for the routing resource among nets, while $delay\_cost_n$ is the delay of routing resource n. The reader is referred to [9] for further discussion on this cost function.

Turning now to our modification of the VPR router, for a routing segment, n, we use the following cost function:

$$Cost_n = (1 - Crit_i) \cdot [cong\_cost_n \\ + PF \cdot power\_cost_n \\ + AF \cdot power\_cost\_infringe_n] \\ + Crit_i \cdot delay\_cost_n \qquad (4)$$

where PF and AF are empirically determined scalar weighting terms, $power\_cost_n$ is a term to guide power critical nets to use routing conductors which are likely to operate in a low-power mode, and $power\_cost\_infringe_n$ is used to guide nets *away* from the "friend" conductors of a potentially used routing conductor which is likely to operate in lower power mode. For the sake of brevity, in the remainder of this section we will focus on the form of these two terms as they relate to the pulsed-signalling power reduction technique; for a detailed description of the router cost functions for the charge recycling and capacitance optimization techniques, the reader is referred to [3] and [4], respectively. For the pulsed-signalling power reduction technique, the term $power\_cost_n$ is given by:

$$power\_cost_n = \begin{cases} 1 & : \sum\limits_{j \in F(n)} \frac{C(n,j)}{C(n)} occ(j) - N_S > 0 \\ 0 & : otherwise \end{cases}$$

where $C(n,j)$, $C(n)$, $occ(j)$, and N_S are as defined in Section 4.2. The term $power\_cost\_infringe_n$ is equal to:

$$\sum_{j \in F(n)} \frac{C(n,j)}{\sum\limits_{k \in F(j)} C(j,k)occ(k)} \cdot occ(j) \cdot power\_cost_j \cdot (1 - max\_crit_j) \tag{5}$$

where max_crit_j is the worst case criticality over all nets currently vying for j.

The motivation for the modification to the cost function is as follows: while routing a circuit, we wish to maximize the number of active conductors which can be put into pulsed-signalling state in order to reduce leakage power. In general, when routing connection i, we need to consider two cases: 1) connection i has sufficient timing margin, or 2) connection i is timing critical. For the former case, we strive to optimize the routing for two different situations. First, we attempt to guide nets to use segments with a sufficient number of unoccupied neighbours; the term $power\_cost_n$ attempts to optimize for this goal, since it estimates whether or not the noise on conductor n exceeds N_S. Any routing conductor n whose $power\_cost_n$ is equal to 0 may be used in pulsed-signalling mode. Conversely, if $power\_cost_n$ is greater than 0, it is unlikely to operate in pulsed-signalling mode, therefore we attempt to avoid using it. The second goal is to avoid injecting excessive noise onto tracks which may otherwise potentially be used in pulsed-signalling mode. This optimization goal is dealt with by the term $power\_cost\_infringe_n$: in evaluating conductor n, we examine all neighbours j of n which are used, and assess the likelihood of j operating in pulsed-signalling mode. If j is likely to be used by a low criticality net (given by the $1 - max\_crit_j$ term) and yet has $power\_cost_j > 0$ (i.e. there was an opportunity for j to operate in pulsed-signalling mode and yet it cannot due to excessive noise), we should assign some cost to using n. This cost is scaled by $C(n,j)/\sum\limits_{k \in F(j)} C(j,k)occ(k)$, since the cost of j not operating in pulsed-signalling mode should be distributed over its neighbours and weighted according to the noise-injected by each of j's neighbours. Finally, if the current net has high criticality, then it is unlikely that i can be used in pulsed-signalling mode due to its inherent delay penalty, and as such we opt to focus on optimizing i's delay.

5.2 Routing Wire Mode Selection

After routing and timing analysis have completed, we are in a position to determine the operating modes of the routing conductors in the chip. For the capacitance optimization technique, mode selection is trivial, since all unused conductors are automatically tristated. For the charge recycling power reduction technique, we formulated the mode selection problem, where power is to be optimized subject to timing constraints, as a mixed integer linear program (MILP). The reader is referred to [3] for further details. For the pulsed-signalling technique presented in this work, we again seek to optimize (leakage) power, subject to timing and maximum injected noise constraints. Algorithm 1 provides pseudocode for the greedy approach we used in this study to solve this problem. With the core objective of minimizing leakage power, the goals of the algorithm are to determine which of the used routing conductors will operate in pulsed-signalling mode, which of the unused routing conducts will act as *shields* to help isolate used con-

---

Algorithm 1: Routing wire mode selection

Input: a set W of routing conductors, a timing graph $G(V, E)$

Output: a data structure $states(i)$ mapping routing conductor i to its state

```
1  begin
2      states(i) ← unknown for all i ∈ W
3      /* Build the set of used wires */
4      WU ← {x | x ∈ W ∧ occ(x) = 1}
5      /* Build the set of unused wires */
6      WN ← {x | x ∈ W ∧ occ(x) = 0}
7      /* First determine the state of used conductors */
       foreach i ∈ WU in descending order of selects(i)
       do
8          if noise(i) > N_S or slack(G,i) < t_D then
9              states(i) ← ungated
10         else
11             states(i) ← gated
12             /* Update G to reflect state of i */
13             update_timing_graph(G, i, t_D)
14             /* Compute noise margin */
15             nm ← noise(i) − N_S
16             foreach j ∈ F(i) ∩ WN in descending order
               of selects(j) do
17                 if C(i,j)/C(i) < nm and states(j) ==
                   unknown then
18                     /* conductor j can potentially be
                       gated, don't set its state yet */
19                     nm ← nm − C(i,j)/C(i)
20                 else
21                     /* use j as a shield */
22                     states(j) ← ungated
23                 end
24             end
25         end
26     end
27     /* Now finalize the states of unused conductors */
       foreach i ∈ WN do
28         if states(i) == unknown then
29             states(i) ← gated
30         end
31     end
32  end
```

---

ductors operating in pulsed-signalling mode from adjacent noise sources, and which of the unused conductors can be set in low-leakage, tristated mode. In the pseudocode shown $noise(i)$ is the worst case total injected noise on conductor i, and is equal to $\sum_{j \in F(i)} occ(j) \cdot C(i,j)/C(i)$, $selects(i)$ is the number of MUXes in the fanout of i where i connects to a selected input pin, $slack(G, i)$ returns the timing slack available for the connection associated with routing conductor i given timing graph G, update_timing_graph(G, i, t) is a routine (not shown for the sake of brevity) which *incrementally* updates the timing graph G when the delay of the connection associated with routing conductor i is increased by t seconds (i.e. the routine only updates edges that are affected, and avoids a complete timing analysis). Recall that t_D is the delay penalty of operating in pulsed-signalling mode (as mentioned previously, this is $80ps$), and the other terms are as described previously. It should be noted that since it can be shown that typically the input pins of a routing multiplexer which have the greatest leakage current are the selected input pins (the pass-transistors connected to these pins are "on", thus these pins have low impedance), the worst case leakage power of a routing conductor is approximately proportional to $selects(i)$. As such, we use this quantity as an estimate for leakage power where appropriate in the algorithm.

The algorithm takes as input the timing graph for the circuit being optimized, and a set W for all the used and unused routing wires in the circuit. The output of the algorithm is the *state* for each routing conductor i, and is equal to either *gated* or *ungated*. A used routing conductor will operate in pulsed-signalling mode if its state is *gated*, and will operate in conventional mode if its state is *ungated*. An unused routing conductor will be tristated if its state is *gated*, and will act as a shield if its state is *ungated*. While we wish to maximize the number of used conductors that are operating in pulsed signalling mode, we also wish to maximize the number of unused conductors in tristate mode, as they lead to reduced leakage.

The first part of the algorithm determines the state of all the used routing conductors in the circuit. We visit these conductors in descending order of their estimated leakage power (using $selects(i)$ as an estimate). For each routing conductor i, we assess if either the injected noise onto i is greater than N_S or if sufficient timing slack is unavailable, in which case i cannot be used in pulsed-signalling mode, and therefore its state is set to *ungated*. Otherwise, i can be used in pulsed-signalling mode and will have its state set to *gated*, whereafter G is updated by increasing the delay of the connection associated with conductor i by t_D seconds. Following this, we compute the *noise margin* for conductor i, denoted nm in the pseudocode, which is the difference between the total noise injected onto i and N_S. If this is non-zero, then *some* of the unused neighbouring conductors of i may b tristated, leading to reduced leakage. We determine which of the unused conductors $j \in F(i)$ may be potentially tristated by visiting them in descending order of their estimate leakage power (again using $selects(j)$ as an estimate), and then assessing if the injected noise onto i from j is less than the current value of nm. If this quantity is less than nm, then j may potentially be tristated, however we leave its state as *ungated*, and revisit the conductor after all used conductors have been visited. If instead the noise injected from j onto i is greater than nm we set the state of j to *ungated*, and thus j will act as a shield.

After the states of all used conductors are determined, we visit each unused conductor i whose state is still set to *unknown*. These conductors are either not adjacent to any used conductors, or the determination of their state was deferred until this phase of the algorithm. This would only occur when an unused conductor is adjacent to ungated used conductors and/or gated used conductors with sufficient noise margin. As such, all of these conductors can be tristated, meaning $states(i) = gated$.

While the above approach is greedy, as will be discussed in the next section, our results appear to indicate that it works well. Nonetheless a less greedy approach will likely improve the quality of results further, but investigation of such approaches is left for future work.

6. EXPERIMENTAL STUDY

In order to assess the merits of the proposed power reduction techniques, we used the set of benchmark circuits packaged with VTR [11]. Our baseline architecture contains unidirectional wire segments which span 4 CLB tiles, uses the Wilton switch block [14], and has logic blocks with ten 6-LUTs/FFs per CLB. All benchmark circuits were routed on the baseline architecture to determine the minimum number of tracks per channel needed to route each circuit successfully (W_{min}); all routing buffers in the baseline architec-

ture are conventional. For each circuit, we then computed $W = 1.3 \times W_{min}$ to reflect a medium-stress routing scenario – standard approach in FPGA architecture research. The computed W value for each circuit was used for all experimental runs of the circuit. We used the ACE switching activity estimator tool [7] to compute switching activity for each signal in each benchmark circuit, as this information is needed for the charge recycling and capacitance optimization techniques. For the pulsed-signalling technique, we consider an additional set of experiments. FPGA vendors develop FPGA *families* (such as Stratix from Altera or Virtex from Xilinx) which are a set of different sized FPGAs all having the same fundamental routing and logic architecture, but have different numbers of CLBs, hard blocks, I/O capabilities, etc. While the different members of a family may have vastly differing logic capacities, their routing architecture (and thus channel width) remains constant; this is a practical approach since it allows a vendor to allocate design resources to develop a single tile (for example containing a single CLB and associated routing channels), and then stitch a varying number of these tiles together to form the different members of each family. As such, a more realistic scenario is to assume a *fixed channel width*, W_{max}, which we set to be 10% larger than the largest channel width for the benchmarks considered in this study. Thus, for the pulsed-signalling technique, we experiment with with $W = 1.3 \times W_{min}$ and $W = W_{max}$.

In our experiments, we assess the interconnect dynamic power reduction, static power reduction, and area overheads. For each of the techniques, the associated router cost functions contain scalar terms which were optimized, however for the sake of brevity we exclude details and the optimization of these terms (the reader is referred to [3] and [4] for more detail). The results presented here therefore reflect power reductions obtained with optimized cost functions; a circuit-by-circuit breakdown of our results is provided in Table 1. The critical path degradations were negligible for all three power reduction techniques, thus for the remainder of this section, we focus solely on power reduction and area overhead results.

6.1 Power Reduction

For the capacitance optimization technique, dynamic power reduction ranges from 10 to 19% with a geometric mean of 13.5 %; this is assuming the ratio between coupling capacitance (C_C) and "plate" capacitance (C_P) is 2; greater power reductions are possible as this ratio increases (see [4] for further discussion). This is in addition to a reduction in interconnect static power of approximately 15.2% (geometric mean across benchmarks). The charge recycling technqiue offers similar dynamic power reduction, ranging from 13 to 19% with a geometric mean of just under 16%.

Turning now to the reductions afforded by the proposed pulsed-signalling technique, we see that active leakage (i.e. leakage in the used routing conductors) can by 26% on average when a circuit is targetted towards an FPGA with channel width $1.3 \times W_{min}$, while total leakage in the routing network (including leakage from unused conductors) can be reduced by approximately 31%. For the fixed channel width experiments (circuits target an architecture with channel width of W_{max}), the active leakage reduction dramatically increases to $\sim$62% on average, however the increase in total routing leakage reduction is less dramatic as in this case it is now $\sim$37% on average. The justification for these results are as follows: since for most circuits in our benchmark set, $1.3 \times W_{min}$ is *significantly* less than W_{max} (due to the fact that the logic counts for the designs in the benchmarks may vary by over an order of magnitude, in addition to varying levels of routing complexity), when routing designs at

Table 1: Power reduction and area overhead results.

Circuit	Effective Capacitance Optimization			Charge Recycling		Pulsed-signalling					
						W = 1.3 x Wmin			W = Wmax		
	Routing Dynamic Power Reduction [%]	Routing Static Power Reduction [%]	Routing Area Overhead [%]	Routing Dynamic Power Reduction [%]	Routing Area Overhead [%]	Active routing leakage reduction [%]	Total routing leakage reduction [%]	Routing Area overhead [%]	Active routing leakage reduction [%]	Total routing leakage reduction [%]	Routing Area overhead [%]
blob_merge	10.4	13.2	4.7	13.6	24.8	26.0	31.5	20.9	61.7	37.6	20
boundtop	13.3	13.6	4.7	16.5	24.5	25.5	31.4	20.7	69.8	40.0	20
ch_intrinsics	19.2	15.5	5.1	17	27	24.6	31.1	22.8	64.2	36.0	20
diffeq1	16.4	16.7	5.1	17.4	26.8	24.7	30.3	22.6	60.5	36.3	20
diffeq2	17.6	18	4.9	13.3	25.7	23.5	28.5	21.7	60.3	38.0	20
LU8PEEng	10.6	12.7	4.6	15.9	24	23.3	31.5	20.3	51.8	35.6	20
mkDelayWorker32B	13.2	18.1	4.5	16.5	23.8	25.2	30.0	20.1	62.0	36.6	20
mkPktMerge	16.5	21	4.4	12.9	22.9	27.5	31.5	19.3	62.7	39.4	20
mkSMAdapter4b	12.4	15.2	4.7	16.5	24.7	24.8	30.6	20.9	59.6	36.0	20
or1200	12.4	16.3	4.6	18.7	24.1	26.0	30.6	20.4	61.8	36.7	20
raygentop	12.9	13.9	4.8	15.8	25.1	28.0	31.2	21.2	60.0	37.9	20
sha	11	13.3	4.7	15.9	24.8	25.5	31.0	20.9	67.9	40.0	20
stereovision0	12	13.8	4.4	16.6	23.1	27.0	32.0	19.5	69.5	37.4	20
stereovision1	11	14.3	4.6	14.2	24.2	29.0	30.8	20.4	74.0	38.0	20
stereovision2	12.9	14.1	4.6	14.9	24.1	31.8	30.8	20.4	48.0	34.2	20
stereovision3	19.2	15.8	6.2	15.1	32.4	25.2	30.5	27.4	53.0	34.7	20
mean	13.8	15.3	4.8	15.7	25.1	26.1	30.8	21.2	61.7	37.2	20.0

W_{max}, the increased number of unused routing conductors means that the used routing conductors may more easily be spaced apart from one another when nets are being routed. This explains why the active leakage reduction increased so dramatically. On the other hand, a larger channel width means that the ratio between unused conductors to used conductors increases, meaning that the net impact on total routing leakage from used routing conductors is diminished. This explains why while active leakage reduction increased almost three-fold going from $W = 1.3 \times W_{min}$ to $W = W_{max}$, total routing leakage reduction increased by approximately ~21%.

6.2 Area Overhead

Of the three power reduction techniques, the capacitance optimization technique offers the lowest (routing) area overhead of just under 5% on average. Given that for commercial architectures routing area is approximately 50% of total FPGA core area [8], this means that total core FPGA area grows by under 2.5%. The routing area overheads for the charge recycling and pulsed-signalling are similar at 25% and ~20%, respectively, which translates to a total core area overhead of just over ~10% for both techniques.

It is important to consider the impact which these area increases will have on routing power. For the capacitance optimization technique, a ~2% increase in tile area corresponds to $\sqrt{1.02} \approx 1.01\times$ increase in tile dimensions, meaning that increase in dynamic power resulting from the increased tile size is less than 1%. Similarly, the charge recycling and pulsed-signalling techniques will result in a $\sqrt{1.1} \approx 1.05\times$ increase in tile dimensions. For the charge recycling technique, this effective power overhead is less than the power saved, although further optimization of the circuitry and/or technique is required for the power savings to be more meaningful. On the other hand, given the significant power savings from the pulse-signalling technique, a ~5% increase in routing dynamic power for a 30-40% decrease in routing leakage power is a favourable tradeoff. Assuming static power is 1/3 dynamic power, these numbers indicate that total routing power can still be reduced by ~10%. For many designs that run at lower clock rates, the dynamic power overhead will decrease, while the leakage power reduction will stay the same, meaning that total routing energy savings will increase.

7. CONCLUSIONS AND FUTURE WORK

This paper presented three novel techniques to reduce power consumption in FPGA interconnect. The techniques showed the interconnect dynamic power can be reduced by 10-20%, while leakage power can be reduced by almost 40%. Because of the fact that all of the techniques fundamentally require the same set of conditions to reduce power, namely that routing conductors which consume a lot of power (i.e. if used by a net with high switching activity and/or connected to many selected input pins of downstream routing multiplexers), and because the circuitry required for the techniques are all similar to one another, it is likely that these techniques may be combined to allow for signiciant net decrease in dynamic and leakage power consumption in FPGA interconnect. As assessment of the net benefits in combining a set of these techniques is an interesting avenue for future research. In addition, future work will aim to improve CAD tools to improve quality of results and reduce tool runtime.

8. REFERENCES

[1] C. Chiasson and V. Betz. Should FPGAs abandon the pass-gate? In *IEEE FPL 2013*.
[2] R. Ho et al. High speed and low energy capacitively driven on-chip wires. *IEEE JSSC*, 43(1):52–60, Jan 2008.
[3] S. Huda et al. Charge recycling for power reduction in FPGA interconnect. In *IEEE FPL 2013*.
[4] S. Huda et al. Optimizing effective interconnect capacitance for FPGA power reduction. In *ACM/SIGDA FPGA 2014*.
[5] ITRS. ITRS 2011 Report.
[6] I. Kuon and J. Rose. Measuring the gap between FPGAs and ASICs. *IEEE TCAD*, 26(2):203–215, Feb. 2007.
[7] J. Lamoureux and S. Wilton. Activity estimation for field-programmable gate arrays. In *IEEE FPL 2006*.
[8] D. Lewis et al. Architectural enhancements in Stratix V^{TM}. In *ACM/SIGDA FPGA 2013*.
[9] L. McMurchie and C. Ebeling. Pathfinder: A negotiation-based performance-driven router for FPGAs. In *ACM/SIGDA FPGA 1995*.
[10] A. Putnam et al. A reconfigurable fabric for accelerating large-scale datacenter services. In *ACM/IEEE ISCA 2014*.
[11] J. Rose et al. The VTR project: Architecture and CAD for FPGAs from verilog to routing. In *ACM/SIGDA FPGA 2012*.
[12] L. Shang et al. Dynamic power consumption of the Virtex-II FPGA family. In *ACM/SIGDA FPGA 2002*, 2002.
[13] T. Tuan and B. Lai. Leakage power analysis of a 90nm FPGA. In *IEEE CICC 2003*.
[14] S. J. Wilton. *Architecture and algorithms for field-programmable gate arrays with embedded memory*. PhD thesis, 1997.

Scaling Up Physical Design: Challenges and Opportunities

Guojie Luo[1,3]
gluo@pku.edu.cn

Wentai Zhang[1]
rchardx@pku.edu.cn

Jiaxi Zhang[1]
zhangjiaxi@pku.edu.cn

Jason Cong[2,3,1]
cong@cs.ucla.edu

[1]Center for Energy-Efficient Computing and Applications, School of EECS, Peking University
[2]Computer Science Department, University of California, Los Angeles
[3]PKU-UCLA Joint Research Institute in Science and Engineering

ABSTRACT

Due to the continuous scaling of integration density and the increasing diversity of customized designs, there are increasing demands on the scalability and the customization of EDA tools and flows. Commercial EDA tools usually provide an interface of TCL scripting to extract and modify the design information for a flexible design flow. However, we observe that the current TCL scripting is not designed for the complete netlist extraction, resulting in a significant degradation in performance. For example, it takes over 20 minutes to extract the complete netlist of a 466K-cell design using TCL. This extraction may be repeated several times when interfacing between the existing EDA platforms and the actual distributed EDA algorithms. This drastic decrease in efficiency is a great barrier for customized EDA tool development. In this paper, we propose to build a distributed framework on top of TCL to accelerate the netlist extraction, and use the distribution detailed placement as an example to demonstrate its capability. This framework is promising in scaling out physical design algorithms to run on a cluster.

CCS Concepts

•Hardware → Physical design (EDA); Methodologies for EDA; •Computing methodologies → *Parallel algorithms; Distributed algorithms;*

Keywords

Physical Design; Detailed Placement; FPGA; TCL; Distributed Computing; Spark

1. INTRODUCTION

The computational demand of physical design and EDA tools keeps growing, due to the increasing complexity of elec-

ISPD'16, April 03-06, 2016, Santa Rosa, CA, USA

© 2016 ACM. ISBN 978-1-4503-4039-7/16/04. . . $15.00

DOI: http://dx.doi.org/10.1145/2872334.2872342

tronics designs. The semiconductor industry is involved in the new applications including medical technology, automotive, robotics, and energy systems, which in turn exposes some complex design problems and thus needs greater computational power [8].

The EDA vendors have already adopted a distributed storage solution for data management [5, 6]. Some EDA tools provide multi-threaded solutions to relieve the runtime issue. However, the emerging and mainstream distributed computing infrastructures are not fully adopted by EDA tools, due to the cost of rewriting software and the unclear pricing models. In the meanwhile, EDA users have various needs for customized tools in their flow. In addition to the core physical design steps, users may develop additional tools for their specific needs. There are strong needs for powerful and extensible framework to design EDA tools and flows.

A related topic is putting EDA tools and solutions in the cloud [30]. These recent efforts mainly spread across the applications of training, demonstrations, and web-based collaboration. These can be viewed as the interaction-intensive end of the design platform, which create opportunities and hide the complexity for the development of parallel and distributed computing tools in the compute-intensive end. And there is another example in academia, called bX [27], to provide computational power for regression testing of EDA algorithms.

Here, we investigate a distributed computing framework for EDA algorithms and flows. We take advantage of the progress in the computational engines (e.g., Spark [37]) in the big data ecosystem, and design a framework capable of interfacing the existing commercial EDA platforms. In this way, the academia will be able to design more distributed EDA algorithms and test with industrial-grade design examples; and the industry will have a low cost to migrate some of the design tools to this distributed framework. The interface implements design query and modification through TCL scripting supported by mainstream EDA tools. TCL scripting is a good candidate to implement a general interface across commercial EDA tools, and there have been some practices of customized in-house EDA tools developed using TCL [35, 16]. However, we observe that existing TCL support is not designed for high-throughput queries. The extraction of the whole netlist takes an ineligible amount of time. We propose a distributed parser to efficiently read design data from existing EDA platforms, and provide a solution to maintain data consistency when interact distributed

EDA algorithm with existing tools. We also demonstrate the capability of this framework using a distributed detailed placement algorithm.

The remainder of this paper is organized as follows. Section 2 states the background and related work. Section 3 proposes the design and details of a distributed EDA framework with an application example of detailed placement. Then Section 4 describes the experimental results. Section 5 discusses the challenges and opportunities for a scalable EDA framework.

2. BACKGROUND AND RELATED WORKS

First, we summarize the latest efforts in putting EDA in the cloud. In the meanwhile, we give a short introduction to the techniques like Spark and Docker in the big data and cloud ecosystem. Though it may not be an urgent task for the EDA companies to take advantage of the progress in these techniques, it is about time to design new distributed physical design algorithms for scalability. In the next section, we will propose a distributed computing framework that can build on top of existing EDA platforms.

A concept related to the scalability of EDA tools is the cloud EDA. The EDA vendors have been investigated the opportunity of offering the solutions in the cloud [30]. Cadence provides Hosted Design Solutions [14] as a production design environment in the private cloud. Synopsys has put its functional verification solution VCS in the cloud [19]. And Mentor Graphics has a cloud-based SystemVision [7] for modeling and design of electro-mechanical systems. Besides, there have been multiple companies putting their products in the cloud, including Altium, OneSpin, Plunify, Tabula, etc. Recently, IBM provides its high-performance services for EDA through SiCAD [21].

On the other hand, the MapReduce [13] programming model and infrastructure have been used widely for scalable data processing in the big data ecosystem. Users of MapReduce implements all the computations using only two functions, map and reduce, where a unit computation takes the input of <key,value> pairs and generates the output of another set of <key,value> pairs. Though the MapReduce model seems less flexible and has lower peak performance [29] than the traditional message-passing model [17], it increases the productivity and has even better performance for the programs written by non-experts in distributed computing. Spark [37] is an open-source data-parallel computation engine using the MapReduce programming model. Different from Hadoop [34], a previous open-source implementation of MapReduce, Spark enables efficient iterative algorithms and interactive queries by keeping data in memory using the Resilient Distributed Datasets (RDDs). Moreover, it supports general computation DAGs and allows optional specification of data partitioner to avoid data movement. Since most EDA algorithms are iterative, Spark is a suitable engine to scale out EDA tools.

Linux container is a lightweight virtualization technique, which provides an isolated kernel namespace for the processes, file system and network without running a full OS on virtual hardware. Docker [4] is a representative implementation. The comparative study of virtual machines (VMs) and containers shows that containers have equal or better performance than VMs and lower overhead in OS interaction [15] . The basic idea of container is illustrated in Figure 1. We will show in the next section that container is useful to manage existing EDA platforms in the environment of Linux clusters.

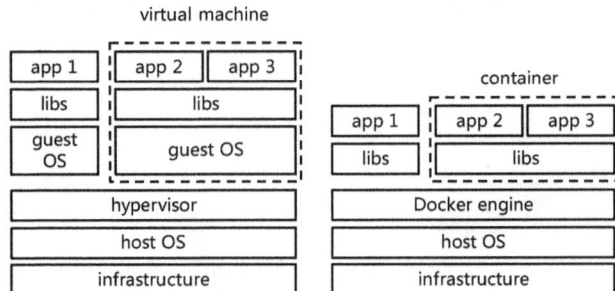

Figure 1: Virtual machine vs. container.

Inspired by the techniques above, we propose a distributed EDA framework for the scalability of physical design algorithms. Comparing with existing cloud EDA solutions, it is a computational infrastructure that can deploy either in the public cloud or private cloud.

3. FRAMEWORK DESIGN

3.1 Overview

The overall design of our proposed framework for distributed EDA algorithms and flows is illustrated in Figure 2. Existing EDA platforms are supported using TCL scripts for design data extraction and modification. The design data and the FPGA architecture or technology information are presented on top of the distributed computing engine of Spark. While we can follow OpenAccess as the data model of post-synthesis design, it is promising to design and develop portable physical design algorithms and flows in the distributed computing engine of Spark.

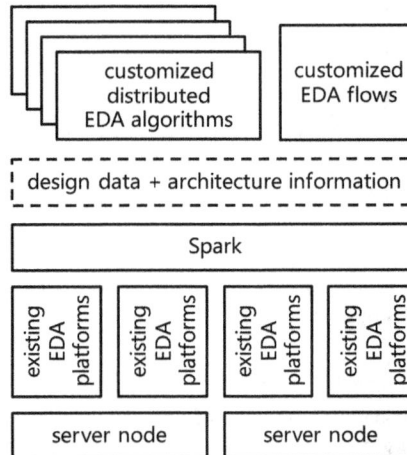

Figure 2: The distributed EDA framework.

3.2 Interfacing Existing EDA Platforms

TCL is a de facto standard for mainstream commercial EDA products. One has to import the design data from existing EDA platforms to the distributed computing framework using TCL scripts. The outline of the parser code is shown in Listing 1, which is implemented for the Xilinx Vivado platform. The scripts are only slightly different for the Altera Quartus platform.

Listing 1: Extract netlist from Vivado using TCL

```
1  foreach cell [get_cells ...] {
2    puts ...
3  }
4  foreach net [get_nets ...] {
5    foreach pin [get_pins -of $net] {
6      var cell [get_cells -of $pin]
7      puts ...
8    }
9  }
```

However, we observe the TCL execution on existing FPGA EDA platforms is relatively slow. For example, it takes over 20 minutes to extract the complete netlist of a 466K-cell design using TCL. This extraction may be repeated several times when interfacing between the existing EDA platforms and the actual distributed EDA algorithms. And this runtime cannot be directly reduced given more computing resources. In order to solve this issue and make the distributed computing framework meaningful, we propose a parallel parser to accelerate the execution of TCL scripts. The parser design is illustrated in Figure 3. In this example, four instances of Vivado execute on two server nodes. In this implementation, the parser reads partial data from each instance, and then combine and convert the design to the in-memory RDD in Spark. The RDD can be partitioned into sub-designs for further MapReduce steps, with an example shown in the next subsection.

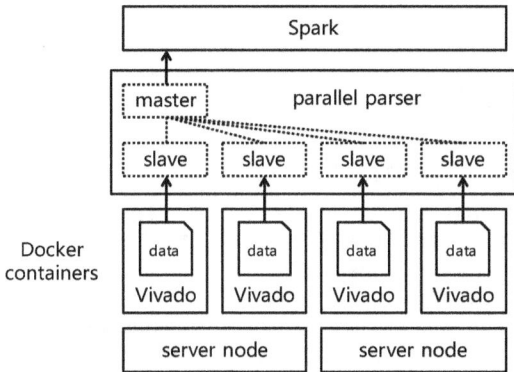

Figure 3: Parallel reads for efficient parsing.

After a design is processed by a distributed algorithm in Spark, the result has to be written back if a conventional step in Vivado is needed. This procedure is briefly listed in Figure 4. First, as shown in Figure 4a, the updated design (from data v0.1 to v0.2) in Spark is written back to a single instance of Vivado. Second, the outdated instances (data v0.1) are stopped and removed; at the same time, the remaining instance can run a conventional step in Vivado to obtain a further updated design (data v0.3), as shown in Figure 4b. Last, the remaining instance can be replicated as in Figure 4c, so that the parallel parsing can be performed to run another distributed algorithm in Spark. The instances of Vivado are managed using the Docker technique, where they can be killed or replicated conveniently. The checkpoint and restore operations are able to save and restore the

in-memory data, and thus can be used to replicate a live instance [31].

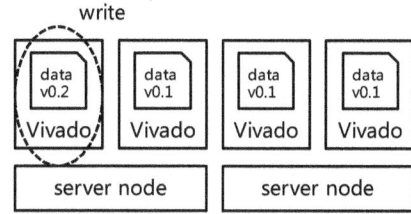

(a) Write data back to a single instance when a conventional step in Vivado is needed.

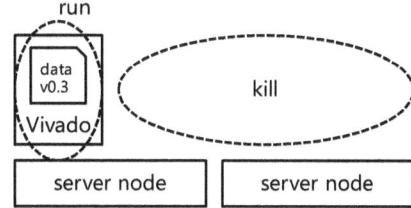

(b) Kill the outdated instances, and run a conventional step in the remaining instance.

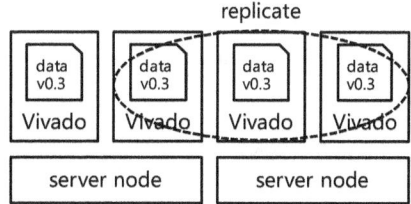

(c) Replicate the instance with the latest data, and get ready for the next parallel parsing.

Figure 4: Writing strategy for data consistency.

In this way, we are able to develop new distributed algorithms in Spark on top of Vivado. The runtime of the TCL-based parser is accelerated by parallel reads from multiple identical instances of Vivado. The data consistency for data write-backs can be guaranteed using the Docker technique to management the Vivado instances. This methodology is straightforward to be applied to any other mainstream EDA platforms that support TCL scripting.

3.3 Example Application: Detailed Placement

The detailed placement algorithms [23, 12, 28] usually include global swapping and local swapping. As an illustrative example, we implement a brute-force algorithm of local swapping on Spark to examine the capability of the distributed EDA framework.

The information produced by previous TCL parsing stage contains the lists of the cells, nets, initial placement, and feasible placement locations. The netlist and the placement region is processed and partitioned into "DP tile" structures after a few MapReduce steps. Each DP tile consists of its partial netlists and subregion information needed by the regional local swapping algorithm. The set of DP tiles is the RDD for a map operator to do parallel swapping. This map operator takes a DP tile as the input and generates a new DP tile after local swapping.

Compared with the conventional sequential solution, our method partitions the whole FPGA into $N \times N$ DP tiles and performs local swapping in each tile. During the swapping in each individual tile, we sweep a sliding window and enumerate all possible permutations of the cells in this window to pick a partially best solution. A size of 3×2 and 2×3 are selected for the sliding window, and the $6! = 720$ permutations of each window can be examined in a reasonable amount of time. After completing one iteration, the best permutation of cells is committed, and the sliding window moves to next position. We send all the tiles in N rounds, and a group of map operations process N tiles in parallel. These N tiles are chosen in a way that there are not any pair of tiles on the same row or column, so that the estimation of wirelength improvement in each tile is consistent. The partitioning and local swapping scheme are illustrated in Figure 5.

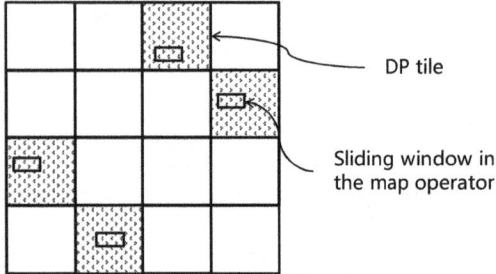

Figure 5: Distributed detailed placement scheme.

4. EXPERIMENTAL RESULTS

Our experiments are run on a Linux cluster with four nodes, each with two 6-core Intel Xeon Processor E5-2620 v3 at 2.40GHz and 64GB memory. The distributed computing engine is powered by Spark 1.5.2 and HDFS of Hadoop 2.6.3. The four nodes are connected by Gigabit Ethernet.

The summary of the test cases is described in Table 1. The test cases are obtained from the Titan benchmarks [24]. They are synthesized and placed using Xilinx Vivado 2015.3 targeting VC707 (part name XC7VX485TFFG1761-2). The total number of logic cells and a short description are also included in the table.

Table 1: Summary of the test cases

name	#cells	description
SLAM_spheric	87K	spherical coordinates algorithm for SLAM
bitcoin_miner	222K	Two-core version of the bitcoin FPGA miner
guassianblur_d1	466K	One of the pipelined loops for 3D Gaussian convolution

4.1 Distributed TCL Parser

After synthesis and placement, the next step in our experiments is to load the data from Xilinx Vivado to memory. We use TCL scripts to extract the design information.

The parsing time of the three test cases in Vivado is illustrated in Figure 6. The part of "load design" is a one-time execution to load a design in Vivado. The parts of "foreach cell" and "foreach net" correspond to the execution of TCL scripts in Listing 1. These two parts are usually executed multiple times when there are multiple interactions between the Spark program and the Vivado services. The runtime of

TCL execution is too long for such interactions, and hurts the speedup from any distributed algorithm in Spark.

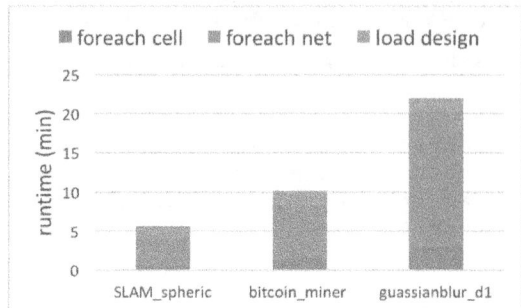

Figure 6: Decomposition of parsing time.

Thus, we use the parallel parser as illustrated in Figure 3 previously, and achieve about $3\times$ speedup with $3\times$ memory using four instances of Vivado. The TCL runtime and memory consumption are shown in Table 2. The runtime can be further reduced using more Vivado instances.

Table 2: TCL runtime time and memory consumption using four instances of Vivado.

test case	TCL time		memory	
	(min)	decr.	(GB)	incr.
SLAM_spheric	1.0	4.0×	6.4	3.2×
bitcoin_miner	2.1	3.9×	8.0	3.2×
guassianblur_d1	6.9	2.9×	11.0	3.0×

The current support of live replication of Vivado instances using Docker and CRIU [1] is experimental. The experiments in [10] show that it takes about 9 seconds to checkpoint and restore a container with 1GB memory. These features are under development by the communities of Linux containers and we can expect a runtime improvement in the near future.

4.2 Distributed Detailed Placement

The distributed detailed placement algorithm is written in Python, and is executed by the command "spark-submit –executor-memory 4G dplace.py".

The runtime results of the distributed detailed placement are listed in Table 3, and the quality of wirelength improvement is similar to the sequential version. The results show great potentials in speedup in the distributed computing.

Table 3: Runtime of distributed detailed placement with different number of parallel tiles

test case	runtime (min)	
	1 tile	48 tiles
SLAM_spheric	36	18
bitcoin_miner	51	20
guassianblur_d1	611	25

5. CHALLENGES AND OPPORTUNITIES

In the previous sections, we demonstrate a proof-of-concept for a distributed EDA framework to scale out the physical design algorithms. In this section, we highlight the challenges and opportunities to attract the efforts of the physical design community to design and develop new distributed algorithms.

The following are the necessary components to make the distributed EDA framework for scalable physical design generic and useful.

Algorithmic kernels. These algorithmic kernels are preferred to be either a map operator in the MapReduce distributed computing paradigm for the partitioned design data, or a composed series of MapReduce operations. There have already been some widely-used physical design tools developed. FLUTE [11] is one of such examples, which is adopted by most global routers in the ISPD routing contests [26, 25] to construct rectilinear Steiner minimal trees for multi-pin nets. The algorithmic kernels are analogous to the cognitive computing services for language, speech, vision and data on IBM Bluemix [3]. It is necessary and challenging to build and maintain a library for such algorithmic kernels.

Standard interfaces. The standard interfaces include the ones connecting some algorithmic kernels to form a complete EDA algorithm, as well as the ones connecting existing EDA platforms and the distributed computing framework. Though the format of raw design data will keep changing due to new design rules and new objectives, it is feasible to provide a conversion operator as an algorithmic kernel for backward compatibility. The relatively stable standard interfaces across different EDA platforms and raw design data will extend the lifetime of an algorithmic kernel and help the growing of the algorithmic library. OpenAccess [18] sets a good example of an open-source data model and API for physical design. Given the necessity of a distributed computing framework to scale out physical design, it is about time to re-define a new set of standard interfaces in such context.

Flow composition. The current implementation of OpenAccess only supports the flow composition by tool-by-tool inter-operation. Given the algorithmic kernels and standard interfaces, the distributed computing framework will be able to support both tool-by-tool inter-operation (macro-flow composition) and the connection of algorithmic kernels (micro-flow composition). The former one is conventional, and it will help the innovations in EDA design flow when there are sufficient amount of tools supported in the framework. The latter one is promising to keep up the innovations in EDA algorithms. For example, there have been a series of routibility-driven placement contests [33, 32, 36, 9]. Most of these algorithms share similar algorithmic kernels, and varies in some of these kernels and the detailed tuning of the flow. Such research activities can attract boarder attentions, if the existing kernels and flows can be reused; so that a group new to this area does not need to start from scratch but can focus on the innovation of the critical kernels (e.g., the routability estimator, the inflation strategy, the placement objective, etc.).

The distributed computing framework have potential benefits in the following aspects.

Scalability. There are extensive efforts to develop the distributed computing engines like Spark and Tachyon [22], which are motivated by big data applications. The porting of EDA algorithms on new distributed engines can take advantage of such progress in the big data ecosystem, and keep up with the scaling of design complexity in the long run. Though there are results [29] showing that Spark is one order of magnitude slower than MPI for specific data sets, it has a data management infrastructure better in handling node failure and data replication. Moreover, these emerging distributed engines lower the barrier to get involve with distributed computing, and bring more EDA experts to implement algorithmic kernels and flows in the framework.

Reproducible results. It is hopefully the algorithmic kernels and flows can be encapsulated with its dependent dynamic linking libraries using the Linux container technologies like Docker. In this way, they are executable in any mainstream Linux clusters without configuration or compilation issues and generate reproducible results. There is also an opportunity to provide "cloud" services for such distributed EDA framework, so that the design data, benchmarks and design flows can be shared in the community similar to GitHub [2]. Moreover, when the flows are executed in the cloud by the masses on some existing benchmarks, it is possible to apply the idea of data deduplication to skip the execution of the first few stages if a flow has been executed before. It will save runtime for the development of late-stage physical design algorithms.

Collaborative innovation. The collaborative innovation comes with the standard interfaces and execution of the algorithmic kernels and flows in the distributed computing framework. And it is promising to bridge the gap between industry and academia. The opportunity of "cloud" services to share design data, benchmarks and design flows is a way to boost collaborations. On one hand, when the results of the algorithmic kernels and a design flow from academia are reproducible, it will be easier for the industry to try the flow and get direct access to the new ideas from academia. On the other hand, since the framework is compatible with existing EDA platforms, the industry can set up an evaluation system like ImageNet [20] for academia to submit their tools and flows in an executable form, with industry-grade design data without worrying about sensitive data leakage.

Education. The distributed computing framework creates opportunities for instructors to provide a design flow to students in a quick way. The students are not only able to see an example of the whole design flow (the highest-level of a composed flow) conveniently, but will also be much easier than nowadays to replace a design step with their own algorithm. The lower barrier to getting familiar with design flows and experiment on EDA algorithms is promising to attract more students understand the EDA field.

6. CONCLUSION

In this paper, we propose a distributed computing framework for extreme-scale EDA algorithms development. Furthermore, we outline the challenges and opportunities of how such framework will benefit the innovations in both EDA algorithms and flows, as well as the collaboration between industry and academia.

Specifically, our proposed framework enables the design and development of new distributed EDA algorithms while being compatible with commercial EDA design platforms. This framework uses TCL language to interact with existing EDA platforms, and converts the design information to a distributed in-memory data structure in Spark. The current TCL support in existing EDA platforms is mainly designed for customized flows and lightweight customized tools. As a result, we observe that the extraction of the complete design information using TCL takes a significant amount of time. And this will cancel out the speedup from the distributed EDA algorithms in our proposed framework according to Amdahl's law. To solve this issue, we start multiple instances to open the same design in multiple server nodes, and extract the design data in a distributed way. The design data is stored in memory for further processing in the distributed computing engine of Spark. To demonstrate the proposed framework, we implement a distributed detailed placement algorithm and show a substantial speedup.

In the end, we summarize the challenges and opportunities to scale out physical design algorithms in a distributed framework. It is promising that such framework will accelerate the innovations in both large-scale EDA algorithms as well as new EDA design flows.

7. ACKNOWLEDGMENTS

This work is partly supported by National Natural Science Foundation of China (NSFC) Grant 61202073, Research Fund for the Doctoral Program of Higher Education of China (MoE/RFDP) Grant 20120001120124, and Beijing Natural Science Foundation (BJNSF) Grant 4142022.

8. REFERENCES

[1] CRIU, a project to implement checkpoint/restore functionality for Linux in userspace. http://www.criu.org/. [Online; accessed Feb 5, 2016].

[2] GitHub. https://github.com/. [Online; accessed Feb 5, 2016].

[3] IBM Watson Developer Cloud. http://www.ibm.com/smarterplanet/us/en/ibmwatson/developercloud/. [Online; accessed Feb 5, 2016].

[4] What is Docker? https://www.docker.com/what-docker. [Online; accessed Feb 5, 2016].

[5] EMC Isilon Storage Best Practices for Electronic Design Automation. Technical Report H11909, EMC Corporation, 2013.

[6] EMC Isilon NAS: Performance at Scale for Electronic Design Automation. Technical Report H13233.1, EMC Corporation, 2014.

[7] systemvision.com: A Cloud-based Engineering Community for System Modeling & Design. Technical Report MGC 04-15 1033380-w, Mentor Graphics Corporation, 2015.

[8] R. I. Bahar, A. K. Jones, S. Katkoori, P. H. Madden, D. Marculescu, and I. L. Markov. Workshops on Extreme Scale Design Automation (ESDA) Challenges and Opportunities for 2025 and Beyond. Technical report, 2014.

[9] I. S. Bustany, D. Chinnery, J. R. Shinnerl, and V. Yutsis. ISPD 2015 Benchmarks with Fence Regions and Routing Blockages for Detailed-Routing-Driven Placement. In *Proceedings of the 2015 Symposium on International Symposium on Physical Design (ISPD'15)*, pages 157–164, New York, New York, USA, 2015.

[10] Y. Chen. Checkpoint and Restore of Micro-service in Docker Containers. In *Proceedings of the 3rd International Conference on Mechatronics and Industrial Informatics*, number Icmii, pages 915–918, Paris, France, 2015. Atlantis Press.

[11] C. Chu and Y. C. Wong. FLUTE: Fast lookup table based rectilinear steiner minimal tree algorithm for VLSI design. *IEEE Transactions on Computer-Aided Design of Integrated Circuits and Systems*, 27(1):70–83, 2008.

[12] J. Cong and Min Xie. A Robust Mixed-Size Legalization and Detailed Placement Algorithm. *IEEE Transactions on Computer-Aided Design of Integrated Circuits and Systems*, 27(8):1349–1362, 2008.

[13] J. Dean and S. Ghemawat. MapReduce: Simplified Data Processing on Large Clusters. In *Proceedings of the 6th Conference on Symposium on Opearting Systems Design & Implementation - Volume 6*, OSDI'04, page 10, Berkeley, CA, USA, 2004.

[14] L. Drenan. Cadence Hosted Design Solutions: Software-as-a-service capability for the semiconductor industry. Technical Report 702 6/13 SA/DM/PDF, Cadence Design Systems, 2013.

[15] W. Felter, A. Ferreira, R. Rajamony, and J. Rubio. An updated performance comparison of virtual machines and Linux containers. Technical Report RC25482 (AUS1407-001), IBM Research, 2014.

[16] J. Friesen. An approach for better debuggability of Tcl- driven EDA methodologies. In *CDNLive Silicon Valley 2015*, 2015.

[17] W. Gropp, E. Lusk, N. Doss, and A. Skjellum. A high-performance, portable implementation of the MPI message passing interface standard. *Parallel Computing*, 22(6):789–828, 1996.

[18] M. Guiney and E. Leavitt. An introduction to openaccess an open source data model and API for IC design. In *Proceedings of the Asia and South Pacific Conference on Design Automation (ASP-DAC'06).*, pages 434–436, 2006.

[19] D. Hsu. EDA in the Clouds: Myth Busting. *Synopsys Insight*, 2011.

[20] Jia Deng, Wei Dong, R. Socher, Li-Jia Li, Kai Li, and Li Fei-Fei. ImageNet: A large-scale hierarchical image database. In *Proceedings of the 2009 IEEE Conference on Computer Vision and Pattern Recognition (CVPR'09)*, pages 248–255, 2009.

[21] R. C. Johnson. IBM Renting Its EDA Tools, 2015.

[22] H. Li, A. Ghodsi, M. Zaharia, S. Shenker, and I. Stoica. Tachyon: Reliable, Memory Speed Storage for Cluster Computing Frameworks. In *Proceedings of the ACM Symposium on Cloud Computing (SOCC'14)*, pages 1–15, New York, New York, USA, 2014.

[23] Min Pan, N. Viswanathan, and C. Chu. An efficient and effective detailed placement algorithm. In *Proceedings of the IEEE/ACM International Conference on Computer-Aided Design (ICCAD'05)*, pages 48–55, 2005.

[24] K. E. Murray, S. Whitty, S. Liu, J. Luu, and V. Betz. Timing-Driven Titan: Enabling Large Benchmarks and Exploring the Gap between Academic and Commercial CAD. *ACM Transactions on Reconfigurable Technology and Systems*, 8(2):1–18, 2015.

[25] G.-J. Nam, C. Sze, and M. Yildiz. The ISPD global routing benchmark suite. In *Proceedings of the 2008 international symposium on Physical design (ISPD'08)*, page 156, New York, New York, USA, 2008.

[26] G.-J. Nam, M. Yildiz, D. Z. Pan, and P. H. Madden.

ISPD placement contest updates and ISPD 2007 global routing contest. In *Proceedings of the 2007 international symposium on Physical design (ISPD'07)*, page 167, New York, New York, USA, 2007.

[27] A. Ng and I. Markov. Toward Quality EDA Tools and Tool Flows Through High-Performance Computing. In *Proceedings of the Sixth International Symposium on Quality of Electronic Design (ISQED'05)*, pages 22–27, 2005.

[28] S. Popovych, H.-H. Lai, C.-M. Wang, Y.-L. Li, W.-H. Liu, and T.-C. Wang. Density-aware Detailed Placement with Instant Legalization. In *Proceedings of the 51st Annual Design Automation Conference on Design Automation Conference (DAC'14)*, pages 1–6, New York, New York, USA, 2014.

[29] J. L. Reyes-Ortiz, L. Oneto, and D. Anguita. Big Data Analytics in the Cloud: Spark on Hadoop vs MPI/OpenMP on Beowulf. *Procedia Computer Science*, 53(1):121–130, 2015.

[30] L. Stok. The Next 25 Years in EDA: A Cloudy Future? *IEEE Design & Test*, 31(2):40–46, 2014.

[31] M. Tessel, M. Crosby, and D. Mónica. Full Sail Ahead: What's Next For Container Technology. In *LinuxCon + CloudOpen + ContainerCon NA 2015*, 2015.

[32] N. Viswanathan, C. Alpert, C. Sze, Z. Li, and Y. Wei. The DAC 2012 routability-driven placement contest and benchmark suite. In *Proceedings of the 49th Annual Design Automation Conference (DAC'12)*, page 774, New York, New York, USA, 2012.

[33] N. Viswanathan, C. J. Alpert, C. Sze, Z. Li, G.-J. Nam, and J. A. Roy. The ISPD-2011 routability-driven placement contest and benchmark suite. In *Proceedings of the 2011 international symposium on Physical design (ISPD'11)*, page 141, 2011.

[34] T. White. *Hadoop: The Definitive Guide*. O'Reilly Media, 4th editio edition, 2015.

[35] L. Wu. Accelerating Physical Design Flow in Laker with TCL Applications and Third Party Tool Integration. In *SNUG Taiwan 2015*, 2015.

[36] V. Yutsis, I. S. Bustany, D. Chinnery, J. R. Shinnerl, and W.-H. Liu. ISPD 2014 benchmarks with sub-45nm technology rules for detailed-routing-driven placement. In *Proceedings of the 2014 on International symposium on physical design (ISPD'14)*, pages 161–168, New York, New York, USA, 2014.

[37] M. Zaharia, M. Chowdhury, T. Das, A. Dave, J. Ma, M. McCauly, M. J. Franklin, S. Shenker, and I. Stoica. Resilient Distributed Datasets: A Fault-Tolerant Abstraction for In-Memory Cluster Computing. In *Proceedings of the 9th USENIX Symposium on Networked Systems Design and Implementation (NSDI'12)*, pages 15–28, San Jose, CA, 2012.

Routability-Driven FPGA Placement Contest

Stephen Yang, Aman Gayasen, Chandra Mulpuri, Sainath Reddy, Rajat Aggarwal
Xilinx Inc.
2100 Logic Drive
San Jose, CA 95124
stepheny,amang,chandim,sainath,rajata@xilinx.com

ABSTRACT

The advances of FPGA technology and increasing size of FPGA designs pose great challenges on FPGA design tools. Deep research on FPGA physical design problems is paramount to improve industrial tools. This contest is the first ISPD contest on FPGA CAD tools. Routability driven FPGA placement, in context of large designs modern FPGA architecture, is one of the best topics to start the effort.

KEYWORDS

FPGA; Placement; Routability; Congestion; Contest

1. INTRODUCTION

FPGA (Field Programmable Gate Array) placement is a classic problem in Electronic Design Automation field. It is one of the key steps in FPGA design flow, directly impacting the completion of the design flow and the performance of the resulting FPGA. With the advances of FPGA hardware technology and wide spreading applications, there are more and more challenges imposed on FPGA placement problem [1].

In year 2005, ISPD hold the first placement contest. 10 teams from worldwide universities research groups participated and competed for the prizes. Since then ISPD has hold 11 different contests, topics covering placement, global/detail routing, gate sizing and clock tree synthesis. These contests greatly stimulated academic research activities. A number of high-quality academic tools with novel ideas and sophisticated algorithms have presented in the past decade.

Yet ISPD has never done any CAD contest on FPGA related problems. Given the difficult and unique challenges, FPGA placement problem serves as a perfect topic for ISPD contest. This contest attracts both classical FPGA placement research groups, as well as standard-cell/mixed-size placement research groups. The former groups have deep understanding on FPGA architecture and FPGA specific algorithms like packing, timing-driven placement and graph routing. The latter groups were used to face large scale placement problem, dealing with hundreds of thousands or even millions of movable objects. Attacking FPGA problem from two different angles can greatly move academic

research forward and lead to effective and efficient FPGA oriented algorithms.

As the world's leading provider of FPGAs, Xilinx Inc. took the responsibility to co-organize this FPGA placement contest. The contest benchmarks are based on industry leading 20nm Virtex UltraScale architecture. The size of the benchmarks reflects the typical modern high-end FPGA designs. The well-defined contest evaluation metrics have the key elements of FPGA design tool: wirelength, routability and runtime are all considered. We believe that this first FPGA placement contest will serve as the beginning of the prosperous research of FPGA physical design, attracting more young talents into the challenging and exciting EDA field.

2. BACKGROUND

There are many challenges in modern FPGA placement problem.

First, multiple objectives need to be considered during FPGA placement. Traditional FPGA placer took total wirelength as the main cost function. Nowadays, FPGA placer has to optimize the following objectives: wirelength, congestion, timing, power, utilization etc. Optimizing all the objectives at the same time is very hard, yet modern FPGA designs do need all of them to stay competitive.

Second, FPGA resource constraints have been the biggest challenge for FPGA placement. Various resources including LUT, flip flop, block RAM, DSP, distributed RAM need to be placed at different sites on the device. Large unit resources like block RAM and DSP are discrete --- their available sites are scarce and are often far away from each other. Placer needs to handle the multi-resource problem in a smooth fashion to be able to achieve good results.

The next challenge is clock. Modern FPGAs have complex and sophisticated clocking architecture. Designs with many clocks can fall into hard dilemma: the placement without clock consideration will eventually failed in clock rule checking, whereas posing the clock constraints early greatly hurt the placement quality. Since the clocking architecture is unique on each FPGA family, there is no generic solution that can fit all situations.

The last but not least challenge is on tool runtime. FPGAs in many applications replaced ASIC because their ease of design and fast turn-around time. This poses great tool runtime requirement. Unlike ASIC tools that can run overnight or days to get the results, FPGA tools will be abandoned if they cannot complete most jobs in a couple of hours. The runtime for placer often needs to be within an hour. This is a very challenging goal considering the ever grown FPGA design size. The above runtime number is only for traditional FPGA designs. As FPGAs get used more and more as software develop platform (e.g., SDAccel from Xilinx), the runtime target is even higher.

ISPD'16, April 3–6, 2016, Santa Rosa, California, USA.
© 2016 ACM. ISBN 978-1-4503-4039-7/16/04…$15.00.
DOI: http://dx.doi.org/10.1145/2872334.2886419

In addition, many FPGA specific rules/constraints pose more restrictions on FPGA placement, including I/O placement, physical synthesis compatibility, data path, large modules like carry chain or cascaded BRAMs/DSPs, and processor area in some FPGA device.

3. FPGA ARCHITECTURE

Xilinx FPGAs [2], an example of which is illustrated in Figure 1, consist of an array of programmable blocks of different types, including general logic (CLB), memory (BRAM) and multiplier (DSP) blocks, surrounded by a programmable routing fabric (interconnect) that allows these blocks to be connected via horizontal and vertical routing channels. This array is surrounded by programmable input/output blocks (IO) that interface the chip to the outside world.

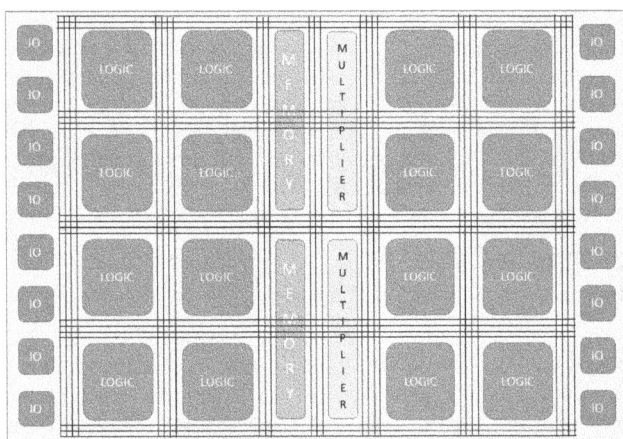

Figure 1. Example of Xilinx FPGA Architecture

This array has a configuration memory (SRAM) beneath it, which, when loaded with appropriate bits, programs the blocks and the interconnects to behave a certain way, as illustrated in Figure 2.

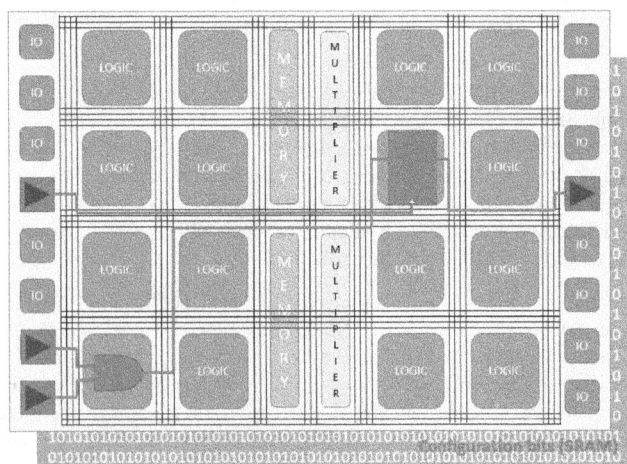

Figure 2. Example of Programming the Xilinx FPGA

Given a logic design that the user wants to implement on the FPGA, the Xilinx Implementation Tool flow (Vivado) converts the design into the appropriate set of configuration bits (Bitstream) which is loaded onto the SRAM to make the FPGA behave as the design. There are usually multiple steps involved in this tool flow, the main ones being, Synthesis, Placement, Routing, and Bitstream generation. Synthesis tool infers the design logic in terms of the logic blocks available within the FPGA. Placement tool places these inferred logic blocks on the various sites of physical logic blocks present in the FPGA. Routing tool connects up the pins of these physical logic blocks using the programmable interconnect routing structures in the FPGA. Bitstream generation tool then proceeds to generate the set of configuration bits that program these logic blocks and interconnect routing structures to behave as the design intended.

The general logic block (also referred to as the configurable logic block, or CLB), is the main resource for implementing general-purpose combinatorial and sequential circuits. The CLB is made up of the logic elements themselves, which are grouped together into a slice. These logic elements are of the type lookup tables (LUTs) or sequential elements (FFs). Each CLB contains one slice. Each slice provides sixteen LUTs and sixteen flip-flops. The slices and their CLBs are arranged in columns throughout the device. There are, however, certain restrictions pertaining to how these LUTs and FFs can be used within each slice. These are explained in detail in the "Placement Evaluation Flow" section under "Legalization Rules" subsection.

In the specific Xilinx FPGA we're targeting for this contest, the XCVU095-ffva2104-es2 device, we have 67,200 CLB/SLICE locations, 880 usable IO locations, 770 DSP locations, and 1730 BRAM locations. More information on this device, and the architecture in general, can be obtained from [5].

4. BENCHMARKS

The benchmarks for ISPD 2016 placement contest have been generated using an internal netlist-generation tool based on Generate NetList (Gnl). The tool allows us to create netlists of different placement and routing complexities by varying the number of components and their interconnection. Additionally, it provides control over the type of components (primitives) used in the netlist. For ISPD benchmarks, we have restricted the primitives to be Look-Up-Tables (LUTs), Flip-Flops (FFs), DSP blocks (DSPs), and Block RAMs (BRAMs). The target device is xcvu095, part of the Virtex UltraScale [3] family.

The following properties of the netlist were varied among the ISPD benchmarks.

1) Number of instances. We have created benchmarks that utilize 55% to 83% of the LUTs available. We have also varied the number of DSPs, BRAMs, and FFs to create medium to highly utilized designs.

2) Rent exponent. Interconnection complexity has been varied by creating netlists of different Rent exponents. This is important to test the routability aspect of the placement solution.

3) Number of resets. FPGA architecture limits the number of unique reset nets per Slice. Hence, by varying the number of resets we test how well the placer can support such restrictions.

Table 1 captures the characteristics of the benchmarks.

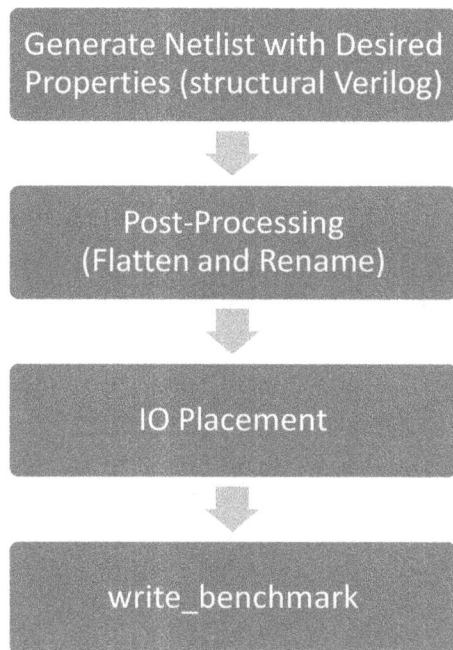

Figure 3. Benchmark Generation Flow

Figure 3 explains the flow used for generating these benchmarks. First, we generate structural Verilog using our netlist-generation tool. The input to this tool is a configuration file, which specifies the desired parameters in the netlist. The structural Verilog file is post-processed to create a flattened design, without any hierarchies. Along with dissolving hierarchies, we also rename the instances and nets in this step. Next, we run Vivado placer to place IO ports of the design. Finally, we write the benchmark in Bookshelf format. The Bookshelf format list the instances in the design in a ".nodes" file and their interconnection in a ".nets" file. It also writes IO placement in a ".pl" file. Library cells are separately listed in a "*.lib" file.

5. PLACEMENT EVALUATION
5.1 Placement Interface
Contestants are expected to write the output of their placement tool in a specific (.pl) file format. Placer's output placement file should contain locations of all the instances in the design. The location of an instance has three fields: x-coord, y-coord (to determine the SITE) and BEL (index within the SITE). Figure 4 shows the BEL number for LUTs/FFs placed inside a SLICE SITE.

For BRAM and DSP instances, since there are no BELs within a SITE, the BEL index remains 0.

The following is a snippet of a placement file:

inst_1000 165 161 3	# (this instance is a LUT)
inst_1003 165 161 12	# (this instance is a FF)
inst_1100 29 0 0	# (this instance is a DSP)
inst_1200 34 0 0	# (this instance is a BRAM)

The placement output (.pl) file, will be given as an input to Xilinx Vivado tool using the flow.tcl file, which is available as part of each benchmarks archive. Vivado Placer will then read these instance placements, and check for legal placement on every

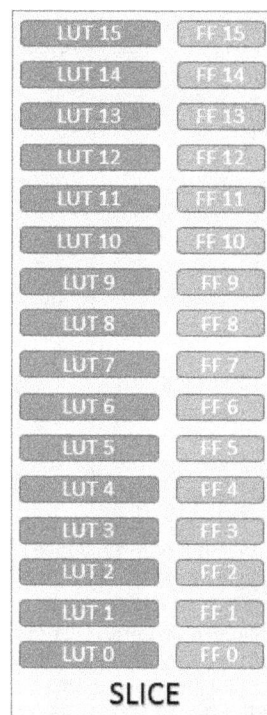

Figure 4. BEL offsets within a SLICE

instance. In case of illegal placement, Vivado Placer will error out with a reason behind the illegality for each instance. If the placement is legal, Vivado router starts and completes routing, or report unroutable design. If routing completes successfully, the following message indicates total routed wirelength: "Total Routed Wirelength: xxxxx (Vertical xxxx, Horizontal xxxx)". In case of unroutable placement, the following message shows up: "CRITICAL WARNING: [Route 35-162] xxxx signals failed to route due to routing congestion."

5.2 Legalization Rules
Each SLICE site provides sixteen LUTs and sixteen FFs. There are, however, certain restrictions pertaining to how these LUTs and FFs can be used within each SLICE.

Using LUTs in a SLICE:

- The 16 LUTs within SLICE are conceptual LUTs that can only be fully used under certain conditions:
- When implementing a 6-input LUT with one output, one can only use LUT 1 (leaving LUT 0 unused) or LUT 3 (leaving LUT 2 unused) or ... or LUT 15 (leaving LUT 14 unused)
- When implementing two 5-input LUTs with separate outputs but common inputs, one can use {LUT 0, LUT 1} or {LUT 2, LUT 3} or ... or {LUT 14, LUT 15}
- The above rule of coming LUTs with separate outputs but common inputs, holds good for 5-input LUTs (as mentioned above) or fewer input LUTs as well
- When implementing two 3-input (or fewer input) LUTs together (irrespective of common inputs), one can use {LUT 0, LUT 1} or {LUT 2, LUT 3} or ... or {LUT 14, LUT 15}

Using FFs in a SLICE:

- There are 16 FFs per SLICE (two per LUT pair), and all can be used fully under certain conditions:
- All FFs can take independent inputs from outside the SLICE, or outputs of their corresponding LUT pair (FF 0 can take LUT 0 or LUT 1 output as input, ..., FF 15 can take LUT 14 or LUT 15 output as input)
- All can be configured as either edge-triggered D-type flip-flops or level-sensitive latches. The latch option is by top or bottom half of the SLICE (0 to 7, and 8 to 15). If the latch option is selected on a FF, all eight FFs in that half must be either used as latches or left unused. When configured as a latch, the latch is transparent when the clock input (CLK) is high.
- There are two clock inputs (CLK) and two set/reset inputs (SR) to every SLICE for the FFs. Each clock or set/reset input is dedicated to eight of the sixteen FFs, split by top and bottom halves (0 to 7, and 8 to 15). FF pairs ({0,1} or {2,3} or ... or {14,15}) share the same clock and set/reset signals. The clock and set/reset signals have programmable polarity at their slice inputs, allowing any inversion to be automatically absorbed into the CLB.
- There are four clock enables (CE) per SLICE. The clock enables are split both by top and bottom halves, and by the two FFs per LUT-pair. Thus, the CEs are independent for: {FF 0, FF 2, FF 4, FF 6}, {FF 1, FF 3, FF 5, FF 7}, {FF 8, FF 10, FF 12, FF 14}, {FF 9, FF 11, FF 13, FF 15}. When one storage element has CE enabled, the other three storage elements in the group must also have CE enabled. The CE is always active High at the slice, but can be inverted in the source logic.
- The two SR set/reset inputs to a SLICE can be programmed to be synchronous or asynchronous. The set/reset signal can be programmed to be a set or reset, but not both, for any individual FF. The configuration options for the SR set and reset functionality of a register or latch are: No set or reset, Synchronous set (FDSE primitive), Synchronous reset (FDRE primitive), Asynchronous set (preset) (FDPE primitive), Asynchronous reset (clear) (FDCE primitive). The SR set/reset input can be ignored for groups of four flip-flops (the same groups as controlled by the CE inputs). When one FF has SR enabled, the other three FFs in the group must also have SR enabled.
- The choice of set or reset can be controlled individually for each FF in a SLICE. The choice of synchronous (SYNC) or asynchronous (ASYNC) set/reset (SYNC_ATTR) is controlled in groups of eight FFs, individually for the two separate SR inputs.

Some of these FF Packing rules are illustrated in Figure 5.

More information on the CLB composition can be obtained from [4].

5.3 Evaluation Metrics

- For each design in the benchmark suite, the placers will be ranked based on the contest evaluation metric. The final rank for a placer will be the sum of the individual ranks on all the circuits. The placer with the smallest total rank wins the contest.
- The placement runtime must be 12 hours or shorter.
- The placement must be legal (legalization rules are described in the previous section).

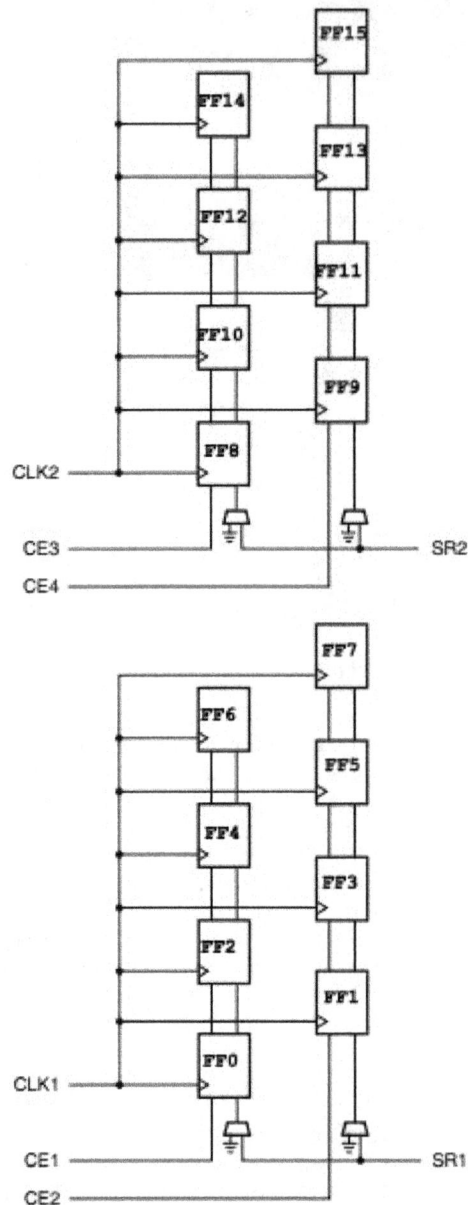

Figure 5. Flip Flop control signals connectivity within a SLICE

- The placement has to be routed by Vivado router, and the router has to complete the job within 12 hours. Routing is regarded as failed if it takes more than 12 hours to complete.
- PlacementScore=RoutedWirelength*(1 + Runtime_Factor)
  - Vivado router reports total routed wirelength. This is the base of the score.
  - Total placement and routing runtime will be used in computing P&R_Runtime_Factor;
  - Runtime_Factor= -(Runtime - Median_Runtime) / 10.0
  - There is 1% scaling factor for every 10% runtime reduction/addition against the median runtime of all place+route solutions;
  - Runtime factor is between -10% and +10%

o Although runtime is a part of the contest metric, the "Total Routed Wirelength" will be the dominant component. In other words, a placer will not get a significant advantage if it is extremely fast compared to the median runtime of all the placers participating in the contest.

- The failed place/route job will get the lowest rank on this design. In the presence of multiple failures, the break-tie factors are: placer failure or router failure, router runtime, number of unrouted nets, number of illegal placements.

6. ACKNOWLEDGMENTS

The authors would like to thank Dr. Ismail Bustany and Dr. Steven Li for their valuable suggestions on the contest details.

7. REFERENCES

[1] R. Aggarwal, 2014. *FPGA Place and Route Challenges*. In Proc. of International Symposium on Physical Design.

[2] Xilinx, "UltraScale Architecture", http://www.xilinx.com/products/technology/ultrascale.html

[3] Xilinx, "Virtex UltraScale FPGAs", http://www.xilinx.com/publications/prod_mktg/ultrascalevirt ex-product-table

[4] Xilinx, "UltraScale Architecture Configurable Logic Block User Guide", http://www.xilinx.com/support/documentation/user_guides/u g574-ultrascale-clb.pdf

[5] Xilinx, "UltraScale Architecture and Product Overview", http://www.xilinx.com/support/documentation/data_sheets/ds 890-ultrascale-overview.pdf

[6] GNL: http://users.elis.ugent.be/~dstrooba/gnl/

Design	#LUTs	#FFs	#BRAMs	#DSPs	#I/O	#Control Sets	Rent exponent
Design1	300K (55%)	241K (22%)	400 (23%)	200 (26%)	453 (54%)	651	0.5
Design2	300K (55%)	241K (22%)	400 (23%)	200 (26%)	453 (54%)	651	0.6
Design3	350K (65%)	259K (24%)	800 (46%)	300 (39%)	533 (64%)	1271	0.7
Design4	400K (74%)	304K (28%)	800 (46%)	500 (65%)	533 (64%)	1271	0.6
Design5	400K (74%)	292K (27%)	800 (46%)	500 (65%)	533 (64%)	1271	0.7
Design6	450K (83%)	338K (31%)	1000 (58%)	400 (52%)	603 (72%)	2091	0.55
Design7	450K (83%)	339K (31%)	1000 (58%)	400 (52%)	603 (72%)	2091	0.65

Table 1. Benchmark statistics

*Number in parenthesis indicates the utilization as percentage of available resources in the FPGA [6]

Generating Routing-Driven Power Distribution Networks with Machine-Learning Technique

Wen-Hsiang Chang
o0000032@yahoo.com.tw

Li-De Chen
mark920435@livemail.tw

Chien-Hsueh Lin
c871111116.eecs99@nctu.edu.tw

Szu-Pang Mu
genius548@gmail.com

Mango C.-T. Chao
mango@faculty.nctu.edu.tw

Dept. of Electronics Engineering & Institute of Electronics, National Chiao-Tung University, Hsinchu, Taiwan

Cheng-Hong Tsai
jhtsai@globalunichip.com

Yen-Chih Chiu
yc.chiu@globalunichip.com

Global Unichip Corporation(GUC), Hsinchu, Taiwan

ABSTRACT

As technology node keeps scaling and design complexity keeps increasing, power distribution networks (PDNs) require more routing resource to meet IR-drop and EM constraints. This paper presents a design flow to generate a PDN that can result in minimal overhead for the routing of the underlying standard cells while satisfying both IR-drop and EM constraints based on a given cell placement. The design flow relies on a machine-learning model to quickly predict the total wire length of global route associated with a given PDN configuration in order to speed up the search process. The experimental results based on various 28nm industrial block designs have demonstrated the accuracy of the learned model for predicting the routing cost and the effectiveness of the proposed framework for reducing the routing cost of the final PDN.

1. INTRODUCTION

Building a power distribution network (*PDN*) for advanced ICs needs to meet two main constraints: the IR-drop constraint and the electro-migration (*EM*) constraint, associated with the circuit performance and the circuit reliability, respectively. The IR-drop constraint defines the maximum acceptable IR-drop between the power sources and the underlying cells induced by the PDN while the EM constraint defines the maximum acceptable current density on the PDN. As the process technologies keep moving forward, meeting both constraints requires even higher routing resource than before due to the smaller tolerable noise margin (resulting from the aggressive scaling of support voltage) and the higher current density (resulting from the faster operating frequency and smaller transistor dimensions). Such routing resource occupied by PDNs may interfere the routing

ISPD'16, April 03-06, 2016, Santa Rosa, CA, USA

© 2016 ACM. ISBN 978-1-4503-4039-7/16/04...$15.00

DOI: http://dx.doi.org/10.1145/2872334.2872353

of underlying standard cells and increase the overall routing overhead. Therefore, to design a routing-friendly PDN under both IR-drop and EM constraints can further speed up the design closure at the physical-design stage.

One important tool for PDN design is to estimate the worst-case IR-drop and EM of a given PDN. Once the current load of each node at the PDN is given, the IR-drop of each node can be computed by solving the linear system of the conductance matrix, such a process is called the modified nodal analysis (*MNA*). Since the size of the conductance matrix is $N^2 \times N^2$ for a $N \times N$ power mesh, performing MNA can take long time. Several techniques such as [1] [2] [3] [4] [5] [6] were proposed to speed up MNA by random-walk method [1] [2], mixed solver [3], preconditioned krylov-subspace iterative method [4] or utilizing the locality of the PDN [5] [6]. A more aggressive line to speed up the IR-drop analysis is to utilize some simplified equations to estimate the worst-case IR-drop by assuming power sources, uniform grid and uniform current-load distribution [7] [8] [9] [10] [11]. However, these simplified estimations can only provide a loose bound of the worst-case IR-drop and hence usually lead to significant over-design for the targeted PDN or multiple rounds of redesign.

In conventional design flow, PDNs are built before placement of standard cells. At this design stage, [8] [9] attempted to minimize IR-drop (and/or EM) based on a given total metal area of the PDN while [10] [11] attempted to minimize the total metal area of the PDN based on a given IR-drop (and/or EM) constraint, by using different number of power stripes and different stripe widths with uniform or non-uniform power stripes. However, the current load at this design stage is assumed to be uniformly distributed over the targeted PDN, which can be significantly different from the real current-load distribution after placement. As a result, the PDN still needs to be redesigned after placement.

Another research line focuses on optimizing PDNs based on given placement of standard cells. At this design stage, [12] [13] [14] [15] [16] attempted to minimize the total metal area of the PDN based on a given IR-drop (and/or EM) constraint by using different number of power stripes and different stripe widths with non-uniform power stripes. As opposed to building PDNs before placement, building PDNs after placement can estimate its IR-drop and EM with a current-load distribution closer to the sign-off condition, and hence the optimality of the PDN obtained at this design stage can sustain.

No matter at which design stage a PDN is built, almost all previous works utilized the total metal area of a PDN as the only routing-cost index to measure a PDN's impact on the underlying routing. However, such a routing-cost index can only reflect the amount of metal occupied by a PDN, not directly proportional to the degree of how the PDN affects the final underlying routing. [7] introduced the idea of using the number of the available routing tracks left by the PDN as the routing-cost index. Unfortunately, this index still cannot directly translate to the result of global route or detail route.

In this paper, we develop an automatic design flow to generate an optimal PDN that can minimize the resulting total wire length of global route (and in turn detail route as well) while satisfying both IR-drop and EM constraints for a targeted block design with a fixed placement. In this design flow, a machine-learning model is used to efficiently predict the total wire length of global route associated with a given PDN configuration based on the given placement. This routing-cost model is learned from the previous global-route results of various block designs and various PDN configurations. With the learned model, we can iteratively modify the PDN configuration while effectively and efficiently estimating its routing cost as well as its worst-case IR-drop and EM. The experiments based on various 28nm industrial block designs demonstrate not only the accuracy of the learned routing-cost models but also the effectiveness and efficiency of the proposed design flow on generating a routing friendly PDN.

2. TARGETED PDN DESIGN

2.1 Design Environment

First, PDNs in our design flow are built after the placement of the block design is finished. Therefore, a PDN should be designed to optimize the routing based on the given placement. Second, we target only the PDNs with uniform power stripes, meaning that the stripe width and the pitch between two stripes are the same for a power layer. Third, the block designs used in paper are flip-chip designs, where power sources are evenly allocated to the top metal layer of a PDN. Fourth, we use Cadence Encounter [17] as our platform for performing all physical-design actions. A PDN is built by automatically generating its tcl script for Encounter.

2.2 Layer Structure of PDN

The process technology used in this paper is a 28nm technology with 8 metal layers, including 1 AP (aluminum-pad) layer at the 8th layer (Metal-8) and 1 low-sheet-resistance metal layer at the 7th layer (Metal-7). We use four metal layers including the AP layer, Metal-7, Metal-6 and Metal-1 to build a PDN. Figure 1 illustrates the layer structure of our targeted PDNs, which is a commonly used structure in practice. The AP layer is originally designed for RDL (redistribution layer) routing in flip chips and then become frequently used for building PDNs since RDL routing usually consumes only a small portion of the AP layer. The use of the AP layer can effectively reduce the IR-drop for

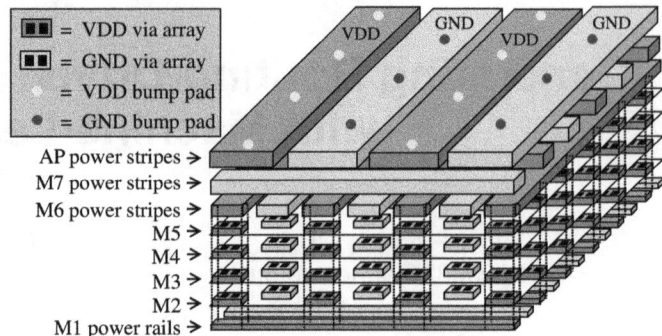

Figure 1: Layer structure of our targeted PDN.

a PDN due to the low sheet resistance and large maximum allowable metal width of the AP layer.

Metal-7 in this case is another metal layer mainly utilized for building PDNs due to its low sheet resistance. Metal-7 can also be used for the interconnect routing between different block designs but seldom used for the cell routing within the targeted block design. Therefore, designers usually set a ratio of Metal-7 that can be used for building the PDN. The rest of Metal-7 is reserved for the block-level interconnect routing. A similar usage ratio is set for the AP layer as well. As a result, the ratio of the AP layer and Metal-7 used for building a PDN is fixed but the stripe width and the number of stripes for the AP layer and Metal-7 can still be adjusted. At the same time, Metal-1 is used for building the power rails directly connected to the standard cells and hence its configuration in a PDN is fixed. Metal-6 is the layer that can be adjusted most flexibly for our PDNs. The usage ratio, the stripe width and the number of stripes can all be adjusted for improving routing cost, IR-drop or EM.

As shown in Figure 1, a via array is placed on the intersection of two stripes at different layers and the dimension of the via array is the same as that of the intersection. This high usage rate of vias on the intersection of two stripes can enhance the design reliability.

2.3 Irredundant Stripe Width

In our design flow, we use only the *irredundant stripe widths* when setting a stripe width of Metal-6, Metal-7 or the AP layer in a PDN configuration. The idea of irredundant stripe widths was proposed by [7]. Once an irredundant stripe width is used, its spacing to the next possible adjacent wire is exactly the minimum spacing defined in the library. Figure 2 illustrates two layout configurations of using a redundant stripe width and an irredundant stripe width, as shown in Figure 2(a) and Figure 2(b), respectively. In Figure 2, w_{ps} denotes the width of a power stripe and $S(w_{ps})$ denotes the minimum spacing between the power stripe and its adjacent wire allowed by the design rules, which is a function of the stripe's width represented by a table in the LEF file. RW denotes the width of an interconnect wire, which is a fixed value for a metal layer set in the APR tool and usually assigned to the minimum allowed width. P_{track} denotes the pitch between two routing tracks.

As Figure 2 shows, both PDN configurations occupy four routing tracks while the irredundant stripe width in Figure 2(b) is significantly larger than the redundant stripe width in Figure 2(a). It is because that the spacing between the power stripe and its adjacent wire in Figure 2(b) is ex-

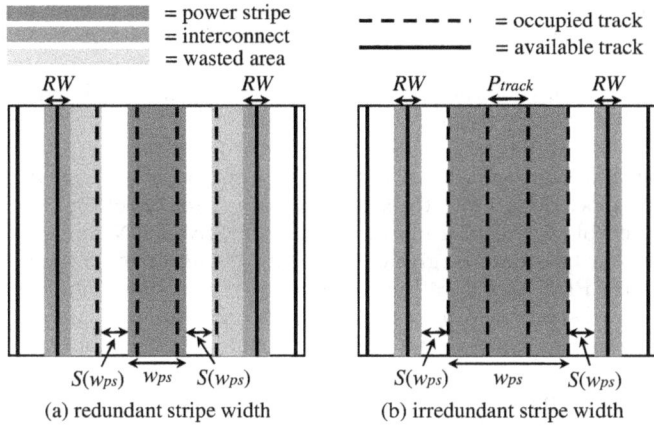

Figure 2: A redundant and irredundant stripe width using the same number of routing tracks.

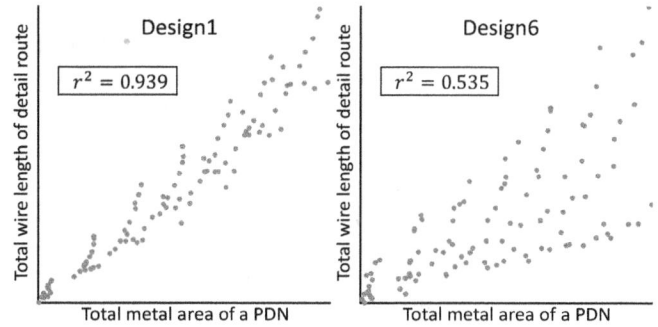

Figure 3: The total wire length of detail route versus the total metal area of a PDN for D1 and D6.

actly the minimum allowed spacing, and hence no space is wasted in between a power stripe and an interconnect wire. As a result, using irredundant stripe widths is always better than using other redundant stripe widths.

An irredundant stripe width w_{ps} can be computed by solving Equation 1, T_{ps} is the number of tracks occupied by the stripe. For example, in both Figure 2(a) and Figure 2(b), T_{ps} is equal to 4.

$$w_{ps} + 2S(w_{ps}) = (T_{ps} + 1) \times P_{track} - RW \qquad (1)$$

In other words, different metal layers can have different sets of irredundant stripe widths due to the spacing rules. For a given metal layer, different irredundant stripe widths can be computed by setting different value of T_{ps}. Note that the use of irredundant stripe width can not only provide more routing tracks with the same PDN metal usage but also reduce the solution space for setting the stripe widths in a routing-driven PDN configuration.

3. OUR MOTIVATION

Detail route is a time-consuming procedure in physical design. If we attempt to apply various PDN configurations based on a given placement and identify the one that can result in the least total wire length of detail route, we need a faster evaluation of routing cost than detail route. The total metal area of a PDN is a super fast approximation to correlate the routing cost imposed by a PDN, which is commonly used as the cost function to be minimized in the previous works of generating routing friendly PDNs [10] [11] [12] [13] [14] [15] [16]. Table 1 first lists the coefficient of determination (r^2) between the total metal area of a PDN and the total wire length of detail route resulting from the corresponding PDN for each of our 28nm industrial block designs, where 105 PDN configurations are sampled for each design. Figure 3 further plots the total wire length of detail route versus the total metal area of a

PDN for the designs with the highest and lowest r^2, i.e., D1 and D6, respectively.

As the result shows, the r^2 between these two features can be as low as 53.5%. More importantly, even for the design with the highest r^2 93.9%, still various PDNs with a smaller total metal area result in a larger total wire length of detail route than other PDNs (as shown in Figure 3). For the design with the lowest r^2 53.5%, the total metal area of a PDN can barely reflect the total wire length of detail route. These results demonstrate that the total metal area of a PDN is not an effective index to predict the total wire length of detail route. Using the total metal area of a PDN as a cost function for optimization can easily lead to a PDN that may generate a significantly larger total wire length of detail route than the optimal solution. Note that to obtain the above results are extremely timing consuming since we need to apply detail route for 105 different PDNs for each block design. The runtime for the largest block design is around 50 days. A strong computation farm is used to help us collect the detail-route result.

In practice, the result of global route is another index to correlate the result of detail route. Table 2 lists the coefficient of determination (r^2) between the total wire length of global route and the total wire length of detail route, where the average r^2 over the 8 designs is 99.2%. This result demonstrates that the total wire length of global route is indeed a more accurate and reliable feature to correlate the total wire length of detail route.

Table 2: r^2 between the total wire length of global route and the total wire length of detail route.

design	D1	D2	D3	D4	D5	D6	D7	D8	avg.
r^2	0.996	0.997	0.994	0.998	0.988	0.969	0.997	0.996	0.992

Even though global route is considered as a much shorter process than detail route, global route is still not fast enough to be applied to every possible PDN configuration for estimating its routing cost. Table 3 lists the average runtime of global route on each industrial block design, where the runtime for large block designs can be more than one

Table 1: r^2 between the total metal area of a PDN and the total wire length of detail route.

design	D1	D2	D3	D4	D5	D6	D7	D8	avg.
r^2	0.939	0.928	0.829	0.926	0.650	0.535	0.896	0.868	0.829

Table 3: Average runtime of global route.

design	D1	D2	D3	D4	D5	D6	D7	D8
runtime	44m	92m	36m	25m	18m	5m	61m	25m

hour. Note that for our targeted 28nm technology, there are more than 40 and 12 different irredundant stripe widths for Metal-6 and Metal-7, respectively. For Metal-6, the number of power stripes can range from 10 to 2000+ depending on the irredundant stripe width in use. The total possible PDN configurations can be easily more than hundreds or even thousands, meaning that applying global route to every possible PDN can take more than hundreds or thousands of hours for large block designs.

In this paper, our main idea is to collect the previous results of global route and then learn a model based on these previous results to quickly predict the result of global route for each untried PDN. In other words, we can replace the inefficient global route with a much faster learned routing-cost model during the search of the best routing-driven PDN. In the following section, we will introduce the machine learning techniques used in our framework for building the routing-cost model.

4. PREDICTING ROUTING COST WITH MACHINE LEARNING TECHNIQUES

4.1 Problem Formulation

The input of a model-fitting problem is a set of n training samples, where each training sample i has m *predictor features* (denoted as X_i) and one *response feature* (denoted as y_i). The objective is to express the response feature of a new test sample t (denoted as y_t') by a function of only the predictor features. For our routing-cost model, the response feature is the total wire length of global route. The predictor features are related to the properties of a PDN or the targeted block design. In our framework, we apply the Gaussian process regression [18] as our core machine-learning technique to learn the routing-cost model due to its ability of expressing a complex high dimensional function while providing stable prediction accuracy.

4.2 Generating Training Samples and Predictor Features

To create training samples for model fitting, we run total 50 times of global route based on different random placements and PDN configurations for each block design in our database. Each time the result of global route forms a training sample. Each training sample contains one response feature, the total wire length of global route, and several basic predictor features including the features of the PDN and the features of the block design and the placement.

The features of the PDN include the total metal usage of stripes per metal layer, the number of effective routing tracks occupied by a stripe (associated with stripe width), the number of stripes, the size of a via array and the number of via arrays. The features of the block design and the placement include the number of cells, the number of nets, the distribution of the number of terminals for a net, the total half perimeters of all nets and the number of available area for each layer (excluding the existing blockages). All the placement and global route are performed by Cadence Encounter [17].

Based on the above basic predictor features, we further create more new predictor features by taking the square or square root of a basic predictor feature or by multiplying or dividing two existing predictor features. The number of

those derived predictor features plus the original predictor features is around 16K. Then, the training samples with all the predictor features are the input of our regression problem. Note that the value of each predictor feature is normalized to the interval from 0.5 to 1.5.

When building a routing-cost model for a new targeted block design, we will use the training samples of each previous block design plus three extra training samples of the targeted block design using three representative PDN configurations based on the given placement. These three representative PDN configurations include (1) the smallest number of tracks occupied by a stripe and the highest total Metal-6 usage of stripes (set to 35%), (2) the largest number of tracks occupied by a stripe and the highest total metal usage of stripes and (3) the median number of tracks occupied by a stripe and the median total metal usage of stripes. The use of three training samples also means that the runtime of the proposed design flow needs to include the runtime of performing global route for these three training samples as well.

4.3 Gaussian Process Regression

Gaussian process regression [18] can be viewed as an extension of Bayesian linear regression [19], which provides more flexible class of models over functions and is considered as a more powerful regression technique than the traditional linear regression models. Before introducing Gaussian process regression, let's quickly review Bayesian linear regression.

For a standard linear regression problem $y = \mathbf{x}^T \mathbf{w}$, Bayesian linear regression is an effective regression method to derive the *maximum a posteriori* of $\mathbf{w}$. In Bayesian linear regression, the prior $\mathbf{w}$ is a Gaussian distribution $\mathcal{N}(\mathbf{0}, \Sigma_p)$, where Σ_p is the covariance of the $\mathbf{w}$. If the training data's predictor features $X = [\mathbf{x}_1, \mathbf{x}_1, ..., \mathbf{x}_n]^T$ and response feature $\mathbf{y}$ are given, the response feature y_* for a given $\mathbf{x}_*$ of a test data point is a Gaussian distribution with mean μ and variance σ^2 as shown in Equation 2 and Equation 3, respectively, where $A = \sigma_n^{-2} X^T X + \Sigma_p^{-1}$, and σ_n is the variance of the Gaussian noise.

$$\mu = \frac{1}{\sigma_n^2} \mathbf{x}_*^{\mathbf{T}} A^{-1} X \mathbf{y} \qquad (2)$$

$$\sigma^2 = \mathbf{x}_*^{\mathbf{T}} A^{-1} \mathbf{x}_* \qquad (3)$$

An potential problem of Bayesian linear regression shown in Equation 2 and Equation 3 is the limited expressiveness resulting from the use of only one dimension of $\mathbf{x}$. This problem can be overcome by projecting $\mathbf{x}$ into some high dimensional space using the basis function $\phi(\mathbf{x})$. After replacing X with $\phi(X)$ in Equation 2 and Equation 3, we can obtain Equation 4 and Equation 5, where $k(\mathbf{x}, \mathbf{x}') = \phi(\mathbf{x})^T \Sigma_p \phi(\mathbf{x}')$.

$$\mu = K_*(K + \sigma_n^2 I)^{-1} \mathbf{y} \qquad (4)$$

$$\sigma^2 = K_{**} - K_*(K + \sigma_n^2 I)^{-1} K_*^T \qquad (5)$$

$$K = \begin{bmatrix} k(\mathbf{x_1}, \mathbf{x_1}) & k(\mathbf{x_1}, \mathbf{x_2}) & \dots & k(\mathbf{x_1}, \mathbf{x_n}) \\ k(\mathbf{x_2}, \mathbf{x_1}) & k(\mathbf{x_2}, \mathbf{x_2}) & \dots & k(\mathbf{x_2}, \mathbf{x_n}) \\ \vdots & \vdots & \ddots & \vdots \\ k(\mathbf{x_n}, \mathbf{x_1}) & k(\mathbf{x_n}, \mathbf{x_2}) & \dots & k(\mathbf{x_n}, \mathbf{x_n}) \end{bmatrix}$$

$$K_* = \begin{bmatrix} k(\mathbf{x_*}, \mathbf{x_1}) & k(\mathbf{x_*}, \mathbf{x_2}) & \dots & k(\mathbf{x_*}, \mathbf{x_n}) \end{bmatrix}$$

$$K_{**} = k(\mathbf{x_*}, \mathbf{x_*})$$

For a given process $f(\mathbf{x})$ to be predicted, Gaussian process regression first models $f(\mathbf{x})$ as a Gaussian distribution with the mean function $m(\mathbf{x})$ and the covariance function $k(\mathbf{x}, \mathbf{x}')$ as defined in Equation 6.

$$f(\mathbf{x}) \sim \mathcal{N}(m(\mathbf{x}), k(\mathbf{x}, \mathbf{x}'))$$
$$= \mathcal{N}(\mathbb{E}[f(\mathbf{x})], \mathbb{E}[(f(\mathbf{x}) - m(\mathbf{x}))(f(\mathbf{x}') - m(\mathbf{x}'))]) \quad (6)$$

Due to the consistency property of Gaussian process regression, any finite number of Gaussian distributions have a joint Gaussian distribution. Given training data X and a test data point $\mathbf{x}_*$, the training response feature $\mathbf{y}$ and the predictive response feature y_* (which are both viewed as a Gaussian distribution) can form a joint Gaussian distribution as shown in Equation 7.

$$\begin{bmatrix} \mathbf{y} \\ y_* \end{bmatrix} \sim \mathcal{N}\left(m \begin{bmatrix} X \\ \mathbf{x}_*^{\mathbf{T}} \end{bmatrix}, \begin{bmatrix} K + \sigma_n^2 & K_*^T \\ K_* & K_{**} \end{bmatrix} \right) \quad (7)$$

Then by conditioning the joint Gaussian distribution of the training data set X and $\mathbf{y}$, Gaussian process regression can obtain the distribution of y_* with its mean μ and variance σ^2 as shown in the Equation 8 and Equation 9.

$$\mu = m(\mathbf{x}_*) + K_*(K + \sigma_n^2 I)^{-1}(\mathbf{y} - m(X)) \quad (8)$$
$$\sigma^2 = K_{**} - K_*(K + \sigma_n^2 I)^{-1} K_*^T \quad (9)$$

In Gaussian process regression, different mean functions and covariance functions can be chosen to learn the prediction target $f(\mathbf{x})$. Bayesian linear regression can be viewed as a special case of Gaussian process regression when $m(\mathbf{x}) = 0$ and $k(\mathbf{x}, \mathbf{x}') = \mathbf{x}^T \Sigma_p \mathbf{x}'$. In our framework, linear mean function and polynomial covariance function are applied as the predictive model.

4.4 Experiments of Routing-Cost Models

Our experiments are conducted based on 8 industrial block designs implemented by the same 28nm cell library. For each block design, 50 training samples are generated as described in Section 4.2. To learn the routing-cost model for a targeted block design, the training data includes the training samples of the other 7 block designs (350 samples combined) and 3 training samples of the targeted block design. Then we validate the learned routing-cost model based on 100 untried testing samples, where each testing sample is generated with a random PDN configuration under the given placement of the targeted block design.

In the following experiment, we first compare the accuracy of our routing-cost models generated by Gaussian process regression (denoted by GP) with those generated by other popular model-fitting techniques including Bayesian linear regression [19] (denoted as Bayesian), stepwise regression [19] (denoted as Stepwise), Ridge linear regression [20]

(denoted as Ridge) and SVM regression [21] (denoted as SVM). Table 4 lists the R square and mean error of the routing-cost models learned by each model-fitting technique for each block design, where the reported R square and mean error are calculated based on only the 100 untried testing samples for each block design. The results based on training samples are not included in Table 4. Also, the errors in percentages are reported by the difference between the predicted and real response features over the range of the real response features among all testing samples. The instance count and the dimension of each block design are also reported in Table 4.

Note that we have tried different settings for the other model-fitting techniques and reported their best result in Table 4. For Bayesian, we have tried different $\frac{1}{\sigma_n^2}$ (ranging from 0.01 to 100) and Σ_p^{-1} (ranging from 0.01 to 100). For Stepwise, we have tried different significance level (ranging from 0.01 to 0.15) and stopping criteria for R square (ranging from 0.1 to 0.00001). For Ridge, we tried different settings of λ (ranging from 0.0001 to 100). For SVM, we tried nu-SVR and epsilon-SVR with various parameters settings including different kernel functions, different cost value (ranging from 0.01 to 100), different nu value (ranging from 0.005 to 50) and different epsilon value(ranging from 0.001 to 10).

As the result shows, Gaussian process regression can result in an average R square of 0.985 over 8 block designs, significantly higher than that resulting from Bayesian (0.911), Stepwise (0.909), Ridge (0.910) or SVM (0.893). The average error resulting from Gaussian process regression is 2.28% over 8 block designs, which is around half of that resulting from each of the other model-fitting techniques. Also, Gaussian process regression can constantly outperform all other model-fitting techniques, meaning that its R square is always the highest and its average error is always the lowest for each block designs. This result demonstrates that the total wire length of global route can only be described by a high dimensional model, such as Gaussian process regression, instead of using only linear models, such as Bayesian, Stepwise and Ridge , or an importance-sampling-based method, such as SVM.

5. ROUTING-DRIVEN PDN DESIGN FLOW

5.1 Overview of Proposed Design Flow

Figure 4 shows the overview of the proposed design flow for generating an optimal routing-driven PDN, which consists of two main procedures: (1) the procedure of learning the routing-cost model and (2) the procedure of identifying optimal PDN configuration. The model-learning procedure first reads in the database of the targeted design (includ-

Table 4: R square and mean error of the routing-cost models learned by each model-fitting technique.

block design	design information		R square					mean error				
	instance #	dimension	GP	Bayesian	Stepwise	Ridge	SVM	GP	Bayesian	Stepwise	Ridge	SVM
D1	1073k	1491um*840um	0.988	0.956	0.969	0.953	0.986	2.29%	3.70%	3.32%	3.83%	2.56%
D2	2835k	1647um*2493um	0.996	0.927	0.907	0.929	0.959	1.24%	6.04%	6.71%	5.97%	4.29%
D3	1759k	2049um*1283um	0.991	0.949	0.955	0.947	0.954	1.95%	4.58%	4.29%	4.65%	4.16%
D4	695k	2152um*1142um	0.977	0.961	0.935	0.958	0.747	3.40%	4.75%	5.33%	4.90%	13.22%
D5	773k	1331um*705um	0.983	0.950	0.966	0.943	0.923	2.21%	4.50%	3.43%	4.83%	5.31%
D6	74k	694um*450um	0.979	0.919	0.911	0.921	0.736	2.42%	4.78%	5.05%	4.72%	8.59%
D7	2239k	3350um*4836um	0.985	0.847	0.833	0.847	0.894	2.32%	7.28%	7.22%	7.31%	5.93%
D8	564k	1959um*1067um	0.984	0.783	0.796	0.784	0.945	2.45%	9.06%	8.81%	9.03%	4.58%
avgerage			0.985	0.911	0.909	0.910	0.893	2.28%	5.58%	5.52%	5.66%	6.08%

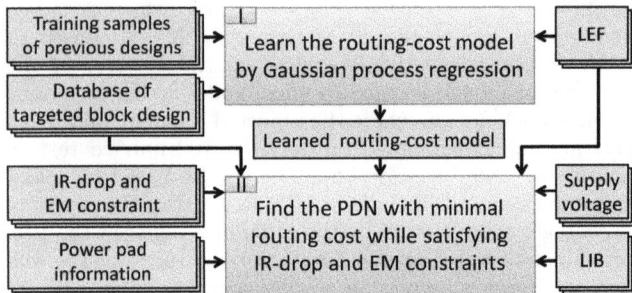

Figure 4: Overview of the proposed design flow.

ing a given placement) and generates 3 training samples by applying global route with the 3 representative PDN configurations. Then based on the training samples of the previous block designs and the three sample of the targeted block design, a routing-cost model can be learned by Gaussian process regression. The LEF information is used for building a proper PDN configuration or calculating some predictor features (such as effective routing tracks and via size). The other details of this model-learning procedure was described in Section 4.

In addition to the learned routing-cost model and the database of the targeted block design, the PDN optimization procedure also needs other inputs, such as the targeted supply voltage, the IR-drop and EM constraints, the locations of power pads and the Lib file, to perform the analysis of IR-drop and EM for a given PDN configuration. In this procedure, a public solver [22] [23] is used to perform MNA. A simple converter is developed to convert a given PDN configuration to its corresponding conductance matrix in conjunction with the MNA solver. The longest runtime of performing one MNA with the solver is less than 10 minutes for all the PDN configurations and block designs used in our experiments.

With the learned routing-cost model and the MNA solver, we can efficiently estimate the total wire length of global route and obtain the worst-case IR-drop and EM for a given PDN configuration. Based on this quick evaluation of a PDN configuration, we further develop an algorithm in Section 5.2 to search for the best PDN configuration that can result in the minimal total wire length for global route while satisfying both IR-drop and EM constraints. The identified optimal PDN configuration will be outputted as a tcl script that can be directly loaded into the Encounter design database by sourcing the tcl script.

5.2 Searching Optimal PDN Configuration

Figure 5 shows the procedure for searching the optimal routing-driven PDN configuration based on our learned routing-cost model. The parameters to be adjusted during the search for a PDN configuration include the stripe width of Metal-6, Metal-7 and the AP layer, denoted as W_{M6}, W_{M7} and W_{AP}, and the number of stripes for Metal-6, Metal-7 and the AP layer, denoted as N_{M6}, N_{M7} and N_{AP}.

The search procedure (Line 2-3) first calculates all the valid irredundant stripe widths for Metal-6, Metal-7 and the AP layer by solving Equation 1 (shown in Section 2.3) with different settings of T_{ps} and the LEF information. For each of the AP layer and Metal-7, we further identify the irredundant stripe width whose number of occupied tracks per

```
Searching procedure for PDN configuration
1  begin
2    for each of M6, M7, and AP
3      Create irreducdant stripe width list
4    W_AP = irreducdant stripe width with min track/width ratio
5    N_AP = TUR_AP*TT_AP / T_ps(W_AP)
6    W_M7 = irredundant stripe width with min track/width ratio
7    N_M7 = TUR_M7*TT_M7 / T_ps(W_M7)
8    for each irredundant stripe width of M6, W_M6
9      Nmax_M6 = TUR_M6*TT_M6 / T_ps(W_M6)
10     Nmin_M6 = 2
11     while Nmin_M6 ≤ Nmax_M6
12       N_M6 = (Nmax_M6 + Nmin_M6) / 2
13       Calculate IR-drop, EM and routing cost
14       if No violation on IR-drop and EM
15         Record PDN configuration with least routing cost
16         Nmax_M6 = N_M6 - 1
17       else if EM of AP or M7 is over constraint and there is
18              a wider irredundant stripe width for AP or M7
19         Use a wider irredundant stripe width for AP or M7
20       else
21         Nmin_M6 = N_M6 + 1
22   Output the recorded PDN configuration
23 end
```

Figure 5: Procedure for searching optimal PDN configuration under IR-drop and EM constraints.

stripe (the corresponding T_{ps}) divided by the irredundant stripe width is minimum. Such a width represents the most cost-effective width in term of the occupied routing tracks for the targeted layer and will be used as the initial values of W_{AP} (Line 4) and W_{M7} (Line 6). Next, as mentioned in Section 2.2, designers will provide a preferred total usage rates for the AP layer and Metal-7, denoted as TUR_{AP} and TUR_{M7}, which represents the ratio of tracks used for building the PDN at the specified layer. Then the initial values of N_{AP} and N_{M7} can be set as on Line 5 and Line 7, respectively. TT_{AP} and TT_{M7} represent the total number of tracks on the corresponding layer. $T_{ps}(W_{AP})$ and $T_{ps}(W_{M7})$ represent the number of tracks used by a stripe with the corresponding width.

Unlike W_{AP} and N_{AP} (or W_{M7} and N_{M7}), whose values are determined by each other due to a fixed usage ratio, W_{M6} and N_{M6} can be adjusted independently and hence form a wider solution space on Metal-6. From Line 8 to Line 13, we will try to identify the optimal N_{M6} for every valid irredundant stripe width W_{M6} based on a binary search, where $Nmax_{M6}$ and $Nmin_{M6}$ represent the boundary of the untried solutions for the binary search. For each searched PDN configuration, we will estimate the total wire length of global route with the learning routing-cost model and perform MNA to obtain the worst-case IR-drop and EM based on the PDN formed by the current W_{M6}, W_{M7}, W_{AP}, N_{M6}, N_{M7} and N_{AP} (Line 13). If no violation of IR-drop or EM exists, meaning too much of Metal-6 may be used, we will record the result of the current valid PDN configuration and then try to decrease N_{M6} for the next searched configuration (Line 14-16). If any violation exists, we will check whether the violation is an EM violation at Metal-7 or the AP layer. If yes, we will increase the stripe width for the layer of the EM violation if a wider width exists for the layer (Line 17-19). For all otherwise cases, we will increase N_{M6} (Line 20-21). After trying all valid irredundant stripe widths for W_{M6}, we will output the PDN configuration that results in the least routing cost and also satisfies both IR-drop and EM constraints (Line 22).

Table 5: Comparison among PDNs generated by different design flows.

block design	wire length without PDN (μm)	proposed flow			[7]			PDN-Metal Search			comparison	
		(i) increased wire length (μm)	worst IR-drop (mv)	worst EM	(ii) increased wire length (μm)	worst IR-drop (mv)	worst EM	(iii) increased wire length (μm)	worst IR-drop (mv)	worst EM	$\frac{(ii)-(i)}{(ii)}$	$\frac{(iii)-(i)}{(iii)}$
D1	14,086,137	679,025	24.4	99.7%	902,679	22.7	86.9%	750,872	24.9	99.6%	24.8%	9.6%
D2	39,135,337	372,462	20.8	98.7%	1,061,667	10.5	94.5%	398,486	24.2	99.5%	64.9%	6.5%
D3	17,466,048	155,426	19.9	99.6%	465,581	14.8	98.2%	174,107	24.0	99.4%	66.6%	10.7%
D4	10,611,887	70,229	17.0	98.7%	146,108	7.5	51.0%	75,344	22.8	98.5%	51.9%	6.8%
D5	9,198,430	32,854	14.9	97.4%	70,286	12.4	71.3%	45,105	24.0	99.9%	53.3%	27.2%
D6	611,924	6,725	21.6	98.8%	10,562	15.9	78.6%	10,680	24.7	99.6%	36.3%	37.0%
D7	30,902,626	70,843	18.4	99.9%	239,951	6.3	53.7%	80,195	25.0	99.1%	70.5%	11.7%
D8	15,535,391	83,496	17.7	97.4%	238,756	10.1	88.2%	97,293	23.1	99.2%	65.0%	14.2%
average			19.3	98.8%		12.5	77.8%		24.1	99.4%	54.2%	15.5%

5.3 Experiments of Routing-Driven PDN

In the following experiment, we first compare the PDN generated by our proposed flow with that generated by [7], which uses irredundant stripe widths to build PDNs with their derived analytical models to compute sufficient total metal width that can guarantee meeting the IR-drop and EM constraints for each metal layer. We also report the PDN generated by using the total metal area of a PDN as the routing-cost model while using the same PDN search procedure as shown in Figure 5, denoted as *PDN-Metal Search*.

Table 5 lists the *increased wire length* of detail route, worst-case IR-drop and worst-case EM (current density) resulting from the proposed design flow, [7] and *PDN-Metal Search*, respectively. The increased wire length of detail route is the difference between the total wire lengths of applying detail route with and without the given PDN. The total wire length of applying detail route without any PDN represents the minimum baseline of the total wire length that must be spent for detail route based on the given placement, which is also reported in the second column of Table 5. The IR-drop constraint is set to 25mV. The maximum allowable EM (current density) can be different for each layer as defined in the LEF file. We first normalize the worst-case current density by dividing it with the maximum allowable current density for each layer and then report the largest normalized value among all layers in Table 5.

As the result shows, when compared to [7], the increased wire length resulting from our proposed design flow is smaller for each block design and 54.2% less in average. Also, the worst EM of our generated PDNs are all close to 100%, showing that the PDN search in our proposed flow is mainly constrained by the EM constraint rather than the IR-drop constraint. On the other hand, [7] still leaves significant margin on both IR-drop and EM constraints for most designs. This result shows that using an analytical model in [7] may usually lead to over-design for PDN.

Compared to *PDN-Metal Search*, the increased wire length resulting from our proposed design flow is always smaller for each block design. Their difference in the increased wire length ranges from 6.5% to 37.0%. Figure 6 shows the scatter plots of using the total metal area of a PDN and the predicted routing cost of our learned model to correlate the total wire length of detail route (instead of that of global route), respectively, for each block design. By visually comparing the scatter plots of the two estimation methods, we can find that our learned routing-cost model correlates with the final routing result significantly better than the total metal area of a PDN and hence can effectively reduce the increased wire length for detail route. The above results demonstrate the advantage of building an accurate routing-cost model for searching an optimal routing-driven PDN in our proposed flow.

Table 6 first compares the runtime of our proposed flow with that of *PDN-Metal Search*. As the result shows, the longest runtime of the proposed flow is 673 minutes (a little more than 11 hours) among the 8 block designs, which is considered affordable for designs with more than 2-million instance count. On the other hand, despite using a super

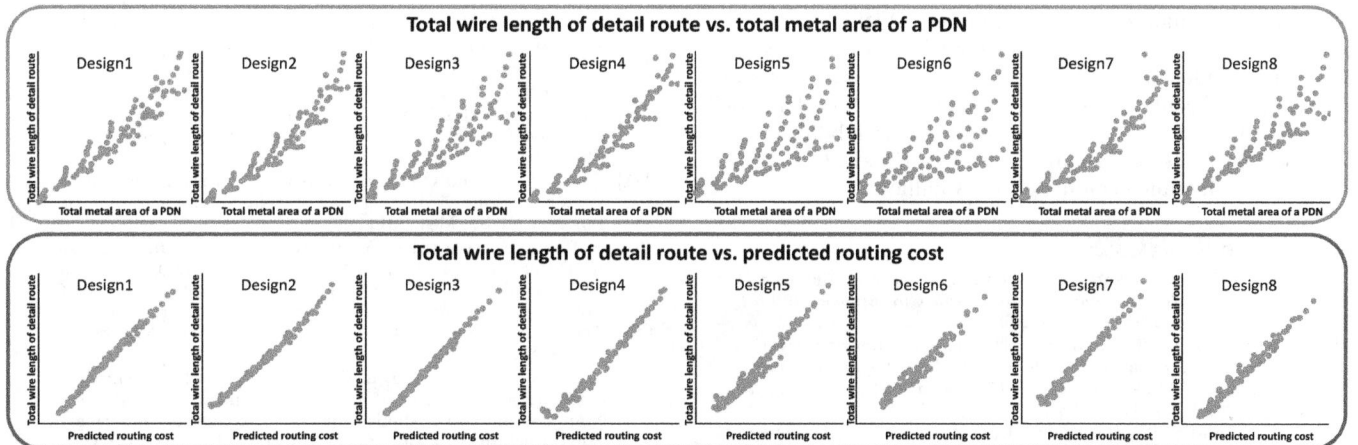

Figure 6: Scatter plots of using total metal area of a PDN and our learned routing-cost model to correlate total wire length of detail route.

Table 6: Runtime of different design flows.

block design	proposed flow (i)	PDN-Metal Search (ii)	Global-Route Search (iii)	comparison (ii)/(i)	(iii)/(i)
D1	321m	163m	12131m	0.51	37.8
D2	656m	354m	35590m	0.54	54.3
D3	325m	191m	10883m	0.59	33.5
D4	261m	160m	8510m	0.61	32.6
D5	118m	38m	5546m	0.32	47.0
D6	62m	21m	1391m	0.34	22.4
D7	673m	464m	23217m	0.69	34.5
D8	208m	107m	7607m	0.51	36.6
average				0.51X	37.3X

fast routing-cost model, *PDN-Metal Search* still needs in average 0.51X of the runtime of the proposed flow. It is because performing MNA to obtain the worst-case IR-drop and EM also requires significant runtime, which cannot be avoided in *PDN-Metal Search*. This result also implies that the runtime of building our learned routing-cost model, including performing 3 times of global route for the representative PDN configurations, is in average about the same as performing MNA in our flow. Note that we exclude the runtime of generating the training samples for the other block designs because those training samples should be collected in the past whenever a global route could be applied. This also shows the advantage of saving useful statistics of previously developed designs for future use.

Table 6 further lists the estimated runtime if we directly apply global route to estimate the routing cost for a PDN in our search procedure, denoted as *Global-Route Search*, by using the average runtime shown in Table 3. As the result shows, the longest runtime of *Global-Route Search* is 35590 minutes, i.e., around 24.7 days, which is unacceptably long for any design-optimization process in practice. This result again demonstrates the importance of building an accurate and fast routing-cost model for searching the best routing-driven PDN.

6. CONCLUSION

In this paper, our main objective is to apply advanced machine-learning techniques to build an accurate and fast routing-cost model. We have demonstrated that the routing-cost model learned by our applied Gaussian process regression can highly correlate the total wire length of global route while constantly and significantly outperforming other popularly used model-fitting techniques. With the learned routing-cost model, we further developed a search procedure to effectively identify the PDN configuration that can result in the minimal routing overhead while meeting both IR-drop and EM constraints. The effectiveness and scalability of the proposed flow has be validated based on 8 industrial block designs with instance count up to 2.8 millions.

7. REFERENCES

[1] H. Qian, S. Nassif, and S. Sapatnekar, "Random walks in a supply network," in *Design Automation Conference, 2003. Proceedings*, pp. 93–98, June 2003.

[2] B. Boghrati and S. Sapatnekar, "Incremental power network analysis using backward random walks," in *Design Automation Conference (ASP-DAC), 2012 17th Asia and South Pacific*, pp. 41–46, Jan 2012.

[3] H. Qian and S. Sapatnekar, "A hybrid linear equation solver and its application in quadratic placement," in *Computer-Aided Design, 2005. ICCAD-2005. IEEE/ACM International Conference on*, pp. 905–909, Nov 2005.

[4] T.-H. Chen and C. Chen, "Efficient large-scale power grid analysis based on preconditioned krylov-subspace iterative methods," in *Design Automation Conference, 2001. Proceedings*, pp. 559–562, 2001.

[5] E. Chiprout, "Fast flip-chip power grid analysis via locality and grid shells," in *Computer Aided Design, 2004. ICCAD-2004. IEEE/ACM International Conference on*, pp. 485–488, Nov 2004.

[6] S. Kose and E. Friedman, "Fast algorithms for ir voltage drop analysis exploiting locality," in *Design Automation Conference (DAC), 2011 48th ACM/EDAC/IEEE*, pp. 996–1001, June 2011.

[7] W.-H. Chang, M.-T. Chao, and S.-H. Chen, "Practical routability-driven design flow for multilayer power networks using aluminum-pad layer," *Very Large Scale Integration (VLSI) Systems, IEEE Transactions on*, vol. 22, pp. 1069–1081, May 2014.

[8] R. Jakushokas and E. Friedman, "Methodology for multi-layer interdigitated power and ground network design," in *Circuits and Systems (ISCAS), Proceedings of 2010 IEEE International Symposium on*, pp. 3208–3211, May 2010.

[9] R. Bhooshan, "Novel and efficient ir-drop models for designing power distribution network for sub-100nm integrated circuits," in *Quality Electronic Design, 2007. ISQED '07. 8th International Symposium on*, pp. 287–292, March 2007.

[10] P. Gupta and A. Kahng, "Efficient design and analysis of robust power distribution meshes," in *VLSI Design, 2006. Held jointly with 5th International Conference on Embedded Systems and Design., 19th International Conference on*, pp. 6 pp.–, Jan 2006.

[11] H. Chen, C.-K. Cheng, A. Kahng, Q. Wang, and M. Mori, "Optimal planning for mesh-based power distribution," in *Design Automation Conference, 2004. Proceedings of the ASP-DAC 2004. Asia and South Pacific*, pp. 444–449, Jan 2004.

[12] S. S.-Y. Liu, C.-J. Lee, C.-C. Huang, H.-M. Chen, C.-T. Lin, and C.-H. Lee, "Effective power network prototyping via statistical-based clustering and sequential linear programming," in *Design, Automation Test in Europe Conference Exhibition (DATE), 2013*, pp. 1701–1706, March 2013.

[13] X.-D. Tan, C.-J. Shi, D. Lungeanu, J.-C. Lee, and L.-P. Yuan, "Reliability-constrained area optimization of vlsi power/ground networks via sequence of linear programmings," in *Design Automation Conference, 1999. Proceedings. 36th*, pp. 78–83, 1999.

[14] X. Wu, X. Hong, Y. Cai, Z. Luo, C.-K. Cheng, J. Gu, and W. Dai, "Area minimization of power distribution network using efficient nonlinear programming techniques," *Computer-Aided Design of Integrated Circuits and Systems, IEEE Transactions on*, vol. 23, pp. 1086–1094, July 2004.

[15] S. Boyd, L. Vandenberghe, A. El Gamal, and S. Yun, "Design of robust global power and ground networks," in *Proceedings of the 2001 International Symposium on Physical Design*, ISPD '01, (New York, NY, USA), pp. 60–65, ACM, 2001.

[16] H. Su, J. Hu, S. Sapatnekar, and S. Nassif, "Congestion-driven codesign of power and signal networks," in *Design Automation Conference, 2002. Proceedings. 39th*, pp. 64–69, 2002.

[17] Cadence, "Encounder user guides version 13.11-s031_1."

[18] C. E. R. . C. K. I. Williams, *Gaussian Processes for Machine Learning*. Cambridge,MA,USA: the MIT Press, 2006.

[19] K. P. Murphy, *Machine Learning: A Probabilistic Perspective*. Cambridge,MA,USA: the MIT Press, 2012.

[20] R. T. Trevor Hastie and J. Friedman, *The Elements of Statistical Learning - Date Mining, Inference, and Prediction*. Springer, 2001.

[21] C.-C. Chang and C.-J. Lin, "Libsvm: A library for support vector machines," *ACM Trans. Intell. Syst. Technol.*, vol. 2, pp. 27:1–27:27, May 2011.

[22] S. Balay, S. Abhyankar, M. F. Adams, J. Brown, P. Brune, K. Buschelman, L. Dalcin, V. Eijkhout, W. D. Gropp, D. Kaushik, M. G. Knepley, L. C. McInnes, K. Rupp, B. F. Smith, S. Zampini, and H. Zhang, "PETSc users manual," Tech. Rep. ANL-95/11 - Revision 3.6, Argonne National Laboratory, 2015.

[23] S. Balay, W. D. Gropp, L. C. McInnes, and B. F. Smith, "Modern software tools for scientific computing," ch. Efficient Management of Parallelism in Object-oriented Numerical Software Libraries, pp. 163–202, Cambridge, MA, USA: Birkhauser Boston Inc., 1997.

Hyperspherical Clustering and Sampling for Rare Event Analysis with Multiple Failure Region Coverage

Wei Wu
UCLA, EE Department
Los Angeles, CA
weiw@seas.ucla.edu

Srinivas Bodapati
Intel Corporation
Santa Clara, CA
srinivas.bodapati@intel.com

Lei He
UCLA, EE Department
Los Angeles, CA 90095
lhe@ee.ucla.edu

ABSTRACT

Statistical circuit simulation is exhibiting increasing importance for circuit design under process variations. It has been widely used throughout the design of standard cell circuits (SRAM, Flip-Flop, etc.) to maximize yield, i.e. to minimize the failure probability. Existing approaches cannot effectively analyze the failure probability when failed samples are distributed in multiple disjoint regions, nor handle the circuits with a large number of variations. To tackle these challenges, the proposed hyperspherical clustering and sampling (HSCS) approach first identifies multiple failure regions through a reweighted spherical k-means algorithm, which clusters failed samples on a set of hyperspheres, rather than the high dimensional open space. Next, a modified mixture importance sampling is designed to draw samples at those clusters to achieve multiple failure region coverage. The proposed HSCS is evaluated using both mathematical and circuit-based examples. It achieves about 3-order speedup over Monte Carlo with the same level of accuracy, while other importance sampling based approaches either fail to converge or converge to wrong results. Furthermore, HSCS demonstrates excellent robustness by generating consistent results in multiple replications.

CCS Concepts

•Hardware → **Process variations; Yield and cost modeling;**

Keywords

Process Variation, Yield, Clustering, Failure regions

1. INTRODUCTION

As integrated circuits (ICs) scale to smaller footprints than ever before, circuit reliability has become an area of growing concern due to the uncertainty introduced by process variations [1, 2, 3, 4, 5]. For highly duplicated standard cells, or critical circuit modules, such as PLLs, which stabilize the clock for the circuit system, an extremely rare failure event could lead to catastrophe of the entire chip.

ISPD'16, April 03-06, 2016, Santa Rosa, CA, USA
© 2016 ACM. ISBN 978-1-4503-4039-7/16/04. . . $15.00
DOI: http://dx.doi.org/10.1145/2872334.2872360

In general, deterministic analysis of rare-event is infeasible [6]. Modern statistical circuit simulation approaches consider process variations and statistically simulate the circuit to estimate the probability that a circuit does not meet the performance metric. Among those approaches, Monte Carlo (MC) analysis remains the gold standard [7]. It repeatedly draws samples and evaluates circuit performance via transistor-level simulation. Even though the circuit simulation has been considerably accelerated [8, 9, 10], it is, however, extremely time-consuming because millions of samples need to be simulated to capture one single failure when the failure is a rare event.

Instead of sampling randomly with standard MC, more efficient approaches only sample the statistically likely-to-fail case [6, 11, 12, 13, 14, 15, 16, 17, 18]. These approaches, however, become less effective while analyzing circuits with a large number of variation parameters, or dealing with problems that failed samples are spread in multiple disjoint failure regions, which is becoming common in real circuit designs [16, 18, 19, 20].

(1) **Importance Sampling:** As a classic modification of MC, importance sampling (IS) modifies the MC sampling strategy. A critical step of IS is to construct a new "proposed" sampling distribution under which a rare event becomes less rare so more failures can be captured. Previous work investigated different approaches [11, 12, 13, 14]. For example, mixture importance sampling (MixIS) [11] mixes a uniform distribution, the original distribution, and a shifted distribution centered around the failure region. Method in [12] spherically searches the failure sample with minimal L2-norm (min-norm), then shifts the sample mean to the min-norm point. [14] shifts the sample mean to the centroid of the failure samples. All these approaches are related to mean shifting and assume that all failed samples are located in one region. However, in reality, failed samples may spread in multiple disjoint regions. In this scenario, the existing IS approaches cannot effectively cover all the failure regions, hence, leading to inaccurate and inefficient estimations.

(2) **Classification:** Approaches in this category tackle the problem from a totally different angle. As a representative example, statistical blockade (SB) [6] utilizes a classifier to block samples that are unlikely to fail, leaving only likely-to-fail samples to simulate. More recently, recursive SB [15] and REscope [16] are proposed to tackle problem with multiple failure regions. However, recursive SB assumes that each failure region is associate with different label, which does not hold for several circuits [19, 20]. Alternatively, REscope [16] relies on support vector machine (SVM) with radial basis function (RBF) kernel to identify failure regions, but SVM works as a black box model and is out of user's

control. Excessively training the SVM to identify multiple regions could easily lead to overfit.

Among others, [17, 21] uses a set of sample "chains" to explore the failure region with the aid of the Markov Chain Monte Carlo (MCMC) method. However, it is difficult to cover the entire failure region with several chains of MCMC samples, particularly when tens or hundreds random variables are considered. Multi-cone approach [18] deterministically breaks the original sample space into multiple non-overlapping cones, and sums up the analytically calculated failure probability in each cone. It does consider multiple failure regions, but the number of cones grows exponentially to the dimensionality, limiting it only effective for low dimensional problems.

In this paper, a hyperspherical clustering and sampling approach, HSCS in short, is proposed to effectively handle the challenges of both multiple failure regions and high dimensionality. As the first step, HSCS identifies multiple failure regions by grouping the failure samples into multiple clusters. Instead of clustering in a high dimensional open space, we sample spherically and develop a weighted spherical k-means algorithm to identify clusters only on a set of hyperspheres. Searching for min-norm points in these clusters is much easier than conventional spherical IS. Next, a modified mixture importance sampling shifts the sample mean to the min-norm points of multiple clusters so as to cover multiple failure regions.

HSCS is evaluated and compared with MC and other IS based implementations in terms of accuracy, efficiency, and robustness. On a small 2-dimensional problem with mathematically known distribution, HSCS yields very accurate results compared with mathematically calculated groundtruth. On a 70-dimensional charge pump circuit, HSCS is about 3 orders faster than MC and provides the same level of accuracy, while other IS based approaches either fail to converge or converge to wrong results. Furthermore, on both examples, HSCS demonstrates excellent robustness by generating consistent results in multiple replications.

The remainder of this paper is organized as follows. In Section 2, the rare event model problem and IS are reviewed. In Section 3, we expatiate the proposed algorithm, including spherical presampling and hyperspherical clustering step, and the modified MixIS step. In Section 4, HSCS is verified on a mathematically known distribution and a 70-dimensional charge pump circuit. This paper is concluded in section 5.

2. BACKGROUND

2.1 Rare Event Analysis

Let $f(X)$ be a probability density function (PDF) for a multivariate random variable X (e.g., a set of process variable parameters) which is the input of a measurement process as shown in (1); the output Y is an observation (e.g. memory read/write time, amplifier gain) with input X:

$$\underbrace{X}_{\text{variable}} \Rightarrow \boxed{\text{Measurement, SPICE, etc.}} \Rightarrow \underbrace{Y}_{\text{observation}} \quad (1)$$

In statistical circuit simulation, it is of great interest to estimate the probability of Y from a small subset $\mathcal{S}$ of the entire sampling space. For example, $\mathcal{S}$ can be the "failure region" for a circuit design and includes all samples that fail to meet the performance specification. Therefore, the probability $P(Y \in \mathcal{S})$ can be estimated as:

$$P(Y \in \mathcal{S}) = \int I(X) \cdot f(X) dX \quad (2)$$

where Y is the observation/performance with the input variable X and the indicator function $I(\cdot)$ outputs 1 only when $Y \in \mathcal{S}$, 0 otherwise. Note that the integral in equation (2) is intractable because $I(X)$ is unavailable in analytical form. Therefore, sampling based method must be used. For example, the MC method enumerates as many samples of X as possible (e.g., $x_1, \cdots, x_n$) according to $f(X)$ and evaluates their indicator function values to estimate $p(Y \in \mathcal{S})$ as:

$$\tilde{P}(Y \in \mathcal{S}) = \frac{1}{n} \sum_{i=1}^{n} I(x_i) \xrightarrow[n \to +\infty]{a.s.} P(Y \in \mathcal{S}). \quad (3)$$

Here $\tilde{P}(X \in \mathcal{S})$ is an unbiased estimate from sampling method and can be very close to $p(X \in \mathcal{S})$ with a large number of samples.

2.2 Importance Sampling

When $Y \in \mathcal{S}$ is a rare event, standard MC method becomes extremely inefficient. Importance sampling (IS) improves the efficiency by shifting the sample mean and sampling more statistically likely-to-fail (important) cases.

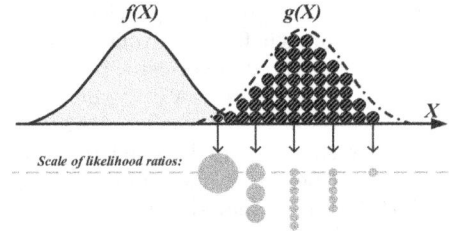

Figure 1: Likelihood ratios in mean-shift importance sampling

As illustrated using a 1-dimensional example in Figure 1, mean-shift IS samples from a proposed distribution $g(X)$ that tile towards $\mathcal{S}$ where a rare-event becomes less rare to happen:

$$P_{IS}(Y \in \mathcal{S}) = \int I(X) \cdot \frac{f(X)}{g(X)} \cdot g(X) dX \quad (4)$$

$$= \int I(X) \cdot w(X) \cdot g(X) dX. \quad (5)$$

Here, $w(X)$ is the likelihood ratio for each sample of X. $w(X)$ compensates for the discrepancy between $f(X)$ and $g(X)$ and unbiases the probability estimation under $g(X)$. Sampling based methods can be used to evaluate above integral as:

$$\tilde{P}_{IS}(Y \in \mathcal{S}) = \frac{1}{n} \sum_{j=1}^{n} w(\tilde{x}_j) \cdot I(\tilde{x}_j) \xrightarrow[n \to +\infty]{a.s.} P(Y \in \mathcal{S}). \quad (6)$$

where $\tilde{x}_j$ $(j = 1, \cdots, n)$ follows the distribution $g(X)$ rather than $f(X)$ because more likely-to-fail events can be sampled.

It is obvious that the samples closer to the nominal value are more desirable [12] because they are associated with greater probability $f(X)$ and likelihood ratio $w(X)$, hence have more significant impact on the estimated failure probability $\tilde{P}_{IS}$. In practice, most of the existing approaches shift the sample mean to the point that is closest to the origin on the accept/fail boundary, which is also known as the minimum-norm (min-norm) point [12]. However, the mean-shift IS implementations suffer from the following two drawbacks:

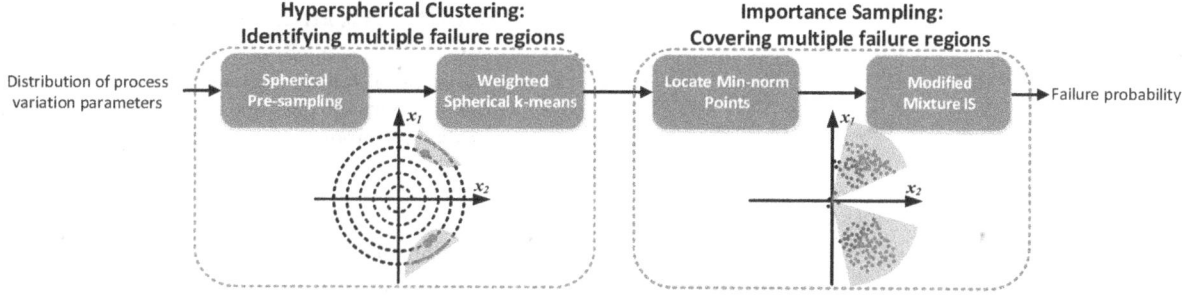

Figure 3: The HyperSpherical Clustering and Sampling (HSCS) algorithm consists of two phases: 1) hyperspherical clustering, 2) multiple mean-shift importance sampling.

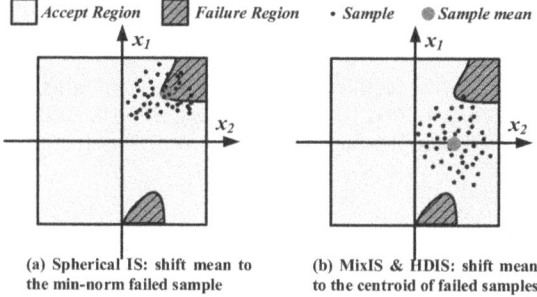

(a) Spherical IS: shift mean to the min-norm failed sample

(b) MixIS & HDIS: shift mean to the centroid of failed samples

Figure 2: Existing mean-shift importance sampling implementations do not handle problems with multiple disjoint failure regions

First, they search the min-norm points by constructing an accept/fail boundary in the open space, which may take prohibitively long runtime, especially at high dimensionality.

Moreover, while existing approaches [11, 12, 13, 14] shift the sample mean to a more important point, they totally neglect that failed samples might be distributed in multiple disjoint regions. As illustrated in Figure 2, one shifted distribution might be insufficient to cover all the failures, hence leading to a biased estimation of $\tilde{P}_{IS}(Y \in \mathcal{S})$ in (6).

To improve the mean-shift IS, the remaining challenges turn out to be 1) identifying failure regions in high dimensional sample space, 2) effectively sampling to cover multiple failure regions.

3. HYPERSPHERICAL CLUSTERING AND SAMPLING

3.1 Algorithm Overview

In this section, we present the proposed hyperspherical clustering and sampling approach (HSCS). It consists of two major phases, (1) hyperspherical clustering, (2) importance sampling around multiple min-norm points, as illustrated in Figure 3. HSCS takes in the process variation parameters, and outputs the estimated failure probability $\tilde{P}_{IS}$ based on given requirements on performance metric Y.

To accurately estimate $\tilde{P}_{IS}$, we attempt to cover more samples that are closer to the nominal value. During the clustering phase, a weighted clustering algorithm is designed to bias the cluster centers towards those samples. In the second phase, sample means are shifted to the min-norm points of multiple clusters for two purposes: 1) capture more samples with greater weights, 2) cover the failed samples in multiple failure regions.

In the remaining part of this section, we will elaborate each phase of the algorithm.

3.2 Hyperspherical Clustering

The hyperspherical clustering phase includes a spherical presampling step and a weighted hyperspherical k-means step to cluster the failed samples. Algorithms in this phase are targeted to find the direction of failure regions, so that statistical approaches can be applied afterwards to estimate the failure probability with a better failure region coverage.

3.2.1 Spherical Presampling

In order to identify multiple failure regions, it is intuitive to collect a number of likely-to-fail samples (typically samples in the quantile of the performance distribution), and to cluster them into several aggregations according to their locations in the sample space. However, clustering samples that are randomly generated in high dimensional open space is challenging. Even in the same cluster, samples may still be far apart from each other. In this scenario, a cluster centroid does not necessarily mean more failed samples, leading to meaningless clusters.

Alternatively, we restrict the samples to a few hyperspherical surfaces by sampling spherically. In this scenario, clustering algorithms can be performed on a more restricted area rather than the high dimensional open space.

As illustrated in the left part of Figure 3, samples are randomly generated on hyperspheres with gradually increasing radius to capture samples in the quantile. During the implementation, we generate 1000 samples on each hypersphere surface and stop expanding the hypersphere until 5% or more samples on the current hypersphere surface fall in the 1% quantile.

3.2.2 Weighted Hyperspherical K-means

Conventional clustering algorithms (e.g. k-means) group samples to optimal clusters by minimizing the sum of Euclidean distance [22] between samples and their corresponding cluster centers, as defined in (7).

$$EuclideanDistance(X^{(1)}, X^{(2)}) = \left\| X^{(1)} - X^{(2)} \right\| \quad (7)$$

$$CosineDistance(X^{(1)}, X^{(2)}) = 1 - \frac{X^{(1)^T} X^{(2)}}{\left\| X^{(1)} \right\| \left\| X^{(2)} \right\|} \quad (8)$$

As we generate samples on hyperspheres, Euclidean distance makes less sense because the distance between samples and the origin is the same. It is more desirable to cluster samples based on the directions those samples pointing to rather than Euclidean distance. Therefore we use cosine distance, defined in (8), as the distance metric, leading to a hyperspherical version of k-means algorithm.

Furthermore, a naive hyperspherical k-means algorithm only makes use of the samples on the outermost hypersphere, without incorporating the failed samples captured on the inner hyperspherical surfaces, which are usually associated with greater likelihood ratio according to (4), i.e. higher importance. To take full advantage of all the failed samples, we propose a weighted hyperspherical k-means algorithm. Each failed sample is normalized to unit length and associated with a weight calculated based on its probability density. With a targeted number of clusters k, the proposed algorithm returns the cluster assignment for each input failed sample.

Algorithm 1 Weighted Spherical K-Means Algorithm

Input: A set of M failed samples: $\mathcal{X} = \{X^{(1)}, X^{(2)}, ..., X^{(M)}\}$
   Sample weights: $w^{(1)}, w^{(2)}, ..., w^{(M)}$
   Number of initial clusters: k
Output: Cluster label for samples: $\mathcal{Y} = \{y^{(1)}, y^{(2)}, ..., y^{(M)}\}$
   Updated number of clusters: k
1: Randomly initialize the unit length cluster centroids $\mathcal{U} = \{\mu^{(1)}, \mu^{(2)}, ..., \mu^{(k)}\}$;
2: **repeat**
3:   **Cluster Assignment** (update $\mathcal{Y}$):
    For each sample $X^{(i)}$, set $y^{(i)} = \underset{j}{\arg\max} \; X^{(i)^T} \mu^{(j)}$;
4:   **Remove Empty Clusters** (update k)
    Remove $\mathcal{X}_j$ if $\mathcal{X}_j = \{X^{(i)}|y^{(i)} = j\} = \emptyset$;
    Update number of cluster k;
5:   **Weighted Centroid Update** (update $\mathcal{U}$):
    For cluster k, let $\mathcal{X}_j = \{X^{(i)}|y^{(i)} = j\}$, update centroid as
    $\mu^{(j)} = \sum_{X^{(i)} \in \mathcal{X}_j} w^{(i)} X^{(i)}$;
    $\mu^{(j)} = \mu^{(j)} / \|\mu^{(j)}\|$;
6: **until** $<\mathcal{Y}$ remains unchanged$>$
7: Return $\mathcal{Y}$ and k;

As the first step of Algorithm 1, a set of initial cluster centroids are randomly generated. Next the algorithm iteratively updates the cluster label assigned for all samples, cleans up empty cluster, and recalculates the centroids, until the label assignment remains unchanged after one iteration. During the cluster assignment step, the algorithm checks the cosine distance between a sample and all cluster centroids. The cluster j that maximizes $X^{(i)^T} \mu^{(j)}$, which is equivalent to minimizing the cosine distance, will be selected. Moreover, we assign samples different weights in the centroid update process in step 5, therefore the centroids are biased to samples with higher importance.

One caveat is that k-means searches for the cluster assignment $\mathcal{Y}$ in a greedy fashion, resulting in convergence to the local optimal instead of guaranteeing global optimum. The proposed weighted hyperspherical k-means is not an exception. In practice, we start from multiple set of randomly initialized cluster centroids $\mathcal{U}$, and choose the one leading to minimal sum of cosine distance as the solution. Hence, the final solution could be more prone to take the global optimum.

Also, the number of clusters, k, is unknown before the clustering. In practice, we try a number of different k and choose the one with a trade off between the model complexity and goodness of fit. In the machine learning community, k is empirically chosen to be $\sqrt{M}$ [23], where M is the total number of samples to be clustered. More discussion on choosing k is included in the experiment section with concrete example.

3.3 Multiple Mean-Shift Importance Sampling

The previous phase generates normalized cluster centers, i.e. the direction of failure regions. In this phase, we locate the min-norm points of multiple failure regions and apply a modified mixture importance sampling (MixIS) approach to sample in all the failure regions and to estimate the overall failure probability.

3.3.1 Locating the Min-norm Points using Bisection

To locate the min-norm points more accurately and efficiently, we only search towards the direction of the clusters given that they have been identified.

Mathematically, all the samples in the same cluster can be covered by a cone defined in (9).

$$\mathcal{C} = \{X | CosiceDistance(X, \mu) \leq d_{max}\} \quad (9)$$

As illustrated in the right part of Figure 3, the opening angle of cone $\mathcal{C}$ is constrained by d_{max}, the largest cosine distance between failed samples in this cluster and the cluster centroid μ.

Algorithm 2 Locate min-norm points for each cluster with bisection

---

Input: Minimal radius of existing failure samples, R
Output: Radius of min-norm point: R_{min}
1: $R_{max} = R$;
2: $R_{min} = 0$;
3: **repeat**
4:   $R = (R_{max} + R_{min})/2$;
5:   simulate a small set of samples at Radius $= R$ in current cluster;
6:   **if** any failed sample captured **then**
7:     $R_{max} = R$;
8:   **else**
9:     $R_{min} = R$;
10: **end if**
11: **until** $R_{max} - R_{min} < R_{threshold}$
12: Return R;

Next, we apply bisection to search the minimal radius that leads to a failure in each cone, as presented in Algorithm 2. Starting with a lower bound of 0, and upper bound at the minimal radius of the existing failure samples, the algorithm bisects the radius and only simulates a small number of samples at this radius. It will reduce the upper bound to search the lower half region if any failure is captured during the simulation, otherwise, it will go to the upper half.

After locating the minimal radius R_i of a cone, the min-norm point of the corresponding cluster is calculated as $Cm_i = \mu_i * R_i$, where μ_i is the normalized cluster center that indicates the direction of this cluster.

3.3.2 Modified Mixture Importance Sampling

Next, we modifie the MixIS and shift the sample mean to all these min-norm points found in the previous step. The proposed distribution $g(x)$ is defined as

$$g(X) = \alpha f(X) + (1 - \alpha) \sum_{i=1}^{k} \beta_i f(X - Cm_i) \quad (10)$$

where $\beta_i = \frac{\sum_{X^{(i)} \in \mathcal{X}_k} w^{(i)}}{\sum_{\forall X} w^{(i)}}$ is the weight for each failure region (cluster), which is calculated based on the sum of sample weights in the cluster.

Note that we also keep a small ratio (α) of $f(x)$ in the proposed distribution $g(x)$, so that IS likelihood ratio

$$\frac{f(X)}{g(X)} = \frac{f(X)}{\alpha f(X) + (1-\alpha)\sum_{i=1}^{k}\beta_i f(X - Cm_i)} < \frac{1}{\alpha} \quad (11)$$

is bounded by $1/\alpha$. It prevents the likelihood ratio from going to infinity at certain X, and preserves the numerical stability of the modified MixIS.

4. EXPERIMENT RESULTS

The proposed HSCS is first evaluated using a mathematically known 2-dimensional normal distribution with 2 disjoint failure regions. Next, we verify HSCS using a more realistic high-dimensional charge pump circuit, which is known to have multiple failure regions.

4.1 Evaluation on Mathematically Known Distribution

On a sample space with 2-dimensional normal distribution, two disjoint failure regions, S_1 and S_2, are defined as follows:

- $S_1 = \{X\,|\,\|X\| > 3.8 \text{ and } \phi(X) \in [\frac{2}{3}\pi, \frac{3}{4}\pi]\}$
- $S_2 = \{X\,|\,\|X\| > 3.9 \text{ and } \phi(X) \in [\frac{4}{3}\pi, \frac{3}{2}\pi]\}$

where $\|X\|$ is the 2-norm of the sample, i.e. the Euclidean distance between the sample and the origin, and $\phi(X)$ is the phase of the 2-D sample. These two failure regions are illustrated in Figure 4[1].

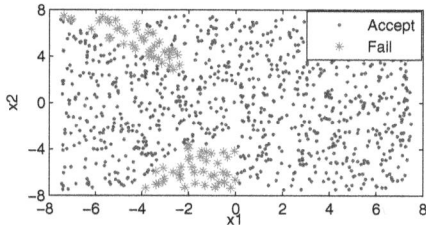

Figure 4: 2-dimensional sample space with two disjoint failure regions S_1 and S_2

Since the PDF and the failure regions are mathematically known, the failure probability can be calculated by integrating PDF function in (12),

$$P_F = \int_{X \in \{S_1, S_2\}} f(X)dX \approx 7.199e-5 \quad (12)$$

leading a failure probability of 7.199e-5, which is close to 4 sigma.

As the first step, HSCS gradually increases the radius of the sphere to search for failed samples and stops expanding until enough failed samples are collected. As illustrated in Figure 5, the presampling step converges at 4-sigma sphere in this particular example.

Obviously, those failed samples are aggregated in two separate regions in Figure 6(a). The weighted hyperspherical k-means updates the cluster assignments in a greedy fashion by always assigning a sample to its closest centroid. Hence, if the initial centroids are improperly selected, it is possible

[1]Figure 4 is plotted using uniformly distributed samples for better illustration.

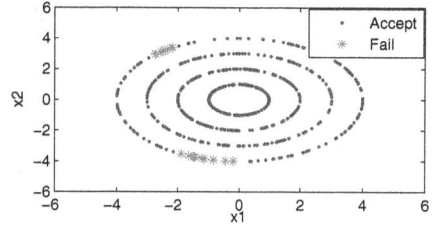

Figure 5: Spherical presampling to collect failed samples

that the iterative cluster assignments end up with assigning all samples in one cluster as illustrated in Figure 6(b), while leaving the other cluster empty (the empty cluster is removed in step 3 of Algorithm 1).

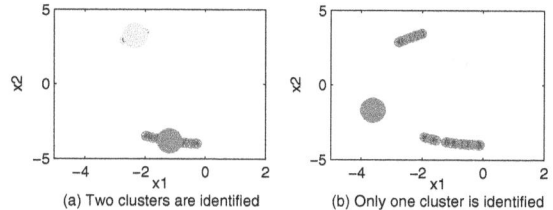

(a) Two clusters are identified (b) Only one cluster is identified

Figure 6: Spherical k-means might converge to local optimal with "improper" initial centroids

This problem has been well addressed in the machine learning community by randomly creating multiple set of initial centroids and applying the same cluster algorithm to all these set of samples. Only the cluster assignment with best optimization target, i.e. the smallest sum of cosine distance, will be chosen.

Next, bisection is applied to locate the min-norm points. In this example, we generate 20 samples only at each Radius. In each cluster, the algorithm ends up with 5 iterations and converges to radius at 3.9375 and 3.8125, which are very close to the groundtruth.

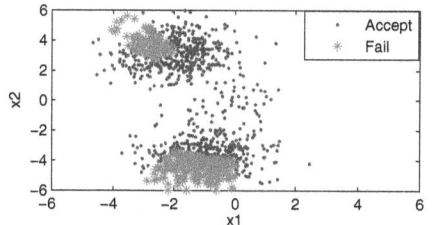

Figure 7: Sample coverage of the modified mixture importance sampling

The modified mixture importance sampling shifts the sample means to the min-norm points of both failure regions. Samples drew by importance sampling in Figure 7 indicate that both failure regions are accurately and fully covered.

The failure rate is estimated at 7.109e-5 using HSCS, which is quite close to the mathematically calculated ground truth, 7,199e-5. As a stochastic algorithm, we also run the HSCS with 100 replications to verify the stability. The estimated failure probability ranges from 5.54e-5 to 9.05e-5, with an average of 7.21e-5.

4.2 Experiments on Charge Pump Circuit

4.2.1 Charge Pump Circuit and Experiment Setting

We also evaluate the proposed HSCS using a charge pump (CP) circuit, which is a critical sub-circuit of the phase-locked loop (PLL), as illustrated in Figure 8. CP adjusts the frequency of the output clock signal, CLK_{out}, via a charge/discharge capacitor and voltage controlled oscillator (VCO).

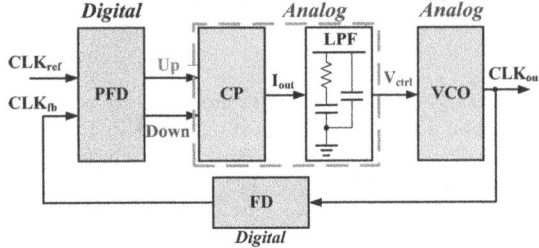

Figure 8: A block diagram of PLL

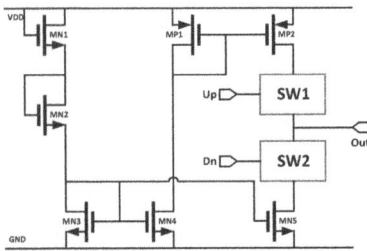

Figure 9: Simplified schematic of the charge pump

A simplified schematic of the charge pump consisting of two switched current sources is presented in Figure 9. Ideally, MN3, MN4, and MN5 on the bottom of Figure 9 are designed with the same dimension. The drain current flowing through these three NMOS transistors should be identical because they are imposed the same gate voltage. The same current also flows through MP1 since it shares the same branch with MN4. Similarly, on the top of Figure 9, two PMOS transistors form another current mirror, so that the current can be copied from MP1 to MP2. In this scenario, the charge current flowing through MP2 should be identical to the discharge current through MN5 when both switches are turned on, leading to zero net current.

In reality, it is, however, difficult to guarantee those transistors exactly the same dimension because of the process variation effects during chip fabrication. Mismatches on these transistors, especially on MP2 or MN5, could result in a nonzero net current at the output node. It could cause large fluctuation at the control voltage, also known as "jitter", which severely affect the PLL system stability. In the following experiments, we consider a failure if there is a big enough mismatch between the charge and discharge current, mathematically, $\max(\frac{I_{Charge}}{I_{Discharge}}, \frac{I_{Discharge}}{I_{Charge}}) > \gamma$, where γ is a threshold of this performance metric.

For experimental purpose, a CP circuit is designed using PTM 22nm high performance technology model [24] and simulated in HSPICE. The CP circuit is a typical circuit known to have multiple failure regions [19, 20, 16]. We analyze this circuit with two different process variation setups.

- In the first setup, we map the variations to threshold voltage (V_{th}), and only model the V_{th} of MP2 and MN5 as variation source. Hence, the failure regions can be visualized in a 2-dimensional space.

- A more comprehensive model with 10 parameters, including flat-band voltage (V_{fb}), threshold voltage (V_{th0}), gate oxide thickness (t_{ox}), mobility (μ_0), etc., are considered as variation source for each of those 7 transistors in Figure 9. Variations in those two digital switches are not accounted. In the second setup, there are a total of 70 variation parameters in the circuit, which is a relatively high dimensional problem.

In addition to the HSCS, Monte Carlo (MC) is included as the gold reference of the experiment. We also implement the high-dimensional importance sampling (HDIS) [14] and spherical importance sampling (SpIS) [12] for accuracy and efficiency comparison. The HDIS and Spherical IS are two typical mean shifting approaches that shift the sample mean to the centroid and min-norm point of the failure region respectively.

The efficiency is evaluated by counting the total number of simulations required to yield a stable failure rate. All the aforementioned approaches converge at the same criterion, i.e. the relative standard deviation of the estimated failure probability, $\sigma_r = \frac{std(p_f)}{p_f}$, gets smaller than 0.1.

4.2.2 2-D Setup with Visualized Failure Regions

In this setup, instead of investigating very rare failure event, we configure the threshold γ to target a 5% failure probability. Under this configuration, two failure regions can be easily visualized when we plot the accepted MC samples against failed ones in 2-dimensional sample space, as shown in Figure 10(a).

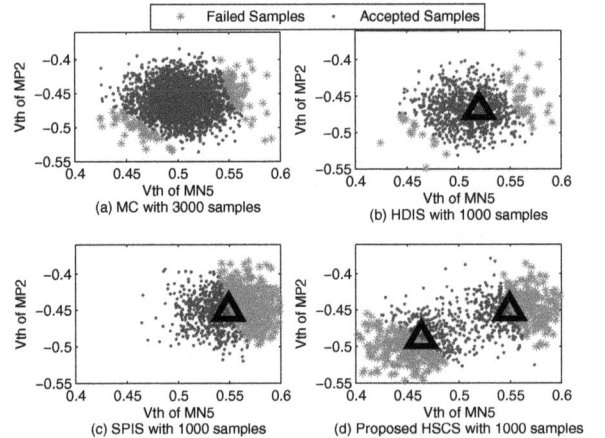

Figure 10: Multiple failure region coverage test MC, HDIS [14], Spherical IS [12], and HSCS

With only 1000 samples, the coverage of HDIS, Spherical IS, and the proposed HSCS are illustrated in Figure 10(b), (c), and (d), respectively. Sample means of these 3 importance sampling approaches are marked as upward-pointing triangulars in the Figures.

It is easy to notice that HDIS fails to shift the sample mean to any of the failure regions. As illustrated in 10(b), it attempts to draw samples around the centroid of the failed samples. The centroid of those failed samples, however, falls almost close to the origin, which is obviously not in the failure region, leading to a poor coverage on those truly "important" samples.

Spherical IS shifts the sample mean to the existing sample with minimal norm. It correctly locate the min-norm point, as shown in Figure 10(c), but Spherical IS only samples one failure region while leaving the other one totally untouched.

The samples drew by the proposed HSCS are plotted in Figure 10(d). Samples generated during presampling and min-norm points searching are not included in this Figure. While the majority of samples are centered at the min-norm points of those two failure regions, HSCS still preserves a few samples around the origin to keep a small ratio of the original distribution according to equation (10) and avoids numerical instability in likelihood ratio calculation.

4.2.3 Hyperspherical Clustering with 70 Process Variation Parameters

In the following discussion, we model 10 process variation parameters on 7 transistors shown in Figure 9 in the CP circuit, leading to a 70-dimension problem. Transistors in two digital switches are not considered.

To collect enough samples for clustering, we generate 1000 samples at each hypersphere surface and gradually increase its radius and search for the samples on the 1% quantile. Until 6 sigma hypersphere, a total of M = 144 samples are collected, including 41 failed samples captured on 5 sigma hypersphere, and 103 failed samples on 6 sigma hypersphere. The weighted spherical k-means algorithm is applied on these 144 samples to group them into clusters. Note that the actual number of clusters (k_{actual}) generated by the algorithm could be small than k_{target}, as some clusters may become empty during the cluster assignment and are removed.

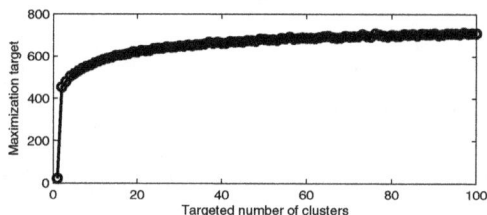

Figure 11: Clustering maximization objective while changing the targeted number of clusters

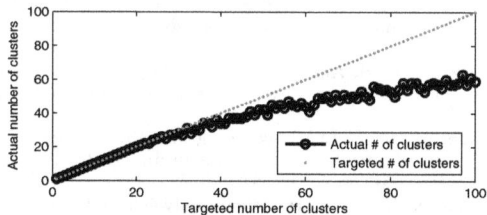

Figure 12: Number of actually clusters may be small than the targeted number of clusters

To determine the optimal number of clusters, we start with different k_{target} and evaluate the value of the maximization objective (also referred as profit) under those k_{target}. As shown in Figure 11, there is a big jump when k_{target} increases from 1 to 2. Afterwards, the slope becomes gentler and almost flat when k_{target} reaches 30.

A lot of information can be interpret from this Figure. First, the big jump indicates that the failed samples are located in two major clusters. When we use two centroids instead of one, the samples becomes much closer to the centroids, leading to a remarkable increase in the profit. Of course, these two big clusters can be further decomposed into smaller ones, but the profit generated by increasing k_{target} is smaller. When k_{target} is beyond 30, we do not benefit from increasing the cluster numbers.

The number of actually generated clusters k_{actual} is plotted against k_{target} in Figure 12, which helping us understand Figure 11 better. When k_{target} is small, the algorithm generates whatever number of clusters we ask for. Therefore, k_{actual} is overlapped with k_{target}. However, excessively increasing k_{target} results in a lot of redundant clusters, which are not assigned any samples and removed from the targeted clusters. These redundant clusters account for the gap between k_{actual} and k_{target}. In this particular problem, any k_{target} between 2 and 30 could be reasonable. As expected, the empirical guess, $k = \sqrt{M} = 12$ falls in this range.

4.2.4 Accuracy, Efficiency, and Robustness

The HSCS is also compared with MC, HDIS [14], and SpIS [12] in terms of both efficiency and accuracy. Their convergence curves are plotted in Figure 13[2], including one figure for the estimated failure probability (P_{fail}) and the other one for deviation of the estimation.

To generate the groundtruth, MC takes nearly 16 million simulations to get confident estimation of P_{fail} at 4.904e-5. The HDIS converges with only 4.9e4 samples (11k samples for pre-sampling and 38k for IS), but unfortunately, to a wrong estimation as shown in Figure 13(a). The Spherical IS is terminated since it does not show any sign of convergence after 7.4e5 samples being simulated. The poor performance of HDIS and SpIS is not a surprise because they fail to draw samples to comprehensively cover the failure regions, hence leading to fluctuant or event deviated estimations. More quantitative results of these approaches are presented in Table 1. Contrasting to HDIS and SpIS, the proposed HSCS achieves very promising estimation about 2.3e4 samples. In short, it estimates P_{fail} at MC accuracy with ∼3 order speedup.

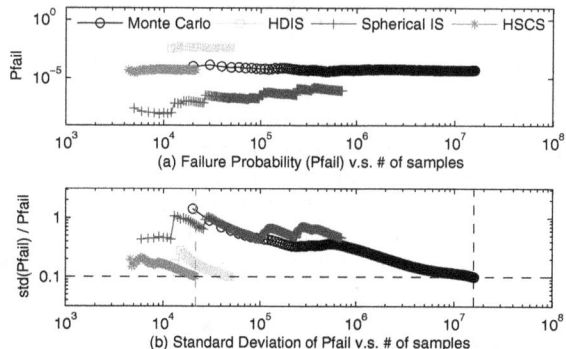

Figure 13: Convergence curve of Monte Carlo, HDIS, Spherical IS, and the proposed HSCS

---

[2]Note that the convergence curves of HDIS, SpIS, and HSCS start from different points because they need different # of samples in the presampling step.

Table 1: Accuracy and efficiency evelution on 70-dimensional charge pump circuit

	Monte Carlo	HDIS [14]	SpIS [12]	Proposed HSCS with 10 replications
failure probability	4.904e-5	3.9e-3	8.788e-7	3.89e-5 ~ 5.88e-5 (mean **4.82e-5**)
Total #sim. runs	1.584e7	3.8e4	>7.4e5	4.6e3 ~ 5.5e4 (mean **2.3e4**)
#sim.　for presampling	-	1.1e4	4e3	4.2e3
#sim.　for IS		3.8e4	>7e5	410 ~ 5.1e4 (mean 1.9e4)

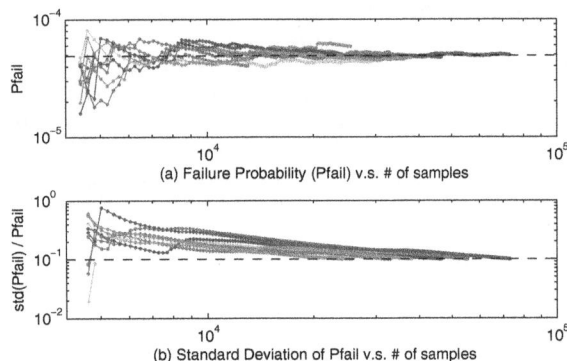

(a) Failure Probability (Pfail) v.s. # of samples

(b) Standard Deviation of Pfail v.s. # of samples

Figure 14: Robustness test of HSCS with 10 replications

To ensure that HSCS can consistently generate accurate estimation, we executed the same program with 10 replications and presented their convergence curves in Figure 14. We notice that the failure probabilities estimated by these replications converge to the ground truth, the dashline in Figure 14(a). As detailed in Table 1, the estimated failure probability ranges from 3.89e-5 to 5.88e-8, with an average of 4.82e-5. This is very close to the MC result. Also, it only takes an average of 2.3e4 samples to converge the simulation, which is about 3 orders faster than MC.

5. CONCLUSION

In this paper, HSCS is proposed to tackle the challenging statistical circuit simulation problems with multiple failure regions and high dimensionality, which are the shortcomings of the existing importance sampling and classification based approaches. HSCS first applies spherical presampling and clustering to identify multiple failure regions. Next, it locates the min-norm points of each failure region and leverage a modified MixIS that shifts the sample mean to those min-norm points. Therefore, the importance samples cover multiple failure regions. In the experiments on a 70-dimensional charge pump circuit, HSCS achieves ~3 orders speedup over MC providing the same level of accuracy, while other IS based approaches either fail to converge or converge to wrong results. Furthermore, HSCS demonstrates excellent robustness by generating consistent results in multiple replications.

6. REFERENCES

[1] S. R. Nassif, "Design for variability in DSM technologies [deep submicron technologies]," in *ISQED*, 2000, pp. 451–454.

[2] K. Agarwal and S. Nassif, "The impact of random device variation on SRAM cell stability in sub-90-nm cmos technologies," *IEEE Trans. on VLSI Systems,*, vol. 16, no. 1, pp. 86–97, 2008.

[3] S. Wang, A. Pan, C. O. Chui, and P. Gupta, "Proceed: A pareto optimization-based circuit-level evaluator for emerging devices," in *ASP-DAC*. IEEE, 2014, pp. 818–824.

[4] G. Leung, S. Wang, A. Pan, P. Gupta, and C. O. Chui, "An evaluation framework for nanotransfer printing-based feature-level heterogeneous integration in vlsi circuits," 2015.

[5] S. Wang, H. Lee, F. Ebrahimi, P. K. Amiri, K. L. Wang, and P. Gupta, "Comparative evaluation of spin-transfer-torque and magnetoelectric random access memory," *IEEE Trans. Emerg. Sel. Topics Circuits Syst.*, 2016.

[6] A. Singhee and R. A. Rutenbar, "Statistical blockade: a novel method for very fast monte carlo simulation of rare circuit events, and its application," in *DATE*, 2008, pp. 235–251.

[7] C. Jacoboni and P. Lugli, *The Monte Carlo method for semiconductor device simulation.* Springer, 1989, vol. 3.

[8] X. Chen, W. Wu, Y. Wang, H. Yu, and H. Yang, "An escheduler-based data dependence analysis and task scheduling for parallel circuit simulation," *IEEE Trans. Circuits Syst. II, Exp. Briefs*, vol. 58, no. 10, pp. 702 –706, oct. 2011.

[9] W. Wu, Y. Shan, X. Chen, Y. Wang, and H. Yang, "Fpga accelerated parallel sparse matrix factorization for circuit simulations," in *Reconfigurable Computing: Architectures, Tools and Applications.* Springer, 2011, pp. 302–315.

[10] W. Wu, F. Gong, R. Krishnan, L. He, and H. Yu, "Exploiting parallelism by data dependency elimination: A case study of circuit simulation algorithms," *Design Test, IEEE*, vol. 30, no. 1, pp. 26–35, Feb 2013.

[11] R. Kanj, R. Joshi, and S. Nassif, "Mixture importance sampling and its application to the analysis of SRAM designs in the presence of rare failure events," in *Proceedings of the 43rd DAC*, 2006, pp. 69–72.

[12] L. Dolecek, M. Qazi, D. Shah, and A. Chandrakasan, "Breaking the simulation barrier: SRAM evaluation through norm minimization," in *ICCAD*, 2008, pp. 322–329.

[13] K. Katayama, S. Hagiwara, H. Tsutsui, H. Ochi, and T. Sato, "Sequential importance sampling for low-probability and high-dimensional SRAM yield analysis," in *ICCAD*, 2010.

[14] W. Wu, F. Gong, G. Chen, and L. He, "A fast and provably bounded failure analysis of memory circuits in high dimensions," in *19th ASP-DAC*, 2014, pp. 424–429.

[15] A. Singhee, J. Wang, B. H. Calhoun, and R. A. Rutenbar, "Recursive statistical blockade: an enhanced technique for rare event simulation with application to sram circuit design," in *21st Intl. Conf. on VLSI Design.* IEEE, 2008, pp. 131–136.

[16] W. Wu, W. Xu, R. Krishnan, Y.-L. Chen, and L. He, "REscope: High-dimensional statistical circuit simulation towards full failure region coverage," in *Proceedings of the 51st DAC*, 2014.

[17] C. Dong and X. Li, "Efficient SRAM failure rate prediction via gibbs sampling," in *Proceedings of the 48th DAC*, 2011.

[18] R. Kanj, R. Joshi, Z. Li, J. Hayes, and S. Nassif, "Yield estimation via multi-cones," in *Proceedings of the 49th DAC*, 2012.

[19] P. Mukherjee, C. S. Amin, and P. Li, "Approximate property checking of mixed-signal circuits," in *Proceedings of the 51st DAC*, 2014.

[20] P. Mukherjee and P. Li, "Leveraging pre-silicon data to diagnose out-of-specification failures in mixed-signal circuits," in *Proceedings of the 51st DAC*, 2014.

[21] S. Sun and X. Li, "Fast statistical analysis of rare circuit failure events via subset simulation in high-dimensional variation space," in *ICCAD*, 2014, pp. 324–331.

[22] J. A. Hartigan and M. A. Wong, "Algorithm as 136: A k-means clustering algorithm," *Applied statistics*, pp. 100–108, 1979.

[23] K. V. Mardia, J. T. Kent, and J. M. Bibby, *Multivariate analysis.* Academic press, 1979.

[24] S. Sinha, G. Yeric, V. Chandra, B. Cline, and Y. Cao, "Exploring sub-20nm finfet design with predictive technology models," in *Proceedings of the 49th DAC*, 2012.

A Machine Learning Based Framework for Sub-Resolution Assist Feature Generation

Xiaoqing Xu, Tetsuaki Matsunawa†, Shigeki Nojima†, Chikaaki Kodama†
Toshiya Kotani†, David Z. Pan
ECE Department, Univ. of Texas at Austin, Austin, TX, USA
Toshiba Corporation, Semiconductor & Storage Products Company, Yokohama, Japan†
{xiaoqingxu, dpan}@cerc.utexas.edu
{tetsuaki.matsunawa, shigeki.nojima, chikaaki1.kodama, toshiya.kotani}@toshiba.co.jp

ABSTRACT

Sub-Resolution Assist Feature (SRAF) generation is a very important resolution enhancement technique to improve yield in modern semiconductor manufacturing process. Model-based SRAF generation has been widely used to achieve high accuracy but it is known to be time consuming and it is hard to obtain consistent SRAFs on the same layout pattern configurations. This paper proposes the first machine learning based framework for fast yet consistent SRAF generation with high quality of results. Our technical contributions include robust feature extraction, novel feature compaction, model training for SRAF classification and prediction, and the final SRAF generation with consideration of practical mask manufacturing constraints. Experimental results demonstrate that, compared with commercial Calibre tool, our machine learning based SRAF generation obtains 10X speed up and comparable performance in terms of edge placement error (EPE) and process variation (PV) band.

CCS Concepts

•Hardware → VLSI design manufacturing considerations;

Keywords

Sub-Resolution Assist Feature (SRAF), Machine Learning

1. INTRODUCTION

As the technology node continues scaling down, the $193nm$ wavelength photolithography with low $k1$ value is the mainstream technique to achieve smaller feature size. However, low image contrast and complex target pattern shapes make it extremely difficult for low-$k1$ lithography to obtain acceptable lithographic process windows [1]. Besides the design for manufacturability techniques, like multiple patterning and litho-friendly layout design, mask optimization through resolution enhancement techniques (RETs) remains as the key strategy to improve the lithographic process window

ISPD '16, April 3–6, 2016, Santa Rosa, California, USA.
© 2016 ACM. ISBN 978-1-4503-4039-7/16/04. . . $15.00
DOI: http://dx.doi.org/10.1145/2872334.2872357

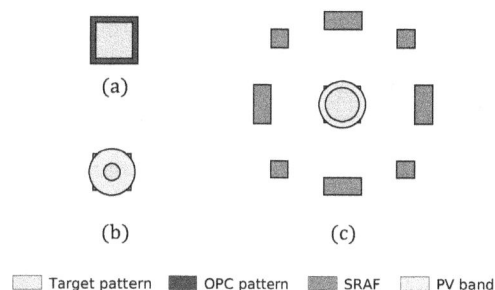

Figure 1: (a) An isolated contact, (b) printing with OPC, (c) printing with SRAF generation and OPC.

and the yield of the volume production in advanced technology nodes [2–6]. Major RETs include source mask co-optimization, sub-resolution assist feature (SRAF) generation and optical proximity correction (OPC). Among them, the SRAF generation is particularly important to improve the lithographic process window of target patterns. The key physical mechanism behind is that, without printing themselves, the small SRAF patterns would deliver light to the positions of target patterns at proper phase so that the printing of target patterns will be more robust to the lithographic variations. The lithographic process window is quantified with the process variation (PV) band area, which should be minimized to obtain a robust mask optimization solution. An example demonstrating the benefit of SRAF generation is shown in Fig. 1. An isolated target contact with the OPC pattern is shown in Fig. 1(a) and the target pattern is optimized only with OPC in Fig. 1(b), while the optimization in Fig. 1(c) is done with both SRAF generation and OPC. It can be clearly observed that much smaller PV band area is achieved in Fig. 1(c). Therefore, fast SRAF generation with high quality is of great importance for the mask optimization.

Multiple SRAF generation approaches, including model-based and rule-based approaches, have been developed and widely used in standard mask optimization flows. The rule-based approach is widely adopted due to its fast execution time and acceptable performance for simple designs and regular target patterns [1, 7, 8]. However, the rule-based SRAF is hard to deal with complex two-dimension (2D) shapes as it requires significant engineering efforts to setup and maintain the rule table [7]. Model-based SRAF generation methods can be divided into two categories based on the lithographic computations involved. One is to use simulated aerial images to seed the SRAF generation [9–12]. The other is to apply inverse lithography technology (ILT) and compute the image contour to guide the SRAF generation [13, 14]. Despite better lithographic performance and generalization capabilities compared to the rule-based approach, the model-based SRAF is known to be very time-consuming and it is difficult to achieve the same SRAFs around the same layout configurations, i.e. consistent SRAFs [1, 7].

Recently, the machine learning technique has been introduced to the computational lithography domain, with applications to lithographic hotspot detection [15–19] and OPC [20–23]. The machine learning technique calibrates a mathematical model with respect to an objective from the training data set based on accurate lithographic computations. Then, the calibrated model can predict the objective values, like a hotspot or non-hotspot for the hotspot detection and the shifting distance of an edge segment for the OPC, on the testing data. The machine learning technique usually demonstrates a trade-off between computational efforts and lithographic performance, which makes it particularly interesting for the SRAF generation problem. However, to the best of our knowledge, there is no prior art in applying the machine learning technique to the SRAF generation issue. In this work, we propose the first machine learning based framework for the SRAF generation. Our methodology can achieve fast yet consistent SRAFs with high quality in a 2D grid plane. Our main contributions are summarized as follows:

- A machine learning based framework is proposed for the SRAF generation, where a classification model is calibrated for SRAF predictions using model-based SRAFs as the training data.

- We propose a robust feature extraction scheme by adapting the concentric circle with area sampling considering SRAF-specific constraints. We further propose a novel feature compaction technique taking advantage of illumination source symmetry properties to reduce the training data size and improve the SRAF consistency.

- Logistic regression and decision tree models are calibrated for fast SRAF predictions due to the large data set size and high feature vector dimension. Different from conventional label predictions, we propose predictions with probability maxima in the 2D grid plane to generate manufacturing-friendly SRAFs.

- Our machine learning based framework achieves 10X speed-up in layout windows with comparable lithographic performance, compared with an industry strength model-based approach.

The rest of this paper is organized as follows. Section 2 introduces the standard mask optimization flow and related evaluation metrics. Section 3 gives the basic definitions and problem formulations. Section 4 explains the details on the feature extraction/compaction and model calibration. Section 5 shows how to generate SRAFs from the classification model while accommodating the mask manufacturing rules. Section 6 demonstrates the effectiveness of the proposed framework with comprehensive results. Section 7 concludes the paper.

2. PRELIMINARIES

2.1 Mask Optimization Flow

A standard mask optimization flow consists of several stages, including SRAF generation, OPC, mask manufacturing rule check (MRC) and lithography compliance check (LCC) as shown in Fig. 2(a) [1]. Depending on the outcome of MRC and LCC, iterative optimizations may be applied to achieve legal mask patterns. The MRC will check whether mask patterns satisfy a set of mask manufacturing rules. The LCC means lithography simulations are performed to check whether lithographic constraints are satisfied. In the stage of SRAF generation, small SRAFs will be added and isolated patterns on the mask will become dense patterns as shown in Fig. 1(b). SRAFs will not be printed themselves but will benefit the lithographic process windows of target patterns. In the next stage, OPC will shift the edges of OPC patterns to compensate for the optical proximity effects. Then, for the MRC, we assume the target patterns are MRC-clean and some typical mask manufacturing rules are applied to the SRAFs since this work mainly focuses on the SRAF generation. Typical mask manufacturing rules for SRAFs include maximum width (max_width) rule, minimum space (min_space) rule and maximum length (max_length) rule. The LCC will introduce a lithographic process window involving a set of {focus, dose} conditions [24]. Lithography simulations at various conditions are performed to check whether the metrics, such as PV band and edge placement error (EPE), meet the criteria.

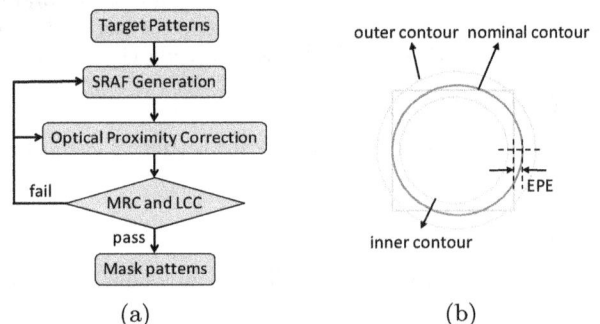

(a)   (b)

Figure 2: Mask optimization: (a) mask optimization flow, (b) lithography simulation contours.

2.2 Evaluation Metrics

We introduce several metrics to evaluate the performance of mask optimization results. An example of lithography simulation results is shown in Fig. 2(b). Inner and outer contours are explicitly drawn to demonstrate the lithographic printing variations due to the imposed {focus, dose} conditions. Nominal contour represents the lithographic printing at the best {focus, dose} condition. To quantify the lithographic variations, we define PV band and EPE as follows.

Definition 1 (PV Band) *Given the lithography simulation contours at a set of {focus, dose} conditions, the process variation (PV) band is defined as the area between the outer contour and inner contour.*

Definition 2 (EPE) *Given the lithography simulation contour at the best {focus, dose} condition, i.e. nominal contour* and a measurement point, the edge placement error (EPE) is defined as the distance between the target pattern contour and nominal contour.

Thus, in Fig. 2(b), the area between the outer contour and inner contour is the PV band. A measurement point is drawn with a dashed line orthogonal to the vertical edge of the target pattern in Fig. 2(b) and the EPE can be explicitly quantified. The SRAF consistency is an important issue since it is closely related to the process variations on wafer [1]. Consistent SRAFs are preferred around the same target pattern configurations because different SRAFs lead to different OPC results, which potentially introduce extra process variations. We define the consistent SRAF generation as follows.

Definition 3 (Consistent SRAF generation) *Consistent SRAF generation means the same SRAF patterns should be generated for the same target layout configurations.*

3. PROBLEM FORMULATION

The machine learning based SRAF generation framework works on a 2D grid plane with a specific grid size. The training data consist of a set of layout clips, where each layout clip includes a set of target patterns and model-based SRAFs. With the 2D grid plane and the training patterns, training samples can be extracted at each grid point. To clearly explain the training data, we define the SRAF label as follows.

Definition 4 (SRAF label) *Given model-based SRAFs on the 2D grid plane, the SRAF label of a grid is 1 or 0, where 1 denotes an SRAF is inserted at that grid and 0 vice versa.*

Specifically, a training data point includes a feature vector and an SRAF label. The feature vector represents the optical conditions of the grid point with respect to the target patterns. With the training data, we define the classification-based SRAF as follows.

Problem 1 (Classification-based SRAF) *Given the 2D grid plane and training patterns with model-based SRAFs, feature vectors and SRAF labels of all grid points are extracted and a classification model is calibrated to predict the SRAF insertion at each grid of testing patterns.*

In the testing phase, the classification model can predict the SRAF label at each grid for testing patterns. Those grids with SRAF labeled as 1 can not directly be treated as the final SRAFs and further simplifications are needed to generate SRAFs accommodating mask manufacturing rules. Thus, we define the SRAF generation as follows.

Problem 2 (SRAF Generation) *Given the classification model and test patterns, SRAFs are generated while accommodating the mask manufacturing rules.*

4. CLASSIFICATION-BASED SRAF

4.1 Data Preparation

4.1.1 SRAF Label Extraction

Given training patterns with model-based SRAFs on a 2D grid plane, we need to extract the training data, including

the SRAF label and feature vector for each grid. As shown in Fig. 3(a), a 2D grid plane is imposed on the target patterns and model-based SRAFs. The coordinates of each grid are determined by the pre-set grid size. A SRAF box is introduced at each grid to decide the SRAF label from model-based SRAFs. Specifically, the SRAF box is a rectangle and the size is a parameter, which could be different from the grid size. The SRAF label of the grid is 0 if no model-based SRAF covering the SRAF box on the grid. The SRAF label is 1 when there is a model-based SRAF covering the entire SRAF box area. Therefore, the grid size of the 2D grid plane decides the granularity of the training data extraction while the SRAF box provides an alternative control on the SRAF label extraction accuracy. The SRAF label extraction will give a set of labels for all the grids, denoted as $\{y_0\}$.

In addition, an OPC region and an SRAF region are explicitly drawn in Fig. 3(a) to demonstrate SRAF-specific constraints. SRAF generation is not allowed in the OPC region since it is reserved for the OPC stage after the SRAF generation. Since the optical interference happens within some specific lithographic interaction window, the SRAF generation outside of the pre-determined SRAF region can be ignored. Both OPC region and SRAF region are created by expanding the edges of the target patterns by some specific distance. We define the distance of expansion for the OPC region and SRAF region as d_{opc} and d_{sraf}, respectively.

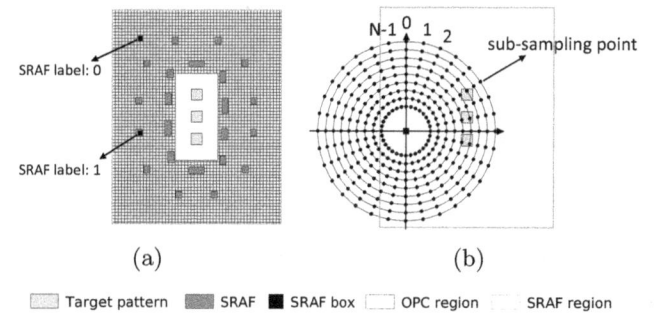

Figure 3: (a) SRAF label extraction and sampling constraints, (b) CCCAS at one grid point.

4.1.2 Feature Extraction and Compaction

The layout feature extraction plays an important role in the classification model calibration and prediction. The SRAFs benefit the printing of target patterns by delivering light to the positions of target patterns at proper phase. Thus, we need a layout feature that represents this physical phenomenon. The concentric circle with area sampling is an ideal candidate since it represents the information related to the concentric propagation of diffracted light from mask patterns [22]. We adapt it to the constrained concentric circle with area sampling (CCCAS) by incorporating the OPC region and SRAF region constraints discussed in Section 4.1.1. The CCCAS at one grid is illustrated in Fig. 3(b), where each circle centers at the grid and the minimum and maximum radius of the CCCAS are determined by d_{opc} and d_{sraf}, respectively. After transforming target patterns into the bitmap on the 2D plane, the CCCAS yields a $M \times N$ matrix, denoted as X_0, where M is the row number and N is the column number. As shown in Fig. 3(b), the column index of X_0 starts at the positive Y-axis with 0 and increases clockwise to $N-1$. The sub-sampling points, denoted as the black dots in Fig. 3(b), sharing the same angle to the origin are on the same column of X_0. The row index of X_0 starts with 0 at the circle with the smallest radius and increases to $M-1$ as the circle radius becomes larger. The sub-sampling points on the same circle is on the same row of X_0.

The consistent SRAF generation is an important issue, which means the same SRAFs will be generated surrounding the same target pattern configurations, i.e. the same optical conditions [7]. For example, in Fig. 4, the four grids are on axial symmetric positions of the grid plane with respect to the target patterns. If we assume the annular shape for the illumination source, the optical conditions of these four grids are the same and consistent SRAF generation scheme will give the same SRAF results. However, since the CCCAS at these four grids are different, denoted by different colors in Fig. 4, it is difficult for a classification model to achieve the same SRAF predictions. To achieve better SRAF consistency, we propose a novel feature compaction technique taking advantage of the illumination source symmetry. As shown in Fig. 4, this feature compaction technique transforms the CCCAS of symmetric grids into the CCCAS of the same grid, denoted as g, in the lower left of the grid plane. The sampling region of the grid (g) can be divided into four quadrants, i.e. I, II, III and IV. The target patterns mainly locate at the quadrant I of the sampling region of the grid (g), while target patterns mainly locate at different quadrants for other symmetric grids. For clearer explanations, we define the main quadrant as follows.

Definition 5 (Main Quadrant) *The main quadrant for a grid is defined as the quadrant of the CCCAS region where target patterns mainly locate.*

By flipping the CCCAS of other symmetric grids with X or Y-axis as shown in Fig. 4, target patterns will always locate at the quadrant I of the sampling regions for symmetric grids, which leads to the same CCCAS results. Then, the classification model will give consistent SRAF predictions for axial symmetric grids.

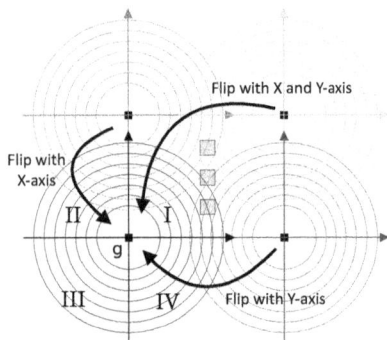

Figure 4: Feature compaction based on symmetry.

The details of the feature compaction technique are explained in Algorithm 1. The 2D feature matrix from CC-CAS contains the bitmap value at each sub-sampling point. The bitmap values of sub-sampling points within each quadrant of the sampling region correspond to a set of columns in the 2D feature matrix. Thus, the main quadrant should have the maximum summation of bitmap values at the 2D feature matrix. From lines 3 to 9, we scan through the four quadrants of the CCCAS region and decide the main quadrant. The flipping of 2D matrix is performed in line 10 to

---

Algorithm 1 Feature Compaction
___
Input: A $M \times N$ feature matrix X_0;
Output: Optimized feature vector x_0;
1: Define $main\_quadrant = 1$ as the main quadrant;
2: Define $max\_sum = 0$ as the maximum summation;
3: **for** $index = 0$, $index < 4$, $index$++ **do**;
4:     Define $sum = $ summation of X_0 from column $index \times N/4$ to column $(index + 1) \times N/4$;
5:     **if** $sum > max\_sum$ **then**;
6:         $max\_sum = sum$;
7:         $main\_quadrant = index + 1$;
8:     **end if**
9: **end for**
10: Flip X_0 based on $main\_quadrant$;
11: Flatten X_0 into a vector x_0 and return x_0;

---

transform the main quadrant to quadrant I as demonstrated in Fig. 4. For practical implementation, the flipping of 2D matrix can be achieved with simple column index switching. In line 11, the 2D feature matrix is flattened into a one dimension (1D) feature vector for the classification model calibration. It shall be noted that, the illumination source symmetry-based feature compaction scheme can be easily extended to other symmetric scenarios, such as rotational symmetry. Overall, the feature extraction and compaction will yield a set of 1D feature vectors with $M \times N$ dimensions.

4.2 Model Training

With the SRAF labels and feature vectors, a classification model is calibrated for SRAF predictions. In particular, the size of training data set and feature vector dimension can both be very large because high sampling accuracy is needed for classification-based SRAF. Moreover, the large training and testing data set sizes make the classification-based SRAF problem difficult to adopt support vector machine (SVM) and other advanced classification models from the perspective of calibration and prediction runtime. Thus, we adopt decision tree (DTree) and logistic regression (LGR) models for SRAF predictions with reasonable performance and runtime.

Decision Tree The DTree model is simple yet powerful, which partitions the feature space into a set of rectangles and calibrate a simple model (like a constant label for classification model) in each one [25]. Specifically, the DTree model calibration is to construct a decision tree from labeled training data in the top-down manner, using a metric to decide the best splits of set of training data at each step [25]. For this application, the Gini index metric is used to decide the best splits at each step of calibration with the CART (Class and Regression Trees) algorithm. With the Gini index, the DTree classifier can estimate the probability of a label for each data sample by calculating the fraction samples of that label in a leaf [25].

Logistic Regression The LGR adopts the logistic function as the probabilistic estimation for each label of the training or testing data. The model calibration is typically achieved with the maximum likelihood method [25]. The LGR model is especially powerful for binary classification, which makes the calibration and prediction scalable to large data set. Due to the large training data set in classification-based SRAF issue, $L2$ regularization is added to the LGR model to avoid overfitting. The LGR model provides the direct probabilistic estimation of labels for each data sample.

5. SRAF GENERATION

5.1 Predictions with Probability Maxima

The typical prediction with a binary classification model will be a label, i.e. 0 or 1, for each testing data. With the label prediction for each grid, clusters of grids will be labeled as 1, denoted as yellow grids, as shown in Fig. 5(a). After the label prediction, clusters of grids in Fig. 5(a) cannot be directly treated as SRAFs because they may violate the mask manufacturing rules or be printed due to large critical dimensions. Instead of using SRAF label for the grid prediction, we propose predictions with probability maxima to simplify the clusters of SRAF grids. When a classification model is calibrated, the probability of the label to be 1, denoted as p_1, can be calculated for LGR and DTree as explained in Section 4.2. Then, a probability map on the 2D grid plane can be attained as shown in Fig. 5(b). To simplify the clusters of grids for SRAF generation, we only insert SRAFs at grids with probability maxima. A grid with probability maximum means the probability (p_1) at that particular grid is larger than that at any other neighboring grids. The idea of predictions with probability maxima originates from the model-based SRAF approach. Model-based SRAFs are generated using the guidance map from lithographic computations [9–12]. A guidance map is also grid based and has intensity assigned to each grid, where SRAFs will only be inserted at those intensity maxima. Thus, we adopt the similar idea during predictions with probability maxima since model-based SRAFs are used as the training data for the classification model calibration.

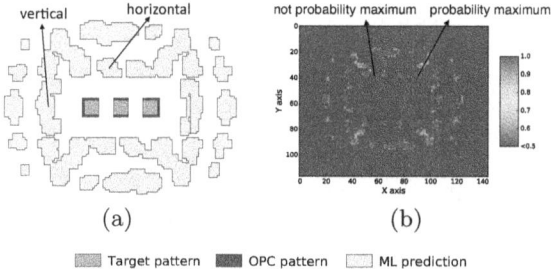

Figure 5: SRAF predictions: (a) label predictions, (b) predictions with probability maxima.

5.2 SRAF Simplification

Using predictions with probability maxima, clusters of grids will be predicted as SRAFs on the 2D grid plane but the mask manufacturing and SRAF printing issues are not fully resolved. The SRAF simplification phase aims at simplifying these clusters of grids into SRAFs satisfying the mask manufacturing rules. A greedy simplification scheme is proposed by grid merging and shrinking the SRAFs into rectangular shapes while accommodating mask manufacturing rules.

The overall algorithm of SRAF generation is shown in Algorithm 2. In lines 1-2, we predict SRAFs at grids with probability maxima from the classification model. In line 3, the grids with probability maxima are merged into polygons, which is followed by the spacing rule check and shrinking the polygons to remove violations in line 4. From line 5 to 14, each polygon is processed to generate a rectangular SRAF. Particularly, in line 7, the main direction of SRAF is detected based on the bounding box of target patterns. In

line 8, the bounding box of the polygon is shrunk to achieve a rectangular SRAF parallel to that of target patterns. As illustrated in Fig. 5(a), the main direction of the polygon on the top is horizontal while the main direction on the left is vertical, both of which are parallel to the bounding box of target patterns. With the SRAF simplification, the mask manufacturing-friendly SRAFs can be generated for testing patterns.

Algorithm 2 SRAF generation

Input: A 2D grid plane, a classification models, a set of mask manufacturing rules;
Output: The mask manufacturing friendly set $SRAF$;
  1: Compute the probability of label 1 for each grid;
  2: SRAF predictions at grids with probability maxima;
  3: Merge SRAF grids into a polygon set $SRAF_{pg}$;
  4: Spacing rule check and shrink polygons in $SRAF_{pg}$ to remove violations;
  5: **for** each $polygon$ in $SRAF_{pg}$ **do**;
  6:    Define $BBox$ as the bounding box of $polygon$;
  7:    Detect the main direction of $polygon$ as $direction$;
  8:    Shrink $BBox$ size based on $direction$;
  9: **end for**
 10: Rule check and shrink rectangles in $SRAF$ to remove violations;
 11: Return $SRAF$;

---

6. EXPERIMENTAL RESULTS

We have implemented the machine learning framework in Python and accelerated with Cython [26] and parallel computations. The optical model, model-based SRAF, MRC/LCC recipes and the SRAF simplification are implemented using Calibre script language with the industry-strength setup. All experiments are performed on an 8-core Linux machine with 3.4GHz Intel(R) Core and 32GB memory. For the optical model, the wavelength (λ) and numerical aperture (NA) are set as $193nm$ and 1.35, respectively. The annular illumination source is used with outer sigma as 0.9 and inner sigma as 0.6. Compact model 1 from Calibre is adopted as the resist model. In the LCC, the outer/inner contours are generated using lithographic process window conditions as a focus variation of $\pm30nm$ and a dose variation of $\pm3.0\%$. For model-based SRAF generation, process window conditions above are considered and SRAF manufacturing rules are set as max_width $= 40nm$, min_space $= 60nm$, max_length $= 90nm$. We test the SRAF generation framework on two types of contact patterns. One type is dense contact arrays with contact width and space fixed as $70nm$. We have dense contact patterns because redundant vias are needed to improve yield during layout design. The other type is sparse contact patterns, where the contact width is $70nm$ but the space between contact holes is random and the minimum space is $70nm$. For CCCAS, the grid size is set as $10nm$, the SRAF box size is set as $40nm$ and radius step size is $s_r = 15nm$. For SRAF-specific constraints, d_{opc} and d_{sraf} are set as $100nm$ and $600nm$, respectively.

6.1 Model Training

A set of training patterns and model-based SRAFs are needed to extract the training data and calibrate the classification model for SRAF predictions on both dense and sparse testing patterns. From the extensive experiments, the training patterns in Fig. 6 yield the best training and testing accuracy. For the dense contact patterns in Fig. 6(a), the width and space are fixed as $70nm$. The width of sparse contact patterns in Fig. 6(b) is $70nm$, while the space is $350nm$.

In particular, since the training patterns are symmetric and feature compaction scheme has been proposed, we only need to sample the lower left part of the layout clip for training data. This is beneficial for the classification model calibration since the training data size can be reduced by 3/4 without losing the critical SRAF information. The training data set statistics are summarized in Table 1. For CCCAS, the number of circle is set as $M = \lfloor (d_{sraf} - d_{opc})/s_r \rfloor = 33$. The number of sub-sampling points in each circle is set as $N = 32$ to guarantee sampling accuracy for sparse contact patterns. Then, the feature vector dimension is $M \times N = 1056$. By combining the training data from dense and sparse patterns, we have 14609 training samples. We have 95412 testing samples from dense patterns and 803756 testing samples from sparse patterns.

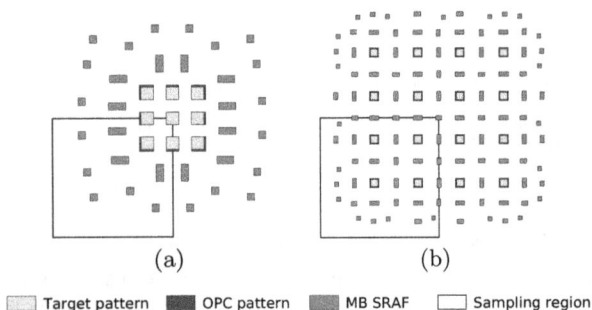

Figure 6: Training layout: (a) dense contact patterns, (b) sparse contact patterns.

The data set statistics demonstrate the high feature vector dimension and large training data size. The feature vector dimension is difficult to be further reduced since each sub-sampling point contains the information related to the target patterns. Moreover, each training data sample within the lithographic interaction window is considered valuable, so there is little redundancy within the training data set. As discussed in Section 4.2, advanced classification models, such as support vector machine, are not applicable to the classification-based SRAF domain due to large training and testing data sets. In practice, we find that the reasons are twofold. First, the training of advanced classification models has high complexity, which is not as scalable as the simple classification models to large training data set. Second, advanced classification models have more complex prediction model calibrated, which means the testing time for each testing sample would be longer than that of simple models. Since the grid based approach is used here, the runtime overhead accumulates and even becomes unaffordable over the huge amount of testing samples extracted from testing patterns. [1]

We further compare different classification models, including DTree and LGR, for the SRAF generation framework and data statistics are shown in Table 2. The F_1 score is computed as:

$$F_1 \; score = \frac{2 * precision * recall}{(precision + recall)} \qquad (1)$$

where *precision* is the number of true positive results divided by the number of all positive results and *recall* is

---

[1] Our implementation of the support vector machine with linear kernels shows much longer runtime than LGR and DTree, which leads to the overall SRAF generation runtime longer than that of the model-based SRAF from Calibre.

the number of true positive results divided by the number of positive results that should have been returned [27]. In particular, $F_1 \; score$ is best at 1.0 and worst at 0.0 for comparison. Since either label 1 or label 0 can be treated as positive result, we compute the $F_1 \; score$ for both labels, denoted as $F_1 \; score(1)$ and $F_1 \; score(0)$, respectively. From Table 2, although DTree achieves better $F_1 \; score(1)$ and $F_1 \; score(0)$ on training data, the testing $F_1 \; score(0)$ and $F_1 \; score(1)$ are worse than LGR on dense patterns by 0.081 and 0.006, respectively. We only see a difference within 0.01 in $F_1 \; score$ for sparse testing patterns. This means LGR is better than DTree due to its better testing accuracy and LGR is less prone to the overfitting with large training data set and high dimension feature vectors. In addition, the model calibration time and testing time on sparse testing patterns for LGR are less than DTree but the difference is non-significant. Moreover, we observe the $F_1 \; score(1)$ is much better than $F_1 \; score(0)$ on all testing data for both classification models. This means that most grids with SRAFs of testing patterns are labeled as 1 correctly but some other grids without SRAFs that should be labeled as 0 are incorrectly labeled as 1. This also proves the necessity of predictions with probability maxima and the SRAF simplification stage later on, which essentially reduces the number of grids labeled as 1 and potentially improves the $F_1 \; score(0)$ for testing data.

6.2 SRAF Generation

6.2.1 SRAF Simplification

We add testing layout clips to demonstrate the strength of predictions with probability maxima and SRAF simplification schemes. Since the LGR based approach performs better than the DTree based approach, we only show the SRAFs from LGR predictions for clear explanations. As illustrated in Fig. 7, we compare the SRAFs generated using different machine learning (ML) predictions, i.e. label predictions and predictions with probability maxima, followed by the SRAF simplification phase. Predictions with probability maxima can simplify the clusters of grids labeled as 1, i.e. breaking large clusters into small clusters, which benefits the SRAF simplification stage. Thus, the SRAFs generated using predictions with probability maxima in Fig. 7(b) are much better than those in Fig. 7(a) in terms of PV band from the LCC.

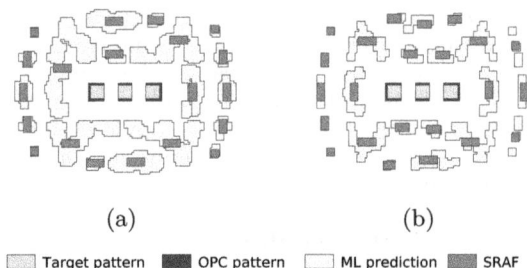

(a)   (b)

Target pattern   OPC pattern   ML prediction   SRAF

Figure 7: SRAF generations: (a) label predictions, (b) predictions with probability maxima.

6.2.2 SRAF Consistency

We further demonstrate the benefit of SRAF consistency improvement from the feature compaction technique in Sec-

Table 1: Data set statistics

feature vector dimension	# of training samples	# of testing samples from dense patterns	# of testing samples from sparse patterns
1056	14609	95412	803756

Table 2: Comparisons on different classification models

Model	Training			Dense Testing Patterns			Sparse Testing Patterns		
	F_1 score(1)	F_1 score(0)	Calibration time(s)	F_1 score(1)	F_1 score(0)	Runtime(s)	F_1 score(1)	F_1 score(0)	Runtime(s)
DTree	0.9983	0.9855	5.66	0.9499	0.3319	3.83	0.8787	0.2646	50.44
LGR	0.9938	0.9462	1.06	0.9557	0.4132	3.83	0.8724	0.2629	41.47

tion 4.1.2. The SRAF generation from model-based method using Calibre [Calibre, v2015.2_36.27], LGR without feature compaction and LGR with feature compaction are shown in Fig. 8(a), (b) and (c), respectively. Since annular illumination source is used, axial symmetric grids share the same optical environment and the consistent SRAF generation should yield the same SRAFs at axial symmetric grids. The feature compaction scheme would transform the feature matrices extracted from axial symmetric grids to the same feature vector. Therefore, the SRAFs in Fig. 8(c) are more consistent than those in Fig. 8(b). Moreover, we have even achieved SRAFs with better consistency than the model-based method shown in Fig. 8(a).

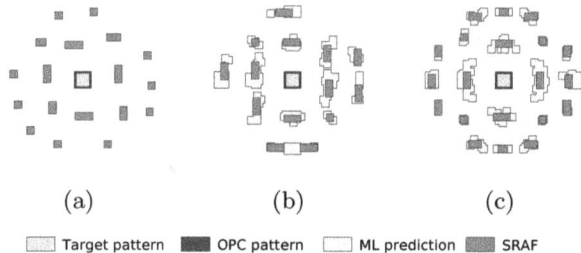

(a) (b) (c)

Target pattern   OPC pattern   ML prediction   SRAF

Figure 8: SRAFs for the isolated contact pattern: (a) model-based, (b) LGR without feature compaction, (c) LGR with feature compaction.

We further demonstrate the SRAFs from LGR predictions on both dense and sparse testing patterns as shown in Fig. 9. The layout clip of dense contact patterns is defined as $m \times n$ dense contact patterns, if the layout clip contains a contact array with m rows and n columns. Fig. 9(a) and (b) show two cases of redundant vias in real designs. The LGR based SRAF generation can obtain acceptable SRAFs on these dense contact patterns but the degradation of SRAF consistency is observed. The reasons are twofold. First, the training data with model-based SRAFs are not perfectly consistent as shown in Fig. 6. Then, it is difficult to guarantee the consistent SRAF generation with the classification model calibrated with these training data. Second, the CC-CAS results may be slightly different for axial symmetric grids due to the grid error within the 2D grid plane. Fig. 9(c) illustrates a small layout clip of random contact patterns, which proves the capability of the machine learning based SRAF generation on random sparse contact patterns.

6.3 Lithography Compliance Check

To evaluate the practical lithographic performance, we combine the SRAF generation with a complete mask optimization flow as shown in Fig. 2, where model-based OPC and LCC are performed using Mentor Calibre tool. We compare the model-based, LGR and DTree approaches in

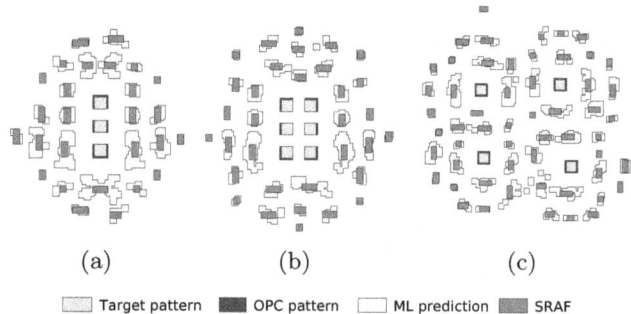

(a) (b) (c)

Target pattern   OPC pattern   ML prediction   SRAF

Figure 9: Testing contact patterns: (a) 3×1 dense contact patterns, (b) 3×2 dense contact patterns, (c) sparse contact patterns

terms of PV band and EPE on both dense and sparse testing patterns. Specifically, we collect the PV band value for each contact and the EPE value at the center of the four edges of each contact at nominal conditions. The mean values are summarized and compared in Table 3. We add the PV band without SRAFs to better demonstrate the benefit from SRAF generation. The model-based approach reduces the PV band from 3.3064 to 2.7705, which is 16.21% reduction compared to no SRAF insertion. Meanwhile, we obtain 13.37% and 14.09% PV band reduction from DTree and LGR, respectively. The LGR based SRAF generation achieves better performance as expected because LGR model is less prone to overfitting compared to DTree model. In particular, there is only 2.12% PV band degradation from model-based approach to LGR based approach. We take the absolute values when calculating the EPE mean to avoid the cancellations between positive and negative values of EPE. The LGR based SRAF generation yields the smallest EPE mean value, which even outperforms the model-based approach. This means there is some trade-off between PV band and EPE because different SRAF results lead to different OPC results. It is very difficult to improve the PV band and EPE simultaneously with a robust mask optimization flow.

Table 3: PV band and absolute of EPE

Mean value	No SRAF	Model-based	DTree	LGR
PV band ($.001 um^2$)	3.306	2.771	2.864	2.841
Absolute of EPE (nm)	3.636	0.539	0.523	0.501

We collect the PV band and EPE values for each contact and further plot the data in histograms as shown in Fig. 10. Fig. 10(a) shows that SRAF insertion significantly improves the PV band and model-based SRAF gives the best performance. The LGR based approach is slightly worse than model-based method but performs better than DTree based method. Fig. 10(b) shows that LGR based SRAF generation achieves the best EPE performance.

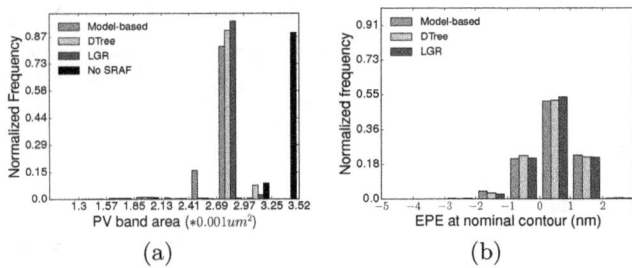

Figure 10: Comparison among different schemes: (a) PV band distribution, (b) EPE distribution.

6.4 Run Time

We compare our machine learning based SRAF generation with the commercial Calibre tool, i.e. model-based SRAFs. The mask optimization techniques, including SRAF generation and OPC, usually apply to small layout windows due to the high computational cost [2]. Therefore, we choose small layout windows with dense contact patterns for runtime comparisons between different SRAF generation approaches. In Fig. 11, different dense contact patterns, denoted as $m \times n$ contact patterns explained in Section 6.2.2, are used for runtime comparisons. The areas of these layout windows considering SRAF regions are in the range from $1um^2$ to $2um^2$. The runtime for the machine learning based approach includes runtime for feature extraction and compaction, predictions with probability maxima and SRAF simplification.

The average runtime for model-based SRAF, LGR based SRAF and DTree based SRAF are $5.14s$, $0.41s$ and $0.41s$, respectively. Although we are using a different programming language and database from commercial tool, we still obtain over 10X speed-up from machine learning based SRAF generation compared to the model-based approach in Calibre [Calibre, v2014.4_18.13]. We also check the runtime of the model-based OPC from different SRAF generation approaches and ensure that they are approximately the same.

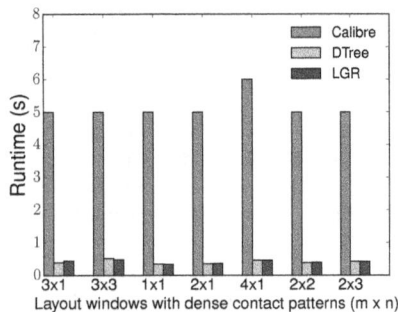

Figure 11: Run time comparison among different schemes on different layout windows.

7. CONCLUSION

A machine learning based framework for SRAF generation is demonstrated for the first time. A robust feature extraction scheme is proposed by adapting the CCAS considering SRAF-specific constraints. We further propose a novel feature compaction technique to reduce the training data size and improve the SRAF consistency. Predictions with probability maxima are proposed to achieve mask manufacturing-friendly SRAFs. Experimental results show that LGR based SRAF generation obtains 10X speed-up in layout windows and better EPE with affordable degradation in PV band, compared to the commercial Calibre tool.

8. ACKNOWLEDGEMENT

This work is supported in part by SRC and NSF. The authors would like to thank the memory lithography group (MLG) in Toshiba Corporation for the helpful discussions and feedback on this work.

9. REFERENCES

[1] Y. Ping, S. McGowan, Y. Gong, Y. M. Foong, J. Liu, J. Qiu, V. Shu, B. Yan, J. Ye, P. Li et al., "Process window enhancement using advanced ret techniques for 20nm contact layer," in Proc. of SPIE, 2014, pp. 90 521N–90 521N.

[2] S. Banerjee, Z. Li, and S. R. Nassif, "ICCAD-2013 CAD contest in mask optimization and benchmark suite," in IEEE/ACM International Conference on Computer-Aided Design (ICCAD), 2013, pp. 271–274.

[3] J.-R. Gao, X. Xu, Y. Bei, and D. Z. Pan, "MOSAIC: Mask optimizing solution with process window aware inverse correction," in ACM/IEEE Design Automation Conference (DAC), 2014, pp. 52:1–52:6.

[4] Y.-H. Su, Y.-C. Huang, L.-C. Tsai, Y.-W. Chang, and S. Banerjee, "Fast lithographic mask optimization considering process variation," in IEEE/ACM International Conference on Computer-Aided Design (ICCAD), 2014, pp. 230–237.

[5] A. Awad, A. Takahashi, S. Tanaka, and C. Kodama, "A fast process variation and pattern fidelity aware mask optimization algorithm," in IEEE/ACM International Conference on Computer-Aided Design (ICCAD), 2014, pp. 238–245.

[6] J. Kuang, W.-K. Chow, and E. F. Young, "A robust approach for process variation aware mask optimization," in Proc. Design, Automation and Test in Eurpoe, 2015, pp. 1591–1594.

[7] J.-H. Jun, M. Park, C. Park, H. Yang, D. Yim, M. Do, D. Lee, T. Kim, J. Choi, G. Luk-Pat et al., "Layout optimization with assist features placement by model based rule tables for 2x node random contact," in Proc. of SPIE, 2015, pp. 94 270D–94 270D.

[8] C. Kodama, T. Kotani, S. Nojima, and S. Mimotogi, "Sub-resolution assist feature arranging method and computer program product and manufacturing method of semiconductor device," Aug. 19 2014, US Patent 8,809,072.

[9] K. Sakajiri, A. Tritchkov, and Y. Granik, "Model-based sraf insertion through pixel-based mask optimization at 32nm and beyond," in Proc. of SPIE, 2008, pp. 702 811–702 811.

[10] R. Viswanathan, J. T. Azpiroz, and P. Selvam, "Process optimization through model based sraf printing prediction," in Proc. of SPIE, 2012, pp. 83 261A–83 261A.

[11] J. Ye, Y. Cao, and H. Feng, "System and method for model-based sub-resolution assist feature generation," Feb. 1 2011, US Patent 7,882,480.

[12] S. D. Shang, L. Swallow, and Y. Granik, "Model-based sraf insertion," Oct. 11 2011, US Patent 8,037,429.

[13] L. Pang, Y. Liu, and D. Abrams, "Inverse lithography technology (ilt): a natural solution for model-based sraf at 45nm and 32nm," in Proc. of SPIE, 2007, pp. 660 739–660 739.

[14] B.-S. Kim, Y.-H. Kim, S.-H. Lee, S.-I. Kim, S.-R. Ha, J. Kim, and A. Tritchkov, "Pixel-based sraf implementation for 32nm lithography process," in Proc. of SPIE, 2008, pp. 71 220T–71 220T.

[15] J. A. Torres, "ICCAD-2012 CAD contest in fuzzy pattern matching for physical verification and benchmark suite," in IEEE/ACM International Conference on Computer-Aided Design (ICCAD), 2012.

[16] D. Ding, X. Wu, J. Ghosh, and D. Z. Pan, "Machine learning based lithographic hotspot detection with critical-feature extraction and classification," in IEEE International Conference on IC Design and Technology (ICICDT), 2009.

[17] D. G. Drmanac, F. Liu, and L.-C. Wang, "Predicting variability in nanoscale lithography processes," in ACM/IEEE Design Automation Conference (DAC), 2009, pp. 545–550.

[18] Y. Yu, G. Lin, I. Jiang, and C. Chiang, "Machine-learning-based hotspot detection using topological classification and critical feature extraction," IEEE Transactions on Computer-Aided Design of Integrated Circuits and Systems (TCAD), vol. 34, no. 3, pp. 460–470, 2015.

[19] T. Matsunawa, J.-R. Gao, B. Yu, and D. Z. Pan, "A new lithography hotspot detection framework based on adaboost classifier and simplified feature extraction," in Proc. of SPIE, 2015, pp. 94 270S–94 270S.

[20] A. Gu and A. Zakhor, "Optical proximity correction with linear regression," IEEE Transactions on Semiconductor Manufacturing, vol. 21, no. 2, pp. 263–271, 2008.

[21] R. Luo, "Optical proximity correction using a multilayer perceptron neural network," Journal of Optics, vol. 15, no. 7, p. 075708, 2013.

[22] T. Matsunawa, B. Yu, and D. Z. Pan, "Optical proximity correction with hierarchical bayes model," in Proc. of SPIE, 2015, pp. 94 260X–94 260X.

[23] X. Ma, B. Wu, Z. Song, S. Jiang, and Y. Li, "Fast pixel-based optical proximity correction based on nonparametric kernel regression," Journal of Microlithography, Microfabrication and Microsystems, vol. 13, no. 4, pp. 043 007–043 007, 2014.

[24] P. Gupta, "What is process window?" SIGDA Newsl., vol. 40, no. 8, pp. 1–1, Aug. 2010.

[25] T. Hastie, R. Tibshirani, J. Friedman, and J. Franklin, "The elements of statistical learning: data mining, inference and prediction," The Mathematical Intelligencer, vol. 27, no. 2, pp. 83–85, 2005.

[26] S. Behnel, R. Bradshaw, C. Citro, L. Dalcin, D. Seljebotn, and K. Smith, "Cython: The best of both worlds," Computing in Science Engineering, vol. 13, no. 2, pp. 31 –39, 2011.

[27] C. Goutte and E. Gaussier, "A probabilistic interpretation of precision, recall and f-score, with implication for evaluation," in Advances in information retrieval. Springer, 2005, pp. 345–359.

Author Index

Aggarwal, Rajat 117, 139

Akopyan, Filipp A. 59

Anderson, Jason H. 123

Berggren, Karl K. 37

Bigalke, Steve 99

Bodapati, Srinivas 153

Chang, Jae-Byum 37

Chang, Wen-Hsiang 145

Chang, Yao-Wen 47

Chao, Mango C.-T. 145

Chen, Li-De 145

Chen, Pengwen 11

Cheng, Chung-Kuan 11

Chiu, Yen-Chih 145

Choi, Hong Kyoon 37

Cong, Jason 131

Das, Sabya 117

Do, Hyung Wan 37

Domic, Antun 61

Ewetz, Rickard 81

Flach, Guilherme 73

Fogaça, Mateus 73

Ford, Greg 63

Gayasen, Aman 139

Groeneveld, Patrick R. 35, 113

He, Hao 91

He, Lei 153

Hu, Jiang 91

Huang, Hantao 19

Huda, Safeen 123

Johann, Marcelo 73

Kang, Ilgweon 11

Knechtel, Johann 3

Kodama, Chikaaki 161

Koh, Cheng-Kok 81

Kotani, Toshiya 161

Lienig, Jens 3, 99

Lin, Chien-Hsueh 145

Lin, Zhi-Wen 47

Lu, Ang 91

Lu, Jingwei 11

Luo, Guojie 131

Matsunawa, Tetsuaki 161

Monteiro, Jucemar 73

Moroz, Victor 55

Mu, Szu-Pang 145

Mulpuri, Chandra 139

Nijssen, Raymond 57

Nojima, Shigeki 161

Otten, Ralph 115

Ou, Jiaojiao 39

Pan, David Z. 39,161

Reddy, Sainath 139

Reimann, Tiago J. 65

Reis, Ricardo 65, 73

Ren, Fengbo 19

Ross, Caroline A. 37

Ryckaert, Julien 89

Schlichtmann, Ulf 27

Sze, Cliff C. N. 65

Tan, Chuan Yean 81

Tsai, Cheng-Hong 145

van Ginneken, Lukas P.P.P. 109

von Beuningen, Anja 27

Wang, Zhiyong 117

Wong, Martin D. F. 107

Wu, Wei 153

Xu, Xiaoqing 161

Yang, Stephen 139

Yu, Bei 39

Yu, Hao 19

Zhang, Jiaxi 131

Zhang, Kevin 1

Zhang, Wentai 131

Zhuang, Hao 11

Zhuo, Cheng 19